Table of Contents

KU-065-783

Introduction   vi

Chapter One   **Fundamentals of Lighting Design**   1

Motivation   2
Cheating   5
Visual Goals of Lighting Design   9
Lighting Challenges   13
Your Workspace   15
Creative Control   16

Chapter Two   **Lighting Basics and Good Practices**   19

Starting the Creative Process   20
Types of Lights   24
Adjusting Controls and Options   40
Exercises   51

Chapter Three   **Shadows and Occlusion**   55

The Visual Functions of Shadows   56
The Appearance of Shadows   62
Shadow Algorithms   73
Occlusion   91
Faking Shadows and Occlusion   102
Exercises   108

Chapter Four   **Lighting Environments and Architecture**   111

Creating Daylight   112
Working with Indoor Natural Light   124
Practical Lights   138
Night Scenes   143
Distance and Depth   144
Exercises   155

Chapter Five   Lighting Creatures, Characters, and Animation   **157**

Modeling with Light   158
Three-Point Lighting   164
Functions of Lights   167
Issues in Lighting Character Animation   182
Exercises   199

Chapter Six   Cameras and Exposure   **201**

F-Stops and Depth of Field   202
Shutter Speed and Motion Blur   214
Film Speed and Film Grain   222
Photographic Exposure   223
Matching Lens Imperfections   230
Exercises   236

Chapter Seven   Composition and Staging   **239**

Types of Shot   240
Camera Angles   244
Improving Your Composition   253
Framing for Film and Video   259
Exercises   264

Chapter Eight   The Art and Science of Color   **267**

Working in a Linear Workflow   268
Color Mixing   278
Developing Color Schemes   285
Using Color Balance   294
Working with Digital Color   301
Exercises   309

[d i g i t a l]
LIGHTING &
RENDERING

Third Edition

New Riders

VOICES THAT MATTER™

JEREMY BIRN

Digital Lighting and Rendering, Third Edition
Jeremy Birn

New Riders
www.newriders.com

To report errors, please send a note to errata@peachpit.com

New Riders is an imprint of Peachpit, a division of Pearson Education.

Notice of Liability

The information in this book is distributed on an "As Is" basis, without warranty. While every precaution has been taken in the preparation of the book, neither the author nor Peachpit shall have any liability to any person or entity with respect to any loss or damage caused or alleged to be caused directly or indirectly by the instructions contained in this book or by the computer software and hardware products described in it.

Trademarks

Many of the designations used by manufacturers and sellers to distinguish their products are claimed as trademarks. Where those designations appear in this book, and Peachpit was aware of a trademark claim, the designations appear as requested by the owner of the trademark. All other product names and services identified throughout this book are used in editorial fashion only and for the benefit of such companies with no intention of infringement of the trademark. No such use, or the use of any trade name, is intended to convey endorsement or other affiliation with this book.

ISBN-13: 978-0-321-92898-6
ISBN-10:   0-321-92898-9

9 8 7 6 5 4 3 2 1

Printed and bound in the United States of America

Chapter Nine   Shaders and Rendering Algorithms 311

Shading Surfaces   312
Anti-Aliasing   325
Raytracing   330
Reyes Algorithms   341
Global Illumination   343
Caustics   352
Exercises   356

Chapter Ten   Designing and Assigning Textures   359

Download this chapter from the Registered Products tab on your Account page at www.peachpit.com. See the Introduction in the book for further details.

Chapter Eleven   Rendering in Layers and Passes for Compositing   361

Rendering in Layers   362
Rendering in Passes   378
Matching Live-Action Background Plates   399
Managing Colors in Your Composite   405
Choosing Your Approach   407
Exercises   409

Chapter Twelve   Production Pipelines and Professional Practices   411

Production Pipelines   412
Lighting on Larger Productions   435
Advancing in Your Career   441

Appendix   Getting a Job in 3D Graphics

Download the appendix from the Registered Products tab on your Account page at www.peachpit.com. See the Introduction in the book for further details.

Index   443

Introduction

To help you make better 3D renderings, this book fuses information from several fields. In these pages, you will find practical advice based on professional film production experience, concepts and techniques from live-action cinematography, design principles from traditional visual arts, and plain-English explanations of the latest science behind the scenes.

Who Should Read This Book?

You should read this book when you have at least a working knowledge of how to use a 3D software package and are interested in taking your 3D rendering further.

- For professional users of 3D rendering software, this book is designed to help with real-world production challenges and contribute to the ongoing growth of your lighting and rendering work.

- For students of computer graphics, this book will help you develop professional lighting and rendering skills.

- For dedicated 3D hobbyists, this book can help you improve the artistic quality of your 3D renderings and learn more about professional approaches to graphics production.

I wrote this book to be clear, but not condescending. I have made every effort to define terms the first time I use them, and to illustrate every concept and technique with figures and sample renderings. This book is designed to complement, rather than replace, your software's manuals and help files. Most of the information you find here is not in your software manual, even if some of it should be.

Software Requirements

This book covers techniques and concepts that you can apply in almost any 3D rendering software. I also recommend that you have 2D paint and compositing software on hand.

3D Software

I don't care whether you use Blender (open-source software from www.blender.org), Maxon Cinema 4D, Side Effects Houdini, NewTek LightWave 3D, Autodesk Maya, Autodesk Softimage, Autodesk 3ds Max, or any other brand of software that lets you light and render 3D scenes. You can use the renderer that comes with your software package or separate rendering software like Solid Angle's Arnold, NVIDIA Mental Ray, Pixar's RenderMan, or Chaos Group's V-Ray. No single program is going to support every feature, function, and rendering algorithm described in this book, so hopefully you won't mind learning about a few functions that aren't in your particular software yet. Most sections show several alternate approaches or workarounds so that you can achieve any effect that I describe, no matter which program you use.

Being non-software-specific doesn't mean that this book doesn't discuss individual programs, though. If there's a noteworthy feature in any particular 3D program, or a technique that you need to do differently in one program than in another, I mention it when it comes up.

This book is dedicated to the idea that, if you are aware of the art and computer graphics principles that go into a rendering, and you apply a little bit of creative problem solving, you can accomplish great work in almost any rendering package.

2D Software

You should complement any good 3D system with 2D software that can create and manipulate texture maps, and composite together layers and render passes. You will find that a paint program such as Adobe Photoshop (which I have used in many texture-creation examples in this book) is useful, although free alternatives such as GIMP (www.gimp.org) or Paint.NET (www.getpaint.net) will also work just fine. You may also find a dedicated compositing program (such as The Foundry's Nuke, eyeon Fusion, or Adobe After Effects) useful when you are compositing together render passes, although you can also do basic compositing in your paint program

About This Edition

This is the third edition of the popular book *Digital Lighting & Rendering*. The first edition became the standard text on the art of 3D lighting and rendering, and introduced many artists to the field. Since it was published in 2000, it has met with great critical and commercial success. A second edition was released with major updates in 2006. I am sincerely grateful to each teacher who has chosen to use my book, everyone on the Internet who has posted a recommendation, and every artist who has shown my book to a friend or colleague.

Now I have written this new third edition to make sure that the book advances along with changes in technology, software, and the industry. A great deal has changed since the second edition.

I have added sections to cover new technologies and growing trends, such as physically based lights, physically based shaders, Ptex (per-face texturing), and unbiased rendering. In addition, there's a new focus on the linear work-flow, why you need one, and how to maintain it.

I've also updated several chapters to reflect how it's becoming common to use global illumination in feature film lighting, as a part of your character lighting, and also to light environments and architecture. I'm not trying to force everyone to use global illumination for everything, though. I have also expanded the coverage of occlusion, using the occlusion sandwich technique, and more advanced approaches to occlusion passes.

I still cover old-school lighting techniques such as depth map shadows in this edition. Although depth map shadows are going out of style for many purposes, a lighting technical director should still know what they are good for, how to adjust them, and how to fix bias issues and light leaks. Though the third edition retains the same chapter organization as the second edition, it has grown longer in places and contains new sections on lighting atmosphere, participating media, and underwater scenes; new examples of compositing; expanded coverage of simulating natural light; and new character lighting situations. I've also included new sections on approaches lighting teams can use to work together in lighting feature films, the state of the computer graphics industry, and new advice for developing your show-reel and finding a job.

In computer graphics, we say our work is never really completed, only abandoned. Shots can always be better, and perfectionists can always find something to tweak and revise a little more—and of course it is the same with books. Crashing into a deadline is what finally forces us to let go of the projects we love. After releasing a book, being able to revisit and revise all the material again gives me great pleasure. It is with great pride that I abandon this new edition to you.

Downloading Additional Files

With the purchase of this book you have access to an entire chapter on texture mapping, the art of adding variation and detail to 3D surfaces that goes beyond the level of detail modeled into the geometry. This chapter, along with an appendix ("Getting a Job in 3D Graphics") are available for download at the publisher's website. If you have purchased the ebook version, the material will already appear within the book and no download is necessary.

To access the download, visit the Peachpit website (peachpit.com), sign in, and register this book. Once you are registered, go to Account, select the Registered Products tab, and click the "Access Bonus Content" link. Copy the download to any location you prefer on your system.

Also, throughout the book, you will find references to many of the 3D scenes used as examples. Feel free to download and experiment with those scenes for your own personal work. You can access them at www.3dRender.com.

CHAPTER ONE

Fundamentals of Lighting Design

The craft of lighting design was practiced for centuries prior to the advent of computer graphics in fields that included theater, painting, photography, and finally cinematography. 3D artists have a great deal to learn from the traditions of earlier lighters. This chapter introduces some of the key terms and concepts in the field of lighting design, and looks ahead to some of the important issues and challenges that will be raised in this book.

Motivation

Before you add a light to your scene, you should know its *motivation,* the cause or original source of a light. You can think of motivation as the *story* behind each light.

You probably wouldn't begin to animate a character without knowing what the character was doing or trying to do, and you probably wouldn't paint a texture map without knowing what material you were trying to create. Yet many people add lights to their scenes in just this sort of random manner, without thinking about what kind of light they are trying to depict or why it might be there.

Motivation should inform every decision you make while adjusting your lights. Once you know a light's motivation, you know what qualities of light you are trying to depict and what kind of light sources you should study or think about when you are creating an appearance in 3D.

Off-Screen Space

Off-screen space is the area that isn't visible in your shot, such as the space above the camera. The illumination, shadows, and reflections you see in a photograph are often motivated by off-screen sources, rather than by light sources visible within the frame. An important part of your job in designing lighting for any scene is to imagine what exists in off-screen space so that you can illuminate your scene with lights that appear to be motivated by real light sources.

To see how lighting can be shaped by off-screen space, take a look at the four photographs in Figure 1.1. The objects in the frame don't change, and yet, based on the off-screen light, you can tell a great deal about where each picture was taken.

How can you make the lighting in your 3D scenes communicate as much to the viewer as the light in these photographs does? How do you make light tell such a story that the viewer can even imagine what exists outside of the frame? To find these answers, start by studying the visible qualities of light from each kind of light source.

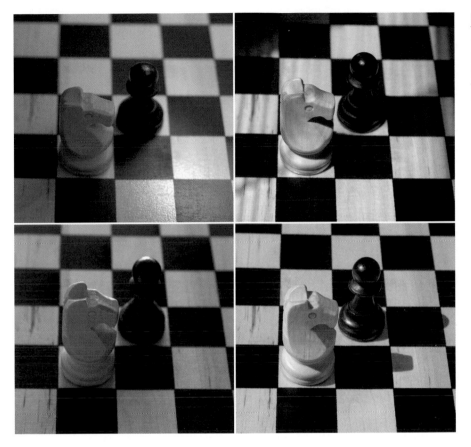

[Figure 1.1]
You can recognize a scene lit by a lamp (upper left), by light through a window (upper right), under a cloudy sky (lower left), and in direct sun (lower right).

Qualities of Light

We recognize different sources of illumination by the different *qualities of light* they add to the scene. The main qualities of light that we notice in a picture are color temperature, brightness, softness, throw pattern, and angle.

- Every type of light source has a distinctive *color temperature*, which helps determine the color of the light. Chapter 8 explores the art and science of color, has charts of real light sources' color temperatures, and explains how the colors we see are all relative to their context and the white balance of the camera.

- *Brightness*, like color, is all relative to how the camera is adjusted—in this context it is based on the exposure settings of the camera. Chapter 6 describes a real camera's exposure process and how to light your 3D scenes to simulate real cinematography.

- *Softness* is a function of several settings on a light: The *penumbra* of a spotlight sets the softness of the edge of its cone; the *decay* or *drop-off* of a light sets how it fades away with distance; and most important, *soft shadows* create the impression of soft, diffused light, whereas crisply defined shadows indicate hard light. Figure 1.1 shows both the hard-edged shadows of the chess pieces lit by direct sun and the much softer shadows that are cast by the cloudy sky. Chapter 3 discusses several approaches to rendering hard and soft shadows, and when you can replace shadows with occlusion.

- The *throw pattern*, or the shape of a light, is another noticeable quality. Figure 1.1 also shows the throw pattern the sunlight makes after it has been filtered through Venetian blinds. Chapter 2 discusses projecting cookies from your lights to simulate different throw patterns.

- A light's *angle* tells you where it is coming from. For example, the light from the late afternoon sun comes from a lower angle than light in the middle of the day. A lighting designer controls the angle to help determine the visual function of a light, such as whether it functions as a key light, a kicker, or a rim. Aiming lights at the correct angle to achieve different visual functions and different looks for your characters is described in Chapter 5.

Almost any adjective you use to describe light can be considered a quality of light. I sometimes consider animation, such as whether a light is flickering or consistent, to be a quality of light. I have even heard other people describe the level of contrast as a quality of light, although I consider the amount of contrast in an image to be a function of the brightness and softness of the lights in the scene.

The one thing that ties all these qualities of light together is that you can study them in real life and work to imitate them with the lights in your

3D scene. In order to know which kinds of light you want to study in real life, you need to imagine what kinds of light sources motivate your scene's illumination.

Direct and Indirect Light

Direct light shines straight from an original source, such as a lightbulb or the sun, to an object that it illuminates. *Indirect light* is light that has reflected or bounced off at least one surface before it indirectly illuminates other objects. For example, if a floor lamp aims light at the ceiling, then the circle of light on the ceiling is direct light. The light that has reflected off the ceiling to softly illuminate the rest of the room is indirect light.

Direct light sources are usually the motivation for most of the brighter lights in your scene, but indirect light, such as light that has bounced off the ground or a wall, is also a motivation for light that can fill in the rest of your scene with soft illumination. Chapter 4 explains how to set up extra lights to simulate indirect light bounces in an environment, as well as how to use global illumination functions that simulate indirect light bounces for you.

Cheating

Cheating is an intentional departure from what's motivated; it is performed in a way so that it should not appear noticeably wrong to the audience.

Cheating in 3D

As a simple example of cheating, Figure 1.2 shows a scene with a candle as the main light source. A point light in the middle of the candle flame is lighting the whole scene. The Buddha statue on the right side of the screen is lit a bit by the candlelight, but only along one side of its face.

Figure 1.2 looks believable enough, but the Buddha statue in the foreground is not very well lit. The light from the candle illuminates only one side of it, and doesn't provide enough shaping and definition to really display the entire form. Even though the statue is positioned prominently in the frame, the lighting doesn't really emphasize the statue at all.

To improve the lighting on the statue, I duplicated the light positioned at the candle flame and used light linking (discussed in Chapter 2) to link the new light exclusively to the Buddha so that the new light doesn't light anything but the statue itself. Next, I did the actual cheat: I moved the light illuminating the statue forward, more toward the front of the scene. Figure 1.3 shows the cheated light position from the top view. I also brightened the light on the Buddha so that it gets more light from the candle than the other objects in the scene, which is another cheat.

When I render the scene with the candlelight illuminating the Buddha from a cheated position, the statue is much better defined by the lighting, as shown in Figure 1.4.

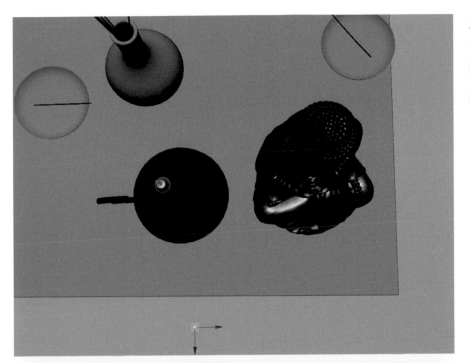

[Figure 1.3]
The point light at the bottom of this view is motivated by the candle flame, but I cheated its position to better light the front of the statue.

[Figure 1.4]
After the cheat, the statue appears better lit by the candlelight.

The objects in the background (a vase and some plates with incense sticks on them) are bright enough that they attract attention to themselves. I went into each of their shaders, darkened their colors, and reduced the brightness of the specular highlights on them. This is another cheat, but it makes them look as if they are farther back from the candlelight, and it helps the Buddha pop out into the foreground more. Figure 1.5 shows the scene with background objects darkened and the Buddha appearing more prominent in the shot.

[Figure 1.5]
Darkening the objects in the background and adding a rim light both help the statue pop out from the scene better.

One more cheat you may notice I added to Figure 1.5 is a rim light on the upper right of the Buddha. (Chapter 5 shows how to aim and use rim lights on characters.) This light could be motivated by some other off-screen candlelight, but really it is just another cheat, an addition to the scene that I thought would help the statue stand out from the environment.

Cheating is performed, to some extent, on almost every project produced in 3D. Shadows cast from one character to another are moved or removed if they are distracting. Light on a character that appears to come from a lamp may actually come from a position far away from the lamp if it lights a character better. Rims of light outline forms perfectly, even if no light is in exactly the right place to motivate them. Even if you start out a project dedicated to physical accuracy and try never to create any cheats, you are likely to have a client, director, or art director who will request visual improvements that require cheats in your scenes.

Cheating in Live Action

Knowing how to cheat and fake things is a crucial part of creating 3D graphics, but it is also an established part of the art of live-action cinematography.

A pool of light on the floor that appears to have come from a window may actually come from a light above the set. An actress running into a dark forest may have her face fully lit when in reality she would have been in darkness. Even the walls of the set are sometimes mounted on wheels (this is called a *wild wall*) so that they can be moved out of the way or rotated independently from other walls.

So why do lighting designers cheat? Why not just make the lighting be as accurate and true-to-life as possible? The short answer to these questions is that lighting and cinematography are arts, not just sciences. A more in-depth answer starts with understanding the *visual goals* that a lighting designer is trying to achieve when lighting a scene.

Visual Goals of Lighting Design

There is more to lighting a scene than simply running a simulation of real-world parameters. Lighting is also designed to achieve certain visual goals that help a viewer better appreciate a scene. How well you accomplish these goals determines how your lighting enhances or detracts from a shot.

Making Things Read

Much like photography, cinematography, and painting, 3D rendering is a process of producing two-dimensional images that depict three-dimensional scenes. *Making things read* means producing images that the audience can interpret as 3D spaces and arrangements of solid objects. To give your renderings solidity and presence, and to fully communicate the three-dimensional form of an object or character to an audience, you need to define your models with careful lighting. Some people call this process *modeling with light* because it is your lighting that lets the viewer perceive an object's 3D form. Defining a character with light is one of the main focuses of Chapter 5.

Making Things Believable

Computer graphics can be rendered in many different visual styles. Some projects require *photorealism* (images that can be mistaken for a photograph), while other projects are stylized in different ways or designed to create more illustrated or cartoon-like looks. Whether or not the visual style you adopt is photorealistic, your lighting still needs to be *believable* to the audience.

A believable image is at least internally consistent, with lights that are balanced in a way that would be motivated in real life. For example, if a beam of direct sunlight is entering a room, the viewer expects the sunlight to be brighter than the light of a table lamp. Even in a cartoon, basic expectations of weight and balance still exist. In fact, sometimes getting small details right in your lighting can even help "sell" a scene that otherwise would be impossible to believe.

Often the key to creating believable lighting is studying real life. Before beginning a project, try to study how light behaves in situations similar to what you will be rendering. In visual effects work, studying the *live-action footage* (the images filmed with a real camera) can show you a great deal about how a subject should appear in an environment. For projects created entirely in 3D graphics, collect *reference images* that you can study to see how color and light appear in a real scene. No matter how you obtain them (whether you photograph the reference images yourself, find them on a photography website, or grab still frames from rented movies), you will find your collection of reference images useful throughout your project; you can use them while pitching your lighting plans to a director or art director, and later compare them with your renderings as you adjust your lighting.

It is a poor artist who blames his tools for his work. Part of making a scene believable is compensating for the failures, flaws, and limitations inherent in your hardware or software. Almost every physical effect discussed in this book, from indirect light bouncing off walls to the translucency in human skin, can be simulated through careful texturing, lighting, and compositing, even when your software doesn't fully or automatically simulate everything for you. When someone sees the picture or animation that you have lit, they want to see a complete, believable picture, not hear excuses about which program you used.

Enhancing Shaders and Effects

Frequently in 3D graphics you find it necessary to add lights to a scene to help communicate the identity of different surfaces and materials. For example, you may create a light that adds highlights to a character's eyes to make them look wetter, or puts a glint of light onto an aluminum can to make it look more metallic. Many effects that, in theory, you could create exclusively by developing and adjusting surfaces and textures on 3D objects are often helped along during production by careful lighting you design to bring out the surface's best attributes. No matter how carefully developed and tested the shaders on a surface were before you started to light, it's ultimately your job to make sure all that is supposed to be gold actually glitters.

Effects elements such as water, smoke, and clouds often require special dedicated lights. The effects department will create the water droplets falling from the sky on a rainy night, but it's your job as a lighting artist to add specular lights or rim lights to make the drops visible. Effects such as explosions are supposed to be light sources, so you need to add lights to create an orange glow on the surrounding area when there's an explosion.

Maintaining Continuity

When you work on longer projects such as feature films, many people are involved in lighting different shots. Even though the lighting is the work of multiple artists, you need to make sure that every shot cuts together to maintain a seamless experience for the audience. Chapter 12 discusses strategies that groups of lighters use to maintain continuity, including sharing lighting rigs for sets and characters, duplicating lighting from key shots to other shots in a sequence, and reviewing shots in context within their sequence to make sure the lighting matches.

In visual effects, continuity becomes a more complex problem, because you need to integrate your 3D graphics with live-action plates. During a day of shooting, the sun may move behind a cloud while one shot is filmed, and it may be brighter outside when another shot is filmed. Although integrating a creature or spaceship with the lighting from the background plate may be the key to making your shot believable, the continuity of the sequence as a whole is just as high a priority, and sometimes you need to adjust your shot's lighting to match the lighting in adjacent shots as well.

Directing the Viewer's Eye

In a well-lit scene, your lighting should draw the viewer's eye to areas that are important to the story, animation, or key parts of the shot. Chapter 7 will cover more about how composition and staging work and what makes a part of the frame attract the viewer's eye or command attention.

Besides making the intended center of interest visible, good lighting avoids distracting the audience with anything else. When you are viewing an animated film, the moment something unintended catches your eye— whether it's a strange flicker or artifact, a highlight where it doesn't belong, or a shadow that cuts across a character—your eye has been pulled away from the action and, worse than that, your attention has been pulled away from the story. Good lighting can add a lot to a film, but first and foremost, you must do no harm when it comes to the viewer's experience of watching the animation.

Emotional Impact

When they are absorbed in the story and watching what happens to the characters in a movie, most of your audience never consciously *sees* your lighting; instead they *feel* it. Helping create a mood or tone that enhances your audience's emotional experience is the most important visual goal of cinematic lighting design.

Chapter 8 focuses on the different moods and associations that color schemes can create for a shot. While staying within what is motivated and believable, you still have room to achieve a range of different looks or moods when you are lighting a scene. Is it very starkly lit, with high contrast and harsh shadows? Is it softly lit, with subtle lighting and soft shadows? Is the scene very colorful with lots of saturated tones, or is it gloomy and desaturated? Is there a point in the scene when the tone shifts and something changes? Knowing the story and, of course, discussing the main points of the scene with the film's director are the keys to planning the type of mood you will try to achieve.

Achieving the visual goals of good lighting design is an artistic process, grounded in the tradition of cinematography, which in turn borrows a great deal from painting. Although this book covers a number of the key technologies that are speeding up or changing the process of lighting, mastering the craft of lighting a 3D scene is, at its heart, a timeless skill whose value will not go away with any new button or switch that will be added to future graphics software.

Lighting Challenges

Lighting is an iterative process. Rerendering scenes with better and better lighting, while getting feedback on your versions, is essential to perfecting your lighting skills. To help you get more practice with lighting, and to get feedback on your scenes as you light them, you can browse through an ever-expanding set of "Lighting Challenge" scenes, which are available for download from this book's companion website, www.3dRender.com, in a variety of file formats. On the Lighting Challenges discussion forum, you can see how other artists have lit each scene; see breakdowns of the lights, the render passes, and other elements of people's work; and, most important, post versions of your own work to get feedback.

Even though the Lighting Challenges were conceived as a sort of online lighting contest in which many people have participated, the wealth of scenes we have generated over the years are ideal for practicing lighting, whether you are going to post your results on our discussion forum or not. As you read this book, you'll notice that I use Lighting Challenge scenes in many of the figures to illustrate many concepts and techniques. These scenes can be rendered many different ways. Figure 1.6 shows several of the entries created by different artists using just the first Lighting Challenge scene, a basic fruit bowl. Feel free to download the scene and take a stab at lighting it yourself.

[Figure 1.6]
The Fruit Bowl Lighting Challenge, as lit by Angel Camacho (upper left), Lazhar Rekik (upper right), Florian Wild (middle left), Andrzej Sykut (middle right), Holger Schömann (lower left), and Ctrlstudio (lower right).

Your Workspace

Before you start work on lighting your 3D scene, pay some attention to the lighting in your own office or the area around your computer.

Working in a room with sunlight coming in through a window, or too bright a glow from ceiling lights or lamps, can limit your perception of the scene you are trying to light. Before you begin lighting a scene, turn your office lights down or off, and make sure no reflections or screen glare is visible on your monitor.

Also take a moment to check that your current monitor is adjusted properly. As a simple approach to calibrating your monitor, visit www.3dRender.com and view the monitor calibration image shown in Figure 1.7 on your screen. Make sure you can read all of the gray numbers at the top and bottom of the image; if any are unreadable, you are missing a part of the dynamic range of your images. Check both the controls on your monitor as well as the software control panel to make sure you don't have the brightness or contrast adjusted to a level that hides bright or dark tones from you.

[**Figure 1.7**] When viewing this image on your monitor, make sure you can read all of the numbers along the top and bottom.

If you are ever creating printed output, the most accurate way to calibrate your monitor is to print a test image first and then adjust your monitor to match the printer's output. The calibration will never be completely perfect for every color, but you should be able to get a reasonably good preview of what you will get if you adjust the monitor side by side with printed output.

If you are creating output for video or television, it pays to view your footage on more than one brand of consumer-grade television set. Many studios do final color correction on expensive, precisely calibrated color monitors that show extremely accurate color reproduction, but don't necessarily match what many viewers see at home. When you see a project on a variety of different televisions, you'll actually get a better idea of how your viewer is likely to see your work.

Creative Control

You probably learned this lesson when dining at seafood restaurants: *If it smells like fish, it is not good fish.*

A similar principle applies in computer graphics: *If it looks like computer graphics, it is not good computer graphics.* When an image is well lit and well rendered, the technology behind the image does not call attention to itself. Viewers notice only a compelling image, a realistic scene, or an innovative new visual style. When viewing a great rendering, the fact that you used a computer in creating the image is not the first thing that strikes a viewer's mind.

When you, the artist, are truly in control of your 3D rendering, then it should be only your hand that the viewer sees in your work, rather than the impression that a computer has made the picture.

The goal of this book is to help you take control of the lighting and rendering process so that every aspect of your rendering is the result of your own deliberate and well-informed decisions. Every chapter will deal with an issue or aspect of lighting and rendering your 3D scenes, and each will discuss how it works and how you can make it work better. In the next chapter, we'll start by discussing how to begin lighting a project, what kinds of light you need to add, and how to adjust the options and controls on your lights.

CHAPTER TWO

Lighting Basics and Good Practices

There aren't many "happy accidents" in 3D graphics. To achieve professional results, you need to be in control of every step of the lighting process, from initial planning through managing revisions of your work. You need to choose the appropriate type of light for each purpose, test-render each light, adjust its controls and options, and create versions of your scene until you can please your client or director.

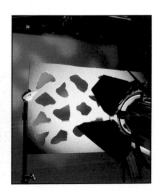

Starting the Creative Process

Where does the lighting process start? The answer varies widely between companies and projects. Sometimes, especially at smaller companies or on smaller projects, it is as simple as having a conversation with the client or director. He may tell you that the scene is set at night, outside the premier of a movie, and he wants a blue or purple gradient for the sky, camera flashes illuminating the characters from all directions, and spotlights sweeping through the sky in the background. From that verbal description, you can sit down and develop some test images to show the director the next day.

Putting images of similar scenes in front of the director can help move along the conversation about your project goals. If you don't have any pre-existing concept art or reference images, then gather images of the type of scene you think the director wants from the Internet, capture frames from rented movies that contain similar scenes, or find pictures in books, magazines, and stock photography catalogs. The sooner you can put some images in front of the director and agree that you are trying for something that looks similar to them, the better your communication about the project will be.

If you are working on visual effects shots, then a common task will be to light 3D models and composite them into a live-action movie. To start this task, you are given the *background plates*, which are the digitized frames that were filmed as a part of the movie. Usually you will also get some reference images of a sphere or other simple objects that were held in front of the camera; you can use these to attempt to match the lighting of the shooting location. Your background plate is your bible in lighting your visual effects shots. You need to observe every detail you can in it—the angle and sharpness of the shadows; the colors, tones, and level of contrast in the scene—and incorporate these observations into your lighting.

If you are working on an animated production, the art department will have started working on the look of the scenes long before you begin to light them. They are likely to have paintings or illustrations of what each scene should look like. The lighting artist will draw inspiration from this art and use it to match the colors and tones, even while making her own decisions about exactly how to implement the lighting design in terms of the many types of lights or options available in 3D graphics.

When to Light

When you are working in the early stages of a project, like modeling, rigging, or layout, you probably don't want to spend too much time on lighting. At most, you want to use a simple lighting rig that allows you to see the models.

By the time animation is being test-rendered, however, it is a good idea to have at least one light casting a shadow. If you render animation without any shadows, it is easy to overlook physical contact mistakes, like a foot that does not make contact with the ground. These kinds of mistakes become apparent in a fully lit scene, so it is best if you can catch them when you are testing animation.

The real lighting process begins when your layout is done: You know where your camera will be positioned and how the shot is composed, your animation is complete, and you can see where the characters will appear throughout the shot. Also, your shaders and textures are finished, so you can see how objects will respond to light.

Sometimes production schedules force you to do lighting work while revisions are being made to the animation or even to the camera. This is an unfortunate necessity. Lighting an incomplete scene wastes some of your time, because often you need to go back and change your lighting (sometimes multiple times) due to changes others make to the animation, shaders, or textures.

The Feedback Loop

Your first rendered output is, at best, a rough draft of what you want to develop into a professional final product. Most of your time in lighting is spent revising and improving the setup—this is where the real work gets done. The art of lighting is essentially the art of *revising* lighting, to craft the best look possible by your deadline.

An essential part of refining your scene is the *feedback loop:* making changes, waiting to see the results of each change, evaluating those results, and then making more changes. The key here is a tight feedback loop, which means you see results as soon as possible after you make changes.

This leads to a quicker work pace and more refined results on a compressed schedule.

How can you get feedback faster? For some types of changes, such as changing the position of a light or adjusting the size of a spotlight's cone, most modern 3D software supports real-time feedback, which shows you the basic illumination, highlights, and shadows as you drag the light. What's visible in real-time is limited, however, and usually it doesn't show you how everything will appear in a final render.

When you are doing software test-renders, you should always think of ways to save rendering time:

- Leave visible in your scene only those objects that you really need to see in each render; hide everything else. If there are any particularly complex models in your scene, sometimes you can use a simpler object as a stand-in while you adjust lights around it.

- If you are adjusting one specific light or shadow, hide all the other lights in your scene so that you are rendering only with that light. Soloing a light gives you a clearer view of exactly what the light is contributing to the scene, but it also saves valuable rendering time by skipping the calculation of the other lights and shadows in your scene.

- You can make most changes while you look at only part of your image—crop a region that shows only what you need to see, rather than rerendering the entire frame.

- Even when lighting film resolution shots, render your earlier tests at a video resolution, and render only a few frames from the shot at full resolution until you have the lighting approved.

- Turn off any functions or effects that aren't part of what you are currently adjusting. You can light a character without making her hair visible in the shot for most of your test renders, and then you can perform only a few tests with hair visible when you are working on the hair lighting. You do not need time-consuming functions such as raytracing, global illumination, or high-quality anti-aliasing turned on during all of your test renders.

While computers keep getting faster, projects continue to get more complex to take advantage of them, so learning to make intelligent choices and think about what you really need to see in each render are skills you'll still need later in your career.

Chapter 11 discusses compositing, another key factor in your feedback loop. If you render elements in separate passes and layers, you can make many changes to your scene in a compositing program; doing so allows you to make some kinds of changes interactively without rerendering.

Naming Lights

Naming becomes twice as important if you are installing lights that more than one person will use or edit. If you expect other people to be able to make sense of your lighting design, or if you want to avoid mistakes when you get confused between one light and another, take care to label everything clearly.

The most informative names refer to the type of light, its motivation, and what it is illuminating. For example, the name "Spec_fromMatch_onEyes" tells you that the light is designed to create specular highlights, is motivated by a match, and illuminates the character's eyes. "Bounce_fromRedCarpet_onSet" describes light bouncing off the red carpet onto the rest of the set. Most studios have much more exacting naming conventions. Exactly which conventions you follow doesn't matter as much as making sure that everyone follows the same set of rules and tries consistently to create helpful names for each light.

Organizing your lights into clearly named groups is also important. If you have some lights you use for similar purposes—such as exterior lights that come in through windows of a set, interior lights on the set, lights you have added around a particular character, or lights associated with a particular effect—then grouping these lights and giving the groups intuitive names makes them easy to find and adjust, and easier to save as separate files and reuse in other shots.

Managing Versions

You will go through many versions of a scene before you achieve a final, approved lighting setup. When you save each version, be sure to save the rendered images, and also save the lights you used to render it. If you have just shown a version of a scene to the client, consider making a folder with a backup of the 3D files and the rendered images from that version; this way, you can go back and retrieve that version if you need to. Sometimes you will go backward—clients do request changes one day and then ask you to revert to a previous iteration the next. Often when you make two versions of something, you are asked to "split the difference" between a previous version and the current one, which makes it vital that you maintain an association between the 3D scenes you use and the images that you show to the client.

When you compare two versions of an image, do so in the same window, flipping back and forth between the old and new images. When you view things side by side, it's often difficult to detect every change. But when you look at them in the same window, even the subtlest changes become visible shifts when you flip between the versions. Viewing a pair of frames in this manner before and after a change is a great way to test your own work, and it is also useful when you need to show the requested changes to a client or director.

Types of Lights

You begin setting up lighting in a 3D scene by choosing which types of light to add. The actual lights that you can use in a 3D program are based roughly on real-world types of light sources. Each has its own uses and advantages, so it pays to know your tools and choose them carefully.

Point Lights

A *point light*, also known as an *omni* or *omnidirectional light*, is the simplest light source to use in 3D graphics. It emits light uniformly in all directions, with all rays of light radiating out from a single point in space. Figure 2.1 is lit by a point light visible on the right side of the image. You can see that all of the shadows radiate away from this point.

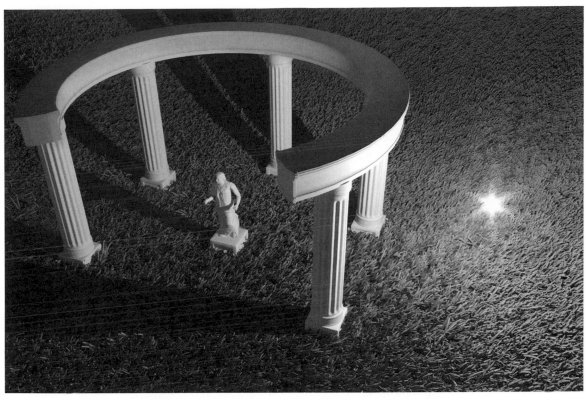

[Figure 2.1] A point light emits light uniformly in all directions, casting shadows that radiate out from the light's position.

A point light in 3D graphics is best compared to a bare lightbulb hanging in the middle of a room; as shown in Figure 2.2, some programs even represent point lights with a bulb icon. Yet unlike a real bulb, a standard point light is infinitely small, so all of the light emitted from it comes from exactly the same point in space.

When point lights are set to cast shadows and you model a light fixture around them, the shadow of the light fixture limits and shapes where the light can shine, as shown in Figure 2.3. However, lighting artists may prefer to use spotlights for this kind of effect, because spotlights provide more control over exactly where the light is aiming.

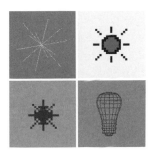

[Figure 2.2]
Icons for a point light in LightWave 3D, a radial light in Electric Image, a point light in Maya, and a point light in Softimage all perform similar functions.

Spotlights

Spotlights (also called *spots*) are a popular type of light in computer graphics, because they can be controlled and adjusted so completely. Just like a point light, a spotlight simulates light radiating from an infinitely small point. However, instead of aiming in all directions, it is limited to a specified cone or beam of light in a certain direction. The spotlight's rotation can determine where the beam is aimed, or a *target* or *interest* may be linked to the light so that the light is always aimed toward the target. Figure 2.4 is lit with a spotlight instead of a point light. Notice that only the objects within the spotlight's cone are lit.

Within the spotlight's cone, the illumination and shadows look similar to the illumination and shadows from a point light. If you think of a point light as an entire pie, then a spotlight is like one slice out of the pie. Because we artists love being in control of exactly where light is aimed in a 3D scene, many of us prefer to order by the slice. You can do almost all of your lighting with spotlights. Even when light needs to be aimed in different directions, you can use several spotlights together, as shown in Figure 2.5.

Spotlights have handy controls that you can adjust to shape exactly where light falls. The *cone angle* determines the width of the spotlight's beam, whereas the *penumbra angle* (also called *falloff* or *spread angle*) determines the softness of the edge around the spotlight's beam.

[Figure 2.4]
A spotlight's illumination is limited to a cone aimed in a specific direction.

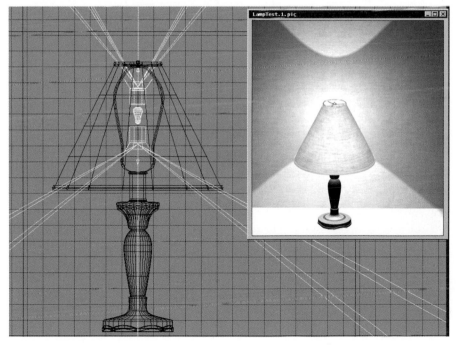

[Figure 2.5]
You can aim multiple spotlights in different directions, which gives the appearance of an omnidirectional light while allowing more control over where the lights are aimed.

A hard-edged spotlight calls attention to itself, projecting a bold circle into the scene. You can use a very small penumbra angle for this kind of effect to simulate a search light aimed from a helicopter at a person running on the ground or a spotlight aimed at a stage performer.

An artist can use spotlights with very soft edges, on the other hand, to subtly "paint" light into different areas of a 3D set. When each spotlight softly illuminates or colors a specific area, and the edges of the overlapping spotlight beams are soft enough, they all blend together. You do not perceive a distinct circle of light from each spotlight. Instead, you see a continuous, softly lit area. Figure 2.6 shows this kind of lighting style. If the spotlights have low penumbra angles for a hard edge, you will see circles of light projected from each light, as shown on the left side of the figure. With larger penumbra angles to soften the beams, you no longer notice the shape of the individual spotlights at all. As shown on the right side of Figure 2.6, soft spotlights can blend together seamlessly to create continuous-looking lighting. Chapter 4 describes how to place lights as shown in this figure.

Spotlights also have an option called *barn doors*. In real life, barn doors are metal flaps mounted in front of a spotlight, as shown in Figure 2.7, which can be folded in front of the light to crop it horizontally or vertically. In 3D graphics barn doors give you the same kind of creative control, enabling you to crop out a square or rectangle of light.

[Figure 2.6] With hard-edged lights (left), you can see every spotlight cone distinctly. When the penumbra angle is increased to create soft spotlight beams (right), the beams merge together so that you cannot distinguish between the individual sources.

[Figure 2.7]
Barn doors also allow a cinematographer to limit the coverage of a spotlight to less than its natural cone angle.

Spotlights are also popular in computer graphics for technical reasons. Because they can be aimed and focused in specific areas, they allow for efficient, accurate shadowing when you are using depth map–type shadows. Your ability to aim a spotlight also helps you aim and position cookies—when you use a light like a slide projector to project a pattern or texture map into the scene.

Directional Lights

A *directional light*, which is particularly useful for simulating direct sunlight, is also known as a *distant*, *direct*, *infinite*, or *sun light* in different programs; the different icons are indicated in Figure 2.8.

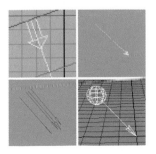

[Figure 2.8]
Common icons for directional lights indicate that parallel rays are being cast in a single direction.

A directional light is different from other kinds of light in that you adjust it mainly by rotating it instead of moving it. The light's position is not what changes the illumination; what matters is the angle of its rotation. A directional light illuminates every object in the scene from the same angle, no matter where the light is located. For example, when a directional light is aimed downward, it illuminates the top of every object in the scene, even the objects located above the light.

In Figure 2.9, the directional light aims down and to the left, causing every object to be illuminated as if it were being lit from the upper right. No matter where the directional light is located in the scene, it fills the scene with parallel rays of light, with all rays aimed in the direction that the light is pointing. Notice that the shadows of all of the columns are parallel to each other, instead of diverging away from the light position like the shadows from the point lights and spotlights.

Directional lights simulate the illumination from a very distant light source like the sun. In real life, the sun can light whole scenes from a uniform angle, just like a directional light. Even across a large area like a football field, goalposts at both ends of a football field can both cast shadows at the same angle and evenly light the entire field.

[Figure 2.9]
A directional light creates parallel shadows and illumination that strike each object from the same angle.

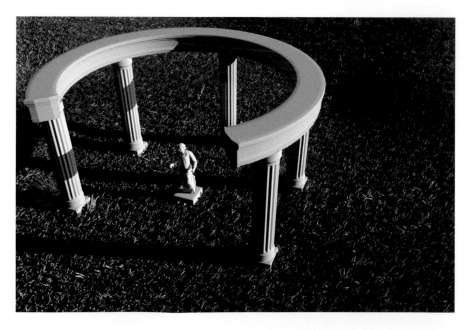

Sky Domes

A *sky dome* (also called an *environment sphere*) is a special light source that provides illumination from all around your scene. Environment spheres are perfect for simulating light from the sky. They also make great *fill lights*, the secondary lighting that you need to fill in areas unlit by your main light source. Figure 2.10 is lit entirely by an environment sphere, with no other light sources added.

When you map environment spheres with an image, the renderer uses the colors from that image to determine the brightness and color of the illumination from each angle. This technique, called *image-based lighting (IBL)*, is covered in Chapter 4. If you have a ground plane in the scene, then the lower half of the sphere could be underground and might not contribute to the illumination. So domes that wrap around the aboveground portion of the scene are sometimes used instead of full spheres.

By themselves, the illumination from sky domes is usually very soft, thus creating very soft shadows. However, sky domes can be combined with a directional light for outdoor scenes. The directional light can represent the sun, coming from one angle, and the sky dome can provide softer illumination from the sky, coming from all of the other angles.

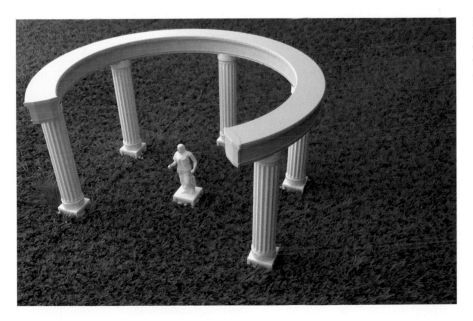

[Figure 2.10]
A sky dome surrounds the scene and lights it with the colors mapped onto the dome.

Area Lights

An *area light* (also called a *rect light*) simulates a panel of light with a specified shape and size, allowing you to create the kind of soft illumination and shadows that you'd expect from any physically larger light source. Contrast area lights with point-source lights (such as a point light or a standard spotlight) in which all light radiates from an infinitely small point. Area lights can be ideal lighting tools for simulating light coming from fluorescent lights in ceiling panels, for adding soft fill light from the sky coming through a window, or for any kind of softer looking illumination that casts natural-looking soft shadows into the scene.

With other kinds of light, such as a point, spot-, or directional light, scaling up the light only scales up the icon, leaving your illumination unchanged. With an area light, however, scaling up the light makes the illumination from the light brighter and softer, and also causes it to cast softer shadows into the scene.

The brightness of an area light is usually dependent on its size. A larger area light can be much brighter than a smaller area light, which is just what you'd expect if you had a larger panel of light emitting more light into a room. Sometimes very small area lights can be too dim to see, unless you greatly boost the intensity or power of the light. An exception to this rule is if an area light has an intensity set in real-world units such as lumens, because in this case, its brightness does not change with its size. If you are using a kind of area light with built-in U- and V-size parameters, then use these parameters to adjust the size of the light source, instead of scaling the whole light.

Area lights are often available in a variety of shapes, including spherical area lights, rectangles, discs, and linear lights (light from a line). If you have a choice, use the shape that best fits the type of light source you are trying to simulate. For example, a linear light can be perfect for simulating a fluorescent tube.

Figure 2.11 is lit with an area light. Notice that the lighting appears softer, with softer shadows than those created with the point light.

A large area light, casting soft shadows, requires more shadow samples to produce smooth-looking shadows that aren't grainy. As you increase the sampling of an area light's shadows, you get higher quality shadows without extra grain, but this begins to slow down your rendering.

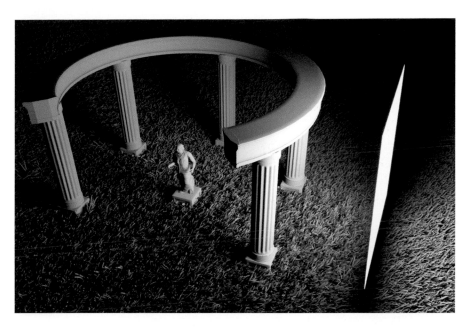

The quality of light and shadows you can achieve with area lights makes them an excellent choice for realistic renderings. They are not the quickest type of light to render, but with faster computers, more and more film productions are biting the bullet and using more attractive area-light shadows, even though they add to overall rendering times.

When lighting the interior of a room with daylight coming in through a window, you can position an area light right outside the window, as shown in Figure 2.12, to simulate soft illumination from the sky flooding in through the window.

The illumination from an area light can simulate soft illumination from the sky outdoors, flooding in from the window, as shown in Figure 2.13. This area light doesn't simulate a sunbeam (a directional light might be better for that), but instead it adds all the soft fill light that comes in through a window from other angles. In many programs, there's even a special kind of area light called a *portal light* designed specifically to be used this way. Portal lights work like regular area lights, only instead of having just one color and brightness setting, they read color and brightness information from a sky dome outside to better simulate illumination coming from whatever is outside of the window.

[Figure 2.12]
An area light can be positioned outside a window to simulate soft sky illumination.

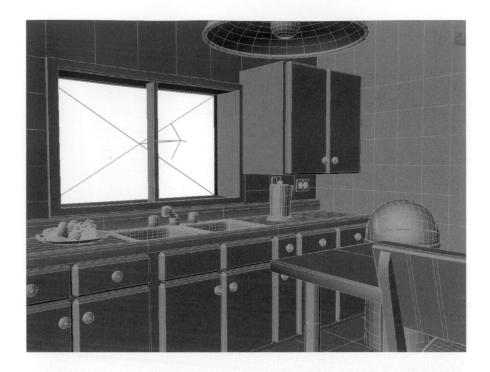

[Figure 2.13]
Illumination from an area light floods through the window to brighten the surrounding area.

Physically Based Lights

Physically based lights (also called *IES lights* or *photometric lights*) are calibrated to match specific, real-world types of light sources. Often they can read IES (Illuminating Engineering Society) data for real light fixtures based on measurements taken from specific brands and models of lightbulbs. IES files are readily available on the Internet for almost every type of manufactured light. You can adjust parameters of a physically based light using real-world units, such as color temperature and lumens. Simply switching to a different IES file simulates a different kind of light. Figure 2.14 shows three lights with different IES data. Notice that each light casts a different pattern of illumination onto the wall.

[Figure 2.14]
Three lights with different IES profiles throw different patterns of illumination on a wall.

Instead of setting a color as an RGB value, the color on physically based lights is usually set as a color temperature. Chapter 8 describes Kelvin color temperatures and has charts of specific color temperature values. Lower numbers in the 1,700–1,800 range are red, 3,000 is yellow, and higher numbers in the 8,000–10,000 range represent blue colors of light.

Instead of setting the power or intensity of the light in units internal to your rendering software, you can set the brightness of a physically based light in *lumens*. Lumens are a measurement of the amount of light emitted from a light source. Many of us are still accustomed to using *watts* to describe the brightness of a lightbulb; for example, on a film set, you would expect a 10k (10,000-watt spotlight) to be brighter than a 2k. Among old-fashioned incandescent bulbs, you probably grew familiar with the difference in brightness between a 60-watt bulb and a 150-watt bulb. However, the wattage of a lightbulb describes only how much electricity the bulb uses, not its light output. More efficient bulbs deliver more light using less electricity. For example, a 60-watt incandescent bulb emits about 890 lumens of light, while a 23-watt compact fluorescent lamp emits about 1,500 to 1,600 lumens. Recently labels have been changed on lightbulb packages so that they advertise their output in lumens, instead of just a number of watts they use.

Don't expect that using physically based lights will automatically increase the realism of every scene. A chain is only as strong as its weakest link, and several links occur between a light source and the final appearance of your image. Light originates from the source, but it must travel through space, reflect off a surface, and be photographed by a camera before it adds to the brightness of an image. Physically based lights can increase realism only if all the other links in the chain are also physically correct. For example, if your scene is not built to an accurate scale, then using a realistic 150-watt lightbulb does not produce realistic illumination. If your scene units are centimeters, then make sure your set is the correct number of centimeters across before you use physically based lights.

Materials or shaders need to be physically based—that is, derived from real materials—rather than just adjusted by sight. You need to use a physically based camera, and most importantly, make sure it is adjusted to a realistic exposure value for your indoor or outdoor setting. A physically based camera model with exposure values set for a sunny exterior scene might render an indoor lamp so dimly that you can't see it. For nighttime or indoor scenes, you might need to adjust the camera's exposure brighter to make the physically correct light visible in your scene.

If these concerns sound like a layer of unnecessary complexity to you, then you have no reason to start using physically based lights right away. Topics such as camera exposure and shaders will be covered in later chapters. For years, physically based lights have been popular in architectural visualization, but they have never become as popular in the film industry. However, as the film industry slowly evolves toward using more global illumination, physically based lights, shaders, and camera models are slowly starting to become more popular as well, at least as a starting point from which cheats and adjustments can be made.

Models Serving as Lights

In some programs, any 3D model in your scene can be designated to function as a light source. With this feature, you can use even nontraditional shapes of light, such as a neon sign, as a true light source, as shown in Figure 2.15.

Any renderer that supports global illumination allows objects to illuminate other objects. When rendering with global illumination (or just final gathering), applying a high incandescence or a bright ambient color to an object's material allows it to function like a light source. To achieve this effect, often you need to assign colors that are brighter than pure white to the incandescence or ambient values. For example, if RGB values of {1,1,1} represent pure white, you can assign RGB values of {10,2,2} to create a super-bright red that illuminates other objects.

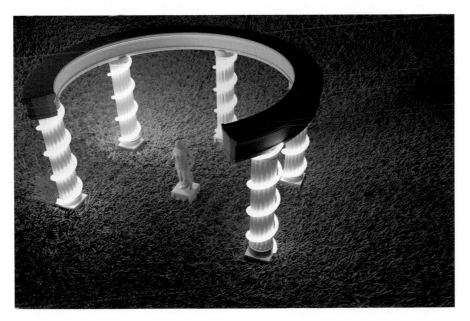

[Figure 2.15]
Even though there are no lights in this scene, helixes modeled around the columns function as light sources that resemble neon tubes.

As it becomes more common to make models serve as lights, some renderers are including a material or shading option designed specifically for this purpose, such as VRay's Light Material. Light Material even has a *direct illumination* option that lets objects serve as light sources when you have global illumination turned off.

It is possible to render a 3D scene in which there are no actual lights and every source of illumination is just a 3D model of a lightbulb, with a material bright enough to let the model illuminate other objects through global illumination. It's tempting to try to work this way, because then you don't need to add any lights in your scene, and illumination all originates naturally from real-looking lightbulbs. However, software today tends to be optimized to light scenes with lights, not with models. You'll probably find that working with lights to light your scene gives you the best control over your illumination and also tends to render more efficiently. The technique of using models as lights is usually reserved for special cases, such as walls illuminated by neon signs, glowing molten metal, fire coming from a dragon's mouth, or glowing force fields. If all you need is a lamp with a lightbulb in it, just place a point light inside the model of the lamp; this is the most efficient and controllable approach.

Ambient Light

In real life, *ambient light* means the light that is all around you. It includes light from the sky, light that reflects back up at you from the ground or floor, and light from any other light source. If you hold out your fist in front of you, you can see light illuminating every side of it, but notice that the light contributes different colors and intensities at different angles. Real-life ambient light is different in every environment, but it's rarely very flat or uniform.

In computer graphics, many programs have an ambient light (sometimes called *global ambience*) that uniformly brightens your objects in an unrealistic way. It makes every side of every surface the same color, robbing your scene of shading and diversity. The general rule with this kind of ambient light is this: Don't use it. Ambient light has been a feature of 3D rendering since long before global illumination was common, and it just doesn't look as good as global illumination, or even as good as the simple techniques you can use to simulate global illumination, discussed in Chapter 4. Really, it doesn't look like anything except a fake way to artificially brighten your entire scene. Figure 2.16 shows the flat, unrealistic shading that comes from using ambient light as a fill light.

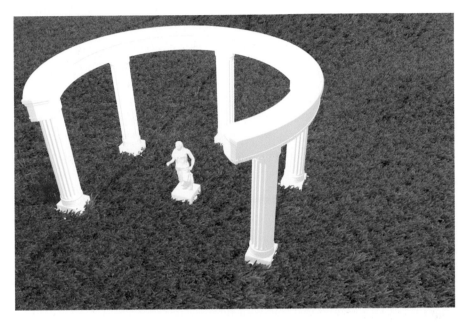

[Figure 2.16]
Ambient light flattens the scene and robs it of richness and shading.

If your scene needs to be brighter, you can add any kind of light discussed in this section to fill in the illumination where it is getting too dark. Any other type of light makes better fill light than a flat, uniform ambience.

Maya has another ambient light option, called *ambient shade*, which makes the ambient light less uniform. At a value of 1, this option makes an ambient light function more like a point light. As you lower the value, the ambient light wraps further and further around each object. When you reduce it to zero, the ambient light produces completely flat, uniform illumination.

You should always start lighting in complete darkness so that when you add your first light and test-render your scene, you see no illumination except what comes from that light. To accurately adjust and control your lighting, it is critical that you get rid of any extra light, including default lights or global ambience.

Adjusting Controls and Options

After you've added a light to your scene, you can adjust a wealth of controls and options on the light. Controls on your light can guide how the light spreads through space in your scene, which objects it illuminates, whether it creates a flat or shiny appearance in objects, and other qualities of illumination.

Soloing and Testing Lights

When you begin adjusting any light, the first step is usually to *solo* the light. This means you hide all the other lights in the scene and render the scene one light at a time. When you isolate each light, you know exactly how it contributes to the lighting and shadows in the scene, and you can accurately adjust the controls and options on the light.

You might be surprised how often you can have a light in your scene that is not actually contributing anything to the lighting. Perhaps all of the illumination is blocked because an object around it is casting a shadow. Perhaps the light is set to decay with distance so that it is not bright enough to see. In a scene with many different lights visible, you can easily get confused about which illumination comes from which light. You can identify and fix this kind of issue only if you solo your lights to test and adjust them one at a time.

If your scene is going to have several very similar light sources in it, such as from a row of similar light fixtures running down a hallway, it's best to create just one of the lights first, solo it, and adjust and test-render it until you are happy with every setting. After you are happy with the way your light looks in one fixture, then you can duplicate the light into all the other fixtures.

The advice to solo each light you work on isn't just advice for beginners. Professionals often adjust light parameters with only one light visible at a time. Even when you need to see more than one light at once, you don't necessarily need to make all the lights in the scene visible. Sometimes you can adjust lighting on one particular character without rendering all the lights on the set, for example. As long as all of your lights are visible when you eventually render your full shot, doing interactive tests with fewer lights visible both speeds up your work and gives you a more precise idea of how each light functions in the scene.

Decay

Decay (also called *attenuation* or *distance falloff*) controls how the intensity of a light decreases with distance. The image on the top of Figure 2.17 is an example of a light with no decay: It lights the farthest column as brightly as the near ones. The image below it is an example of a light with an *inverse square* (also called *quadratic*) decay: It lights the columns near it much more brightly than the distant ones.

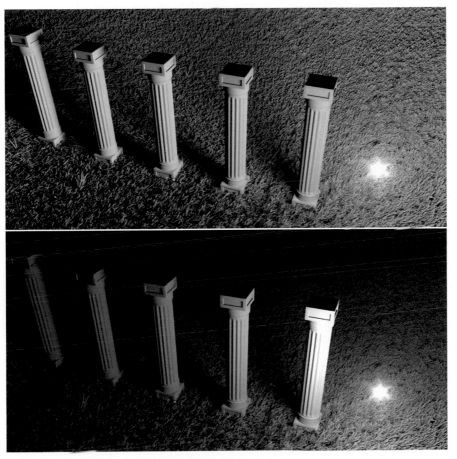

[Figure 2.17]
With no decay (top), the light illuminates each column evenly. With inverse square decay (bottom), objects closer to the light are brighter.

Some software offers a multiple-choice setting between three or four specific types of decay. Another way to adjust decay is by using a numeric value, usually labeled *decay* or *exponent*. The numeric approach is more flexible, because you can enter fractional values. For example, if you want a decay rate that's slightly less than 2, you can type in 1.8. Your main choices are shown in Table 2.1.

Table 2.1
Decay Rates

NUMERIC VALUE	TYPE OF DECAY
0	None
1	Linear (inverse)
2	Quadratic (inverse square)
3	Cubic

Inverse Square Decay

A decay rate of 2, also known as *inverse square* or *quadratic* decay, is the most physically correct decay setting. This is the type of decay seen in real light sources. In real life, decay is a function of light rays geometrically spreading out over space, not of the rays decreasing in energy. Real rays of light can travel huge distances—they can keep traveling for years—without growing any dimmer. However, as they travel farther away from their source, they are spread further apart and become scarcer.

Figure 2.18 shows how a plane moving twice as far from a source gets half as many rays of light over its height; this also happens across the width of a surface, so it will become one-quarter as bright every time you double the distance between the surface and the light. This geometric spreading out of photons is simulated by using an inverse square decay on your lights.

If a light source is visible in your shot, as in Figure 2.19 where a character has just lit a match, or you have modeled a lamp on a table and it is turned on, then it is a good idea to use an inverse square decay. Also, when working with global illumination, inverse square decay is a geometric property of how indirect light is bounced between surfaces, so using it on your primary lights adds to the consistency and realism of the rendering.

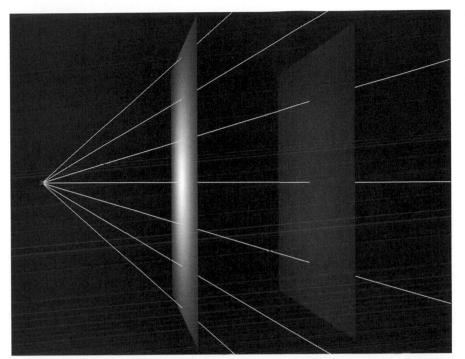

[Figure 2.18]
This diagram shows why twice as many rays of light may hit a nearby surface as would hit a surface at twice the distance. This difference over the height and over the width of a surface makes an object twice as far away receive one-quarter as much light.

[Figure 2.19]
An inverse square decay is useful when a light source (like this match) is visible within a scene. Character by Rini Sugianto.

A light with an inverse square decay usually needs to be much brighter at the source than a light that uses no decay. You need to turn up the intensity or multiplier of the light to get the light to travel a greater distance and illuminate distant objects, but doing so can sometimes make the area immediately surrounding the light appear too bright. Don't be afraid to type in very high numbers for the intensity or multiplier of the light. Especially if the light needs to travel a large distance to reach an object, you may need values in the thousands or millions for some lights.

Chapter 8 talks about the important issue of maintaining a *linear workflow*. Failing to use a linear workflow can affect the look of different decay settings on your lights. If quadratic decay always appears to be too much decay— the light looks too bright near the light source, while it is still too dim at a distance—this could be a problem caused by not using a linear workflow. Instead of choosing a different decay setting, your best approach is to adopt a linear workflow first; then you will see quadratic decay, which is the most physically correct setting, look as natural and believable as it should.

Using No Decay

You will run into situations in which you will not use any decay. These include when you simulate illumination from very distant light sources and when you use directional lights.

If you are simulating a very distant light source, like the sun, then using no decay can be the most realistic setting. For example, the sunbeam entering the room in Figure 2.20 does not get noticeably dimmer between the window and the left side of the table, so no decay is needed.

When using directional lights, it is normal to use no decay. Remember that for directional lights, the position of the light does not matter. It's only the angle defined by a directional light that controls its illumination, because it fills the entire scene with parallel rays of light. Some software doesn't even provide an option to choose different decay settings for directional lights.

Other Decay Settings

Using a decay of 3 (cubic) makes a light decay more rapidly than a real light would in a vacuum. But you can also use this setting to simulate a light in thick fog or under murky water, as shown in Figure 2.21.

[Figure 2.20]
A sunbeam entering a room does not need any decay, because light that has already traveled millions of miles is unlikely to visibly decay in the last few feet.

[Figure 2.21]
Cubic decay can simulate light shining through murky water.

Very high decays can also be useful if you are adding a light that needs to influence only a surface right next to it, such as when you position an extra highlight in a particular place on a car's bumper.

You can use a decay of 1 (linear) as a useful compromise between full inverse square and no decay at all. If you have simulated light bouncing up from the ground, you'll want some decay. However, since inverse square might sometimes appear to be too much, using a linear decay may work well. In addition to different decay settings, many programs also let you set specific distances at which your light attenuates. For example, you could set a light to begin growing dimmer at 50 units and have it disappear completely at 100 units from the light. This might not be physically correct, but it is certainly convenient. If you know that a light should not reach a certain object, setting it to cut off by a specific distance is a more reliable way to limit it than by just using inverse square. Setting a light to decay at a specific distance or region is also a great tool to use in conjunction with visual effects, such as putting a light into a force field or around a shockwave traveling through fog.

Diffuse and Specular Reflection

In real life, diffuse and specular are actually two ways that light can be reflected off a surface. In *diffuse reflection*, light rays are scattered in all directions. Think of light hitting a plaster wall or a piece of fabric, or anything that is not glossy or shiny—that is diffuse light reflectance. *Specular reflection* occurs when rays of light are not scattered at all, but instead they are reflected in parallel, creating a perfectly focused image. A mirror, or anything with a mirror-like reflection, shows you specular light reflectance.

When objects are rendered in 3D graphics, they can reflect the illumination from your light source in both diffuse and specular ways. The diffuse illumination is the primary shading, covering the side of the surface that faces the light. The specular shading usually appears as a smaller highlight, simulating a reflection of the light source itself.

Diffuse and specular light reflection are controlled in two ways. First, the shader that defines an object's surface appearance determines how it will respond to diffuse and specular illumination. A shader on one object could make it very shiny, whereas a different shader could give an object a completely matte finish with no highlights or reflections at all. Second, most software also offers options on the lights themselves, setting whether a light emits diffuse illumination or specular illumination. Figure 2.22 shows the results when a light is set to emit diffuse illumination, specular illumination, or both.

[**Figure 2.22**] A light can emit diffuse illumination (left), specular illumination (center), or both (right).

Most lights are usually set to emit both diffuse and specular illumination. However, there may be times when you want just one or the other. If you want to add highlights to a character's eyes but don't want to make the whole eyeball glow, then you can set a light to emit specular only. If you add an area light to simulate illumination bouncing up from the ground (which creates very soft illumination without a concentrated source), then you can set that light to emit diffuse only so that there won't be unmotivated highlights on the bottom of a shiny surface.

Some renderers allow you to set different levels for a light's diffuse and specular light emission. Instead of having such settings just on or off, you may want to give the sun a specular level of 1.0 to 1.2, give fill lights representing the sky specular levels between 0.3 and 0.5, and give lights representing illumination reflected back from the ground levels between 0 and 0.25. These numbers are just starting points; as you test-render, you will usually want to tweak the diffuse and specular levels for each light.

Sometimes it's useful to make two copies of a light; set one copy to emit only diffuse and the other copy to emit only specular. Replacing one light with two lights like this is called *splitting out* a light. Once you have split out a light into a separate diffuse light and specular light, you can separately adjust the brightness, color, and location of the specular light to tweak the appearance or position of the specular highlight without changing the overall diffuse illumination.

Specular highlights are supposed to look like reflections of a light source. However, in 3D graphics many light sources have an infinitely small size, with light coming from a single point in space. A point source light is infinitely small and has no area. Because of this, an accurate reflection of it would be a point smaller than a pixel, which could not be rendered because it would be too small to see. To correct for this, a cheat is programmed into shaders that adds an adjustable highlight size to each surface, simulating a reflection of a larger light source. The result is that specular highlights are not a true, accurate reflection of a light source. Highlights are not accurately raytraced reflections of lights in the same way that you can see raytraced reflections of other models. Instead, the size and softness of a specular highlight is a cheated rendering of what a larger light source might look like in a reflection.

Light Linking

Let's say you have a light that you want only for a specific purpose, such as adding highlights to a character's eyes. In such a case, consider using *light linking* (also called *selective lighting*), which allows you to associate specific lights with specific objects. Lights that are not associated with an object will not illuminate it at all, no matter how close the light is to the object.

For eye highlights, you can create a point light, set it to emit only specular illumination, and then link the light to the character's eyeballs. If this light is kept reasonably close to the camera position, you're guaranteed that the character's eyes will always have highlights when it looks toward the camera. And because of light linking, you'd know those highlights won't affect anything else in the scene.

You can also use light linking to gain more precise control over how different objects are lit. If you have a light illuminating many objects in your scene, you may find that it looks good on most of the objects, but somehow appears to light other objects with the wrong intensity, color, or angle. Instead of settling for a compromise, split out the light for the objects that aren't lit well. Just make two copies of the light: Use light linking to link one copy to the objects that aren't lit well, and unlink the other light from those objects. When you test-render your scene after splitting out the light, it should appear just the same as it did when you had only one light in that position. After you've checked that the light is split out correctly, adjust it to fix the illumination of the objects that weren't lit well.

One issue you should be careful about is that the default behavior for light linking in some programs also changes the shadow linking so that objects not linked to be illuminated by a light also won't cast shadows in that light. If you are splitting out lights to make subtle tweaks to the lighting on different objects, then turn off shadow linking, or at least do not set it to follow light linking.

Figure 2.23 shows an example of how you can use light linking to gain more precise control over how different objects are lit. There are two different lights used to represent the illumination from the match. One is linked to the character's hand and clothing, but not to his head. This one is positioned exactly at the match flame so that the hand and arm are lit from a realistic angle. The other light is linked only to the character's head, and it is cheated forward so that the match light wraps further around his face.

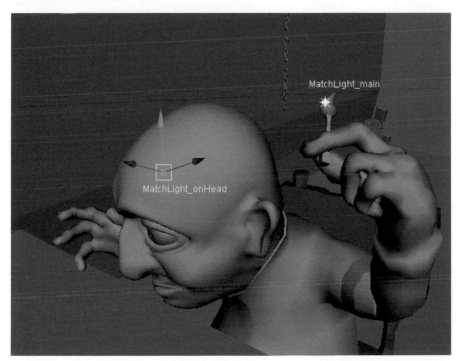

[Figure 2.23]
Light linking allows you to cheat and illuminate different objects using light with different angles, colors, or intensities.

Light linking is a marvelously powerful cheat, but if some objects appear to be getting too much more light than other objects, it can make an unrealistic image. Whenever you set up a scene with light linking, you need to test-render it and make sure that what you've done makes sense and doesn't depart too obviously from what's plausible.

Cookies

In lighting for movies, television, and theater, a *cookie* (also called a *cucoloris* or *gobo*) is a piece of metal, wood, or cardboard with holes or shapes cut out of it. Cookies are designed to break up a light or project a pattern into the scene. The exact origin of all these terms is not clear, but in the early days of movies, when lights were very hot, metal cookie sheets were used to make a cookie. *Cucoloris* could be a contraction of *cookie* and *iris*, and *gobo* could be short for *go-between*. Figure 2.24 shows a real cookie in action.

[Figure 2.24]
A real-life cookie has holes cut out to shape or dapple a spotlight's illumination.

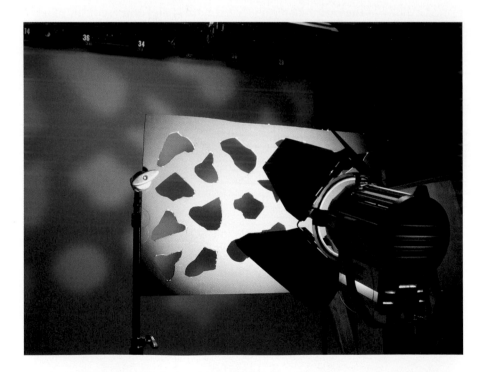

It is possible to model a cookie as a 3D object and put it in front of a light so that it casts shadows. However, a more direct way to create a similar effect in computer graphics is to map an image onto a light. In most 3D programs, the color of a light is mappable with any image you choose. You can use an image similar to the one on the left side of Figure 2.25 as a cookie and map it to the color of a spotlight. On the right side of the figure, you can see the resulting pattern projected into a scene.

[Figure 2.25] A texture map used as a cookie (left) breaks up your lighting as if the sun is being filtered through the trees (right).

Exercises

The following learning exercises provide you with practice creating and adjusting different types of 3D lights. If you don't have any 3D scenes to light, download one of the Lighting Challenge scenes I have made available at www.3dRender.com/challenges in multiple file formats.

1. A great learning exercise (which can be done on your own or as a class homework assignment) is to create a *one-light rendering*. That is, take a given 3D scene and light it with only one light. Some of the Lighting Challenge scenes you can download work well for this. Even a simple scene such as the fruit bowl can be lit well with one light. Do not turn

on global illumination, but do make sure your light casts shadows. Turn on shadows for your light, and turn on raytracing in your render settings if you are using raytraced shadows. Shadows are the subject of the next chapter, but using them at least with default settings will help better divide your scene into lit and unlit regions for this exercise.

With only one light, any area of the scene that falls into shadow is pure black, so a one-light rendering can appear to be a very high-contrast image. See how well the illumination and shadows can define key forms in your scene by bringing contrast to key profiles, or adding shading with a bright side and a dark side to each object. Use any of the light types available, and try to create a pleasant balance between lit and unlit areas of the image.

2. A classic cinematography exercise that has been used in Hollywood studios for many decades is to light an orange. If you can light an orange with shading and definition that bring out its shape and texture, then you have mastered a lot of the keys to revealing the shaping of an actor's face or many other subjects. I have included an orange model as a part of the Fruitbowl Lighting Challenge. Figure 2.26 shows one way you might chose to light an orange.

[Figure 2.26]
The classic cinematography exercise of lighting an orange gives you practice defining a form with light.

3. A great homework assignment for classes learning to use different types of lights is to assign students to match specific images. The instructor works with a 3D scene first and produces a set of images; then she deletes the lights from the scene and gives the 3D scene and the rendered images to the students. Using the lit images as references, students try to light the scene so it matches exactly the illumination they see in each image. As examples, the instructor can create a slash on the back wall of the scene using barn doors on a spotlight, have a scene softly lit by an area light, or use a specular-only light to add bright highlights to some objects. To facilitate matching, the instructor can provide students with the settings she used for the shadows on lights and render settings for the scene. Even matching the lighting in a very simple scene can be challenging, and the more lights that are used, the more challenging it gets.

CHAPTER THREE

Shadows and Occlusion

Setting up shadows takes just as much time and attention as setting up lights. You can think of illumination as one half of your lighting design and of shadows as the other, equally important half. Shadows can add richness to the tones and shading of your image, tie elements together, and improve your composition.

Closely related to shadows, *occlusion* is an overall effect that can look similar to soft shadows and be combined with regular shadows to darken parts of your lighting.

Rendering shadows and occlusion are key technical areas to master. Making the best choices of shadow-casting algorithms, building up a bag of tricks to cheat and manipulate your shadows, and knowing how to optimize your shadows and occlusion for the best possible rendering speed are essential skills for any 3D artist. This chapter will explore both the visual and the technical sides of shadows and occlusion in 3D graphics.

The Visual Functions of Shadows

People commonly think of shadows as obscuring and limiting vision, but they often reveal things that otherwise are not seen. Here are some of the visual functions that shadows serve in cinematic images and computer graphics.

Defining Spatial Relationships

When objects cast shadows onto each other, the spatial relationships between the objects are revealed. For example, compare the scenes in Figure 3.1 before and after shadows are added. Take a look at the version without shadows on the left side; you can't tell exactly where each ball is located. On the right side of the figure, shadows reveal how close some of the balls are to the back wall, which ball is on the ground, and where the balls are in relationship to each other.

[Figure 3.1]
The most basic use of shadows is to show spatial relationships between objects. On the right side of this figure, it is clearer which balls touch the back wall or the floor.

Shadows help show contact between objects when they touch. Any time a character touches or holds something, check to make sure that the object is shadowing the character and that the character is shadowing the object, so that a visible sense of contact is achieved between the character and the object. If you have lights in your scene that aren't set to cast shadows, that is likely to cause problems with physical contact.

Technical issues discussed later in this chapter—such as framing or bias settings with depth map shadows, or shadow linking controls that stop a hand from shadowing a prop—could cause a shadow to be missing where the viewer would expect to see a sense of contact.

The floor of a room can be full of shadows that indicate spatial relationships. From shadows on the floor, you can tell whether a character's foot is in full contact with the floor or is being held above it. For each piece of furniture in a room, you can tell which parts of the furniture are touching the floor and which float above it.

The way shadows visually indicate spatial relationships is both a blessing and a curse. When you render a scene with shadows, they can reveal mistakes and inaccuracies in your animation, for instance if a character's feet are floating above the ground instead of being planted firmly on it. In this kind of situation, an animator may need to edit her animation to fix whatever flaws become visible.

Revealing Alternate Angles

In addition to spatial relationships, a well-placed shadow can also disclose new angles on a subject that otherwise might not be visible. In Figure 3.2, the woman's profile is brought out by a shadow; without it, we would see only the front of her face.

You can think of a light casting shadows as something like a second camera, with its own angle of view and perspective on the character. Most 3D programs enable you to view the scene from a light's point of view to help you position and aim the light. The outline of what you see—the profile of the subject from the light's point of view—shows you the shape that will be rendered as the shadow. When you see how two objects align from a light's point of view, you can also visualize when and where one object will cast a shadow onto another.

[Figure 3.2]
The shadow reveals a character's profile, which otherwise would not be shown in this rendering.

The shadow a character casts should complement, not detract from, how you want your character to look. Be careful that no part of the character is too close to a point source or spotlight, because it could become disproportionately enlarged in the shadow. Also, be sure that any cheats that the animator has created don't look strange from the shadow's perspective. For example, if the animator has stretched a character's arm to an extra-long length to bring the hand into the foreground in a gesture, that cheated pose might look believable from the point of view of the camera, but look strange where the character's shadow is visible on the side wall. To fix this, you may need to change the angle of your shadows, thus hiding the part of the shadow that doesn't look believable.

Enhancing Composition

Shadows can play an important role in the composition of your image. A shadow can lead the viewer's eye to a desired part of the rendering or create a new design element to balance your composition. Figure 3.3 shows how a well-placed slash or other shadow can break up a space, adding variety to what otherwise would be a monotonous rear wall.

[Figure 3.3]
The image on the right is enhanced by a shadow on the back wall, which accentuates the top of the vase in the composition and breaks up the uniformity of the wall.

Adding Contrast

Figure 3.3 also shows how a shadow can add contrast between two elements that might otherwise appear similar in tone. In the right frame, the shadow behind the vase adds depth and definition to the rendering by increasing the contrast between the vase and the similarly colored wall behind it. The vase now pops out much more clearly from the frame so that people will clearly notice its shape, even in a brief shot.

Indicating Off-Screen Space

A shadow can also indicate the presence of off-screen objects. The sense of "off-screen space" is especially important when you are telling a story or trying to set a mood for a small scene. A shadow that appears to have been cast by objects not visible on the screen indicates that there is more to the world you are representing than what's directly visible in the shot. The shadows in Figure 3.4 suggest a great deal about the other elements that might be in the off-screen environment. Sometimes you can use a cookie to simulate shadows from off-screen objects, as discussed in Chapter 2.

[Figure 3.4]
The shadow indicates what might exist in off-screen space.

Integrating Elements

By cementing the relationship between objects, shadows can also create a kind of integration between the elements in a scene. In the fanciful or implausible scenes often created using computer graphics, realistic shadows

[Figure 3.5]
Shadows help integrate otherwise incongruous elements.

may be the only threads of reality available to tie together and sell the whole image. Even the commuting hippo in the subway car in Figure 3.5 looks more natural and present in the scene with shadows underneath him. Building a solid sense of contact between 3D sets and characters, between human actors and digital creatures, or even between 3D characters and real environments, is perhaps the most essential function of shadows. Without this contact, many scenes would fall apart into an apparent collage of disjointed images.

Making Walls Block Light

In real life walls are barriers, keeping outdoor light outdoors, indoor light indoors, and allowing a variety of different colors and tones of light to exist separately in each room or hallway of a building. Figure 3.6 shows what would happen if outdoor lights didn't cast shadows. Without shadows, the sunlight would shine right through the walls and ceiling of the set, instead of just entering in one place, through a window.

[**Figure 3.6**] Lights coming from outside need to cast shadows (left) if they are supposed to stay outside. Without shadows (right), the light shines right through the walls and overexposes the entire interior.

In any scene where you can see more than one area at once—because you look through a window or door into multiple rooms, or up a staircase to another floor, for instance—you expect the light to have different qualities in different parts of the scene. You expect a different brightness and color in different rooms or different levels in a house, and you expect a different light to appear outside than inside. Diversity in lighting appears in real life because different light sources have different brightnesses and colors, and also because different materials can transmit indirect light, such as when light bounces off a colored surface or filters through a cloth curtain or lampshade. To convey this richness and diversity in 3D scenes, you must keep the light in each area separate and use shadows to let walls block the light, except where a window or door allows some of the light to spill through.

The Appearance of Shadows

You have a lot of choices to make when you are adjusting the appearance of your shadows. Shadows may have a different hue than the rest of the scene. An object can cast a big shadow or a small one. Shadows can be bold and black or faint and subtle. Shadows may be crisp and hard-edged or soft and diffused.

Shadow Size and Perspective

The location of a light source relative to the object casting shadows determines the size of the shadows. For example, a light that is far away from your subject casts a shadow similar in size to your subject, as shown on the left in Figure 3.7. Alternatively, moving the light closer to the subject will enlarge the shadow, making the shadow much bigger than the subject itself, as shown on the right side of the figure.

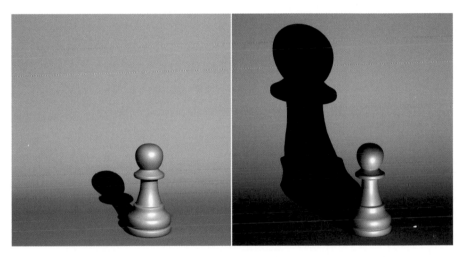

[Figure 3.7]
What size do you want your shadow to be? Move the light farther away for a smaller shadow (left) or up close for a larger shadow (right).

The type of light used matters in this technique. Moving the light closer to an object creates larger shadows when you are using point, spot-, or area lights, but this does not work with directional lights. Directional lights make shadows the same size as the object casting them, regardless of position.

Shadows look different, and even take on different shapes, when cast from different perspectives. For example, something is visibly wrong with the sunbeams on the left side of Figure 3.8. They were produced by putting one spotlight directly outside of each window. You can see how they splay outward, aiming away from the nearby lights. Moving the lights much farther back, as shown on the right side of the figure, to replicate the distance of the light source—the sun, in this case—makes the shadows appear parallel. On the right side of the figure, the left and right sides of the sunbeams appear parallel, as they would in real life. You can also use a directional light instead of spotlights to create parallel sunbeams.

[Figure 3.8] Sunbeams that spread out from an unnaturally close perspective (left) give away the fact that sun lights were placed too close to the windows. Moving lights farther away (right) creates parallel sunbeams.

Shadow Color

In real life, shadows often appear to be a different color than the area around them. For example, outdoors on a sunny day, shadows cast onto a white surface can appear to be tinted blue. The shadows appear blue because the bright yellow light from the sun is blocked from the shadow area, leaving only indirect light and blue light from other parts of the sky.

Shadow Color (the Natural Way)

In a 3D scene, the most natural, realistic way to create colored shadows is to assign different colors to different lights. Take the example of a sunny day; you can create a bright directional light representing the sun and give it a yellow color. Then create other lights representing general illumination from the sky in other directions (fill lights), and give them a blue color.

Where sunlight overlaps the light from the sky, their colors are added together. The hues from the yellow sunlight and the blue sky lights cancel each other out to a certain extent, so they appear almost white in areas where they are both present.

Inside the shadow, however, the sunlight is blocked. This is the only place where you really see the blue color from the fill lights. If you want more color to be visible in the shadows, add more color to the fill lights that illuminate the shadow area. Figure 3.9 shows the natural approach to colored shadows—a yellow sunlight casts hard-edged shadows, and blue fill lights fill in the shadow areas with a cooler tone.

You can look for the appearance of "blue shadows" outside on a sunny day. They are most visible when the sky isn't very cloudy and you have a white surface with shadows cast on it; this makes the light color more prominent than the color of the ground.

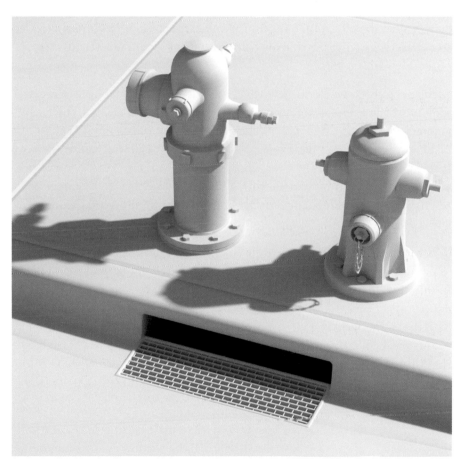

[Figure 3.9]
A blend of warm sunlight and cool blue fill from the sky creates a natural impression of a blue shadow color.

Color contrast between complementary colors such as yellow and blue can give your scene an engaging look. As a creative decision, you can also make colored objects cast shadows in complementary colors to the color of the object. For example, you could make red objects cast a blue shadow by filling in the shadow area cast by the red object with a blue light. The contrast between the object color and the shadow color helps the colored objects pop out visually. Note that adding complementary colors to an object's shadows is an artistic stylization, not something that always happens in real life.

The Shadow Color Parameter

There is a cheat available on most lights called *shadow color,* which artificially adds color to the shadows cast by that light. Pure black is the default shadow color, which means that no extra color or brightness is added to a shadow. Leaving the shadow color parameter set at pure black is the only truly realistic value.

Setting the shadow color to any value other than black is a cheat that can sometimes have unrealistic results. Some people give the shadow color parameter very deep, dark color values that are just a little brighter than black just to cheat in a little extra color into their shadows. Even this can create unrealistic results in some situations, however. Figure 3.10 shows yellow sunlight casting shadows with a blue shadow color. You'll notice the results are not as convincing as using blue fill light to fill in the shadows with a blue color.

What makes the results of using the shadow color parameter so unrealistic? When the shadow color parameter artificially adds color to your shadows, it only tints the places where a shadow is actually cast. The shadow color doesn't affect the dark side of an object where it faces away from the light. This discontinuity is the biggest problem with using the shadow color parameter. Look at Figure 3.10 and you can see that the blue is cast onto the sidewalk, but the unlit sides of the fire hydrants don't get the blue color. This is what makes it look less realistic than the natural approach of using colored fill lights, as shown in Figure 3.9.

Using colored fill lights is the best way to add a little extra color to all the dark tones in your scene. In realistic lighting, the shadow color parameter is a cheat that should be used sparingly, if at all.

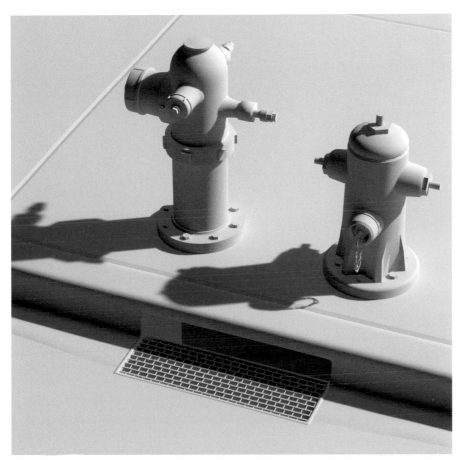

[Figure 3.10]
A fake-looking effect is created by assigning a blue color to the shadow color parameter of a light. Note how the unlit side of the hydrants does not match the tone of the shadow cast onto the ground.

Shadow Color as a Diagnostic Tool

Even if you avoid using the shadow color parameter as a part of your general lighting, it is a handy tool for highlighting a shadow during test renders. Cranking up the shadow color to a bright red, as shown in Figure 3.11, is a great way to isolate exactly where a particular light's shadow is going. Use this whenever there is room for confusion between several overlapping shadows, or if you are not sure which shadow comes from which light. If you make adjustments while the shadow color is bright red, then you can see what you're doing, even with shadows that will appear subtler in the final render. When you're done with your tests, reset the shadow color parameter to pure black.

[Figure 3.11]
Temporarily assigning a bold shadow color makes it easier to see and adjust an individual shadow within your scene.

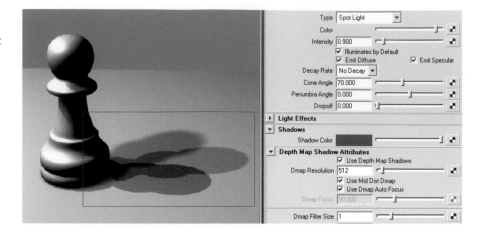

Shadow Color as a Trick to Render "Shadows-Only" Lights

Sometimes you want to add a shadow to your scene, but you don't want to add any light along with it. Most 3D packages enable you to create a *shadows-only light*—a light that doesn't brighten anything, but only adds an extra shadow. This functionality exists as a hack or cheat you can set up, not as a clearly labeled option.

In many programs you can create a shadows-only light by sliding the light color down to pure black and setting the shadow color to a negative value, as shown in Figure 3.12.

[Figure 3.12]
In Maya, you can create a shadows-only light by giving a light a black color and a negative shadow color. Note the RGB values of −1 in mixing the shadow color.

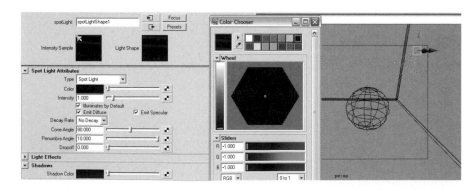

In 3ds Max you aren't allowed to set a color to a negative value, but an alternate technique for making a shadows-only light is to set the light's color to black, the shadow color to white, and the shadow density to –1, as shown in Figure 3.13.

If your software does not support either of the techniques just described, there's another way to create an identical effect. This works in any program that supports negative lights.

Start with two copies of a spotlight in the same place. Give the first light a positive intensity of 1 and set it to cast shadows. Give the second light a –1 intensity but do *not* set it to cast shadows. These two lights work as a pair; the first light adds illumination (except where it is shadowed), and the negative light subtracts all of the illumination added by the first light, effectively canceling it out. The negative light also takes light away from the area where the first light was shadowed.

Shadows-only lights can be tremendously useful if you want to control the exact size, angle, and perspective of your shadow without changing the lighting of the scene. You can even light the scene with several lights that don't cast shadows—such as the red, green, and blue lights in Figure 3.14—and then use a shadows-only light to add a single, consolidated shadow to an object.

Hard and Soft Shadows

By default, most shadows are *hard*—having crisply defined, sharp edges, as shown in Figure 3.15. Overusing hard-edged shadows, even from lights that would be larger or more diffused in real life, produces a cliché look typical of bad 3D renderings and can give your lighting a conspicuously fake appearance.

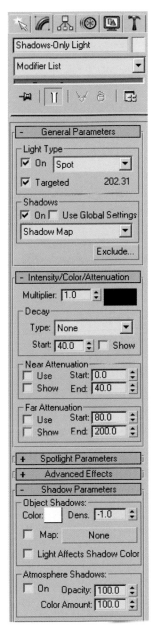

[Figure 3.13]
A shadows-only light in 3ds Max uses a black light color, a white shadow color, and a shadow density of –1.

[Figure 3.14]
Multiple shadows (left) can be replaced by a single shadows-only light (right).

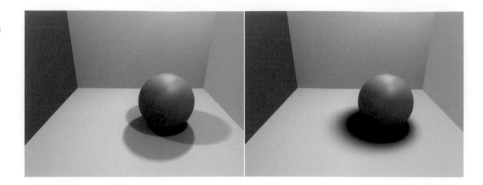

[Figure 3.15]
Hard-edged shadows are a default appearance that only looks plausible when it is coming from a very small point source light.

In most cases, using *soft shadows*—which are less distinct and fade off toward the edges, as in Figure 3.16—tends to look more realistic than using only hard shadows. In Figure 3.16, the spotlight's cone has also been given a larger penumbra angle, which softens the edge of the spotlight beam to match the softer shadows.

[Figure 3.16]
Soft shadows look more natural and convincing as if the light came from a larger light source.

When to Use Hard Shadows

There are some scenarios in which hard shadows are motivated in your scene. Here are some cases in which you will want to use hard shadows as a creative choice:

- To simulate illumination that comes directly from a small, concentrated light source, such as a bare lightbulb

- To represent direct sun on a clear day, which produces fairly hard light

- In some space scenes, where light reaches objects without being diffused through an atmosphere

- To call attention to an artificial light source, such as when a spotlight is focused on a circus performer

- To project shadows with clearly defined shapes, such as when you want your audience to recognize a villain by watching his shadow on a wall

- To create a harsh or inhospitable environment

Even in these cases, the shadows don't need to be 100% perfectly hard. A slightly soft edge to your shadows can make them more realistic. For example, even on the clearest days, the sun never produces completely crisp shadows.

When to Use Soft Shadows

There are many situations in which soft shadows are motivated. Here are some of them:

- To represent natural light on a cloudy day when you do not get very bold shadows.

- To simulate indirect light, such as light that has reflected off walls or ceilings.

- To simulate light that has been transmitted through translucent materials, such as leaves, curtains, or lampshades.

- To make many environments look more comfortable or relaxing and to make most subjects look more natural or organic. Most interior lighting fixtures in a home are designed to either diffuse or bounce light to soften the light from the lightbulb.

- To portray characters favorably or make them look beautiful. Close-up shots of many movie stars, especially female lead actresses in Hollywood movies, are frequently soft-lit.

If you look around and pay attention, you'll find a combination of soft and hard shadows in many situations where, at a quick glance, you might have thought that only a hard shadow existed. For example, on a sunny day you quickly notice the hard shadows from the sun, but if you look more closely, you also see the soft shadows of light from the sky darkening areas underneath large objects such as cars.

The actual settings you use to render hard or soft shadows will depend on the type of light you're using and the type of shadow algorithm you choose.

Shadow Algorithms

Many rendering programs let you choose between two popular techniques to calculate shadows:

- Depth map (also called shadow map) shadows are typically the quickest and most efficient to render, but they have a finite resolution and sometimes need to be adjusted (as described in this section) to avoid artifacts.

- Raytraced shadows are easy to use and accurate at any resolution, but they usually take more rendering time to compute.

This section discusses how to use depth map shadows and raytraced shadows, their advantages and disadvantages, and how to render hard and soft shadows using either technique.

Depth Map Shadows

Depth map shadows are an efficient type of shadow that can be rendered without using up as much memory or rendering time as raytraced shadows. Even though depth map shadows are starting to seem a bit old-fashioned, they are still used in some professional lighting work.

This kind of shadow works by precomputing a depth map to determine where shadows will be rendered. A *depth map* (sometimes abbreviated *dmap*; also called a *shadow map*) is an array of numbers representing distances. Before the renderer even begins rendering the scene viewed by the camera, it computes a depth map from the point of view of each light that will cast depth-mapped shadows. For each direction that the light shines, the depth map stores the distance from the light to the nearest shadow-casting object found in that direction, as shown in Figure 3.17.

During the rendering, the light will be cut off at the distances specified by the depth map so that it does not shine farther than the distance measurement stored for each angle. When rendering a surface under the apple, for example, the renderer only needs to check the depth map to see which parts of the ground are shadowed. This saves a tremendous amount of rendering time, because the renderer doesn't need to keep searching through the scene to find where objects come between the ground and the light.

Figure 3.17 shows only one row of depth measurements, as would exist in one "slice" of a depth map. A depth map would actually run both horizontally and vertically over the area illuminated by the light. For example, a depth map with a resolution of 512 would actually be 512 distance measurements wide by 512 distance measurements high.

Resolution and Memory Use

A single distance measurement within a depth map is stored as a *floating point* value. Floating point values can store just about any number, from tiny fractions to huge distances, while using just 4 bytes to store each value. The resolution of a shadow map is used for both the horizontal and vertical dimensions of the map, meaning the number of bytes used is actually $4 \times (\text{resolution}^2)$. Table 3.1 shows the memory used by common shadow map resolutions, in megabytes.

[Table 3.1] Shadow Map Memory Use

DEPTH MAP RESOLUTION	MEMORY USED
512	1 MB
1024	4 MB
2048	16 MB
4096	64 MB
8192	256 MB

As Table 3.1 shows, increasing your shadow map resolution will rapidly deplete your system's memory. On a well-framed spotlight, a shadow map resolution of 1024 will usually be adequate for a light covering a small area of your scene or shadows that do not need to be very crisp. For shadows covering a larger area of your scene, or for shadows that need to appear crisp and sharp, a resolution of 2048 or 4096 may be needed.

It is usually not a good idea to go above 4096 for depth map resolutions. If you keep raising the resolution of the shadow map, eventually the memory and speed advantages usually associated with shadow maps will disappear, and you'd be better off using raytraced shadows. If you want to stick with shadow maps, then before you go too high with the resolution, be sure to check the framing of the shadow map to make sure it is not covering a bigger area than it needs to.

Depth Map Framing

To make shadow maps work efficiently, you need to frame your shadow map so that it includes the objects that will cast shadows but doesn't include too much extra empty space around the objects.

Spotlights are the lighting tools of choice for most projects that use depth map shadows. You can aim and control a spotlight to put your shadow exactly where you need it. If you use a point light, then the software needs to calculate multiple depth maps in order to calculate the shadows cast in each direction. If you use a directional light, then the depth map shadow might be stretched over too broad an area to optimize its resolution.

If you are lighting with a spotlight, make sure that the cone angle is focused as tightly as possible around the visible area it needs to cover; this way you don't waste samples in your depth map outside of the area that will be visible in your shot. Figure 3.18 shows how a shadow map works efficiently for a narrow cone angle but becomes lower resolution at a wider cone angle, as samples are spread over a wider area. If the light is very far away from your subject, you may need to use a very narrow cone angle. You can check your framing by viewing the subject from the light's point of view to make sure there isn't too much empty space around the subject within your shadow map.

[Figure 3.18]
A spotlight that is poorly aimed, with its cone angle covering too wide an area, wastes most of the samples within a shadow map and produces inaccurate results (left), while a spotlight with a cone tightly focused around the subject uses the shadow map efficiently for an accurate shadow (right).

You may come across situations in which it seems impossible to properly frame a depth map for everything that needs to be shadowed. You certainly don't want to compromise your lighting just to achieve a more memory-efficient shadow map. If your shadow maps are covering parts of the scene that are not visible in your shot at all, then you can use a narrower cone angle to frame the shadow more accurately without hurting your lighting. If a light is linked to only illuminate a single model, then certainly you can focus the light to only cover the model and avoid having it cover too much empty space around the model it lights.

If the sun is lighting a very large scene including a tree, a house, and an animated character, then ideally you'd want a depth map framed neatly around each of these things. In programmable renderers such as RenderMan, studios can implement solutions providing control over which objects are in each shadow map, and which shadow maps a given light uses. In most off-the-shelf 3D software, however, there is no option to specify an arbitrary list of shadow maps that are used by a light, nor is there one to frame each of those shadow maps differently. If your software only lets you use one shadow map that is aligned with the cone of each spotlight, then this kind of ideal framing is impossible. You might have to settle for one huge shadow map covering the tree, the house, and the character all at once, and if that doesn't work well enough, you might have to switch to raytraced shadows instead of relying on shadow maps.

When you are stuck with a shadow map that covers too wide an area, and you can't frame it any tighter because of the number of objects it needs to light, you have several choices:

- Replace your light with several spotlights, each covering a smaller area. This adds a little bit of natural variation to the lighting, which is often a good thing.

- Turn off shadows in the main light, and instead use shadows-only lights to create shadows beneath each object.

- Use different well-focused spotlights for each shadow in a separate shadow pass; then use the shadow pass to darken the scene in compositing software. (Chapter 11 goes into detail about shadow passes.)

- Raise the resolution of the shadow map as high as necessary. Be mindful of the memory and performance hit that this solution will take, though. If test renders show that you need to go above 4096, you may find that a raytraced shadow (discussed later in this chapter) could be more efficient.

Depth Map Bias and Self-Shadowing Artifacts

As shown in Figure 3.19, artifacts such as bands or grid patterns in your shadows are often caused by having a parameter called *depth map bias* set too low. For scenes built on a very large scale, you may need to raise the bias of some shadows to eliminate artifacts.

Bias is a number that gets added to each distance measurement in the shadow map, pushing the shadow-start distance further out from the light. Increasing the bias slides the shadowing effect out a little further away from the surface, casting the shadow so that it doesn't accidentally start too soon and cause artifacts. Artifacts such as banding or grid patterns appear because points on the surface essentially begin shadowing themselves in areas where the limited number of depth samples have underestimated the actual distance from the light to the surface.

[Figure 3.19]
Too low a depth map bias
can cause artifacts as bold
as these or ones that might
appear to be subtler stripes,
grids, or moiré patterns.

Although raising a bias can get rid of artifacts, increasing the bias too much can create visible gaps between the shadows and the objects casting them. Test-rendering is often needed to identify the best bias setting for a particular shadow.

Too low a bias doesn't always appear as distinct artifact patterns. Sometimes the accidental self-shadowing caused by too low a bias just results in a darkening of the illuminated side of some objects. Test-rendering can identify this problem as well: Just render with your light visible with the shadow, then render with the shadow turned off, and compare the results. If the fully illuminated side of your object, where your object is facing the light source, gets darker when the shadow is activated, then your bias may be too low.

Fixing Light Leaks

Too high a bias can sometimes let light "leak" through walls and corners, as shown in Figure 3.20.

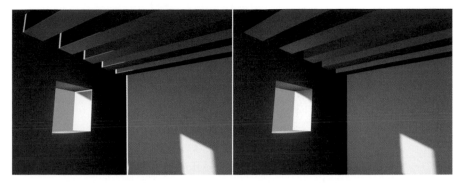

[Figure 3.20]
A depth map bias that's too high, combined with thinly built geometry, can cause light to leak through the corners of the set (left). Lowering the bias (right) is one way to fix this problem.

If you have light leaking through corners, there are some things you should do to isolate and fix the problem:

- Hide all the other lights in your scene so that you are test-rendering only one light.

- If you are using a spotlight, make sure the cone is as narrow as possible to aim it just where it needs to shine.

- Reduce the depth map bias.

- Reduce the filtering or softness applied to the shadow, which extends light into shadow areas in much the same way as an increased bias.

A light leak is not always the fault of the lighting; often it is a problem with your modeling. Here are some tips to fix your models to avoid light leaks:

- Build thicker geometry in your architecture instead of using infinitely thin surfaces. Walls of real houses have a thickness, and yours should too.

- Add a polygon outside a building to block light where it is not needed.

- Make sure that all corners are properly beveled, not perfect 90-degree angles.

- If a part of your geometry isn't casting shadows effectively, try adding another surface, such as a primitive shape, inside the part.

For some beginners, raising the shadow map resolution seems to be their first response to any shadow problem, even though this takes more memory and rendering time. If a problem with your shadows can be fixed by adjusting the bias, which does not add to your rendering time, then get the bias right first. If your shadows are still not working well with a particular model, sometimes you need to fix the model.

Transparency Support

You expect a transparent object to cast a lighter shadow and an opaque object to cast a darker shadow. However, conventional depth map shadows do not respond correctly to transparency and are not any lighter when cast by a transparent object. For example, in Figure 3.21, the top image was rendered using depth map shadows, and you can see that the clear lenses of the glasses cast shadows that are as dark as the shadows cast by the opaque frames. The bottom part of the figure was rendered using raytraced shadows and it shows, for comparison, the type of shadow you would expect to see if transparency were taken into account.

The conventional depth map shadows described here are what you get in most programs, but alternatives do exist. *Deep shadow maps* in RenderMan can support different levels of transparency.

You can work around the lack of transparency support in scenes that have a small amount of glass by setting glass objects so they do not cast shadows. Setting the lenses of the eyeglasses this way is certainly the easiest fix in a case like Figure 3.21. By using light-linking, you can also unlink the glass from some of the shadow-casting lights in your scene. Either of these solutions will work to make sure your depth map shadows don't get blocked by a glass window. However, in scenes featuring glass bottles, wine glasses, or other prominent transparent objects (in which you will probably be raytracing already to achieve reflections and refraction), you may choose to bite the bullet and switch to raytraced shadows.

Soft Shadows Using Depth Maps

You can soften a depth map shadow by increasing a *filter* (also called *dmap filter* or *shadow softness*) setting. This approach blurs your depth map in much the same way that you can blur a two dimensional image in a program such as Photoshop. As with a Photoshop blur, using a larger filter value takes more time to compute, especially when large filter values are used on a higher-resolution depth map.

[Figure 3.21]
A standard shadow map does not take a material's transparency into account, so the glass lenses cast an opaque shadow (top). A raytraced shadow appears lighter where the light passes through glass (bottom).

To achieve very soft shadows, often you get similar results if you lower the shadow resolution instead of just raising the filter value. For example, if your shadow resolution is 1024 and a filter value of 16 isn't soft enough for you, try lowering the shadow resolution to 512 instead of doubling the filter size. The result will be similar, but much faster to render.

When depth map shadows are made soft with a filter setting, they can appear uniformly soft across the entire shadow. Figure 3.22 shows a comparison between a soft shadow map on the left and a raytraced soft shadow on the right. The raytraced soft shadow looks more realistic because it spreads out and gets softer with distance from the object.

If you are using a small amount of depth map filtering, then the shadow being uniformly soft might not be a noticeable problem. If the object casting the shadows doesn't touch the ground, such as the shadow of a fish on the ocean floor, then this kind of softening isn't a problem at all. However, especially when you need to show physical contact, you may prefer to switch to raytraced shadows for the most convincing-looking soft shadows.

[Figure 3.22]
A depth map shadow is softened uniformly from beginning to end (left), whereas a soft raytraced shadow grows softer with distance (right).

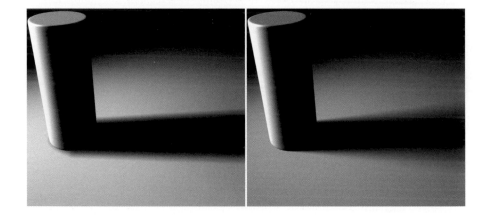

Raytraced Shadows

Raytraced shadows are computed one pixel at a time as you render instead of being precomputed and stored in shadow maps. For each pixel being rendered, the renderer calculates the path that a ray of light would follow from the light source to the pixel being rendered on an object, and it searches along that path to see if any geometry exists that would block the rays. Although raytracing requires some computing time, it has a number of advantages over shadow maps:

- With raytraced shadows, you don't run into many of the problems associated with shadow maps, such as the need to adjust bias to prevent artifacts or fix light leaks.

- Raytraced shadows do not use a fixed-resolution map, so they can always be crisp and accurate in any resolution rendering.

- When you render soft shadows, raytraced shadows can realistically grow softer with distance from an object.

- Raytraced shadows become lighter where a light shines through transparent surfaces and can even pick up colors from colored transparent surfaces such as stained glass windows.

- Raytraced shadows work equally well in scenes using most types of lights, with no efficiency advantage pushing you toward spotlights.

So if raytraced shadows are so wonderful and easy to use, why didn't I write about them first? And why do some feature films still use shadow maps in some situations? There are three simple answers:

1. Raytraced shadows generally take longer to render than shadow maps.

2. Employing raytracing in your scene increases memory use and effectively limits the complexity of the scenes you can render on your computer.

3. Some kinds of subject matter, such as hair, fur, and grass, can be especially inefficient to render with pure raytracing, so some productions still use shadow maps when rendering these subjects.

Because of the superior image quality that is possible, from more naturally diffused soft shadows to more accurate hard-edged shadows, raytraced shadows will always be your first choice. Shadow maps create many potential problems and artifacts, and it's understandable if you try to avoid using them when you can get away with it. However, there still may come times when raytracing is just too slow. This is especially true for complex scenes with large amounts of grass, fur, and vegetation; you may find situations like this where frames take many hours to raytrace but can be completed in minutes using shadow maps. As annoying as shadow maps are to get set up and looking good, they remain a bargain in terms of delivering quick results without using up too much of your system memory. When you are pushing the limits of what you can do with your system's memory and processing power, plain old shadow maps may still seem like the best tool to use for some projects.

How Raytraced Shadows Work

Conventional raytracing works backward in the sense that each ray is computed starting at the camera, instead of starting at the light source as in real life. For each pixel in your image, a ray is traced out from the camera at the appropriate angle until it hits part of a surface that needs to be rendered, as shown by the white lines in Figure 3.23.

[Figure 3.23]
Raytracing starts with primary rays fired from the camera (white). But for raytraced shadows, rays need to be fired from each rendered point toward the light to see if the path is clear (yellow) or blocked and requiring a shadow (red).

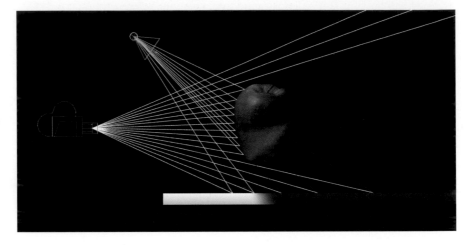

For each point on a surface, the renderer needs to determine which lights will be illuminating that point. If a light uses raytraced shadows, then the renderer needs to trace a path from the surface point to the light. If any polygons are found that block that path, then the light is blocked from the point on the surface. The area where light is blocked from points on the surface forms the raytraced shadow. The yellow rays in Figure 3.23 show rays followed to the light; red rays show rays that were blocked by geometry, indicating that the point being rendered is in shadow.

If more than one light casts raytraced shadows, then the renderer repeats the process of checking through space to see whether any polygons are blocking a ray for each light with raytraced shadows. It repeats all of this at least once for each pixel, and usually more than once per pixel when you are rendering with anti-aliasing (anti-aliasing techniques are discussed in Chapter 9).

The result is that raytraced shadows slow down even the fastest computers. Furthermore, the time you need to raytrace the shadow is only a part of the performance hit you take by raytracing. All of the polygons in your scene may need to be stored in memory in a way that can be checked for ray intersections. Instead of allowing the rendering software to focus on a small part of your scene at one time, when raytracing the process requires continual access to large amounts of data, usually stored in memory in many sorted lists of polygons. Raytracing a large, complex scene can require far more memory than rendering without raytracing.

Trace Depth

One concern of using raytraced shadows is *trace depth,* the idea that raytracing is always limited to a finite number of steps.

Raytracing without limits potentially requires an almost infinite number of calculations, taking a limitless amount of rendering time to compute shadows that are only visible within a reflection of a reflection, or are visible through many ray bounces within a refractive surface. Limits save rendering time, but too low a limit can cause problems with missing raytraced shadows.

Often a shadow appears within a raytraced reflection so that you need to see a reflection of the shadow, or else a shadow is visible through a refractive transparent surface so that the shadow needs to be transmitted through the refraction.

By default, most renderers impose very strict limits on trace depth. In many scenes, you need a shadow to appear within a raytraced reflection so that you see a reflection of the shadow, or you need a shadow to be visible through a refractive transparent surface. For these kinds of cases, raytraced shadows that should be indirectly visible through reflection or refraction are often missing from renderings as a casualty of having too low a trace depth setting.

If your raytraced shadows don't appear within a reflection or don't appear when seen through layers of refractive glass, chances are you've run into a limited trace depth. Figure 3.24 shows the consequences of a shadow not appearing in a reflection.

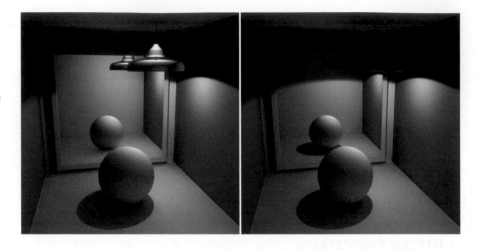

In many cases, trace depth is limited by a setting on each light, but it also can be limited globally in your scene's render settings. If trace depth is set too low in *either* place, this can prevent your raytraced shadows from appearing in reflections or through refractive transparent surfaces.

In Maya, the *Ray Depth Limit parameter* controls the trace depth of each raytraced shadow. It defaults to only 1, which prevents shadows from appearing in reflections, no matter how high the values are set in the Raytracing Quality section of your Render Settings window. Raising the Ray Depth Limit to at least 2 gives you more realistic raytraced scenes.

Note that depth map shadows also appear in raytraced reflections and refractions. You may be surprised that depth mapped shadows appear in raytracing just as well as raytraced shadows do. Depth map shadows don't have a trace depth setting, but this is just because they aren't limited in terms of how deeply into the raytracing they appear.

Trace depth is limited in order to save rendering time. Always look within your reflections or refraction to make sure shadows are visible, but don't raise limits higher than you need in order to make a visible difference.

Soft Raytraced Shadows

Soft raytraced shadows are a beautiful and worthwhile addition to your scene. By default, raytraced shadows from a point source light are very sharp.

In fact, they can often appear *too* sharp—more perfectly crisp than shadows cast by any light in real life. Luckily you have several options for getting soft, natural-looking raytraced shadows. Most programs support several types of area lights or options to soften shadows from a point or directional light.

Area Lights

An *area light* is the most conceptually elegant source for soft shadows, because it is designed to closely resemble the effects of a larger light source in real life. As in real life, a larger light source, such as a fluorescent ceiling panel, casts softer shadows than a smaller light source, such as a bare light-bulb. With area lights, you can simply scale the light larger to make a softer shadow, as shown in Figure 3.25.

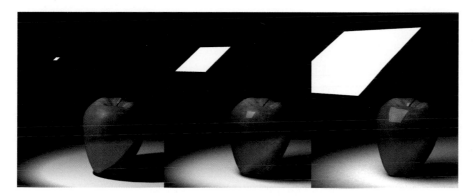

[Figure 3.25]
A small area light (left) makes harder shadows, while scaling the light larger (right) casts softer shadows onto the ground.

In some programs, areas lights are available in a variety of shapes. Common shapes include lines, cylinders, rectangles, discs, and spheres. Each simulates a different shaped light source; for example, a line or cylinder can be a good simulation of light from a fluorescent tube. If fewer shapes are available, often you can scale other shapes to resemble them, such as scaling a rectangular area light down in one dimension to match a line.

Light Radius

Another option for creating soft raytraced shadows in some programs is to use a *light radius* (sometimes called a *virtual radius*) parameter on the light. The light radius creates the impression of a larger light source, like a spherical area light, when the renderer is calculating raytraced shadows.

Increasing the light radius to 3, for example, is the same as using an area light with a 3-unit radius.

Using a light radius parameter does not create any visible change to your rendering when compared to using a round area light. It only changes how you control the softness (by adjusting this parameter instead of scaling the light) and gives you the flexibility to use different kinds of lights, such as spotlights, to create soft raytraced shadows.

Be careful when you place a light with a large light radius parameter near a wall. Even though the light looks as if it is entirely outside of the wall, a portion of the light within the virtual radius you set might actually be inside the wall, causing a light leak from one side of the wall to the other.

Light Angle

When using a directional light, an option for creating soft raytraced shadows is sometimes called *light angle*. As with the light radius setting on a point light or a spotlight, the light angle on a directional light gives you hard shadows when you set it to 0 and softer shadows the higher you raise the number. The difference with light angle is that you are setting the softness of the directional light shadow in degrees instead of units of size for the light.

If your directional light is simulating direct sunlight, then a setting from 1 to 2.5 degrees creates a sufficient degree of softness. If the sun is behind clouds and you want soft, indistinct shadows, then going much higher, to 20 degrees or more, makes more sense.

Sampling

Soft raytraced shadows tend to scatter rays and produce a noisy, dithered pattern, as shown on the left side of Figure 3.26. Turning up the number of shadow samples or shadow rays smoothes out the shadow, although increasing the sampling slows down your rendering, making the raytracer do many times more work when computing the shadow. Increasing your scene's anti-aliasing quality also helps smooth out grainy shadows (and also helps slow down your rendering.)

[Figure 3.26]
Raytraced soft shadows can appear grainy (left), so increased sampling is needed to smooth them out (right).

Hard-edged raytraced shadows don't need many samples; often the number of samples can stay at a default of 1 for shadows that aren't soft. Anything that makes the shadow softer requires more samples. It doesn't matter whether you scale up an area light or increase a light radius parameter; either way the shadow gets grainy if you don't use more samples.

Shadows and Motion Blur

Rendering with motion blur can cause shadows to be blurred when objects or lights move within your scene.

If an object is moving rapidly, the shadows or occlusion cast by that object are affected. Figure 3.27 shows a car speeding down a road. Its shadow on the road is blurred, as you would expect.

A tricky situation is presented when the camera is travelling along with the moving subject, as in Figure 3.28. Because the camera maintains the same speed as the car, the car and its shadow should not appear motion blurred. The ground under the car appears to speed by, but even where the car's shadow is cast onto the motion-blurred ground, the shadow remains crisp.

In situations like this, some renderers tend to blur the shadow when motion blur is applied to the ground. To prevent this, either adjust the renderer to compute shading at more steps per frame, or render the shadow as a separate shadow pass without motion blur.

[Figure 3.27]
When a car speeds by, rendered with motion blur, the shadow it casts on the ground is also blurred.

[Figure 3.28]
If the camera is moving with the car, then the background and street get motion blurred but the car is not blurred much. The shadow cast by the car onto the street also does *not* get blurred much in this case.

Occlusion

To *occlude* something is to block or obstruct it. In computer graphics, *occlusion* is a shading technique that simulates the blocking of light.

Ambient Occlusion

Imagine that your 3D scene is surrounded by a bright white sky that wraps all the way around your models. Some surfaces of your models are fully exposed to the skylight, so those surfaces look white. Other parts of your scene, such as the alleys between buildings or gaps in between objects, are partly hidden from the sky, so those areas appear darker. And underneath a rock, or in the deepest cracks and corners and crevices, surfaces that are completely blocked from the sky appear black. *Ambient occlusion* simulates this kind of soft, overall shading, making surfaces brighter the more exposed to empty air they are, and darker the more they are blocked by nearby objects.

The main idea behind ambient occlusion is *hemispheric sampling,* or look-ing around the scene from the point of view of each point on a surface. Figure 3.29 shows how this happens. In the figure, red dots indicate points on the surface being sampled. Of course, points need to be sampled for each pixel rendered, so there will be more than three. Starting at each point that gets sampled, rays shoot out in every possible direction, as indicated by the yellow arrows in the figure. If all of these rays shoot off into empty space, as is the case with the point on the left side of the figure, then the occlusion returns a pure white value, indicating that the point is not occluded. If rays hit an object, as with the two points that are near the bottom of the sphere, then the more rays that hit, and the closer the object is to the sampled point, the darker the occlusion gets.

At the end of the ambient occlusion rendering process, surfaces that are out in the open are shaded brightest, whereas surfaces right up against another surface, or inside a narrow crevice, become the darkest. Lights don't mat-ter at all to ambient occlusion. Instead, every surface is shaded based on whether it is facing any nearby geometry that might be blocking it.

[Figure 3.29]
Hemispheric sampling starts
at each point on the surface
(indicated by a red dot)
and samples rays out from
each point in all directions
(indicated as yellow arrows).
Points where more of
the rays hit an object are
shaded darker in ambient
occlusion.

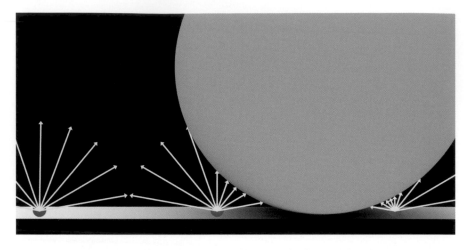

Even though ambient occlusion is just an overall shading technique and not a kind of shadow, it creates an appearance that can look similar to having lights all around your scene that are casting very soft shadows. In most cases, rendering ambient occlusion is much faster than rendering soft raytraced shadows from large area lights or sky domes, so occlusion is a useful technique for creating soft overall shading, without render times that are as slow as you might expect if you used lots of soft raytraced shadows.

Rendering Occlusion Passes

Occlusion is often rendered as a separate pass. This means that you render out a separate image containing just the occlusion. All other aspects of your scene will have to be rendered in other passes and composited together to create a final image.

You don't need to include any lights in your occlusion pass. Ambient occlusion completely ignores any lights in your scene, so no lights are needed or useful.

Adjustments and controls of your occlusion pass are based in your occlusion shader, the material or texture that is actually rendered on each object in the pass. You can adjust several different parameters to control your occlusion.

Maximum Distance

One of the most important adjustments to your occlusion is the *maximum distance*. This sets how far apart two surfaces can be while still occluding each other. When rendering a room, a good rule of thumb is to set the maximum distance to about half the height of the ceiling. You want the occlusion to create a soft gradient running up and down the walls, and you want it to grow darker as it approaches each corner of the room, as shown in Figure 3.30.

If you use too low a maximum distance, then the walls are not covered with gradients. Instead, too low a distance can end up just darkening the corners themselves and leaving most of the walls white, as shown in Figure 3.31.

If the maximum distance is too high, the whole image becomes darker so that no white tones appear in your occlusion pass. You usually don't want the floor to be occluded by the ceiling or by things hanging from the ceiling such as a chandelier, so the maximum distance shouldn't usually include the full height of the room. Test-render your scene to make sure you see gradients running up and down the wall, darkening the corners and appearing white in the middle of the walls.

[Figure 3.30]
A maximum distance of about half the height of the walls creates nice gradients running up and down the walls in an occlusion pass.

Spread

The *spread* or *sampling angle* of your ambient occlusion controls how big a range of angles is sampled from each point. Back in Figure 3.29 the yellow rays were shown spreading out almost 180 degrees from the red sampled points. With a lower spread, the rays are closer together and do not spread out to the sides so much. With a higher spread, they can sample more than a hemisphere, making it more likely that parts of the surface will occlude nearby parts of the same surface.

In test-rendering, at times you will need to increase the spread. If you have a beveled corner in a room, and the bevel or molding appears to be a white stripe inside of the darkened corner, then your spread is too low. On the other hand, if you see artifacts in your occlusion pass that make the square or triangular polygons visible in a curved surface, these are caused by excessive self-occlusion and indicate too high a spread. Try turning it down, and those artifacts should go away.

Sampling

Another control is the number of rays or samples. Take another look at Figure 3.29; the number of samples sets how many of the rays (the yellow lines) are tested from each point. With fewer samples, the occlusion renders very quickly but looks grainy. You can keep the number of samples low while test-rendering and adjusting other parameters, but for your final output, you need to raise this number until the occlusion doesn't look grainy. You might find that 16 samples per pixel works well for a quick test, but you might need 64 or 128 samples per pixel for full quality. As with the sampling of raytraced soft shadows, this is a control you need to test-render carefully to make sure you go as high as you need to avoid grainy-looking renderings, without going so high that you waste rendering time.

Special Cases in Occlusion Passes

In general, you can make an occlusion pass without regard for materials or shaders on different objects. It doesn't matter whether objects are made of rock or metal, fabric or human skin; they can all look the same in an occlusion pass. This is to be expected, because color, texture, highlights, and most other aspects of a material are rendered into other layers. The occlusion is only based on how much each surface is blocked by other surfaces.

There are some special cases, however, in which you need to treat objects with certain kinds of materials or shaders differently when you create an occlusion pass.

Displacement maps are an important special case, because displacement actually changes the shape of the object. If an object is displaced in other passes but is rendered without displacement in the occlusion pass, then the occlusion pass cannot line up with the other passes. Although other kinds of textures can be left out of an occlusion pass, you need to make sure displacement maps are still visible. If your software creates occlusion passes by replacing all of the materials with a new occlusion material, you may need to make an occlusion material with a copy of your displacement map and assign that to your object in the occlusion pass. When you test-render your occlusion pass, take a look at objects that have displacement maps on them. When they are rendered correctly with displacement in the occlusion pass, the occlusion can add definition to the textural detail from the displacement. Figure 3.32 shows a displacement mapped sphere in an occlusion pass.

[Figure 3.32]
While otherwise omitting
textures, an occlusion
pass needs to include
displacement on displaced
objects such as this bumpy
sphere. Mirrors can also
remain reflective in order
to capture the reflections of
occlusion in the mirror.

Mirrors and reflective objects are another special case to consider when you render occlusion passes. A mirror usually doesn't need ambient occlusion, because it doesn't reflect enough diffuse illumination for the ambient occlusion to be noticeable. The image visible in the mirror, on the other hand, should contain occlusion. To make sure that reflections of your occlusion are visible, the surface of a mirror or highly reflective object should not be replaced by an occlusion texture. Instead, you should leave a highly reflective mirror material on the mirror, even in the occlusion pass, so that the occlusion pass contains reflections, as in Figure 3.32.

Transparent and refractive objects are another special case. Clear glass doesn't reflect enough diffuse illumination to require occlusion itself, but what you see through the glass should still receive occlusion. Because of this, you can give transparent objects a transparent shader in the occlusion pass so that you can see the occlusion on other objects through them. If a transparent object has refraction, then it should have the same index of refraction in the occlusion pass to make sure that occlusion is visible through the refraction and that it will align properly with the refracted objects seen in other passes.

Once you have an occlusion pass, what do you do with it? More options for how to composite together different render passes will be discussed in Chapter 11. For now, we'll focus on just one technique—an occlusion sandwich.

Making an Occlusion Sandwich

In compositing, you can combine occlusion with your lighting using an approach that I call an *occlusion sandwich*. Here's a quick overview of the three rendered passes that we will layer together to create an occlusion sandwich:

1. As a solid base layer, start with a *fill light pass*, which appears smoothly and evenly lit, and has no distinct shadows of its own.

2. The middle layer of your occlusion sandwich is your *occlusion pass*. Use a *multiply* compositing operation to combine it with your fill light pass.

3. Add a *key lighting pass*, which contains any lights that need their own distinct shadows. This layer uses an *add* compositing operation. (An *add* is also referred to as a *plus* merge mode in Nuke, or a *linear dodge* layer blending mode in Photoshop.)

Fill Lighting Pass

The fill lighting pass does not need to contain shadows. It only needs to contain soft illumination simulating ambient light and bounce light in the environment. If there are any shadows in this pass, they should be very soft and indistinct so that they can blend seamlessly with the occlusion. In many cases, you'll find that the occlusion replaces your need for soft shadows on your fill light, which can end up saving you a lot of rendering time compared to rendering extra raytraced soft shadows.

Some people use a pure ambient light for the fill light pass. This can work fairly well, because even though the fill light pass looks unnaturally uniform (as you'd expect when something is lit by ambient light), it becomes more varied when multiplied with the occlusion pass. However, if you can give your fill light pass more varied lighting, including different colors of fill and bounce light in different areas, it adds richness and variety to your final scene. Chapter 4 will discuss bounced light and ways to simulate it in more detail.

Figure 3.33 shows an example fill light pass that has red fill light on the left, motivated by the idea that light reflected off the left wall would look red, and blue fill light on the right, motivated by the blue wall on the right.

[Figure 3.33]
A fill pass shows the whole scene lit very evenly with overall lighting that fills even the darkest areas of the scene.

A fill light pass usually doesn't have any black areas. Later, when you multiply it with the occlusion, parts of it will be made darker or could appear black in the final composite, but for now the entire pass should be smoothly lit, showing color and texture from your scene.

When you view the fill light pass by itself, the lack of shadows will be an obvious flaw. However, the plan here is to multiply this pass with occlusion, to simulate the look of very soft shadows on these lights. After that, your key light pass adds illumination from lights that do cast shadows. When all three layers are assembled, the final composite should not show conspicuous signs of missing shadows.

The Occlusion Pass

The occlusion pass is the middle layer of the occlusion sandwich. If you are using the occlusion pass from Figure 3.32, you can multiply that with the fill pass. Figure 3.34 shows how the occlusion is multiplied with the fill if you are putting together the occlusion sandwich in Photoshop.

It is safe to *multiply* an occlusion pass with other render layers, but do not use other compositing functions, such as *add*, *screen*, *mix*, or *over*, to composite an occlusion pass into your scene. An occlusion pass will not contain the color and texture of your models. If you layer your occlusion pass onto your final composite with a function other than multiply, it can desaturate your scene and fade the texture from your surfaces.

[Figure 3.34]
The occlusion pass is layered on top of the fill pass, with the layer blending mode set to multiply.

The Key Lighting Pass

The key lighting pass should contain shadows as normal. This might contain just one light, such as direct sun, or it might contain many lights if the scene has different lamps that need to cast shadows, rim lights that outline a character, or other lights that need full shadowing. However, the key lighting pass will *not* contain fill or bounce light. Figure 3.35 shows a key lighting pass; in this case, it contains only light from the overhead lamp. The shadow areas in this layer are pure black, without any fill light.

[Figure 3.35]
A key pass includes the main light and shadows in the scene, with dark black shadows and no overall fill or bounce light.

[Figure 3.36]
Layer the key pass on top of the fill and occlusion using a linear dodge blending mode; this mode is called add or plus in other programs.

The key lighting pass is added on top of the fill and occlusion, as shown in Figure 3.36. This means that the fill layer has been multiplied by the occlusion, but when the key layer is added on top of the whole sandwich, the key layer does not get darkened by the occlusion. The full occlusion sandwich comes together to form the image shown in Figure 3.37.

[Figure 3.37]
The final composite features the fill pass darkened by the occlusion with the key pass added on top. Note that the key pass is not darkened by the occlusion.

The occlusion pass is sandwiched in between two lighting passes, toning down the fill light before the key light is added. The great thing about using an occlusion sandwich approach is that, for each light in your scene, you get to choose whether it will be darkened by occlusion or not. If you want the light to be darkened by occlusion, include it in the fill light pass. If you don't want it to be affected by occlusion, include it in the key light pass instead.

It is not realistic for all of the lights in your scene to be darkened by occlusion. Occlusion can replace or supplement soft shadows from generalized fill light. A hard, direct light source such as light from the sun should cast its own shadows and does not need to be darkened by occlusion. This distinction is essential to getting the most convincing shading and colors in your final scene.

In the area under a car, for example, you can see the fill light from the sky softly darkened by occlusion. This creates a gradient, allowing the blue to softly fade away as you move farther under the car. The warm key light representing the sun contrasts both in color and in sharpness with the fill. The gradient from blue to black is most visible where the key light is shadowed.

After you've composited together your occlusion sandwich, you always need to do a reality check to make sure the layers are working together. Try adjusting the brightness of your fill light layer and key light layer to see if either of them would look better brightened or darkened. If you need to make extreme adjustments, you can go back to the 3D scene and adjust the intensity or multiplier of some of the lights.

Faking Shadows and Occlusion

Sometimes you want more creative control over your lighting than regular shadows and occlusion provide. This section discusses some handy cheats and tricks to create *fake shadows*—things that look like regular shadows or occlusion, but really aren't. These techniques give you more ways to control the shape and location of your shadows, to darken any area you want in your scene, and even to save some rendering time.

Negative Lights

Negative lights, which are simply lights with their intensity (also called brightness or multiplier) set to a negative number, can be useful tools for darkening parts of your scene. For example, if you wanted to softly darken a corner of a room or the area underneath a table without using any soft shadow or occlusion techniques, you can just put a negative light in the area you wanted to darken.

Generally, a negative light should not be set to cast shadows, nor should it emit any specular light; negative specular highlights would appear as unnatural black dots.

If you want to add a colored tint to the area that you darken, it's OK to give the light a color. However, you have to remember that the light color in a negative light specifies the color that will be subtracted from your scene, not added to it, so you may need to set the light to a complementary color of the tint you'll actually see in the scene. For example, to darken an area and give it a blue cast, you could set the negative light's color to yellow.

You can use almost any type of light as a negative light; a simple point light can work well, especially if you give it a quadratic or cubic decay so that it only darkens the area around the point. Remember that these lights are still emitting their negative light from a specific point, however, so just like a positive light, they affect the surfaces facing them, not surfaces facing away from them. For example, a negative point light might not work well to darken the rear of a character's mouth, because from the center of the mouth it would hit the insides of the teeth, not the outsides of the teeth.

Negative spotlights can be handy for aiming at a specific area of the ground you want to darken with something that looks like a soft shadow. They can even be constrained or grouped to move underneath vehicles and characters for this purpose. Figure 3.38 shows how a negative light can softly darken the area underneath a table.

[Figure 3.38]
On the left, the scene is lit by two lights, one on the left and one to the right of the table. If you feel that the area under the table is too bright, you can add a negative light under the table, as shown on the right side of the figure.

In Maya, there is a kind of light called a *volume light,* which seems ideal for negative lighting. A volume light influences only the area within its own radius or within a selected shape, such as a cube or cylinder, so you can scale the light to surround the exact region you want to darken. With a volume light, you can turn off the Emit Diffuse and Emit Specular options and use only Emit Ambient. This means the volume light softly darkens every surface in the region, without any regard for whether a surface is facing toward the light or away from it.

Negative lights are a somewhat old-fashioned technique to use in modern computer graphics. In most cases, using real shadows and occlusion gives you a better result. However, negative lights remain an option that can still work if you need a quick way to darken an arbitrary area of your scene a little bit. If you use a dim enough light, such as a negative intensity of –0.1 or –0.2, then your negative light can be a very subtle cheat that you can use along with other lights and shadows.

Baking Shadows and Occlusion

Baking is a process of computing the light and shadows that hit a surface and storing them as a texture map. Once illumination has been baked into texture maps, the surface can be rendered very quickly, because lighting and shadows do not need to be calculated.

As an example of baking, suppose that you wanted a soft shadow of a shelf to appear on a wall, as shown in Figure 3.39. Rendering a good-quality soft shadow from an area light can take a significant amount of rendering time, so you might not want to do that at every frame of an animation if there's an alternative that can look just as good. The lighting and shadows can be baked into a texture map that gets applied to the wall.

Once converted into a texture map, as in Figure 3.40, the rendered lighting appears the same, even if the area light isn't present. The only downside is that the shadow does not change automatically if the lighting changes or something on the shelf moves.

[Figure 3.39]
A soft shadow does not need to be recomputed for every frame if it can be baked into a texture map.

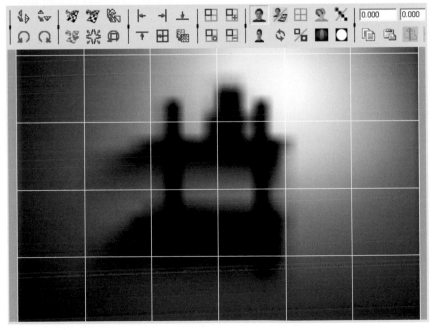

[Figure 3.40]
A texture map on the wall stores a baked shadow.

Be careful about baking anything onto moving characters. The end result of a light-baking process is lighting that essentially seems painted on to surfaces. Limit baked-in occlusion to specific areas where you are sure you want darkening throughout the whole production, such as the throat and nostrils.

For real-time games, a much greater amount of lighting, shadows, and occlusion is integrated into character textures, because it is often the only way possible to achieve certain looks. Even techniques such as global illumination can appear in an interactive game level if you bake your GI solution into textures on the walls and floor.

Shadow Objects

Objects in most programs can be adjusted to cast shadows or not, whether or not they are directly visible in the render. This means that you can always add extra objects to your scene that cast shadows but are otherwise invisible. These are called *shadow objects*.

If you want to make an extra shadow, fill in gaps or holes in an existing shadow, or plug any kind of light leak, adding a shadow object (which could be a primitive cube) can be a simple approach.

Shadow objects are also handy if you plan to do any compositing. For example, if you plan to composite a real car into a 3D environment, you could add a shadow object the shape and size of the car to create proper shadows in the scene.

Shadow objects provide a marvelous degree of creative freedom that goes beyond the control a photographer or cinematographer has when shooting in real life. Cinematographers use all sorts of blockers, flags, and other objects to cast shadows and control where a light can shine, but they have to put them in places that are not visible in the scene. With shadow objects, you can shadow or block any light from any angle or position you want, and the surfaces you add to block the light will never appear in your rendering by accident.

You can also make a pair of two objects in the same place: One is a shadow object (casting shadows but not directly visible) and the other is the regular object that appears in the rendering but is not set to cast shadows. Figure 3.41 shows an example of this: Because the regular object is a flat card textured to look like a tree, the shadows it casts from the side are very thin and un-tree-like. By turning off the tree card's shadow casting and adding a shadow object that is rotated toward the light, acceptable shadows can be cast.

[Figure 3.41] A shadow object (green) helps cast a shadow from the side of the flat card textured as a tree.

Cookies

I discussed cookies in Chapter 2. Simply projecting an image or pattern from a light can often create results that look similar to a shadow, so you should consider cookies as a part of your bag of tricks in faking a shadow.

One source for the texture maps that you could use as a cookie could be the depth map created for a depth map shadow. If your software allows you to save a depth map from a light and then view it, then you should be able to render a shadow of a 3D model of a tree, for example, and then view the depth map of the tree. Save the depth map as a grayscale image, and you can use it as a cookie to project what looks like tree shadows into your scene (see Figure 2.25 in Chapter 2 for an example of a cookie used to add dappled light that looks like the shadow of a tree).

Another way to create textures that you can use as cookies is to set up a simple rendering of the objects that you want to appear in the cookie and bring it into a paint program. You can then convert the alpha channel into a cookie, or even create a multicolored cookie with black for tree branches and dark green for leaf shadows. The possibilities for using cookies to fake shadows are almost limitless, as long as the object that's supposed to be casting the shadow isn't directly visible in your scene.

Use your own judgment regarding whether you need to apply any cheats or manipulations to your shadows. With computers getting faster and production schedules always placing demands on your time, you might not find it worthwhile to spend extra time setting up a fake shadow just to speed up a rendering. If a cheat gives you more convenient and direct control over your output, however, then you may wish to cheat for artistic reasons.

No matter how rarely you use these cheats, learning to manipulate any aspect of your rendering is a valuable skill. You are always better off knowing ten ways to achieve something rather than being boxed in to a single solution.

Exercises

When you pay attention to shadows, the improvement to your renderings can be well worth the effort and experimentation you invest in them.

1. Depth map shadows are not dead. Yes, most of the time you will find that raytraced shadows give you better-looking results, with less tweaking, than depth maps do. But as an exercise, try lighting a scene using only depth map shadows and no raytraced shadows. You can download a scene to light from www.3dRender.com/challenges in a variety of file formats, or feel free to try relighting a scene that you previously lit using raytraced shadows using only depth map shadows. *Hint:* You may find that you need to replace some of the other kinds of lights with spotlights in order to aim and focus the depth maps well.

2. Every type of light, such as spotlights, directional lights, and area lights, casts shadows differently. In the spirit of getting to know your renderer, try creating soft raytraced shadows from each type of light. After you've made the shadows look soft, see how many samples you need to produce a high-quality final image without the soft shadows looking grainy.

CHAPTER FOUR

Lighting Environments and Architecture

To light natural environments and architectural spaces, you need to be aware of the environment around you. Direct light from the sun, soft illumination from the sky, and indirect light blend their colors and tones in subtle ways. This chapter discusses how you can use these three elements to simulate natural light outdoors and indoors, by day or by night. Different kinds of artificial light, from flashlights to desk lamps to streetlights, require equal care to simulate realistic throw patterns and illumination in your scene. You can use atmosphere, from fog and dust in the air to thicker participating media for underwater scenes, to help convey how light

travels through space in your environment. Finally, with global illumination (GI) you can simulate how all of these lights are transmitted from one surface to another, filling your scene with indirectly bounced light. This chapter explores not just how to light with natural and artificial light sources, but how to simulate indirect lighting with or without GI.

Creating Daylight

You can create a simple outdoor lighting setup by adding three elements to your scene: direct sunlight; soft fill light representing light from the sky; and indirect light, simulating light that has bounced off of surfaces in your environment. When you put these three elements together, you can simulate outdoor light at any time of day. This section will explore these three elements and the choices you need to make when creating them.

Adding Sunlight

Think about your scene. What time of day is it? Is there direct sunlight? You'll want to address the sun first, because the sun will be your *key light*—the most important, main light that defines your scene. If sunlight is visible at all, it is often the brightest light in your scene and tends to cast the most visible shadows. You determine the angle of the sun depending on the time of day you are trying to re-create, but remember that your audience doesn't usually know whether the camera is facing east or west, so you have enormous creative latitude in picking an angle for the sun that lights your scene well.

Most of the time, you will use a directional light as the type of light source for the sun. Remember from Chapter 2 that a directional light casts all light and shadows in parallel, which is appropriate for sunlight. If you are using a directional light to cover a full scene with sunlight, you should probably use raytraced shadows to make sure that accurate shadows can be cast by everything in the scene.

Sunlight does not need any decay or attenuation based on distance. The light has already traveled about 150 million kilometers (93 million miles) from the sun to reach your scene, so it is unlikely to wear out appreciably in the last few meters.

Make the sun a yellow color for most of the day; turn it orange or red only during sunrise or sunset. If you test-render your scene with just the sunlight and no other lights, it will appear very yellow and stark, as in Figure 4.1. Before you add any other lights, make sure that you are completely happy with which areas of the scene are in sun and which aren't. In this example, I pivoted the sun around until the statue's head was lit by sunlight and the light came from the side, to bring out the shape of the face instead of flattening it with frontal lighting.

[Figure 4.1]
Sunlight by itself looks yellow and is full of contrast. Here, the sun angle is adjusted to light the main subject well.

Adjusting Raytraced Shadows

The shadows from the sun are the most important shadows in an outdoor scene. Be sure to adjust and test-render the sun shadows, and make sure you like their shape and direction, before you move on to add any other lights.

Shadows from the sun are not completely sharp. Think of the sun as an area light that casts slightly soft shadows. The sun usually fills an area of about 1% of the sky around us, but the shadows from the sun can become considerably softer on a hazy day or around sunset, so you may use values between 1 and 5 degrees for the shadow's light angle.

It is best to leave the *shadow color* parameter of your sunlight set to pure black. You can add a blue cast to the shadow areas later, when you fill in the scene with skylight.

Using Depth Map Shadows

If you are using depth map shadows, you may need to approach setting up sunlight differently. In order to focus a depth map around an appropriate area, you may choose to use spotlights instead of a directional light.

If you use a spotlight to represent the sun, you need to translate the light a large distance away from the rest of the scene so that the shadows it casts will appear parallel. After you accomplish this, set the spotlight cone to a very narrow cone angle so that it only covers the area where its light and shadows are visible in the scene.

One advantage of this approach is that it is easy to aim cookies from a spotlight. If you want a cookie in the sun—to simulate dappled light shining through tree leaves, for example—you can aim and adjust that cookie by moving the light.

One spotlight might not be enough to cover a large area, however. Stretching a depth map over too broad an area can cause it to lose accuracy. If you want to work efficiently with depth maps in cases like this, sometimes you must represent the sun with an array of spotlights, and each must provide light and shadows to one region of the scene. Using multiple depth maps, each with a reasonable resolution such as 1024 or 2048, is usually more efficient than cranking up the depth map resolution above 4096 or 8192.

In some environments you may have no choice but to use depth maps. Complex elements such as grass, fur, or vegetation greatly add to render times and memory use if you try to render them in raytraced shadows. Depth maps can shadow this kind of subject matter more efficiently. Specialized types of depth maps in some renderers, such as the *deep shadow maps* in RenderMan and the *detail shadow maps* in Mental Ray, are optimized for shadowing fine details such as hair and grass.

Adding Spill from the Sun

It is often a good idea to use a second light to represent the spill from the sun. After you have your main sunlight set up and you have test-rendered it to make sure you like what it illuminates and where it casts shadows, you can duplicate a second copy of the sunlight and rename it to become a spill light. Don't rotate the spill light; leave it aimed the same direction as the main sunlight. Set the spill to have much softer shadows than the sunlight so that it spills out beyond the edge of the sunlight into shadow areas, and make the spill dimmer than the sunlight itself.

In some scenes, it is useful to give the spill a richly saturated color. Around sunset, the sun itself might be an ordinary yellow, but the spill could be a rich red or deep orange. In some midday scenes, the sun is so bright that it should appear overexposed and desaturated; in these cases your sun's color might be a pale yellow or appear almost white. If you give the spill light a more saturated color than the sun itself, then the overall impression created by your scene will be that the sunlight has a warm tone.

Figure 4.2 compares the scene from Figure 4.1 with sunlight only (left), and with both sunlight and spill light together (right).

Visually, adding a spill light around the sun extends the sunlight into more angles and helps it wrap further around round objects. Because shadows get softer the farther they are cast from the subject, you can still have black shadows close to the objects that cast them, but shadows cast from more distant objects are more filled in. Overall, having spill light around the sun can add both richness and realism to your scene, compared to the starkness of having sunlight that is not visible at all beyond the edge of the shadows.

[Figure 4.2]
Sunlight by itself (left)
leaves more of the scene
in black shadow. Adding a
spill light (right) fills in the
edges of the shadows with
a warm glow.

[Figure 4.2]
Sunlight by itself (left)
leaves more of the scene
in black shadow. Adding a
spill light (right) fills in the
edges of the shadows with
a warm glow.

Adding Skylight

The soft blue light from the sky is another main aspect of your outdoor lighting. It helps to test-render the sky illumination by itself, with the sunlight and sun spill hidden, before you start to put them all together. A single dome light, as discussed in Chapter 2, is usually the best way to simulate sky illumination in an outdoor environment. The left side of Figure 4.3 shows the scene lit entirely by a dome light.

You can map the dome light with gradients to create shaping and variety in your sky illumination. Often a gradient runs from a lighter blue at the horizon up to a deeper, darker blue at the top of the sky. This simulates a bit of haze that makes the sky look brighter and less saturated near the horizon. Often you want a second gradient to run from the bright side of the sky (where the sun is) toward the darker side of the sky. This adds more variety to sky illumination.

In some programs, the sky dome is just the top half of a sphere and does not include the portion of the sphere that would be underground. In other programs, dome lights wrap all the way around your scene, with half of the dome below the ground. Because the ground shadows any illumination that comes from below it, the color of the bottom half of the sphere shouldn't make a visible difference in your scene. However, you can map the bottom half of the dome to black to prevent potential light leaks if you have holes in your geometry, and possibly to save rendering time in some renderers in case the renderer is optimized to take more samples toward brighter parts of the dome light.

[Figure 4.3]
Sky illumination from a single sky dome softly fills the entire scene (left), whereas adding a kick light (right) adds definition to the shadow side of the objects.

Including an Extra Kick from the Sky

Sometimes you can add more shaping to your scene by augmenting your sky illumination with an extra light. You can use a directional light, set up just like the spill light from the sun, or you can add a spotlight if you want to be able to aim it and focus it on one area. You might give this extra light a blue or gray color, matching whatever colors you see in the sky. This technique not only adds an extra kick of illumination that comes from the sky behind your subject, often on the opposite side from the sun, but it also adds variety and shaping to the side of a subject that isn't lit by the sun and sun spill, as shown on the right side of Figure 4.3. Notice how the dark sides of the statue and columns are better defined when the kick is added.

[Figure 4.4]
This wireframe view shows the sunlight and sun spill (lower right), the sky dome, and the kick from the sky (upper left) positioned around the scene.

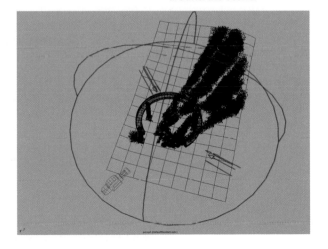

Let's make all of our lights visible now, as shown in Figure 4.4. We now have two directional lights in the same place for the sun and the sun spill (shown in the lower right), a dome light for the sky, and another directional light for a kick from the sky.

Adjusting Color Balance

In a sunlit scene, the warm color of the sun and the cool color of the sky should balance out so that they appear almost white where they overlap. Areas where the sun is blocked so that you see only skylight may look blue. If you render your scene with the sun and all of your skylights visible, you can see the overall color balance of your scene.

You might want a golden yellow overall tint for your scene for a late afternoon or sunset, or a blue tint for dusk or a gloomy overcast day. For a normal daylight balance, however, you don't want your full scene to look blue tinted or yellow tinted overall. You may need to go back and adjust the sun's brightness or color to achieve a natural-looking balance and make it cancel out the blue of the sky.

Figure 4.5 shows the result of rendering with the sun, the spill from the sun, and the sky illumination, all together. Although it still lacks the bounce light that will tie it together, you can see the overall daylight look already appearing in the image.

[Figure 4.5]
Sunlight and skylights are combined to create balanced daylight illumination.

Adding Indirect Light

The sunlight and skylights give you most of your illumination, but a realistic daylight scene also requires *indirect* or *bounce* light. Light that reflects off the ground and other surfaces back up into the scene is called indirect light because it doesn't come directly from a light source. Where sunlight and skylight illuminate the ground and other surfaces in your scene, the brightly lit surfaces themselves need to act like light sources. If light has bounced off the ground, then in many scenes most of your indirect light is aimed upward from the ground, illuminating the bottom of other objects.

You have two basic choices for how to simulate indirect light in your scene. You can add your own bounce lights to simulate indirect illumination, or you can use GI to simulate indirect illumination for you. GI adds indirect illumination to your scene automatically, so you don't need to add any more lights as bounce lights. However, this type of illumination also takes a lot longer to render, especially for scenes like this example that feature grass and vegetation. We'll come back to GI later in this chapter. For now, the straightforward approach to simulating indirect illumination in this scene is to add some bounce light, aimed upward at the scene through the ground, as shown in Figure 4.6.

[Figure 4.6]
Bounce lights (shown in yellow) shine up through the ground to simulate indirect light.

The bounce light makes the biggest difference on the bottoms of objects, brightening up the surfaces that face the ground. Figure 4.7 shows the difference that bounce light adds, if you compare the scene without bounce light to the scene with bounce light.

To simulate indirect light, you need to make some delicate adjustments:

- Most of the time, you should set bounce lights not to emit any specular illumination; you don't want unmotivated specular highlights to appear on the bottom of objects.

- Give your bounce lights colors similar to whatever surface motivates the indirect light. For example, to simulate light reflected off of a green lawn, use a green light.

- To simulate light bouncing off of the ground, position your bounce lights underneath the ground, aimed upward. Use light linking or shadow linking to make sure the ground itself doesn't shadow the light.

- Sometimes bounce lights don't need to cast shadows. If your bounce light casts shadows, then the shadows should be very soft and indistinct. Check inside the mouths, noses, and ears of characters to make sure you don't have unshadowed bounce light visibly shining through them.

- In most scenes, you need more than one bounce light, with different angles and different colors. Even if there's only one ground color, you can use different colors based on the colored lights that hit the ground. For example, if yellow sunlight and blue sky fill both illuminate the grass, then you can have a yellow-green light and a blue-green light bouncing back from the grass onto the rest of the scene.

- Whereas most bounce light in many scenes is light aimed upward, you can actually aim bounce lights in any direction. If bright light is aimed at a wall, you can add a bounce light simulating light bouncing off of that wall. If a floor lamp is aimed up at a ceiling, you can aim a bounce light from the ceiling down onto the rest of the scene.

Because bounce lights are dim and subtle, it's usually a good idea to hide all of your other lights and test-render an image with only the bounce lights so that you can see that they uniformly cover the surfaces of your scene. Make sure you don't see any harsh shadows or sharp highlights in your bounce lighting, because that would give away the illusion that it comes from indirect light reflecting off large surfaces.

Alternate Approaches

You can simulate sky illumination in three alternative ways in modern software: You can simulate the sky with an array of lights coming from different directions instead of using dome lights; you can use a unified sun and sky shader that is available in many programs; or you can use image-based lighting to illuminate the whole scene with a High Dynamic Range Image (HDRI).

Doing Without a Dome Light

If your renderer doesn't support dome lights, or you want a solution that renders faster, use a set of multiple lights to simulate sky illumination.

Start with a directional light that casts very soft raytraced shadows (a light similar to your spill light), but give it a blue color. Test-render your scene and see how it looks with one skylight; then duplicate the light so that lights illuminate your scene from all directions. In an open scene you probably need between four and eight lights to represent fill from the whole sky. Figure 4.8 shows a collection of directional lights arranged to simulate sky illumination.

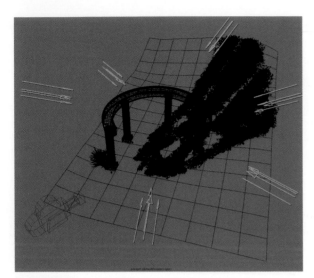

[Figure 4.8]
As an alternative to a sky dome, add several directional lights around the scene.

The lights don't need to have the same brightness and color. You can vary the brightness and color of the lights so that the sun side of the sky is brighter, and the darker side of the sky is a more saturated blue. The lights don't need to be spaced at equal angles, either. Adjust them however they look best in your particular scene. If you see any visible edges to shadows, use softer shadows, or add more directional lights from more angles, to fill in the unlit areas.

Unlike when you use a dome light, using an array of directional lights does not look very good on shiny or reflective objects. If you used six directional lights to simulate light from the sky, you don't want six bright highlights to appear on each shiny object. If you have any shiny, reflective objects in your scene, your best bet is to set the lights not to emit specular illumination and then use a separate environment map for their reflections.

For the very cheapest results, you can use an array of spotlights with depth map shadows instead of directional lights with raytraced shadows. This may not look as natural as other approaches, especially for wide-open scenes surrounded by sky, but it can render very quickly without raytracing. And in situations where only a smaller amount of sky is visible, such as within a canyon, a few spotlights may be all you need to create some sky illumination.

Sun and Sky Shaders

Available at the click of a button in many programs, linked sun and sky shaders allow you to create a sunlight and sky fill all in one step. These shaders simulate many effects for you automatically. For example, when you move the sunlight lower in the sky, it automatically changes color to simulate the color of the setting sun, and the sky's color and brightness changes to match it.

When choosing approaches to lighting, you need to think ahead, beyond the first version that you render. After you render version one, chances are that you will need to show your work to your client, creative lead, director, or art director. At that time, you will get notes on how to proceed to the next version. Even if physically based sun and sky shaders saved you time on lighting the first version, they can sometimes limit your ability to adapt to art direction after that. For example, if you are asked to make the sun a little pinker as it sets, it's easier to directly adjust the RGB color of a light than to look through options labeled "Turbidity" and "Ozone" and adjust them to see how the sun's color happens to respond. Time saved up-front on an easy, preset setup does not always speed up your overall workflow in the long run.

Image-Based Lighting

Image-based lighting (IBL) provides an alternative approach to simulating sky-light. With IBL, you map an image to a sky dome surrounding the scene, and the colors and tones from that image are used to illuminate the scene. Figure 4.9 is a test-render of the scene lit only by a texture map of a sky and clouds.

[Figure 4.9]
This test-render shows a scene lit entirely by IBL instead of lights.

When you use a High Dynamic Range Image (HDRI) format, all of the colors and tones from a real environment can be included in one map for IBL. A huge range of HDRI maps are available for free or for low prices over the Internet, or you can make your own. (Chapter 6 describes how to make your own HDRI.)

IBL holds the promise of great convenience and realism if you happen to have a texture map that perfectly matches the environment you are simulating. IBL also lets you use whatever map you make to represent the environment in reflections, potentially increasing the realism of any shiny or reflective objects in your scene.

In a few ways, it is possible to adjust the lighting on a scene lit by IBL: You can adjust the overall diffuse and specular brightness emitted from your dome light; you can rotate the whole map around to face a different way; you can adjust its overall tint; and you can add conventional lighting to it, aiming extra lights into the scene wherever the illumination from the IBL itself doesn't meet your needs. However, lighting your whole scene based on a premade map is still creatively limiting compared to lighting your scene with fully adjustable individual lights. As with the sun and sky shaders described earlier, sometimes taking this approach makes it easy to create the first version of your lighting, but makes it more difficult to iterate your scene into different versions and adapt your lighting based on creative notes from the director or art director.

Working with Indoor Natural Light

Indoor light can be a mix of natural light that comes in through windows, doors, and skylights, and artificial light sources. The artificial light sources simulated in the scene are called *practical lights*, and those are discussed in the next section. As a first step in moving indoors, start with the natural light—including sunlight, skylight, and indirect light—which you can add to interior scenes in almost the same way as you did outdoors.

Adding Skylight

When adding natural light to an indoor environment, it sometimes makes sense to start with the light from the sky rather than the sun. Sometimes you see a sunbeam coming through a window, other times you don't. Direct sunlight only enters a window when it happens to come from the correct angle. Skylight, on the other hand, always enters through every window, as long as it is daylight outside and you can see out the window.

As it was when we were working with lighting outdoors, sky illumination is a broad, soft light that simulates all of the light coming from every visible part of the sky. It is possible (but not efficient) to put a full sky dome outside of your 3D building and let some of the light from that dome enter through the window; however, this approach can lead to very slow render times, because light from every possible direction is computed, even when most of the sky dome is not visible through the window.

Area Lights in the Windows

Area lights aligned with a window are often the most natural way to simulate sky illumination coming inside. Place a rectangular area light just outside of a window, door, or skylight, and give it a color matching the sky. Of course, if the window is round, you can use a disc-shaped area light, and you can use multiple area lights for more complex groups of windows.

If a background image is visible through the window, then use the color of the sky visible outside to guide the color of your area light. If the outdoor area is a 3D scene, use the color from the outdoor sky fill for the area light in your window.

Some renderers have a special kind of area light called a *portal light*, which is like a regular area light except that it gets the brightness and color from a corresponding sky dome that surrounds the scene. A portal light simulates getting light and color from a sky dome without the inefficiency associated with sampling a full sky dome when only a tiny part of the dome is visible.

Even if you only have one window in the scene, it's OK to use more than one light to simulate skylight from that window. A rectangular area light, matching the shape of the window, is technically a good fit, but sometimes you want to use more lights to help fill more of the room with soft illumination. A spherical area light can create a nice, soft ball of light, emitting soft illumination from just outside the window. In the example kitchen scene, two windows are side by side, so two spherical area lights have been added outside the window, as shown in Figure 4.10.

[Figure 4.10]
Rectangular and spherical area lights are both added to each window. This kitchen model is from Lighting Challenge #2, which you can download from www.3dRender.com/challenges in multiple file formats.

The spherical area lights in this window overlap with the rectangular area light, and they are partially inside the room to help the fill light spill out to a broader angle. Figure 4.11 shows what the window fill looks like from the rectangular area light by itself (left) compared to how the scene looks with the spherical area lights extending the sky illumination (right).

[Figure 4.11]
Rectangular area lights in each window (left) simulate sky illumination around the window, but adding the spherical area lights (right) extends the illumination to fill more of the scene.

Usually it's best to test-render the skylights without any GI activated. The scene will have high contrast but images can render faster, and such an image shows you what the sky fill looks like by itself, without any light in the scene. You may come across exceptions to this rule if a technical option on the area light or portal light requires GI to be turned on, but in general it's best to get a clear look at what the light does by itself when you are first setting it up.

Check the area immediately around the window and make sure surfaces near the window appear to be convincingly lit by the window light. The light should spill out into the room so that any surfaces immediately above, below, or beside the window receive some light from outdoors.

Excluding Window Geometry

If you have a 3D model of glass in the window, then use light linking to remove the glass from your lights. Otherwise a light very close to the glass itself or intersecting with the glass might create unnatural highlights on the glass, or the glass might block or shadow the light.

You can sometimes use shadow linking to remove thin pieces of geometry in the window itself (such as window frames, bars on the window, or blinds) from the fill light's shadow. When a soft area light illuminates the whole room, the shadow of a thin bar on the window spreads out so that it no longer looks like a shadow of a bar; instead it just creates extra noise in the area light, and can require more shadow samples if it isn't removed from the shadow completely.

You may wish to set the clear glass in the window so it does not to cast any shadows. You should not do the same thing for window frames or other opaque geometry, however. Even if you prevent this geometry from casting shadows in the sky fill, you still want it to be able to cast shadows in a sunbeam if sunlight enters the window.

Adding Sunlight

Check your background image (or whatever you see through the window) to see what direction the sun seems to be coming from and if it's sunny outside. Windows don't always have a sunbeam, especially if the sun is coming from the other side of the building.

Create a bright, warm directional light, just as you did for sunlight outside. If you don't want to use a directional light, a spherical or disk-shaped area light can work just as well, but make sure to position it far away from the window to achieve the kind of distant perspective that people expect from sunlight. Test-render your scene to see where the sunbeam is cast into your room, and rotate or move the light until it hits where you want. Figure 4.12 shows the room with a sunbeam added.

[Figure 4.12]
A directional light adds a sunbeam to the room.

Adding Spill Light

The sunlight shouldn't cut off completely at the edge of the sunbeam. Just like when you were working outside, the spill light should be outside the sunbeam, simulating the extra light that comes from the bright parts of the sky around the sun itself. Figure 4.13 shows the difference that spill light can make.

[Figure 4.13]
Compare the sunlight by itself (left) to the addition of a spill light (right)–the spill light adds a warm outer glow around the sunbeam.

If you are using a directional light for your sun, then to create a spill light, you only need to duplicate the directional light, modify the shadows to be much softer, and reduce the intensity of the light. Often it looks good to use a rich, saturated color (more saturated than the sunlight itself) for the spill from the sun.

Adding Indirect Light

When light hits each surface in your interior scene, any brightly lit surface essentially functions as a light source, illuminating other objects with indirect light that has reflected off of it. The floor, the walls, and certainly any object hit by a sunbeam motivate indirect light that needs to illuminate the rest of the scene.

Adding Global Illumination

By far the easiest and most realistic way to render indirect light indoors is by using global illumination (GI). Turning on GI in your renderer allows the color and brightness of each surface in your scene to help illuminate other surfaces around it; this gives you naturalistic results without your having to work to set up extra lights to simulate indirect light.

Figure 4.14 shows the difference that GI makes to the scene. Using only the sky fill, sunlight, and sun spill lights coming through the window, GI extends the natural light from the window to fill the entire room.

[Figure 4.14]
The sunlight and skylights through the window (top) are augmented by indirect light bounces (bottom) when global illumination is turned on.

When you turn on GI, it is not just another source of fill light. When you activate global illumination or indirect illumination in your renderer, you are fundamentally changing how the lighting in your scene works.

Consider a test scene illuminated by a single light source, as shown in Figure 4.15. Without GI, surfaces are only lit by the light source itself. Parts of the scene that don't directly face the light remain black.

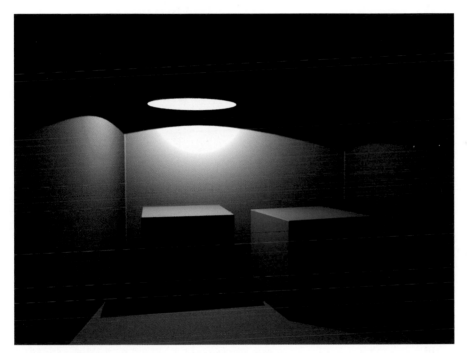

[Figure 4.15]
With no global illumination, a scene lit by a single light source contains solidly black shadow areas.

Figure 4.16 shows the same scene rendered with GI. When you use GI, surfaces are lit by other surfaces. One brightly lit surface can indirectly brighten other surfaces that face it. This is why shadow areas of the scene are brightened and filled in.

One nice feature you can achieve through GI is secondary levels of shadowing, where shadows are created even within other shadows. Look at the three balls in Figures 4.16. Without GI, there you would have only a single level of shadowing, and the balls would be hidden in the shadows cast by the cubes. With GI, you get secondary shadowing, even though the scene only has one light. Not only do the indirect light bounces make the balls visible, they also provide secondary shadowing, casting soft shadows from the balls onto the floor.

Also notice the colors of light that illuminate the three balls: The first ball appears red because of the light that has bounced off of the red wall; the second ball appears green because of light that has bounced off the two green cubes; and the third ball appears blue from the light that has bounced off the blue wall. This feature of GI, the way the indirect light picks up the colors of surfaces that it bounces off of, is called *color bleeding*.

One area where you can inspect any architectural rendering for quality is in the corners, where two walls meet, or where a wall meets the floor or the ceiling.

Corners are the areas where light most closely inter-reflects between walls. As a result, your scene should show continuity at the corners—a continuation of tones from one wall to another, rather than a sudden jump in brightness. GI tends to provide this, so that you can see a smooth, continuous sharing of illumination where two walls meet. When you are lighting without GI, even if you add extra bounce lights to the scene, you need to put in a lot of effort to achieve really convincing corners.

We use the term *local* illumination to describe rendering without GI, and call GI *global* illumination, which refers to how many other surfaces in the scene are taken into account when a surface's illumination is rendered. Without GI, each surface is rendered by itself; this process takes the light sources into account but not the brightness of nearby objects. With GI, illumination is computed taking all the geometry in the scene into account, so light hitting any surface may indirectly brighten other surfaces in the scene. The inclusion of all the geometry in the scene is what gives the "global" perspective to the illumination process.

GI rendering allows indirect light to contribute to diffuse illumination. In other words, GI can indirectly brighten even matte-finished surfaces—surfaces that are not shiny or reflective. With GI turned off, you can still use conventional raytraced reflections for reflective objects, but raytraced reflections by themselves don't transport light from diffuse surfaces to other diffuse surfaces. Only GI gives you true diffuse-to-diffuse light transport. Only GI allows any brightly lit surface to brighten other objects, not just as a reflection but as a light source.

The idea that reflected, indirect light can function as a light source is something that GI lighting has in common with live-action filmmaking. Especially when working outdoors, where bounced sunlight can be a brighter light source than many types of artificial light, filmmakers often use bounce cards or reflectors to light their

[**Figure 4.17**] Reflectors are used to bounce light onto actors or sets.

scenes, instead of doing all of their lighting with lights. On a sunny day, reflectors, as shown in Figure 4.17, can provide all of the fill light filmmakers need when filming scenes outdoors.

Chapter 9 will come back to global illumination to discuss the different types of GI algorithms that your software may support. Although these algorithms can add to the quality of your imagery and may save you many hours of work as a lighting artist, they all come at the expense of slower overall rendering times. As computers get faster and software becomes more advanced and efficient, there are fewer and fewer reasons to render architectural interiors or realistic indoor scenes without using GI. However, for some extremely complex scenes, short-deadline projects, and some types of subject matter—such as hair, fur, grass, and vegetation, which are difficult to include in a full GI solution—the limited nature of rendering time still makes some people work without GI.

Working Without GI

If you want to simulate indirect light without using GI, often the easiest starting point is the *occlusion sandwich* approach, which was discussed in Chapter 3.

Figure 4.18 shows a fill light layer that includes two light colors: Blue light is coming from the window area and warmer light is coming from inside the room where the sunbeam would be hitting.

The fill light layer is a great place to add bounce lighting, because it does not need to include shadows. The occlusion layer adds shading later, but for this layer you can use area lights positioned outside each wall to light the scene. A blue area light is positioned outside of the window and warm colored lights illuminate the scene from other directions. The bright area where the sunbeam hits the table and walls motivates extra bounce light, so extra area lights are added coming from those parts of the scene. Figure 4.19 shows the area lights used in rendering the fill layer.

[Figure 4.18]
A fill light pass is evenly lit, but it does feature some color variation.

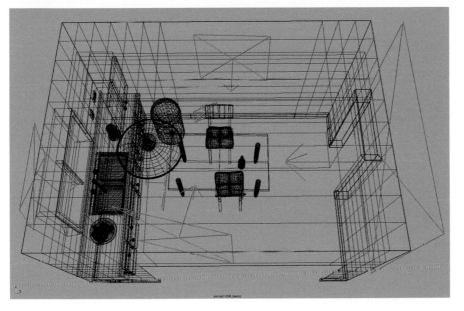

[Figure 4.19]
Area lights from every major surface are used to illuminate the fill pass.

As a quality-control check on your fill light layer, take a look at the corners where two walls meet, or where the walls meet the ceiling or floor. The illumination on the different surfaces should be roughly equal, without any big jump in brightness between the connected surfaces. Although some variation in color and tone is good, the fill light pass should be smoothly, evenly lit, without any high-contrast jumps in the brightness.

Also check your fill light layer to make sure no noticeable specular highlights or extremely bright spots are in the scene. By using broad, soft area lights as fills instead of tiny point-source lights, you help avoid unmotivated highlights that come from what should be bounce light from a wall. The fill layer also should not have any completely black areas unless you are sure an area in your scene would receive absolutely no fill or bounce light.

The middle layer in the occlusion sandwich is the occlusion pass of the room, as shown in Figure 4.20. Note that corners are softly darkened, and alcoves, such as the area under the upper cabinets, go much darker. This shading helps your bounce lighting look more like real global illumination.

[Figure 4.20]
The occlusion pass is the middle layer of the occlusion sandwich.

We already have the lights that go into the key layer of the occlusion sandwich. We render an image lit by the sunlight, sun spill, and sky fill lights, all as described earlier. The result still has dark areas because of the lack of GI, but otherwise it should be a fully lit scene, as shown in Figure 4.21.

[Figure 4.21]
The light pass is mainly just the sunbeam and other direct illumination.

Assemble the occlusion sandwich in your compositing software or a paint program starting with the fill layer as the base. *Multiply* the occlusion layer and then *add* the key layer on top. Figure 4.22 shows the occlusion sandwich assembled in Photoshop.

[Figure 4.22]
The occlusion sandwich assembled as layers in Photoshop. Blend modes are Normal for the Fill layer, Multiply for the Occlusion layer, and Linear Dodge (Add) for the Key layer.

The result is shown in Figure 4.23. Although it might not match the output with global illumination, it gets pretty close, and the scene can be rendered much more quickly.

[Figure 4.23]
The result of the occlusion sandwich looks somewhat similar to global illumination, but it is produced in a fraction of the rendering time.

Practical Lights

Practical lights are the light sources that are visible as models within your scene. Indoor examples of practical lights include lamps, light fixtures, television sets, or any other model you've built that emits light. Outdoors, practical lights include street lamps, vehicle headlights and taillights, illuminated signs, and lights on buildings.

There are two different aspects to simulating the illumination from a practical light. You need to light the source itself (such as the actual lamp or lightbulb), and then you need to light the surrounding set as if the lamp is casting illumination into the scene.

Lighting the Light

If you want to illuminate a bulb model using a light, you can position a point light in the middle of it where a filament would be located, and give the outside of the bulb a translucent shader that gets brighter when backlit by the interior light source. As discussed in Chapter 2, inverse square (also called a quadratic decay rate) is the most physically correct setting for a light. To get realistic variation in brightness across the bulb's surface, give the light source inverse square attenuation.

As an alternative to adding a light within the bulb, you can shade 3D models of lightbulbs with a luminosity, ambient, or incandescence map so that they appear bright without regard to the local lighting. The real drawback to adjusting the shader to make the bulb bright is that when you try to isolate your lights and render with only a single light visible, the glowing shader is still present, even when lights around it are hidden. Bulbs need to be texture mapped if they are to be seen up close. A lit bulb may have a bright middle area, but it can become less bright where the glass is attached to the metal base and near the top, as shown in Figure 4.24.

The immediate area around a light source often requires some dedicated lighting. For example, a lamp surrounded by a lamp shade receives a great deal of bounce light as light is reflected off the interior of the shade. With GI you can allow the lamp shade to bounce light back onto the lamp, or you can add bounce lights to illuminate the lamp itself with simulated indirect illumination.

If you are positioning any light inside a 3D model of a lightbulb and that light casts shadows, then you may want to unlink the light from the bulb model so that it can shine through the bulb and illuminate the surrounding area. Otherwise the bulb model may cast a shadow that effectively blocks any of the light from reaching the rest of the scene.

[Figure 4.24]
A bare lightbulb can feature a gradient making it brightest in the center.

Set Lighting from Practical Lights

Just because you are simulating a single practical light source doesn't mean that you need to light it with a single light in 3D. Often you will observe several different effects on the set from a single practical light and use a light in 3D for each of these effects. For example, the lamp in Figure 4.25 emits a soft glow through the shade, a cone of light aimed up through the top of the shade, and a cone of light aimed down from the bottom. You simulate this using a point light that shines out through the shade, plus spotlights aimed upward and downward to simulate the upward and downward cones.

[Figure 4.25]
The lamp casts a dim glow through the shade, plus harder illumination through the top and bottom openings, and a little spill around the hard circles of illumination.

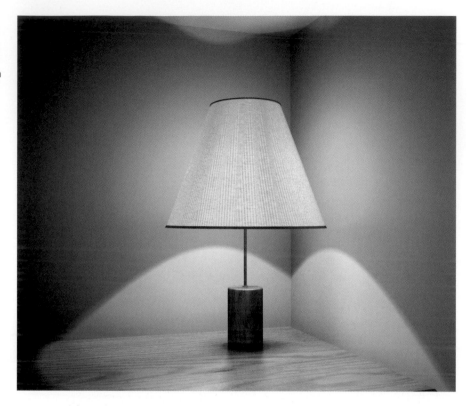

Adding Spill

Often, projecting one spotlight in a particular direction isn't enough. You usually see a broader, dimmer cone of light around the main light source,

[Figure 4.26]
A pair of spotlights are aimed upward, and two more are aimed downward, so that spill can be created around each circle of light.

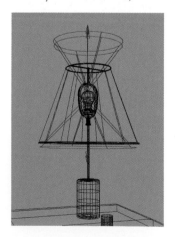

which is a kind of spill light. For example, if you use one spotlight for the illumination cast upward from a lamp, you may need another spotlight, with a broader cone angle and a much dimmer intensity, to add a spill around the area. Figure 4.26 shows how the lighting in Figure 4.25 was created: Two spotlights aim upward and two aim downward, including the main cones and the outer spill lights. The outer spill lights can simulate light that bounces off the lamp shade instead of being aimed directly from the bulb.

Lighting Larger Areas

When you want to add illumination to larger areas of your set, sometimes individual lightbulbs in a light fixture just aren't enough. For example, suppose you have a chandelier in the middle of a room. It may have many individual bulbs within it, and you need one practical light for each bulb in the chandelier. However, turning up the brightness of these lights too high can spread hard-edged shadows all over the set and cause bright highlights on any surface that is shiny or reflective. Instead, you can create a softer type of light motivated by the chandelier, as shown in Figure 4.27, by adding a larger spherical area light above the chandelier.

[Figure 4.27]
One of the "secrets" of lighting design is that the actual light source doesn't have to come from the practical bulbs themselves. Here, a spherical area light (the large orange ball) is responsible for most of the illumination motivated by a chandelier.

You can use shadow linking to prevent the ceiling, and the chandelier itself, from casting shadows in the large area light. This way, the area light fills the room with soft, even illumination, without lots of noise from sampling soft shadows through the complex geometry of the chandelier.

Throw Patterns

The *throw pattern* is the shape or texture of the light that is cast into the scene from a light source. We can recognize distinctive throw patterns from car headlights, flashlights, burning torches, and many other light sources. In real life, often a complex throw pattern is caused by reflection or blocking by structural elements within the light fixture. Figure 4.28 shows a throw pattern cast by a flashlight. Interestingly, when you study different flashlight throw patterns, you see that no two models of flashlight cast exactly the same pattern into the scene.

In 3D graphics, you can create throw patterns by applying a cookie or map on the light source. If you use an image such as Figure 4.28 as a cookie on a light, it will help simulate a flashlight's beam as well as its outer spill light both from the same spotlight. Another way to simulate different throw patterns is to model geometry around the light source. The shape of the geometry can cast a shadow, or the geometry can be transparency-mapped with an image, creating an effect very similar to a cookie directly mapped onto the light.

You can also use a cookie to tint the edges of a spotlight's beam. In many real spotlights, a more saturated or reddish tint appears near the edge of the beam, just before it falls off to black. A cookie with a reddish edge can help simulate this and make softer, more naturalistic throw patterns for your spotlights. If all you want out of a cookie is to tint the outer edges of a spotlight, then you can also use a procedural ramp or gradient texture, and you don't even need to paint a map.

Any time you are tempted to aim a spotlight into your scene and have it add just a plain circle of light, stop and think whether a more complex throw pattern could be more natural looking.

[Figure 4.28] The throw pattern from a flashlight. If you used an image like this as a cookie, then you could simulate both the main light and the spill around it all from one single spotlight.

Night Scenes

You can create night scenes by combining techniques I have described so far in this chapter. You can create natural light coming from the moon and night sky using the same basic principles as with daylight, with just a few modifications. Practical lights, such as streetlights, light from buildings, and car headlights, also add to most nighttime scenes.

You can create light from the moon the same way you did for the sun. Usually light from the moon appears much dimmer than other lights such as streetlights. Only when you get far away from cities and towns does the moon start to become a dominant light source like the sun. Moonlight can appear either blue or yellow. Most often it appears yellow in scenes where light comes only from the moon and the night sky. If you see moonlight in addition to light from lightbulbs, the moonlight appears bluer.

At night, usually light from the sky should be a very soft blue glow. As with light from the moon, you don't want the sky to appear too bright. In cities or indoor scenes, natural light can disappear, and many night scenes are lit entirely by practical lights. At nighttime, even light coming in through a window is as likely to be light from a streetlight or car headlight as it is to be natural light.

The key to lighting night scenes is not to underexpose the entire scene, but to use a lot of contrast. The scene may be dominated by shadows, but you need to break up the darkness with bright highlights and selectively apply rims and glints of light.

You may have noticed that many night scenes in Hollywood movies feature wet pavement, making them look as if it has just rained. This is often the case even in dry cities like Las Vegas. Cinematographers are always looking for ways to capture extra glints of light and reflections in their night scenes. Since they have discovered that spraying water on the streets is a great way to get the city lights to reflect off the street, and since this makes prettier night scenes with more highlights in them, they do this even when it is obviously a cheat.

If you have any surface in your scene that can be reflective, feel free to use it wherever you need more contrast or visual interest. In Figure 4.29, for example, I added an extra light to the porch in the background. I set it to emit specular only and linked it to the street itself, so that it makes the street glisten without adding brightness to the surrounding buildings. I also used light linking to add a light that exclusively illuminates the hanging cables. These extra glints of light create interesting lines and contrast, even within a scene that is made up mostly of dark tones.

[Figure 4.29]
A night scene takes advantage of a wet-looking ground to reflect the practical lights.

Distance and Depth

You can divide up space and show distance with your lighting in many ways. Instead of lighting all parts of a natural environment uniformly, you can depict natural variation in color and tone that exist in different parts of a scene.

Dividing Up Space

Many scenes let you look through a door or stairway so you can view more than one room, area, or floor of a building. Each area of a scene like this can have different lighting. If one room has a window that lets in daylight and another room is lit by a lamp or a ceiling light, then you'd expect the room lit by daylight to be brighter and have cooler, more blue-colored light, whereas the room lit by the ceiling light would appear less bright but have warmer colored illumination, as shown in Figure 4.30.

[Figure 4.30]
Mixing colors of light sources with a dimmer, warmer light in the foreground hallway helps divide the space in this scene.

Even within a room, corners can receive different light than the middle of the room, or there can be a transition of color and brightness between the area around a window and the parts of the room farther from the window.

If you can create a distinction between areas that are in direct sunlight and areas that are in the shade, then that's another good way to divide up your scene. Indoors, parts of your scene can be in a sunbeam while other parts are outside of it. Often, a scene split between sunlight and shade serves to highlight the objects or characters that appear in the sunlight, but this isn't always true. It's possible to have a central subject that stands prominently, entirely in the shade, and have it set apart from a brightly overexposed background that is in direct sunlight. No matter where your center of attention is positioned, it's the contrast between the subject and the background that helps it pop out.

Even small differences between rooms—such as differently adjusted blinds or shades on the windows, or different color curtains or walls can lead to differences in the lighting in different rooms. Although light can flow through doors, windows, and stairways within your scene, the light cast through an opening only lights one part of a room, and where a scene is divided into different spaces you always have the opportunity to vary your lighting.

Defining Depth with Lighting

When designing the lighting for any larger set, you need to choose a strategy for how to portray the distance as you head away from the camera, into the background. Many approaches are possible: You can move from a bright foreground to a dark background, you can have a dark foreground and a bright background, you can alternate light-dark-light, or you can separate areas with color. Different designs work for different spaces. The important part of this issue is that you are creating a two-dimensional image that needs to depict three-dimensional space, so your viewers are able to see the difference between things that are close to camera and things that are farther away.

Figure 4.31 starts with a simple version of this: It has a bright, colorful foreground area, full of warm light, and a background that gets darker and uses cooler, blue tones.

In Figure 4.31, the background itself is broken up into different regions. Although the whole background is dominated by blues and cool tones, the middle hallway is lit from above, with light coming down through a fan, whereas the far background is less saturated, with more blue-colored instrument lights.

[Figure 4.31]
Space can be divided between a brighter foreground and a darker background, among other variations. This scene is Lighting Challenge #18, modeled by Juan Carlos Silva.

Whenever the background is a different color from the foreground, or you have bright light visible in the background, you can think about adding some rim light to the subjects in the foreground motivated by the background light. A few highlights or some rim light that match the background color can help tie together the background and foreground. In this case, the blue rim light along the robot's back also helps separate the robot from the darker background area behind it.

In real cinematography (unlike computer graphics) the camera is a physical object that can cast a shadow. Because of this, objects often appear darker when they get extremely close to the camera. For example, if a door is opened or closed in the foreground, the door itself often looks very dark when it shuts into a position near the camera, as if the scene itself were being wiped to black. Or if a ball is thrown directly at the camera, the ball becomes darker as it reaches the camera and fills the frame. You can avoid this effect in real cinematography in several ways (you can attach a ring light to the camera lens, brightening what's right in front of the camera, for instance), but the convention of objects in the foreground becoming darker, or turning into silhouettes, is seen in many films.

Adding Atmosphere

Atmosphere plays a role in many scenes, tinting and changing the appearance of more distant objects. In any situation in which it might be appropriate, you should look for a chance to use atmosphere to add variation with distance.

- Dust adds to the atmosphere of many outdoor environments and sometimes is visible in the air indoors in barns or old buildings.

- Any room with smoke in it, including rooms lit by torches or candles or places where people smoke or burn incense, can have a lot of visible atmosphere.

- Underwater scenes are essentially scenes with a lot of atmosphere that tints and desaturates and causes distant objects to fade away.

- Almost all outdoor scenes, if you can see all the way to a distant horizon or distant hills, have atmospheric perspective that shifts the more distant parts of the scene into a bluer, less saturated tone, as shown in Figure 4.32.

- Many kinds of weather conditions make the atmosphere more visible. Rain adds the drops themselves, plus extra mist and fog as well. Snow in the air also creates atmospheric perspective as distant objects become whiter.

- Even depictions of outer space sometimes have something like an atmosphere, in the sense that dust particles or the emissions from a rocket can float in space in between the objects in your scene.

[Figure 4.32]
Each successive mountain in this photograph has a lighter, bluer color, thanks to atmospheric perspective.

Modern rendering software offers you a whole range of different approaches for adding atmosphere to your scenes.

One simple, but somewhat limited, option is to turn on a fog effect from an individual light. This allows you to create a visible light beam easily, such as a beam of light coming through a window. However, it can sometimes look unrealistic because in real life, atmosphere tends to be spread through an entire room so that areas in the light or not in the light are all filled with the same amount of dust or smoke. If you set individual lights to emit visible fog effects, then you should also think about adding an overall atmosphere to the whole room, including the areas outside of the light beam.

An efficient approach to adding overall atmosphere to a scene is covered in more detail in Chapter 11. If you render a *depth pass* of your scene, which shows the distance from the camera to each object, then the compositor can use that information to tint, desaturate, or soften distant parts of the scene. This approach lets you simulate the overall look of atmospheric perspective in your scene, although it doesn't visibly respond to each light.

For atmosphere that responds realistically to each light, by forming visibly brighter areas or light beams in the air wherever the light is brightest, you can apply *volumetric fog* shaders, which are available in many programs. Volumetric fog makes the air (or water) in your scene respond realistically to light so that shafts of light or visible light beams can form where light and shadows cut through space, as shown in Figure 4.33. Using volumetric fog can add greatly to your rendering time, but the results often look much more realistic than what you can create in compositing software from an overall depth pass.

Finally, moving into a full particle simulation within your environment is an option that can simulate not only the presence of atmosphere, but also the movement of smoke or dust through the scene, as it responds to wind or character movements. When you fill a dusty barn with a particle system of floating bits of dust, you give a tremendous boost to the dimensionality and realism of the overall space, and you also add to the overall effect of fading out and desaturating more distant surfaces.

[Figure 4.33]
Volumetric fog makes light filtered through stained glass windows visible in the air. This scene is Lighting Challenge #8, modeled by Dan Wade, concept by Gary Tonge.

You can render using a depth of field (DOF) effect that simulates selective camera focus to complement and enhance the effects of atmospheric perspective while diffusing more distant objects and drawing our attention to the foreground (or to whatever object is in focus). If your final scene will be rendered with DOF, then it's a good idea to turn it on when you test your atmospheric effects, because the two effects work together to create the final look of your scene.

Going Underwater

Being underwater is like having a very thick "atmosphere" around you. Even though we are trying to simulate water instead of air in this section, we can apply all of the same rendering techniques to create an underwater environment. Some computer scientists use the term *participating media* instead of *atmosphere* to describe whatever gas, liquid, or solid particles fill space in the scene and influence and respond to illumination.

You begin creating an underwater scene just as if it is above water. Add a directional light to simulate the sun. In a shallow pond or a swimming pool, you might need some fill light from the sky as well, although deeper in the water this might not be necessary. You can aim a bounce light upward to simulate light bouncing off the bottom of the pond to illuminate the bottom of objects. Figure 4.34 shows the humble beginnings of an underwater scene that still looks as if it is above water.

When we look out into an underwater landscape, the entire surface of the water looks just like a rippling mirror above us. Even if you make the water surface both transparent and reflective, giving it a realistic index of refraction of about 0.75 causes it to show mostly reflections. Only one area of the water surface above us, called *Snell's Window*, lets us see through to the sky and the world above the water.

The sunlight in such a scene should appear dappled, as if it is refracted caustics that have passed through the water surface. Although it might be possible to render this in a physically correct manner, you can save time by applying a cookie to the sunlight instead. If you want the sun to appear dappled below the water but not to appear dappled above the water, then you can transparency-map the caustic texture pattern onto a plane at the level of the water surface, and you can set that plane so it casts shadows but is not directly visible in the rendering.

Figure 4.35 shows the scene with the water surface above and the dappled effect on the key light. However, it still doesn't appear to be underwater. What's missing is the atmosphere.

You can use a volumetric fog shader contained within a cube that fills the entire underwater area to add the atmosphere that really makes it look as if we are underwater, as shown in Figure 4.36. You need to tweak this to make sure the fog color (or scatter color) is bright enough to respond to light, which creates shafts of light where the dappled sunlight comes through the scene, and to make sure the shader absorbs light or darkens with distance enough so that the more distant parts of the water fade naturally and don't become too white. The best approach to this process is to set the resolution of your scene very low, with very low anti-aliasing quality and low quality for volumetric rendering; then you render small postage stamp–sized tests until you get the overall colors and brightness right. At this stage, the fill light can be turned down if you want to focus on the shafts of light from the key, or you can turn it up if you can't see enough of the foreground. Only once you like the overall colors and tones in the scene should you move into higher-resolution renderings.

[Figure 4.35]
Adding a reflective water surface and dappled light gets this scene closer, but an essential ingredient is still missing.

[Figure 4.36]
Adding atmosphere (or participating media) to the scene creates the impression of being underwater.

You can add a whole range of different effects beyond this. Sometimes you can use particles to simulate dirt and debris in the water, or add bubbles that float upward. Sometimes you can add pieces of sediment as individual polygons with transparency-mapped textures, thus scattering organic detail through the space.

In a pond, you don't want the view through the water to be too clear. Although the compositor can achieve other effects (blurring based on distance, or blurring what is seen through floating particles or bubbles), using DOF on your camera also helps blur the background and add realism to an underwater scene, as shown in Figure 4.37.

[Figure 4.37]
Rendering with DOF nicely complements the underwater effect.

Exercises

There's no shortage of interesting environments to light and interesting ways to light them. I used several of the Lighting Challenge scenes as examples in this chapter, and most of them can give you experience lighting interior or exterior environments. Try to collect reference images that show a similar interior or exterior space at a similar time of day or night, and study the lighting in your reference image as you light the scene.

1. Between 1888 and 1891, Claude Monet painted image after image of haystacks. He captured the same subject over and over, in different times of day and in different seasons; he captured different lighting and colors each time he went back into the fields. If you're looking for exercises to improve your skills and your portfolio, don't be afraid to relight the same scene several times. Imagine what it would look like at night, early in the morning, or on a foggy day, and relight and rerender the scene.

2. Ambient occlusion is not dead. Some people are so accustomed to using GI that they already regard occlusion passes as a thing of the past. In reality, you will come across many situations in which you might need a faster technique than full GI. If you've never tried the approach that I call the "occlusion sandwich," try using it and see how you like the workflow.

3. Volumetric fog (also called volume shaders or environment fog) is a useful tool that's tricky to set up and adjust well in a lot of renderers. If you haven't done so before, then use your favorite rendering software to try to fill a scene with a fog or haze that responds to light.

CHAPTER FIVE

Lighting Creatures, Characters, and Animation

Good lighting can enhance animation in ways that are analogous to adding music and sound effects. When an animator keyframes a character, the initial animation tests are lacking in both lighting and sound. When the soundtrack is complete, sound effects add definition and solidity to every motion, with every swish through the air, and every footstep and thud created in sync with the animation. Likewise, good character lighting adds definition to the character. Shadows and occlusion create a sense of solid contact where feet meet the ground. Modeling with light defines the character's form and makes the character appear to be present in the environment and actually moving through the space in which he appears.

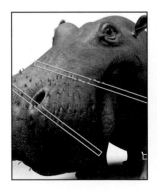  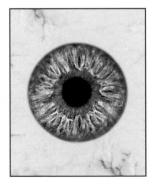 

Like music, lighting helps set a mood and shapes the emotional context of the scene, making a scene look foreboding, hostile, and scary, or bright, sunny, and cheerful. Whether you are adding a glint to a character's eye when she thinks of an idea, making sure the scales on a snake glisten as it slithers past the camera, or highlighting the profile of a character as he dances past a window, you are really completing the process of bringing a creature or character to life.

Modeling with Light

Modeling with light means lighting in a style designed to represent the full three-dimensional form of your models. Even though you are rendering a two-dimensional image, the shades and tones you add through lighting can help people perceive your models in three dimensions.

In real life, curved surfaces tend to get different amounts of illumination from different directions, which creates a gradient that runs across the surface. If a part of your character is round in shape, it should not have flat-looking lighting. A key component to modeling with light is to try to create gradients that indicate the curvature of each surface in a character.

In Figure 5.1, look in the yellow boxes to follow the gradients running across the hippo's head, across its leg, and down its body. The head starts bright above the nose and shifts into a darker tone as it turns toward the jaw. The leg begins with its darkest tone facing the underside of the body, then transitions to a bright central core, and then comes back down again to a medium tone. Along the body, several features and wrinkles are each represented by shifts from bright to dark to bright again. The variety in these gradients conveys the curved shape of all of these forms.

Indicating Directionality

One key aspect of how a form is lit is *directionality*, the cues that tell the audience where the light is coming from. For example, look at Figure 5.2. You can tell just by looking at the character's face that the light is coming from the left side of the screen. The screen-left side of her face is more brightly lit, which creates a gradient that runs to darker tones on the screen-right side of her face.

[Figure 5.1]
Key gradients in shaping the form are enclosed in yellow boxes.

[Figure 5.2]
Light shows directionality. In this case, the brightest illumination is coming from screen left.

Although having a brighter side and a darker side is a good thing, nothing should split the character exactly in half. Figure 5.3 shows a situation where the terminator exactly bisects the form. The *terminator* is the edge of the visible illumination, where the light turns into darkness. When centered, it appears as a boring vertical line and doesn't bring out the roundness of the character.

[Figure 5.3]
It looks unnatural for the light to bisect the face exactly into two halves.

The *core* of the character's lighting is the center of the gradient of shading running across a body. The core tells you whether the light is coming from in front of or behind the character. The darker core, with brighter edges, as shown in Figure 5.4, makes a character look backlit. Even though the character looks as if the brightest lights in the scene are behind her, you can still clearly see gradients running from the bright edges inward across her face.

[Figure 5.4]
Shading with a darker core and brighter edges makes a character look backlit.

Adding Definition

In any action or shot, you must decide which parts of your character most need definition. Based on what's going on or what's important to the story, you need to clearly define some parts of a character with lighting.

When you are defining a character's face, think of it as consisting of multiple planes. Imagine a head simplified into large, flat surfaces that represent the main angles of the head, as shown in Figure 5.5. To define the face well, you need to assign each of the major planes of the face a different shade or tone from your lighting so that you see a shift in brightness or color wherever they intersect. For example, the front of the nose, the side of the nose, and the bottom of the nose should each have a different value. The right side of Figure 5.5 shows the face defined by the illumination hitting every plane.

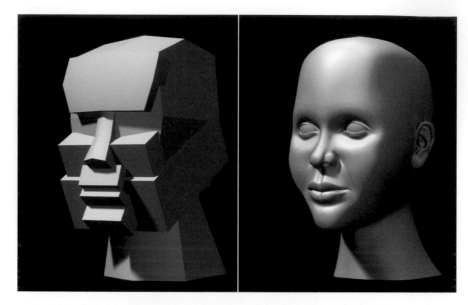

In cinematography, as in real life, a person's outline is not always fully defined. For example, when an actor wearing black pants stands in front of a dark piece of furniture, her legs won't be well defined. However, if her shirt and face are well defined, then she can be lit well enough for the audience to see her performance.

In lighting animated characters, on the other hand, the director of an animated film may consider the entire body important to a character's performance. Often the entire body is animated to anticipate or follow through with an action, and the director may want curves that flow through the entire body to be well defined in lighting. Even when you might think some scenes would look better if parts of a character fell into shadow, communicating the full animated performance to the audience is often more important to the director than simulating more subtle cinematography.

The brevity of a shot is another factor that forces you to add more definition. The shorter a shot is, the less time the audience has to recognize what they are seeing and what's going on. If you are working on a sequence that will be rapidly edited, then you need to work much harder to make sure that everything the audience needs to see is clearly defined with light and contrast. For the same reasons, if you are working with characters who are moving quickly and only staying in each pose for a few frames, you may need to work harder to achieve clear definition in each pose.

If a character (or part of a character) doesn't pop out well enough against a background, you can take several approaches to fix the problem.

- Darken the background behind a character. Sometimes just dimming a light, re-aiming a shadow, moving a prop, or adjusting a shader can create a dark area behind a character.

- If the edge of a character is dark, consider lightening the background behind the character. Sometimes some fog or atmosphere can help push more distant parts of the set into the background and set the foreground apart from it.

- Add a rim light (discussed later in this chapter) to help create a bright defining edge to a character and help it pop out against the background.

- Add light to the character, even if just a part of the character falls into a beam of light, to help the character stand out in a dark room.

Even in a dark, shadowy scene, you must find ways to define a character against a background. If the character is half-lit, then darker parts of the character can blend into a dark background, as shown on the left side of Figure 5.6. As shown in the center of the figure, adding a pool of light behind the character can help the dark parts become more visible so that in the center image, the mouth and forehead are more fully defined in profile. On the right side, another approach is shown: A rim light is added to the character, which also helps define the profile.

[Figure 5.6]
The character lacks contrast against the background, hiding her mouth and forehead (left). Adding light to the background fixes this problem, making her mouth and forehead visible (center). Adding a rim light (right) also makes the profile more visible.

Three-Point Lighting

One of the most basic approaches to lighting a character is with a classic Hollywood lighting scheme called *three-point lighting,* a design that makes it easy to model your subject with light. Variations on three-point lighting can cast a favorable light on anything from a small prop to a movie star.

The three "points" in three-point lighting are actually three roles that light can play in a scene, each serving a specific purpose. The next section goes into more detail about how to create each of these in computer graphics, but let's start with a background on how they are used in photography and cinematography:

- A *key light* creates the subject's main illumination and defines the dominant angle of the lighting. The key light is usually brighter than any other light illuminating the subject and is usually the light that casts the darkest, most visible shadows in your scene.

- A *fill light* softens and extends the illumination provided by the key light and makes more of the subject visible. The fill light can simulate the effect of reflected light or of secondary light sources in the scene.

- A *rim light* creates a "defining edge" to help visually separate the subject from the background. A rim light can glint off the subject's hair and add a defining edge to delineate where the subject ends and the background begins. Graphically, a rim light usually just adds one thin, bright line along the top or side of the character.

Figure 5.7 shows the three points being added one at a time to achieve portrait-style lighting.

At the left side of the figure, the subject is lit only by the key light. This main light illuminates most of her face, and the picture could look acceptably lit if we stopped here. However, part of her face remains black and unlit.

In the center, a fill light is added. Less than half as bright as the key light and coming from the other side of her head, it fills in the area that the key light did not illuminate.

On the right, a rim light is added. The rim light comes from behind the subject and creates a defining outline around her head and shoulders. The rim light adds definition to her silhouette and helps separate her visually from the dark background. Even if her black hair was photographed against a black background, the rim light would bring out her hair's outline, texture, and detail.

Figure 5.8 shows the lighting placement used in this scene. A large 2,000-watt light is used as the key and rim light, with a smaller 1,000-watt light as the fill. The screens mounted in front of the key and fill soften the illumination and shadows.

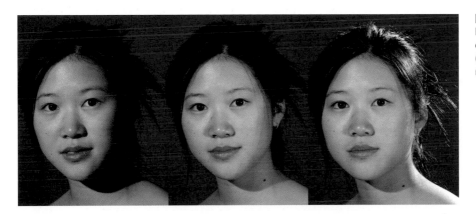

[Figure 5.7]
Photographs show key light only (left); key plus fill light (center); and key, fill, and rim light together (right).

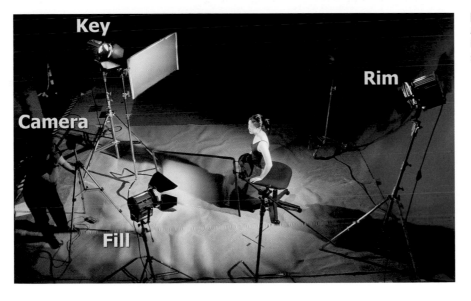

[Figure 5.8]
A three-point lighting setup is arranged around the subject.

Making Variations

You can make many tweaks and modifications to the basic three-point lighting setup. Figure 5.9 shows what happens when we add the rim light on the same side as the key; it adds contrast, reinforces the directionality of the lighting, and creates a more sunlit look.

The difference in brightness between the key and fill lights is called the *key-to-fill ratio*. For example, if the key is twice as bright as the fill, the key-to-fill ratio is 2:1. A ratio of 2:1 gives you very bright, even lighting without much contrast.

In a dramatic production, you don't want everyone lit with the same three-point lighting as if they were anchors on the TV news. A high key-to-fill ratio, such as 5:1 or 10:1, gives you a starker, higher contrast shot. Parts of the scene may become too dark to see clearly, but that may be acceptable to you. Figure 5.10 shows a scene with a 10:1 key-to-fill ratio, with the key and rim lights behind the subject (moving the key behind the subject is sometimes called an *upstage key*). In this shot, only a small fill light was used, and some light has naturally bounced onto the subject's neck and chin. This is not the most conventional three-point lighting, but it does use a key light, fill light, and rim light.

[Figure 5.9] Rim and key can both come from the same direction.

[Figure 5.10] Upstage key and rim light leave a dark core.

Avoiding Formula

Each scene is different. Simply saying that you are setting up three-point lighting is no excuse for adding lights without thinking about a motivation for each one. Nor is it an excuse to position lights around a character that don't work with the lighting being used in the set.

The most important thing to take away from three-point lighting is not a recipe or formula to follow, but the idea that every light in your scene has a specific visual function. Functioning as a key, a fill, or a rim light are three of the visual functions that a light can serve in your scene—other functions are covered in the following pages. As a lighting designer, you should be in control of exactly what each light adds to your image, and be able to name and describe each of your lights according to their function in the shot.

Functions of Lights

The previous section introduced three visual functions that lights can serve, but there are more functions than that. In this section, we will explore the following functions of lights used on characters and tackle how to set them up in computer graphics:

- Key

- Fill

- Bounce

- Spill

- Rim

- Kick

- Specular

To serve these visual functions, you must position a light relative to the camera. Position the camera and compose your shot first, before you aim these lights. If you later change your mind and decide to shoot your scene from a different angle, you also need to adjust the lighting accordingly.

Different studios have different standards for how lights are named. Most common naming schemes start with the function, or sometimes an abbreviation for the functions. If you name your lights something like Key_Sun_onDragon or Fill_Sky_onDragon, then anyone looking at your scene or copying your light rig is able to understand the visual function of each light.

Key Lights

As mentioned earlier, the key light is the main, brightest light in the scene, and it establishes the scene's dominant angle for the illumination and shadows. Choosing an angle for your key light is one of the most important decisions you will make when lighting your subject.

To start with something that you should *not* do, take a look at the left side of Figure 5.11. This shows the flat, poorly defined results you get when you place the key light very close to the camera. Swing the key light at least 30 degrees away from the camera to give the face you are lighting some definition, as shown on the right side of the figure. Don't worry about the fact that part of the face remains pure black where the key doesn't hit it; you can add other lights to fill in the dark areas later. For now, look at how the different planes of the face are delineated by the key light when it comes from a different angle than the camera.

[Figure 5.11]
A centered key light can flatten the subject (left); moving it to the side adds definition (right).

Figure 5.12 shows the angle between the camera and the key light position that are used in the right side of Figure 5.11. Of course, the key can go to the left or to the right, depending on what's best motivated in your scene, but either way you must make the key light angle and the camera angle different. One of the reasons why photographs taken with the built-in flash on a compact camera or phone don't look as good as pictures taken in natural light is that the camera flash acts as a key light that is mounted right next to the lens. When the flash is the main source of illumination on a face, the face is very flatly lit.

In the example shown in Figures 5.11 and 5.12, the amount the key angle was moved away from the camera angle happened to be 51 degrees. Having a key light that also lights and creates highlights in the eyes is nice, but not essential. Sometimes you want a character lit more from the side, and you can add other lights to illuminate the eyes later.

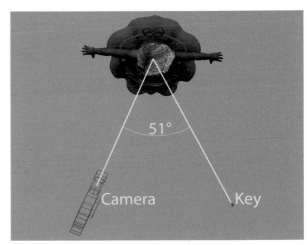

[Figure 5.12] Seen from the top, the key light should reach the character from a different angle than the camera.

Another point of reference to look at when you are adjusting your key light angle is the shadow cast by the subject's nose. Look at the nose shadow in Figure 5.13; you can see that it comes down toward one corner of the mouth. As a general rule of thumb, if you keep the nose shadow aimed at a part of the mouth instead of skewing it off sideways across the cheek, it looks more natural and is less distracting.

We are accustomed to seeing people lit from above, so it is most normal and natural to have light coming from a bit above the character. Light from below your character's face can look unnatural or spooky, as shown in Figure 5.14. It looks especially spooky when hard-edged shadows are cast upward on the face. Very soft low-angle lighting isn't always spooky, though; when it is combined with other lights, it can be really beautiful in some situations, such as when you are simulating soft candlelight from a table in front of the character, or bounce light from a sunbeam on the floor.

[Figure 5.13] When the nose casts a visible shadow, the nose shadow commonly points at a part of the mouth.

[Figure 5.14] Light from a low angle can look spooky.

An opposite problem is sometimes called *raccoon eyes*, when your light reaches a character from such a high angle that her eye sockets become entirely dark, as shown in Figure 5.15. Although you can fix raccoon eyes by adding extra fills on the eyes, more commonly what you want to do is chose a lower angle for your key light.

[Figure 5.15]
Light from a very high angle can create raccoon eyes.

Working in computer graphics, you may find yourself lighting a diverse range of stylized human and animal characters with very different facial structures. Often, you'll need to make them appear to be illuminated as if they were more normally proportioned humans. For example, a character with deeply inset eye sockets or huge, bushy eyebrows is naturally more likely to suffer from raccoon eyes, but it may be your job to aim his key light to light his eyes anyway, or you may need to add another light to illuminate his eye area. As another example, you may need to slide the key lights of characters with very flat faces to the side more to create shaping that shows directionality running across their faces. On the other hand, if you have characters whose eyes are placed on either side of a huge snout, you may need a more frontal key to illuminate both sides of the head.

For animated shots, test-render your key light at several different frames to make sure that you like the angle of its illumination throughout all the main poses. It's a good idea to hide any other lights and turn off global illumination when testing key light angles so that you can render your tests more quickly and see exactly where your key light is illuminating the character. Make sure that you are happy with the illumination and shadows that your key light casts before you move on to add other lights.

Fill Lights

Fill lights extend the illumination beyond the key light to make the rest of the character visible. Whereas the key light might be motivated by the sun or a ceiling light fixture, fill light is often motivated by smaller lamps, indirect light, or the sky.

If you already have a key light aimed at your character that is shadowing your character, then you can simply duplicate the key. This is often the quickest way to create a fill. If you start with a copy of the key, be sure to rename the copy to indicate that it is a fill light, and then swing it around to the position you want fill light to come from.

Here are other things that you should adjust to make a fill light different from a key:

- Reduce the brightness of a fill light to less than half the brightness of the key.

- Give fill lights a different tint from the key. A complementary color (such as a blue fill with a yellow key) will do the most to help define the form of the character.

- In general, make the shadows cast by your fill lights softer than the shadows from the key.

Another approach to adding fill light to your scene is to use dome lights as a source of fill illumination. If you choose this route, be sure that the fill light still comes from a specific direction and that it does not uniformly brighten all sides of the character. To shape and limit the dome light, you can map a gradient image to the dome itself, or add geometry such as ground or walls that will shadow the fill light from some directions.

Your first fill light is usually aimed at the area in the key light's shadow. If you look at your test-render of the key by itself, as on the left side of Figure 5.16, it clearly still has a black area where the key did not reach. On the right, after fill light is added, the illumination continues all the way around the character.

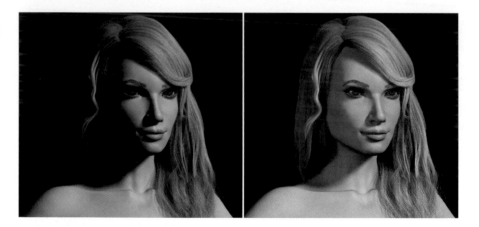

[Figure 5.16]
The key light by itself leaves much of the character black (left), but adding fill light illuminates the whole character (right).

To best fill in the area the key didn't hit, position fill lights on the opposite side of the character from the key light (see Figure 5.17). Often fill light comes from a lower angle than the key. If the key light is coming from a high angle, then the fill may be at about eye level to your character, or perhaps lower.

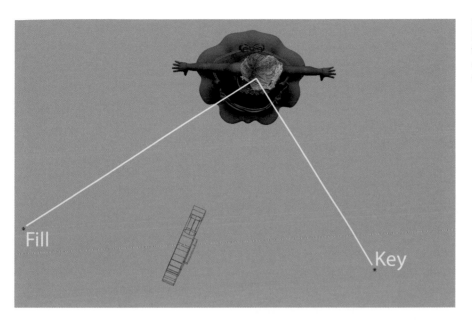

[Figure 5.17]
Seen from the top, the
fill light illuminates the
character from the side
opposite the key.

You may need several fill lights to evenly light your character. Be careful that
the fills don't add up to compete with the brightness of the key, which could
reduce contrast and definition in the character. Very low key-to-fill ratios,
such as 2:1 or lower, make it look like a cloudy day or a fluorescent-lit room.

In addition to the fills that light your whole character, you can also add fill
lights that use light linking to selectively light certain body parts. For example, if your character's teeth are falling into shadow, and looking too dim
and yellow when compared to the white of his eyes, you might add a dim
bluish fill light, linked exclusively to the teeth and gums.

Bounce Lights

Bounce lights for characters are basically the same as bounce lights for sets,
which I described in Chapter 4. Bounce lights can be considered a type of
fill light; the only difference is that they simulate indirect light bounces
instead of other sources of light.

If you already have bounce lights in your environment or are using global
illumination (GI) to simulate bounced light, then a good first step is to
test-render your character with the bounce lights visible or with GI turned

on, and see if you like the results. Remember that GI simulates light bouncing off all surfaces, including walls, not just the ground, so it can add fill light from any angle, not just coming up from below. Bounce lights are a type of fill light, and you will probably need fewer bounce and fill lights in scenes rendered with GI than those without GI.

When lighting a character, you need to be especially careful that all of your bounce lights either cast shadows or are darkened by ambient occlusion so that the inside of the mouth or other interior surfaces don't become too bright. If the bounce light from your set does not use accurate enough shadows, then you should not link that light to your character, and you should dedicate a separate bounce light to the character himself.

A bounce light generally should not cast specular highlights, especially if the bounce light is a point light or a spotlight. Nobody will believe that a small highlight on the lower part of a character's eyeball is motivated by soft indirect light bounced off the entire floor.

The color of a bounce light coming from the ground is based on the color of the ground, as it appears when it is illuminated by the lights in your set. However, carefully check how colored bounce light looks on your character. If the character itself has boldly colored skin, fur, or clothing, make sure that complementary colors don't result in too dim a bounce light. A saturated green bounce light illuminating a bright red shirt or red lipstick might not provide much illumination, for example.

To help breathe a little extra life into a character, sometimes it helps to tint bounce lights on characters a warmer color than you would use on a set because the character's skin also transmits indirect light, and this helps simulate a general impression of warm subsurface scattering. Figure 5.18 shows the difference that adding a warm bounce light below a character's face can make.

Light can sometimes bounce between characters, as well. This is especially true if your characters are out in the sun and are brightly colored. At such times, you should add a bounce light constrained to one character to add a small amount of illumination to another. Of course, this can happen automatically if you render with GI, but even in non-GI renders, adding a little bounce to carry one character's clothing color onto a nearby character can be a wonderful finishing touch.

[Figure 5.18]
Bounce light makes a huge difference. Without bounce light (left) the bottom of the nose and chin go black. With bounce light (right) the character looks more softly and naturally lit.

Spill Lights

Spill lights for characters are basically like a dimmer, softer version of the key light. Spill lights can be considered a type of fill, except that they come from the same direction as the key light and are designed specifically to help the key light wrap around and define the character.

Sometimes a spill light can come from exactly the same position as the key, because if it is a larger area light or has softer shadows, the spill can extend a little further around the character. However, if the key is only lighting the character along one side, or if it is backlighting the character and leaving her face dark, then the spill light can also be moved toward the front of the character to help provide shaping on her face. Figure 5.19 shows the difference this can make: A spill light extends the key illumination further around the face, providing more shaping and visibility for a backlit character. In this example, the key we start with is little more than a kick. This type of effect can happen for portions of a shot when the character turns away from the key light, or when the key on the set clearly comes from behind the character. Adding spill light doesn't light the whole face, so you need some fill and bounce from other angles, but it does extend the light from the key direction to make more of the face visible.

[Figure 5.19]
Without spill light (left) the only key illumination cuts off without reaching much of the face. Adding spill light (right) extends the key illumination to light more of the face.

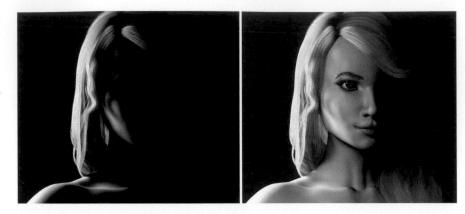

There are many possible motivations for a spill light. It could come from the key light reflecting off a nearby wall, providing a soft echo of the key itself. If the key light is the sun, then the spill might be motivated by a bright area in the sky near the sun or a cloud illuminated by sunlight. However, you shouldn't wait for a natural situation like this to arise and create a spill light for you. When your character's face isn't being lit as well as it could be, extend your key light with a spill to more fully light her face.

Rim Lights

Rim lights are aimed to create a bright line defining the edge of the character. Rim lights have their origin in black and white photography and cinematography. The top portion of Figure 5.20 shows how the foreground and background in a black and white picture can be similar shades of gray (top left), but by adding a rim light (top right), you can help separate the foreground from the background. As shown on the bottom of the figure, you can use rims to add punch to color images as well.

There are many uses for rim lights in computer graphics productions:

- To visually separate characters from backgrounds, especially in darker scenes.

- To add a sense of directionality by brightening the key side of a character.

- To create the impression that a character is backlit by adding rims to both sides of a character.

- To draw the audience's eye to a particular character or action you want to highlight.

- To help match live-action background plates. (This is because many cinematographers like shooting when the sun is low in the sky or is backlighting characters.)

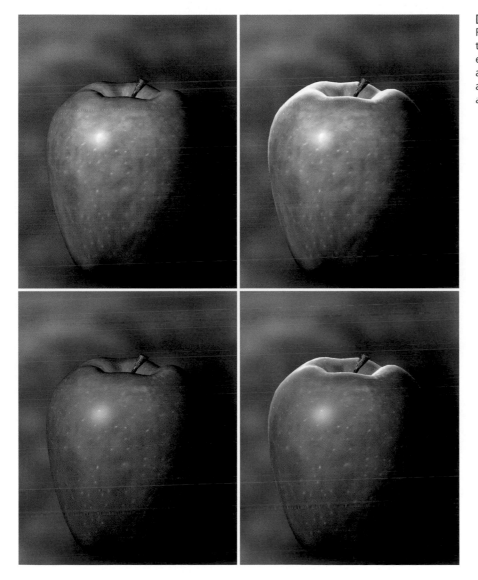

[Figure 5.20]
Rim lights are added in the right images. They are especially useful in black and white imagery but can add punch to color images as well.

Figure 5.21 shows a character lit only by two rim lights, one on the right and one on the left. Graphically, all they are doing is highlighting the outline around her body and hair.

[**Figure 5.21**] The woman is lit entirely with two rim lights. If you call a light a *rim,* then a thin line of light is all it should add to your image.

[**Figure 5.22**]
It's essential to aim rim lights by looking through the camera that will be used when the shot is rendered. You can adjust the position and thickness of the rim light by placing lights within the camera's view.

For some reason, rim lights seem to be one of the least understood types of light. In the work of beginners, I sometimes see lights that are anything from keys to fills to kicks mislabeled as rims. Look at how little of the woman is actually lit in Figure 5.21. What you see in this figure is what people expect if you name a light a *rim* light: They are not lighting much of the front of her at all. Rims add lines to the composition, not larger areas or shapes.

To aim a rim, start with the light positioned behind the character, on the side opposite from the camera, and move it so that you can see the light itself when you look through the camera or perspective view of your scene.

Looking through the actual camera view is essential to aiming a rim light. Don't try to guess its position by looking at just top or side views. It's OK to use another view to get the rim light into a rough position on the opposite side of your character from the camera, but you need to look through the final camera angle of the shot to really aim a rim light.

You can control where the rim light appears on your character by determining where the light icon appears in your camera view. Figure 5.22 shows the two rim lights aimed at the head. If the rim is to the right of your character in the camera view, it will add a rim to the right side of the character. If the rim is above the character in the camera view, it will add a rim to the top of the character. By looking through your camera view, you can even line up rim lights beside specific limbs or parts of the head and shoulders, and you can get a rim on whichever parts of the body you want.

Rim lights need to cast shadows, otherwise the mouth interior or parts of the nose or ears may receive illumination leaking through your character. If you have multiple characters, often they each need their own rim light so that you can position the lights individually. Usually, you should link rim lights to your character so that they illuminate only the character and not the set. To position a rim light correctly, sometimes you will need it to shine through a wall behind the character.

To get a thinner or more subtle rim light, move the light so that it appears closer to the character when you see it in the camera view. To fatten up the rim and make a thicker, more visible line, slide the rim light farther away from the character, heading for the edge of the frame. For a very thick rim, sometimes you may need to move a rim light all the way outside of the camera view, although you can set your viewport to over-scan the camera's view area so that the light is still visible in the camera view window. Be careful about making a rim too thick, or it will stop being a rim and look more like a kick.

Because you make all adjustments to rim lights from your camera's point of view, it is something that you need to do for each shot. A generalized rim position in a light rig can be a starting point, but to really achieve a rim you need it to be behind the character and opposite the camera.

Different kinds of surfaces and shaders respond differently to rim light. Very rough or furry surfaces catch more of a rim light, whereas hard, smooth surfaces may need a thicker or brighter rim to make anything appear. Rim lights can catch in a character's hair or fur and appear much wider than they would appear on the skin itself. It can be especially challenging to add rims to highly reflective surfaces, because they tend to respond to specular highlights and not to diffuse illumination. Sometimes you may need a large area light to add a rim to a highly reflective surface. In some cases, you can adjust shaders to help them receive a rim light better; do this by increasing the diffuse level on a highly reflective surface, or by using a Fresnel effect, which is a shader function that can make the edges of the surface respond to light more than the parts of the surface facing the camera.

[**Figure 5.23**] Kick lights can be much thicker than rims, but they still only illuminate one slice of the character, not her whole face.

Kick Lights

A *kick* is similar to a rim light, but it wraps farther around the character so that it lights one side or edge. Figure 5.23 shows a character lit solely with two kick lights.

A kick light doesn't just create a bright line—it actually illuminates enough of a surface that you can see some of the texture of the surface within the kick. Usually there is shaping within a kick; it moves from its brightest level at the edge of the subject and then fades away toward the center.

Figure 5.24 shows the position of the kick. Kicks are positioned more to the side of a character than rim lights, which are more behind the character.

[**Figure 5.24**]
Seen from above, kick lights are positioned further to the side of the character than rim lights.

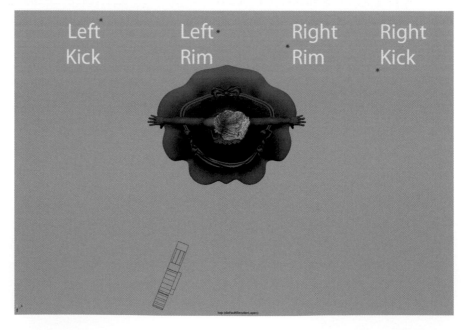

Visually, kicks can perform many of the same functions as rim lights, but they are usually much more apparent. Rim lights are often cheated into scenes in places where they are stylistically needed, but they are not exactly motivated by any light in the scene. Kicks are usually used more sparingly—only in cases where a bright light could more plausibly be present to one side of the character, for instance.

Kicks don't need to be as bright as the ones in Figure 5.23. Sometimes a kick is added to the fill side of a character only to boost the edge brightness a little bit, to help separate it from the background. You can also use kicks to add directionality to a character, adding a bright edge to the key side of the character.

Adding kicks on both sides of a character is acceptable for backlit characters, if the brightest lights are behind her. However, it's not a good idea to make two kick lights look too symmetrical. If you can make one kick thicker or brighter than the other, or you can combine a kick with a rim light, you can create a backlit look that's more natural looking than two identical kicks. Figure 5.25 shows the use of kicks to create backlit character.

[Figure 5.25] Using kicks and rims as the brightest lights on a character makes the character look backlit. Even though the face has spill, bounce, and fill light, it still looks dark in comparison to the light coming from behind the character.

Specular Lights

A *specular* or *spec light* is designed to add an extra highlight to a character. It can be any type of light source that is set not to emit diffuse illumination, but only specular. As noted in Chapter 2, most lights are usually set to emit both diffuse and specular illumination. This generally gives the best results. However, if your character is already getting enough overall diffuse illumination and needs a carefully placed highlight, a specular light lets you add a highlight without brightening the rest of the surface.

If you are trying to make a character look wet, getting just the right highlights on his skin or hair is essential. As shown on the left side of Figure 5.26, reptile or lizard skin can look dry if it has no highlights or reflections, but by adding some extra specular highlights (right), you can fix that problem. To add highlights that rake across a character's skin or hair, position the spec light roughly behind the character, much as you would a rim light.

[Figure 5.26]
Without a specular light, the snake looks flat and dry (left). Adding a specular light (right) makes the snake look more slick and shiny.

As discussed in the "Lighting Eyes" section later on, spec lights are also ideal for adding highlights to eyes. If you want to make sure a highlight appears in eyes, glasses, teeth, or other shiny parts of a character, position the spec light very close to the camera. When a spec light is close enough to the camera position, you can get highlights that remain visible no matter where a character moves during a shot.

Issues in Lighting Character Animation

Even if you are already good at lighting sets and inanimate objects, lighting animated characters presents some new issues. One issue you face is deciding whether the lights that you have already adjusted to illuminate the set are the same lights that should illuminate the characters. Sometimes lights may double as both character lights and set lights. Other times it's best to set up new groups of lights linked exclusively to the characters. Because characters move in the animation, you also need to deal with the dynamics of lighting moving characters and bringing out the best in their performances. Finally, specific lighting issues deal with different body parts, such as making the character's eyes, hair, and skin look good.

Creating Light Rigs

Lights intended to illuminate a specific character are often grouped together to form a *light rig*. A light rig is just a group of lights that can be saved and shared between lighting artists or used in different shots or scenes.

In order for rig lights to be shared between artists you must give each light in the rig a name that identifies its visual function. Use the functions of character lights (such as key lights, fill lights, rims, kicks, etc.) discussed in this chapter in the light names to communicate exactly what each light is supposed to do.

Sometimes characters have lights in their rigs that perform very specific functions, such as adding a gleam or specular highlight to their eyes, or adding shine to the character's hair.

Most rig lights use light linking to exclusively illuminate just the character itself. An exception to this rule would be if a character were something with built-in light sources, such as a car (with headlights and taillights), a robot, or a firefly with a glowing tail. Those practical lights would be included in the character's rig but adjusted to illuminate the surrounding set and other characters as well.

Lights included in a light rig do not need to be made visible in every shot. The light rig could be a toolkit of lights that are usually hidden, with specific lights only made visible when they are needed in a particular shot or sequence.

Using Set Lights to Light Characters

If you've already lit the set or environment in which the characters will appear, you can test-render your scene to see how your characters look when they are lit entirely by the set lights. Sometimes you may like the results. Other times you will see room for improvement in the modeling of the character and will need to make further additions and adjustments.

When you use global illumination and raytraced soft shadows, it gets easier to set up lights once and have the lights illuminate both the sets and the characters. Global illumination works best when light can hit each part of the characters and environment the same way and inter-reflect between them. Once you are using these modern tools, you can at least get a good start to your character lighting by just using the set lights; then only add character lights where you see room for improvement to the modeling or definition of the character.

On the other hand, if you use entirely direct illumination and depth map shadows, you are more likely to want individual lights adjusted with shadows framed around each character. A light that uses depth map shadows works best when you aim it at that character, with the cone angle adjusted so that it only covers the area where it's really needed. Also, you need to adjust depth map shadows differently for different characters; adjust the bias up and down to make sure you do not have any light leaks or missing self-shadows, or switch to a detail shadow map for a furry character's self-shadowing. Because all of the depth map adjustments I described in Chapter 3 need to be tweaked for each character, you are likely to want to use more rig lights than set lights when lighting characters with depth maps.

Splitting Out Lights

The audience expects practical lights, such as a lamp on a desk, to illuminate both the set and the characters. Sometimes, you may like how such lights look when linked to the characters and the set at once. However, at other times, you really want to be able to adjust a light's illumination on a character separately from how it lights the set. In this kind of situation, you need to *split out* a light.

Splitting out a light just means making two copies of it: The original light will still illuminate the set, and your new copy will be linked to your character. After making a copy of your set light, you can change the light names. Usually, I add the character name to the end of the light name. For example, if a practical light from a lamp is named Prac_fromLamp, I name the copy I split out to illuminate the character Jane Prac_fromLamp_onJane. Just make sure that anyone who looks at your scene can tell where the light comes from and what it is lighting.

Once you have two copies of the light, you can use light linking to make the original light illuminate the set only, but link the split-out light exclusively to the character. Once the light is split out, you gain more creative control over a character's lighting, so you can freely adjust the angle, brightness, and color of the light on the character. Of course, you want to keep the split-out light coming from the same general direction, but perfect technical continuity with your set should not outweigh concerns such as modeling with light or defining the character in a way that shows the animation and helps tell the story.

These approaches to character lighting can all be mixed and matched. As long as you like the way the lighting looks, and the overall tone and directionality works visually with the scene, all sorts of combinations are possible. For example, your key light might be a light from the character's light rig, the fill and bounce lights could come from the set lighting and global illumination, and a kick or rim might come from a light that was split out from the set to illuminate the character. No matter how much your character lighting overlaps with your set lighting, how you design the lighting for your characters is your own creative decision.

Making Lights Move with the Character

Lighting creatures and characters that change positions and poses is a far more complex task than lighting static geometry. A light that illuminates a character perfectly at one frame might not light him at all after he steps into a shadow. A carefully aimed rim light that looks great in one frame might overexpose his hair after he turns a different direction.

It is technically possible to group or constrain lights to a character so that the lights move wherever she moves, and no matter where the character goes, all of the lights surround her from the same distance and angle. This ensures that your lighting remains uniform, but it could also look fake if the lights appeared to follow the character around for no apparent reason. In general, this is not an approach you want to take for most lights on a character.

As a cheat, sometimes you can constrain a top-down fill light, or general fill light from sky illumination, to a character without anyone noticing. If you are adjusting your own bounce lights, sometimes you can attach a very dim bounce light to a character—although if the character walks over areas of ground that are brighter, darker, or of different colors, it's best if you set up different bounce lights in different areas and let the character walk through them. Fill lights aimed at a character's eyes are sometimes attached to a character so that they always brighten just the area around the eyes where they are aimed.

Rim lights are a special case, because to achieve a consistent rim lighting effect sometimes you need to animate a rim light as a character moves. Set up the rim light and test-render it at the first and last frames of your animated shot, and any frames in between that represent extreme positions or major stopping points for the character. At each frame, adjust the rim light if needed until it looks good and set a keyframe for the rim light's position.

Your character lighting generally looks more natural if the character is moving through the illumination of the scene and the light sources themselves remain static, as they do in real life. Certainly, for practical lights in a room or sunlight outside, the audience expects your character to be lit differently as he moves through space, and into and out of shadows, so your most dominant light sources should be fixed in position, even if the character gets brighter or darker at different frames of an animated shot.

Lighting Multiple Characters at Once

A single light can illuminate multiple characters, or even a whole crowd, as easily at it illuminates just one character. When the characters are all facing the same direction, like an audience in a theater, the light illuminates each character in the same way. When different characters are facing different directions, it's still possible for them to be lit with the same light, but the light illuminates them differently. For example, the light shown in the lower left of Figure 5.27 could serve as a key light for the character at the top of the figure and as a kick for the other character.

In cases where a light serves as one character's key but as a fill, kick, or rim for another character, sometimes you may want to split out copies of the light for each character. By making a copy of the light for a character and linking it just to that character, you have more creative control over being able to adjust the angle, color, brightness, and softness of the light separately for each character.

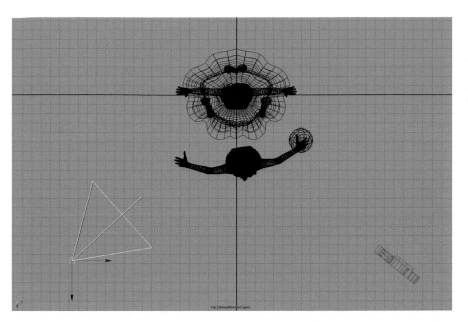

[Figure 5.27]
Seen from the top, the light on the lower left of the image can be a key light for one character and a kick light for the character facing her.

If characters actually touch each other, then you need to cast shadows between them to achieve a solid sense of contact. When you have two characters who are simply near each other, such as when they are engaged in a conversation, you don't always need visible shadows between them. Sometimes, if you have split out separate lights for the two characters, you can use shadow linking as well as light linking so that the characters self-shadow without shadowing the other characters; this prevents the characters from being crisscrossed with too many moving shadows.

Letting the Performance Guide the Lighting

Many scenes contain events that change the emotions of at least one of the characters at some moment during the scene. When this moment happens on screen, it's a good idea to think about how your lighting will reflect this.

In many cases, pivotal moments in a scene are accompanied by either a character moving to a new position or a camera angle change. Because the character position and camera angle are changing, you can often find room to motivate a change to how the characters are lit in the new position, or from the new camera angle, without breaking continuity within the scene.

Contrast is one of the big variables that you can adjust when you work with a dramatic scene. In calmer, happier moments, your character may appear more fully lit, with soft illumination, fill, and bounce light illuminating her entire face. When she is in a more stressful moment, under pressure, or in a heated argument, you might introduce more contrast into the lighting, having her stand in a place with strong light from one side and less fill light on the other half of her face. You can also accentuate contrast by having the background behind a character appear very dark, in contrast to the brighter character in the foreground.

Shadows can help play up drama. If a character is suddenly afraid of another character approaching from behind him, you can cast a shadow from the other character onto him, which makes it clearer that the other character is close by and shows the influence of the scary character on the one who is afraid. Shadows from the set can also fall onto a character. For example, while a character is walking outside, you can have shadows from overhead tree branches fall onto his face; by making his key light flicker across his face in this situation, you make him appear distracted, confused, or upset.

The angle of a light can also increase its dramatic impact. When a character stands up and announces her bold plans to take over the world, you may light her with bounced illumination from a low angle, creating somewhat scary or at least unusual illumination compared to more typical lighting from above. If she is trying to do something sneaky, perhaps it might fit the mood of the scene to have part of her face hidden in darkness, with the outline of her face illuminated by rim light to make it visible.

Finally, color is an essential component to the look of your scene. Chapter 8 of this book is all about color. In general, when you make the whole image look desaturated (with more gray tones overall) the scene appears gloomy or sometimes more frightening than a colorful scene does. Without resorting to image processing, when you light a character with more blue-colored lights, it tends to desaturate warmer flesh tones or make red lipstick appear darker and less colorful. Using bright colors can make a character appear more cheerful and confident. When you use unnatural colors to illuminate a character, such as green light, you can make a character appear sick or create the impression that something might be wrong.

Testing Frames

Because your character lighting is going to change over time, pick out a few representative frames from each shot where you want to develop and test the lighting. Pick the first and last frame, or any frames that are extremes in terms of the character being as far forward or backward as he gets in the shot. If you are planning to make the lighting change at any pivotal moments in the scene—for instance, you want to heighten contrast when a character stands up during a heated argument—then pick some frames before and after this change. Other good candidates worth testing are frames where a character's mouth is open so that you can see how the inside of the mouth looks, and any frames where two people or things come into contact.

Once you have a list of the frames that you want to test, you can move between them while lighting. If you work at one frame and aim a rim light or adjust your key, you will also want to switch to other frames and test-render the shot there to see the results of what you have added or changed.

If you are working at film resolution, normally you aren't able to render all of your frames overnight. Instead, just render a new version of a few main frames at film resolution after you change the lighting. If you need to see your lighting in motion, render the whole shot at a lower resolution, sometimes rendering every second or third frame for longer shots. Being very selective and careful about what you test-render is the key to getting your final rendering of all film-resolution frames done correctly the first time.

Subsurface Scattering

Many shaders in 3D software have a *translucency* parameter, which can make a thin surface such as a leaf, lampshade, or piece of paper appear translucent. However, for thicker objects such as most characters, the translucency of skin is best simulated via more advanced shaders that use subsurface scattering. Figure 5.28 shows a head with a regular, opaque shader (left). When rendered with subsurface scattering (right), the head shows a clear response to the bright rim light behind the left ear.

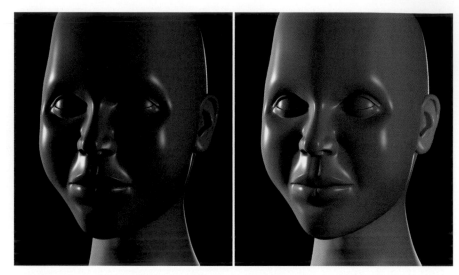

Subsurface scattering simulates the way rays of light are dispersed within translucent materials. No matter how carefully you texture map the surface of your skin, it can still look fake if it doesn't have realistic translucency. On skin, subsurface scattering is visible in three main areas:

- When bright light comes from behind thin parts of the body, such as ears and nose, they can glow red. This is called *forward scattering* because the light enters on the far side of the surface and exits after scattering through to the front.

- The terminator where the light transitions into darkness takes on a reddish glow, also due to forward scattering.

- The edges of shadows on the skin can appear reddish. This is due to back scattering, or light entering the flesh, then coming out near the same point on the surface where it entered. This happens more on fleshy areas such as cheeks.

Figure 5.29 shows these effects in real photographs. For these shots I used very bright light to make the effects particularly pronounced. In most cases subsurface scattering is very subtle. However, human skin is a material with which we are all intimately familiar, and nailing subtle details of its shading is vital to making a lifelike, engaging character.

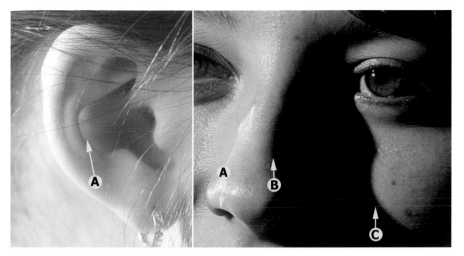

[Figure 5.29]
Three results of sub-surface scattering are light passing through thin parts of the skin such as the cartilage of the ear (A), a red edge on the terminator between the lit side of the skin and the unlit side (B), and red edges to shadows cast on the skin (C).

Once you use subsurface scattering in a skin shader, it is usually a good idea to calculate scattering for all the other parts of the head, such as teeth and eyeballs, as well. Remember that subsurface scattering is a simulation of light passing through a model, so the interior parts of the head should be a part of the equation.

Mapping Variation

An image rendered with subsurface scattering can sometimes make a character's head look as if it is made of wax rather than of flesh and blood. The waxy look is actually a result of using subsurface scattering without painting maps to vary the scattering in different parts of the face. Completely uniform subsurface scattering looks waxy because wax is a very homogeneous material that scatters light uniformly.

Under your skin, you have a mixture of bone, muscle, cartilage, and fat—all of which scatter light differently and are distributed at different depths under your skin. To physically model all of this would be prohibitively complex for an animated production. However, you can reproduce the properties that you observe in real life by painting maps to control your subsurface scattering. For example, you can map a back-scattering effect so it appears more pronounced in areas such as the cheeks, where more flesh is beneath the skin, but paint darker tones on the forehead or chin, where there's bone immediately under the skin. You may need to paint one map to control the depth or scale of the subsurface scattering so you can control how far it penetrates, and paint another to control the colors of the indirect light, if it reveals veins or a tissue texture, for instance.

Faking Subsurface Scattering

An increasing number of shaders and solutions for soft, natural-looking subsurface scattering are becoming available. However, they take time to set up properly and add to your rendering time. In particular, the texture mapping you must do to control parameters of the scattering for different parts of a character can be complex and time-consuming to set up and test. You may be looking for a quicker, simpler way to give a soft look to your characters. Luckily, you can fake some of the visual results of subsurface scattering through simpler adjustments to your shaders and lights:

- Tint the bounce lights on your character a warmer tone. Adding some pink or red helps create the feeling that the skin is tinting indirect light. Warm fill or bounce light is an ideal thing to try first if you are a beginner or are working on a tight deadline, and you don't want your character's skin to look lifeless or dead.

- Using a ramp shader or any shader with adjustable color gradients or remapping, adjust the shader so that its color appears red around the terminator instead of proceeding directly from white to black.

- Colorless wrinkles are a dead giveaway that you are using bump or displacement without subsurface scattering. When you texture map wrinkles onto a character's hands or face, also use your map to color the skin inside the wrinkle red or pink.

No matter what colors appear on the surface of a character's skin, it's what's underneath the skin—mostly red blood—that's most responsible for the tints added by subsurface scattering. Even green-skinned aliens have been rendered successfully with warm scattering tones added in the skin shaders.

Lighting Hair

Often a big concern in rendering hair and fur is how much they can slow down your rendering time. If you are rendering with depth of field (DOF) but a character is in perfect focus, it can save render time to render the character as a separate layer without calculating DOF for that layer. Hair and fur can greatly slow down raytracing, too. It is generally a good idea to exclude hair and fur from raytraced shadows or reflections altogether.

Hair is usually rendered with depth map shadows. As mentioned in Chapter 4, some renderers have special types of shadow maps designed to work well with hair, such as deep shadow maps in RenderMan or detail shadow maps in Mental Ray. Because hairs are so thin compared to individual samples in the shadow map, it is essential that shadow maps be tightly framed to focus on the hair itself. This is one reason to use separate lights to illuminate a character's hair.

By dedicating separate lights to hair, you get more perfect rim lighting on the hair. Hair tends to pick up rim light much more readily than most surfaces, so making a separately aimed, less intense rim light for it can provide a nice rim without making the hair go pure white.

Lighting Eyes

An eye has four main visible parts:

- The sclera—the "white" of the eye

- The iris—the colored part of the eye

- The pupil—the black part in the middle

- The cornea—the clear part covering the sclera, iris, and pupil

Each of these parts requires careful attention in character lighting.

Lighting the Sclera

Even though the sclera is called the "white" of the eye, it doesn't need to be pure white. Figure 5.30 shows an eyeball texture map. It has more pink and red detail as you move away from the center. Using pure white for your sclera might make your character look like a cartoon character. In a realistic character, the sclera also tends to receive shadows from the eyelashes.

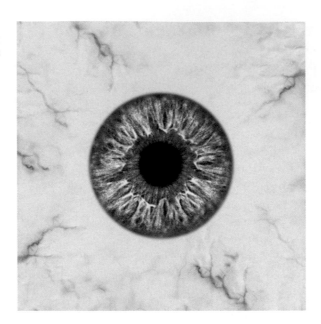

Even though this texture map includes the sclera, iris, and pupil, these parts should not all run together as if they were just differently colored regions on the surface of a sphere. If you model and texture your character's eyes like a painted Ping-Pong ball, they will not look convincing, no matter how you light them. You can make the iris part of the same object as the sclera, but at least build it at a different angle compared to the overall curve of the sclera.

Because the sclera does not need to be exposed to light in order for you to see, and because it is made up of very sensitive tissue that's easily damaged, most animals have their scleras covered by their eyelids. Human eyes look distinctly different from the eyes of other animals because so much of the sclera is exposed and visible. Our exposed scleras make the direction of a gaze readily apparent, even from a distance, which is a useful cue in communication and social interaction. In stylized animation, animals are usually given more human-like exposed scleras, because the exposed sclera is so important to telegraphing the full performance of the character, including eye directions.

Lighting the Iris

The iris doesn't just provide color to the eyes, it also provides depth. Set deep into the eye, behind the cornea, the iris often receives a bright gleam on the opposite side of the eye from where the light enters. Figure 5.31 shows an example of this. Notice that, overall, the eyes are brightest on the right, with highlights on the right side. And yet the irises are brightest on the left, the opposite of the shading of the overall eye.

[Figure 5.31]
The iris gleam is visible on the opposite side of the eye from the eye highlight.

The bright side of the iris is called *iris gleam*. In a real eye, iris gleam is very apparent when eyes are lit from the side and less noticeable when eyes are lit from the front or uniformly lit from all angles. Real iris gleam is actually a caustic pattern, caused by light that has refracted through the lens of the eye and is coming out the opposite side of the lens to illuminate part of the iris. In computer graphics, you can achieve iris gleam in a number of ways. One of the simplest ways was used in the character in Figure 5.31, which is just to model the irises so that they slope inward instead of bulging out into the lens.

Figure 5.32 shows how the eyes were modeled. The outer layer, shown in blue, is the transparent cornea, which includes a bulge in front, which represents the lens. The inner surface of the eyeball, shown in yellow, depicts the sclera and iris. It is not a complete sphere. Instead, the portion that represents the iris dents inward, sloping back toward the center of the eyeball. The direction of the slope catches an iris gleam on the side that's opposite the key light, and this gives more depth to the eye. The iris slopes inward by a large amount on this stylized character. In other characters, a flatter iris, sloping in just slightly, could be used for a more subtle effect. Iris gleam is also faked at some companies through special eye shaders, which create fake gradients (sometimes called *scooping*) on the side of the iris opposite from the eye highlight.

[Figure 5.32]
The iris is connected to the sclera, but it is angled inward to catch gleam from the opposite side of the eye.

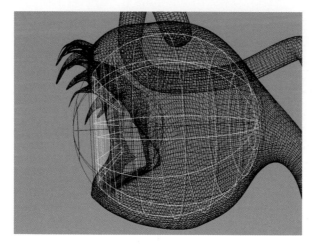

As a general rule of thumb, the iris gleam should not make the iris look brighter than the sclera next to it.

Lighting the Pupil

Generally, the pupil should remain black. When photographs are taken of people using a flash and the camera flash is close to the lens of the camera, light from the flash sometimes reaches all the way back through the pupil of the eye and causes *red eye*. This is an artifact of flash photography that photographers are likely to digitally remove from a photograph to prevent their subject from looking demonic. Red eye won't happen by accident in computer graphics, but sometimes reflections and highlights land right in the center of the eye and make the pupil area look bright and milky, rather than crisp and black.

Highlights that cover the pupil can distract from the character's expression or make the eyes look unhealthy. Try to position your eye highlights and reflections so that the pupil remains black and well defined against the iris. Another key to getting a crisp, black pupil is to make sure that the iris gleam can't brighten the pupils. You can model the pupils as holes cut through the center of the iris, showing through to an all-black surface behind the irises. If you don't cut them out as holes, you can use texture mapping to map their specular color to pure black so that they don't receive any highlights.

Lighting the Cornea

The cornea is transparent, so most of the time it is only visible where reflections and highlights hit it. This makes it one of the most important parts of the eyes for your lighting. Eye highlights help make a character look alive. Without highlights, a character's eyes look unnaturally dry. Even in wider shots, when highlights in a character's eyes might be only a few pixels in size, they are often some of the most important pixels in the image.

Even though reflections and highlights can happen anywhere on an eye, you generally don't want bright highlights right along the upper or lower edge of the cornea, because in that area, many reflections are blocked at least partially by eyelashes and the reflection of the eyelid. Highlights stuck right in the lower edge of the eye can make a character look as if he is crying, with highlights appearing on the welled-up tears.

Often the most convincing place for a highlight is right along one edge of the iris. This accentuates the convex shape of the lens of the eye, as though it is the edge of the lens that has caught the highlight. You can model the lens shape into the cornea as a bulge in front of the iris to help it collect highlights from more angles. Figure 5.33 shows a model for a human eye. The outer cornea model (shown in blue) is not a perfect sphere, but instead it protrudes forward away from the iris, creating the impression that it wraps around a lens in the eyeball.

[Figure 5.33]
The cornea has a slight bulge to simulate a lens in front of the iris.

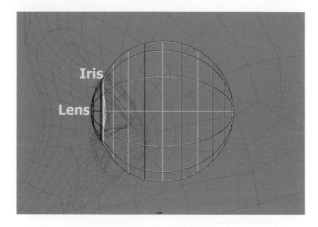

In general, it's best to start lighting the eyes by giving them the same illumination as the rest of your character. Your key light or other lights on the character might contribute a specular highlight that works well enough to provide eye highlights in some shots.

If your key light is not enough to trigger a nice eye highlight, or if the key creates a highlight that lands right over the pupil or is too close to the edge of the eyes, then you can create a new specular light to use for eye highlights. Because the cornea is a separate object, you can use light linking to prevent the key light from illuminating the cornea itself, where the highlights appear. Set a new light to emit specular illumination only, and link it just to the corneas of your character's eyes. Then you can start with the specular light positioned near your key light, but adjust its position as needed to get the specular highlights you want in the eye. To make sure the highlights are visible in any animated shot, you can cheat the specular light very close to the camera. Once it is near the camera, moving the specular light only a small amount to the side or upward can adjust the highlight position in the eye.

Exercises

The illumination striking people and animals is something you can observe as you go through the day, and you can learn different things about it in every environment. Movies and photographs are another source of inspiration worthy of study. Most of all, keep practicing lighting your own characters in ways that best define them and fit with each scene.

1. The exercises section at the end of Chapter 2 suggested a *one-light rendering*. If you are working on finding a good key light position for a character, then this assignment is a great starting point. Render the character lit with only one light and allow blackness wherever the light is shadowed. From a good key light position, a one-light rendering can begin to model the character with its illumination, shadows, and terminator position. If you are happy with your one-light rendering, then you have found a great key light position and can start adding other lights. (As a homework assignment, the images could be submitted in a multilayer Photoshop file, with the base layer showing the scene lit by the key light only, then other layers showing the scene with other lights added.)

2. Many of the Lighting Challenge scenes available at www.3dRender.com/ challenges contain characters you can practice lighting. Once you've lit some characters for still images, though, try lighting characters that are actually animated. If you don't have skills in character animation, even animation you take to a blocking or layout stage can be better suited for character lighting than characters that remain motionless. Because character animation tends to be a full-time job, sometimes the desire to light animated characters is also a reason for lighters to work on group projects.

3. It is not illegal to collect reference images from your favorite movies to study how actors are lit in different scenes. Looking at how live-action cinematographers capture different emotions and different kinds of scenes though lighting can be a great asset. Many digital lighting artists build up a library of still images from live-action movies to use as references and also use them as points of discussion with directors and clients in planning a project. The 1992 documentary *Visions of Light: The Art of Cinematography* is a great video to buy for your collection; it includes clips from many noteworthy films that can serve as a taking-off point.

CHAPTER SIX

Cameras and Exposure

Why does a 3D artist need to know about cameras and exposure? You need to understand how real photography works in order to match or simulate the effects of a real camera in computer graphics. Whether you are rendering visual effects elements that need to be integrated with live-action footage, or are just trying to make a 3D scene look more cinematic and believable, it helps to understand how exposure works in real cameras, and to be able to read the notations in a camera log regarding lenses, f-stops, and shutter angles. Your understanding of real cameras can also help you shoot bracketed sets of shots that are ideal for creating High Dynamic Range Images (HDRIs) to capture the lighting at shooting locations so that you can precisely match it in 3D graphics.

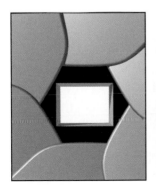

Exposure is the all-important moment when the camera's shutter opens and allows light to reach the sensor or film. The adjustments that a photographer or cinematographer makes to control the exposure also influence the depth of field, motion blur, and other properties of the shot. Three main aspects control a camera's exposure:

F-stops describe how wide the opening is that lets light into the camera. This aspect has a side effect of also controlling the amount of depth of field in your shot, so f-stops and depth of field are discussed together in this chapter.

Shutter speed describes how long the shutter will be open to let in light. This has a side effect of controlling the amount of motion blur in your shot, so shutter speed and motion blur are discussed together.

Film speed describes how sensitive to light the film or sensor is, but as a side effect, it can also add grain or noise to an image.

This chapter discusses each of the three exposure parameters, how to simulate their side effects in the computer, and how other aspects of a camera such as lens imperfections can be simulated for more realistic renderings.

F-Stops and Depth of Field

Depth of field (DOF) determines how much of your scene is in focus. With a narrow DOF, only a narrow slice of your scene remains sharp near a specified focal distance; everything farther from or closer to the camera is blurred. With a deep DOF, more of the scene (sometimes all of your scene) is in focus.

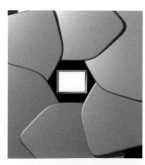

[Figure 6.1]
The camera's aperture dilates with a set of metal flaps. The hexagonal shape being formed here is sometimes seen as a feature in lens flares and bokeh.

A photographer or cinematographer controls a camera's DOF by adjusting the size of the *aperture*, the opening through which light travels in order to enter the camera. The aperture size varies via an arrangement of metal flaps, as shown in Figure 6.1.

The size of the aperture is measured in *f-stops*. In a real camera, the primary function of setting an f-stop is to control how much light reaches the sensor. DOF is a side effect of your f-stop choice.

Low-numbered f-stops, like f/1.4, let in the most light and create a shallow DOF with very few things in focus.

Higher-numbered f-stops, such as f/16 or f/22, let in the least light but create the deepest DOF with more things in focus.

The sequence of f-stops is shown on the lens of a camera in Figure 6.2. Different lenses have different maximums and minimums but often include the f-stops 1.4, 2, 2.8, 4, 5.6, 8, 11, 16, and 22.

What f-stops actually represent in a camera is the ratio between the focal length of the lens and the diameter of the aperture that lets in the light. For example, if you use a 100mm lens at f/4, the aperture will have a diameter of 25mm. Because the light is limited to what fits through a smaller opening, each increase of one f-stop cuts the amount of light hitting the sensor exactly in half.

[Figure 6.2]
The *aperture ring* on a camera lens is used to choose an f-stop. Newer lenses often lack an aperture ring because the f-stop is chosen electronically through the camera, but the f-numbers still work the same way.

Having everything in focus at once, from objects close to the camera all the way to the distant background, is called *deep focus*. On the computer, of course, you have the option of turning off DOF and rendering without it entirely, which gives you infinitely deep focus by default. You do not need to turn on DOF in your software if you want your entire scene in perfect focus. If you want deep focus with just a small amount of blurring on objects that fall out of focus, turn on DOF but use a higher f-stop number such as f/22.

As you move into lower f-numbers, such as f/5.6 for instance, parts of your scene will fall out of focus. Take a look at the left side of Figure 6.3; it was rendered at f/5.6, and you can see that both the candles in the background and the columns in the far background are a bit out of focus.

[Figure 6.3]
A medium aperture of f/5.6 creates a larger DOF (left), while a large aperture of f/1.4 produces very shallow DOF (right).

The lowest f-number, such as f/1.4, specifies the widest aperture opening possible with your lens—the one that lets in the most light. As light enters from a greater range of angles, this creates a very shallow DOF, with fewer objects in focus, as shown on the right side of Figure 6.3. Any subject that steps closer to the camera, or moves farther beyond the focal distance, quickly falls out of focus.

Some renderers support a physical camera model in which the f-stop controls both the DOF and brightness of the image at the same time, but the general approach in most software is that these things are set separately. In most 3D software, the f-stop you select to control DOF does not affect the brightness of your scene. However, you should still remember the photographic relationship between brightness and aperture. A narrower DOF, with fewer things in focus, is usually expected in dark or dimly lit scenes that have been filmed with a lower f-stop number. Deeper focus is more commonly expected in brighter environments, such as a sunny outdoor scene.

Setting the Focus

You can focus the camera at only one focal distance. You need to choose an object to focus on, and measure the distance between the camera and that object.

A great way to check the distance between the camera and the object you want to appear in focus is to adjust the camera's near or far clipping plane so that only the near or far half of the object is visible in your camera's view. After you find the number you want, make sure you return the clipping planes to their original values and use the distance value that you tested as the focal distance for your DOF. Figure 6.4 shows the far clipping plane being adjusted to the middle of the front candle flame, establishing the value that will be used as the focal distance.

It can be more accurate to perform the clipping plane trick than to use a quick display of "distance from camera," which is available as an interface element for the selected object. A distance from camera attribute only displays the distance to the object's center or pivot point, which may not be the exact part of the object where you wanted to focus. Some programs also have a measure tool that works like a measuring tape between two points. You can use this to determine distance between the camera and a desired part of the object; however, this too might be less accurate than checking your focal distance with a clipping plane.

[Figure 6.4]
To focus on the foreground candle and let the candles seen in the background (of the left image) fall out of focus, the far clipping plane is adjusted to bisect the foreground candle flame (right). The clipping planes can then be reset to their old values, but the number chosen can be used as the focal distance.

Be careful not to scale the camera itself if this might scale the focal distance in your software. In some programs, scaling the camera also scales all distances that are parts of the camera, so if you scale up the camera for the purpose of seeing a bigger icon, you might have the unwelcome side effect of throwing your camera to the wrong focal distance.

Pulling Focus

Changing the focus on the camera during a shot is called a *focus pull*. In live-action filmmaking, a crew member needs to pull the focus on the camera if the focal distance is adjusted during the shot. Common types of focus pull are the *follow focus* (adjusting the focal distance to keep an actor in focus when the actor or camera moves) and the *rack focus* (using a focus shift as a transition from focusing on one person or thing to another person or thing). Usually, the focal distances involved are worked out ahead of filming, and desired focal distances are marked, so the focus pull operator can simply rotate the lens from one mark to the other at a designated time. A similar approach usually looks best in computer animation: If your subject moves closer or farther away from the camera during the shot, simply choose two or three keyframes to set the focal distance and let your DOF animate between those. You shouldn't need constant focus tracking at every frame, which could result in jerky or distracting adjustments to the focus.

If the camera is animated, just set keyframes for the focal distance as you set keyframes for the position of the camera itself; this way, all parameters are animated at once. After you set the initial keyframes, go back through your animation curves and check on how the animation moves in and out of each keyframe to make sure it doesn't start or stop mechanically.

When you rotate the lens ring that controls focus on a real lens, the lens does not move linearly through different focal distances. Instead, you use much of the range you have when you rotate the ring to focus on the first few meters of space around the camera; it is only a small remaining part of the rotation that you use to focus from there to infinity. When focus is pulled, even if the ring is turned at a uniform speed, the focus spends more time on the closer distances; it then speeds up greatly when it moves through greater distances.

Most 3D programs provide many options for how you can animate between keyframes. If you settle for linear interpolation between focal distance values, your animated focus changes do not look like a real focus pull. Instead, if you are focusing from near to far, the transition should start out very slow and speed up near the end. Pulling focus from far to near should start moving through the far focal distances more quickly and then slow way down on the distances closer to camera.

Matching Real Lenses

The *focal length* of a lens is the amount of magnification it provides. When a lens has a greater focal length, it is more zoomed in, or *telephoto*, and provides more magnification to your image. A telephoto lens tends to produce a narrower DOF, with a lot of foreground and background blurring. Technically, if you see a larger amount of blurring through a telephoto lens, it is simply because the blurring is magnified along with the rest of the image, but as a result you do see a blurrier looking background at the same f-stop. A wide-angle lens (low focal length) generally has a deeper DOF, with more things in focus. If you simulate an extremely telephoto lens, such as the view through a telescope, the audience expects a narrow DOF.

You use a *macro* lens for close-up photography and shooting very small things. This type of lens tends to have an extremely narrow DOF. Because of this, people have come to associate a very narrow DOF with miniature objects. If you want a part of your animation to look like macro photography of a tiny subject, use a very narrow DOF, which will help convey this effect, as in Figure 6.5.

[Figure 6.5]
A narrow DOF helps simulate the look of a macro lens in "Circus Maximus Irritans," by Péter Fendrik, rendered in Cinema 4D.

Keep in mind that if you render a scene with too narrow a DOF, it can make your characters look like miniatures in a dollhouse instead of life-sized people. Giving your scene a greater DOF makes the scene's scale look more normal.

Lens Breathing

Lens breathing is a term used to describe the tendency of lenses to change their effective focal length when the focal distance is changed. The advertised focal length of a lens (a 50mm lens, for instance) is really only the focal length when that lens is focused at infinity. When the lens is focused on a nearby subject, the focal length slightly increases, so that the lens becomes slightly more telephoto.

Lenses made specifically for cinema instead of still photography are designed to minimize lens breathing, because it is distracting if each focus pull in a movie also noticeably changes the composition of a shot. However, a tiny amount of lens breathing may still be present.

Some camera models in 3D, such as the VRay Physical Camera, include lens breathing. You can see it zooming in slightly when you adjust it to a closer focus distance. Although this can add to realism, remember that lens breathing is considered an undesirable effect in live-action filmmaking, so as technology progresses, we are more likely to see it simulated in 3D graphics and less likely to notice it in live-action films.

Finding the Area in Focus

You might imagine that focus is uniformly distributed around the focal distance, so that if you focus on an object 3 meters away, objects at 2 meters and 4 meters are equally blurry. However, this is not the case.

When a camera is focused to a specific focal distance, you can expect about one-third of the area in focus to be in the foreground, closer than the focal distance, and about two-thirds of the area in focus to be in the background, beyond the focal distance, as shown in Figure 6.6.

[Figure 6.6]
About one-third of the area in focus will be in front of your focal distance, and two-thirds will be beyond it.

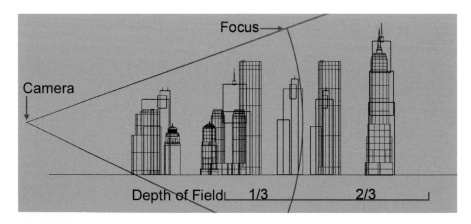

Hyperfocal Distance

When a lens is focused at its *hyperfocal distance*, everything in the background is in focus, no matter how far away it is. In the foreground, focus begins at half the focal distance. For example, in Figure 6.7, if the camera is focused at 200 meters, everything from 100 meters to infinity is in focus. Specifics depend on the lens, but you usually reach the hyperfocal distance when you use a small aperture and focus at least a few meters away. We often see outdoor scenes and landscape photography created with cameras focused at their hyperfocal distance.

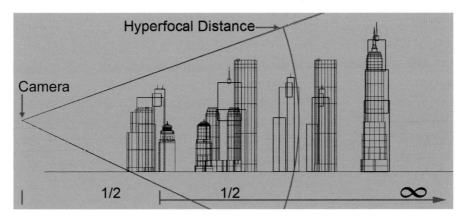

[Figure 6.7]
When a lens is focused at its hyperfocal distance, everything in the background is in focus.

In bright daylight scenes, when the focal distance is more than a few meters from the camera, it is likely that the far distance and the sky will be in focus as well. At night or when you are indoors, backgrounds often fall out of focus. If your background is an image mapped onto a sphere surrounding your scene, leave it fully in focus for most of your daylight shots. If you need to visually separate the foreground from the background, consider adding some mist or haze on your daytime backgrounds instead of blurring them.

Using Bokeh Effects

You've probably seen pictures with out-of-focus backgrounds, where all the lights or bright areas in the background bloom into little balls of light. Instead of just a smoothly blurred area, the out-of-focus parts of the image

[Figure 6.8]
Highlights grow into beads
of light as they fall out of
focus. The bokeh (out-of-
focus quality) of a lens gives
each type of lens a unique
signature.

shimmer or glisten with little beads of light surrounding each highlight, as shown in Figure 6.8. These are called *bokeh effects*. They are an option you can activate that enhances the look of DOF effects. Bokeh (pronounced "bow-kay") is a word derived from Japanese that describes the "out-of-focus" quality of a lens.

Lenses have different bokeh. Some lenses are described as very smooth and creamy; this means the lens blurs things in much the same way as a renderer's default DOF, making areas look like they have been smoothly Gaussian blurred. Other lenses make very defined circles or seem to put rings around bright points of light when they fall out of focus.

Some renderers like Mental Ray can render bokeh effects through a plug-in or lens shader. Other renderers (like VRay) have bokeh options integrated into the main DOF rendering options. Either way, you are provided with a set of controls that influences how out-of-focus features appear in your rendered image. The results are most visible around lights, highlights, or small bright objects that fall out of focus. The background candle flames in Figure 6.9 look like pentagons because of the bokeh effects used.

Each bright spot that falls out of focus can appear to be a bead or circle of light, or can take on a specific shape such as an octagon or hexagon.

For bokeh shapes with a specific number of sides, set the number of *blades* in your shutter to the number of sides you want in each bokeh shape. For example, chose five blades to create a pentagon-shaped bokeh effect. If you chose eight blades, you get an octagon-shaped bokeh effect. Figure 6.10 shows bokeh from the candle flames with zero blades (circular bokeh), six blades, and eight blades.

Another common control for bokeh is the amount of *center bias*, which controls whether the light concentrates in the center of the bokeh features or out on the edges. Figure 6.11 shows bokeh weighted toward the center, with a neutral bias of one and concentrated out in the edges. Note that some photographers consider donut-shaped bokeh (rings that look hollow in the center) to be "bad bokeh," in that they look unnatural and are distracting, and can be considered undesirable lens artifacts.

[Figure 6.9]
Bokeh effects make the background candle flames look like pentagons, simulating a five-blade aperture.

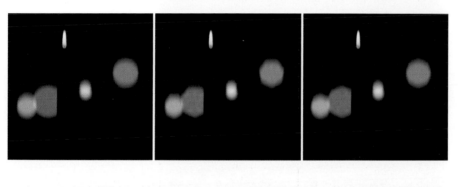

[Figure 6.10]
By varying the number of blades, the bokeh around the flames can be made round with zero blades (left), seven-sided with seven blades (center), or eight-sided with eight blades (right).

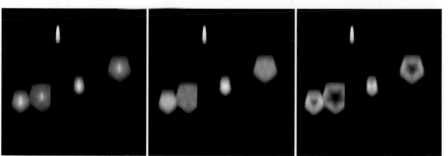

[Figure 6.11]
The center bias of a bokeh effect can weigh the highlights toward the center (left), create a neutral result (middle), or create bokeh that are hollow or darker in the center (right).

For even more control, some renderers support using custom *bokeh maps*. In this case, you provide an image of any shape or color pattern over a black background, and this image becomes the shape for the bokeh. For example, an image of a white hexagon over a black background creates bokeh that looked like a six-blade aperture. If you are matching the bokeh from a specific camera, you can crop out an out-of-focus highlight from a photograph taken with that camera and use that as a bokeh map.

Depth of Field and Hidden Image Areas

Rendering with depth of field can reveal parts of your 3D scene that are not visible if you render without DOF. Figure 6.12 shows how this can work. A candle is positioned just outside of the right edge of the frame so that it is not visible in the top image where the scene is rendered without DOF. With DOF, you can see part of the candle on the far right side of the frame.

[Figure 6.12]
Look carefully at the right edge of the frame. When the scene is rendered without any DOF (top), there's no candle visible on the right side. When the exact same scene is rendered with DOF (bottom), you can see a candle on the right edge of the frame, which had been positioned just outside of the camera's view.

When the camera moves, or when objects enter or leave the frame, blurred objects tend to enter the frame sooner and leave later than you would guess if you were looking at the scene within your 3D program without DOF. This is a natural result of how rays of light are gathered from more angles when you are simulating DOF. However, it does mean that you need to be careful about what objects exist just outside of the frame: Don't assume that something is completely hidden from the audience just because it is outside of your viewport when you compose a shot.

The edges of the frame aren't the only hidden areas that can be revealed with DOF. Other hidden areas that can be revealed are where one object is behind another object, and where an object is near the edge of a wall or just around a corner from the camera.

To save rendering time, some people render without any DOF and then create a fake DOF effect during compositing. A number of plug-ins can even simulate bokeh effects in compositing programs. However, be careful when you use these techniques, because the lack of extra image information behind foreground objects and off the edges of the screen can lead to artifacts where blurred objects pop on and off screen unnaturally. If you fake your DOF in post, you may have to render a larger image, with an extra 100 pixels around each edge, and then crop it down to your final size after adding bokeh effects to ensure that objects enter and leave frame smoothly.

Computational Expense

Rendering with DOF and bokeh can be expensive. When you first turn on DOF, you can see your scene becoming more grainy or noisy, and the only good way to reduce the noise is to turn up the number of samples. However, if you turn up the samples high enough for a noise-free image with shallow DOF, you can greatly slow down your renders.

You should always test-render a region of your image to see how noisy it actually looks with your current DOF settings. In general, the further out of focus a part of your scene falls, the more likely it is to appear noisy. Turn up your samples as high as you need to smooth out the noise, but certainly no higher.

If the full-quality frames you render have a little bit of noise visible in areas that fall out of focus, this is not a big problem. Noise reduction filters available in compositing software such as Nuke or After Effects can smooth out areas that are a little bit noisy. The only side effect of using a noise reduction filter is that it sometimes causes a little more blurring and reduces small details as well as noise. But if you apply the filter to an area that is supposed to appear soft and out of focus already, this should not be a problem.

Shutter Speed and Motion Blur

Motion blur is the directional streaking that results when movement is captured during the exposure. The controls on a real camera that influence motion blur are the shutter speed (in stills) or shutter angle (in motion pictures).

Shutter Speed and Shutter Angle

Shutter speed is a measurement of how long a camera's shutter opens to allow light to expose the film. Shutter speed is usually expressed as a fraction of a second, such as $\frac{1}{125}$. The longer the shutter is open, the more light reaches the film.

Frame Rates

Video and motion picture cameras have a *frame rate,* which is measured in frames per second (fps). The frame rate specifies how many individual frames or images are exposed per second of moving film or video.

Motion picture film is usually shot at 24 fps, which is called *sound speed* because it is the standard speed for film with a synchronized soundtrack. Prior to the invention of sound, camera operators would crank movie cameras at slightly different rates for different shots, which they considered a part of their creative control over the flow of the film. Digital cinema cameras also commonly operate at 24 fps. Movies can also be shot and digitally projected at higher frame rates for smoother motion, although this can take away from the traditional cinematic look to which the audience is accustomed.

Different television standards around the world have different frame rates. The NTSC standard, common throughout North America, uses a frame rate of just less than 30 fps. Two of the world's other major standards, PAL and SECAM, use 25 fps. Switching to HDTV did not eliminate these frame rate differences.

Doubling the amount of time the shutter stays open makes an image twice as bright. A shutter speed of ¼ of a second would allow twice as much light to reach the film as a speed of ⅛ of a second. In the viewfinders and controls of many cameras, abbreviated labels show only the divisor (the second number in the fraction) to indicate a shutter speed. For example, ¹⁄₂₅₀ of a second is labeled 250, or ¹⁄₂₀₀₀ of a second is labeled 2000. In this case, what appear to be the highest numbers actually refer to the smallest fractions of a second.

In a motion picture camera, instead of shutter speed, you are more likely to see a control called the *shutter angle*. The shutter of most motion picture cameras is a revolving disc. The disc rotates 360 degrees for each frame that is exposed. A window behind the disc allows light through to the film when the shutter is open. The shutter angle controls the angle of the opening in the shutter, which can be made narrower by the position of a small metal flap, as represented in Figure 6.13.

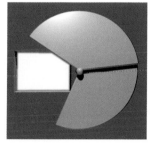

[Figure 6.13]
An opening in a revolving shutter creates the shutter angle. The two halves of the shutter can rotate to make the opening wider or narrower.

A *shutter angle control* is also used to control motion blur in many 3D programs, including RenderMan and Maya.

The common shutter angle of 180 degrees means that the shutter is open half of the time and closed half of the time. At a 180-degree shutter angle, the shutter speed is equal to half of the frame rate. For example, at 24 fps with a shutter angle of 180 degrees, the shutter speed is ¹⁄₄₈ of a second.

The shutter angle divided by 360 tells you what portion of the frame rate is actually being used as the shutter speed. For example, if the shutter angle is 90 degrees, then the shutter is open one-quarter of the time. Therefore, a 90-degree shutter at 24 fps is equivalent to a shutter speed of $1/(4 * 24)$, or ¹⁄₉₆ of a second.

A 360-degree shutter angle is a special case. Going all the way up to 360 used to be impossible with ordinary film cameras, because that meant that the shutter never shut and no time was allowed to advance the film to the next frame. With digital cameras, a 360-degree shutter is now possible, so you can capture the full arc of motion that occurs during each frame. When some films are shot at frame rates higher than the standard sound speed of 24 fps, a 360-degree shutter may be used. This allows more than one frame of the high frame rate version of the film to be combined to create a lower frame rate version that may be shown in some theaters.

In 3D software, you are allowed to type in numbers up to 360 degrees or even higher. When you go above 360 degrees you are capturing extra motion streaks on each frame that actually overlap with the motion that's also captured on other frames.

Different programs have slightly different ways to adjust motion blur. 3ds Max asks for a motion blur duration in frames so that a value of 1 frame equals a 360-degree shutter. If you have a logged shutter angle from live-action footage, divide the shutter angle by 360 to get the value in frames. For example, if a scene was shot with a 180-degree shutter, enter 0.5, which produces results similar to those in Figure 6.14.

[Figure 6.14]
A motion blur of 0.5 simulates a 180-degree shutter angle.

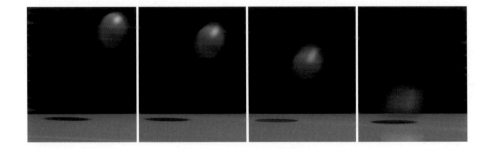

Softimage asks for a shutter open and shutter close time. For example, if you have shutter open at 0 and shutter close at 0.5, that is a 180-degree shutter angle, which samples motion during the first half of the frame duration. If an animator wants to avoid having a particular pose motion-blurred at a particular frame, he can create a half-frame "hold." Making the character (or part of the character) hold still during the interval being sampled produces a crisp image of the pose with no motion blur.

As a rule of thumb, keep your shutter angle between 90 degrees and 180 degrees for the most natural, realistic results. Too low a level of motion blur often makes the action seem jerky or unnatural, while too high a number creates an after-image or trail behind objects as they move.

To simulate the most photorealistic motion blur possible, remember that you often need slower shutter speeds to let in enough light in darker environments, and very high shutter speeds are usually possible only in brightly lit environments.

First Frame Problems

You need to render every frame of an animated shot with consistent motion blur, including the first one. In order to guarantee that the first frame of a shot has normal, consistent-looking motion blur, make sure the animation of a shot begins before the first frame. If the first frame is number 1, then the animation should begin at frame 0 (or earlier) for consistent results.

As a lighting artist, if you are receiving animation from someone else, it pays to check the animation you receive by flipping between the first frame of the shot and the frame before the first frame. For example, if the shot starts at frame number 1, check frame 0. Since frame 0 is not going to be rendered or used in the movie, it's possible that nobody has checked it. However, what changes between frames 0 and 1 affects the motion blur in frame 1. Make sure that things that are supposed to be moving are moving before the first frame, and that nothing jumps into position at the first frame that has been somewhere else immediately prior to the first frame. These are easy mistakes for an animator to make, but become visible only when you render with motion blur.

Because camera motion also causes motion blur, make sure you also check for consistent camera work immediately before and after the animation. When animating a camera position, don't let the camera jump suddenly between frames, as if to simulate a cut; the motion blur will badly distort those frames.

The Comet Tail Myth

Photographs can be created that appear to have trails fading off behind a moving object, but usually what causes these is either a camera flash triggered at the end of the exposure or a subject that stops moving near the end of the exposure. If a subject is moving at a constant rate and is illuminated evenly while the frame is exposed, the motion blur is symmetrical and does not indicate whether the object is moving forward or backward.

Some people imagine that motion blur lags behind a moving object, similar to how a tail appears behind a comet. In reality, motion blur is uniformly bidirectional, meaning that if something is filmed moving continuously from left to right, it will have the same amount of blur on the left side as the right side.

When you look at a single frame from a movie, the motion blur does not indicate which direction something was traveling. If the subject moves at a constant speed throughout the exposure, then the motion blur is not bright in front and does not fade out in the rear like the tail of a comet. Instead it appears as streaks of a continuous brightness, as you can see in Figure 6.15. Even in a slow exposure that captures long streaks of motion blur, the streaks are uniformly bright and consistent along their length; nothing about the motion blur would look different if the cars were driving in reverse.

[Figure 6.15]
This shot would look just the same if all of the cars were driving in reverse. Motion blur does not fade off like a comet tail—it remains constant through the exposure if the brightness and speed of the subject remain constant.

Blurring Rotations

Rapidly rotating objects—such as the blades of a fan, spinning wheels, or a helicopter's propeller—are some of the hardest things to accurately motion blur. Rendering software must slow down and sample the motion several times per frame to render a fully round rotation, instead of a linear streak from one frame's position to the next. Further complicating things, rapid rotations don't always rotate in perfect synchronization with the frame rate, so sometimes a wheel can appear to be rotating backward.

Figure 6.16 illustrates the *wagon wheel effect*—the confusion sometimes caused by actions that repeat at a pace similar to the frame rate. The wagon wheel effect got its name from chase scenes in Western movies, which often featured speeding wagons. In these scenes, the rotating wheels often appeared to spin at the wrong speed, or even backward, when viewed on film. This was because similar-looking spokes changed places while the shutter was closed, making it difficult to follow their motion between frames.

[Figure 6.16]
The wheel turns counter-clockwise between these frames, but to the viewer it looks as if the wheel turns clockwise if you can't tell one spoke from the other.

Often, a cheated solution is the best solution to very rapid rotation. For example, you can replace a spinning fan blade with a flat disk, and transparency map it with a texture that is already blurred to look as if it is spinning. This way a simple textured surface can look like a rapidly spinning blade, without causing rendering headaches in every shot where it appears.

Interlaced and Progressive Scan

Two common standards used in current high-definition television are called 1080i and 720p. They have different resolutions (1,920×1,080 for 1080i and 1,280×720 for 720p), but they also differ in what the *i* and the *p* stand for: *interlaced* and *progressive* scan, which are two different ways of shooting, transmitting, and displaying video signals.

Progressive scan is the simplest to understand. For each frame, the camera's shutter opens only once and captures the full image. The image consists of a number of horizontal *scanlines*, which are horizontal rows of pixels running all the way across the screen from left to right. Scanlines are recorded or transmitted one at a time, from top to bottom. To display each frame, the television or monitor displays each scanline in order, from top to bottom, and then it starts refreshing the image at the top again for the next frame.

Interlaced video is more complex, because each frame consists of two *fields* taken in two different exposures. The first field consists of all of the odd-numbered scanlines, and the second consists of all the even-numbered scanlines, filling in the gaps from the first field. Figure 6.17 shows this process, as an image is drawn from top to bottom on odd-numbered scanlines, and then the even-numbered scanlines are filled in between them.

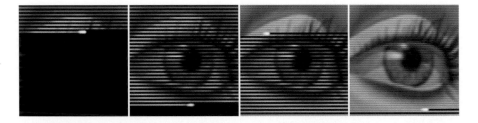

[Figure 6.17]
Two fields are interlaced on a television screen to form a frame. These images show the process of refreshing alternate scanlines, first completing all of the odd-numbered lines, then starting at the top again to fill in the even-numbered scanlines in between.

The rate at which fields are recorded or transmitted is twice the frame rate. For example, if the frame rate is 30 fps, then there are 60 fields per second. To display each frame, the television or monitor first displays each scanline from the first field, from top to bottom, which displays only every other line. Then it goes back to the top and fills in the alternate scanlines from the second field.

Old standard-definition television used interlaced video. The rationale for adopting the format was that motion would be sampled twice as frequently, resulting in a smoother, more accurate reproduction of motion. Instead of having the shutter open only 25 or 30 times per second, it opened and captured a field 50 or 60 times per second. This meant that moving subjects were scanned twice as frequently. Also, the flickering of screens would be less this way, because the electron beams would refresh the screen at twice the frame rate.

In modern times, even many productions that are transmitted as 1080i television signals are shot or rendered with progressive frames. The need to deal with interlaced fields tends to occur when you are trying to match interlaced video shot for live television sports and news programming.

Rendering Fields

Most 3D rendering programs have an option you can choose to render motion in separate video fields. When you activate this, the renderer outputs twice as many image files, rendered at each frame as well as at each half frame, so that the two field images show different points in time but can be interlaced together to form a complete frame. This simulates how a video camera records interlaced video.

By using field-rate video, you can cut the shutter speed in half, and this will halve the amount of motion blur as well. Some 3D artists even turn off motion blur when rendering field-rate video output. The renderings of an animated object in Figure 6.18 illustrate your different rendering choices for fields and motion blur; you can see that the motion blur matters less when rendering on fields.

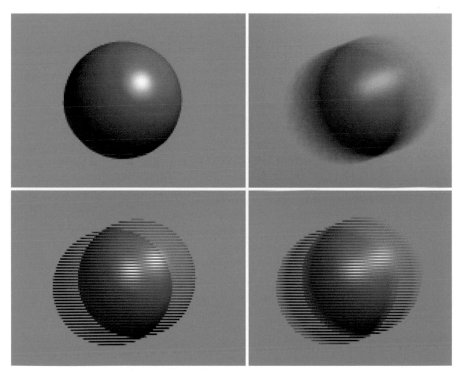

[Figure 6.18]
An animated object with no motion blur or field-rate rendering (upper left) appears static. Motion blur is added to two renderings on the right, and field-rate motion is added to the lower two renderings.

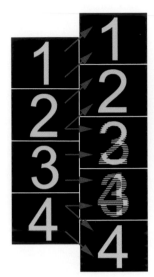

[Figure 6.19]
In 3:2 pulldown, film frames shot at 24 fps (left) alternately contribute two or three fields to produce 30 fps video frames (right).

3:2 Pulldown

When motion pictures, shot at 24 fps, are converted to 30 fps video, they go through a process called *3:2 pulldown*. Every four frames of the original film are converted into five video frames by alternately recording two video fields from one film frame, then three video fields from the next film frame, as shown in Figure 6.19.

3:2 pulldown produces some *jitter frames*—frames made of fields from two different film frames. Because jitter frames contain redundant information (fields also used in adjacent video frames), you will usually want to remove them during visual effects work so that you can perform rendering and compositing on a 24-fps basis. As a final step, you can expand output back to 30 fps by simulating a 3:2 pulldown process in compositing software.

Film Speed and Film Grain

Besides aperture and shutter speed, the third main factor influencing a camera's exposure is the *film speed*. Some film stocks are more sensitive to light than others. A designated film speed measures how quickly a particular film stock responds to light.

Film speed is usually measured in ISO or ASA units. The International Organization for Standardization (ISO) adopted the American Standards Association (ASA) standards for film speeds, so both refer to the same standard units. Low numbers such as 64 ISO or 100 ISO mean the film is less sensitive to light but is likely to be *fine-grain*, with sharp detail and not much visible grain. A high-speed film, such as 800 ISO or 1600 ISO, is more sensitive to light but usually has larger, more visible grain.

Just as you can choose a lower- or higher-speed film for a film camera, you can set a digital camera's ISO setting for similar results. At a lower ISO, the camera is less sensitive to light but the image remains sharp, with very little noise (noise in a digital image means random variation in pixel colors that look similar to grain in film). At a higher ISO, the signal from the imaging chip is amplified, but what amplifies the signal also amplifies the noise. A high-ISO image can lose quality and appear speckled with colored dots.

In visual effects work, compositors add simulated film grain when matching CGI to film stocks used in background plates. If you are simulating film or camcorder footage in an all-3D scene, consider adding more of a grain effect in low-light and indoor scenes than in sunny or outdoor scenes. Most importantly, pay attention to the issue of film speed when you are trying to understand the trade-offs involved in controlling a camera's exposure process.

Photographic Exposure

So far in this chapter, I have discussed three main exposure controls on a real camera: aperture (f-stop), shutter speed, and film speed (ISO).

Photographers refer to each doubling of the amount of light captured as a *stop*. Of course opening to a wider aperture by one f-stop is a stop, but so is using twice as slow a shutter speed or using twice as fast a film speed. Adjusting any parameter to allow the camera to capture twice as much light is called a one-stop increase in the exposure.

Understanding Reciprocity

There is *reciprocity* between the three main exposure controls, which means that you can make trade-offs between them. For example, if a photographer is taking a portrait and wants a soft-focused background behind her main subject, she will choose a wide aperture to achieve a shallow DOF. To compensate for the extra light she lets in by using the wide aperture, she can choose a faster shutter speed. Opening the aperture by two stops, but then using a faster shutter speed by two stops to compensate, brings her back to the same overall exposure value but achieves a shallower DOF.

Exposure modes on most cameras called *shutter priority* and *aperture priority* are made to take advantage of reciprocity. In shutter priority exposure mode, you dial in your desired shutter speed, and the camera automatically adjusts the aperture and ISO to compensate. In this way, you can change the shutter speed without seeing the image get brighter or darker. In aperture priority mode, you dial in your desired aperture, and the camera automatically adjusts the shutter speed and ISO to compensate. This gives you the freedom to change the aperture to whatever f-stop you want without seeing the image get brighter or darker.

Of course, in addition to automatic modes, cameras also have a manual exposure mode where you can set the aperture, shutter speed, and ISO all by yourself. In manual mode, any time you open the aperture by one stop, or choose a stop slower shutter speed, you see the overall exposure value get brighter. In manual mode, you can still take advantage of reciprocity, but you have to do it yourself; click the aperture open by a few stops, then choose a different ISO or shutter speed to compensate if you want to maintain the previous exposure value.

The Zone System

When casual photographers take snapshots, they usually leave the camera in an automatic mode. Automatic exposure adjusts exposure controls in the camera based on the average amount of light in the scene, essentially trying to bring the scene as close as possible to a medium gray. This provides an exposure that is "correct" in the sense that what is visible will be recorded on the film.

A professional photographer, on the other hand, starts designing a photograph based on his own impressions to craft an image that uses the tones he chooses in each area of the frame. Instead of letting the camera bring a snow scene to an average gray level, he might prefer to make the snow white.

To achieve this level of control, photographers practice an approach called the *Zone System*, which describes tones that can be printed in 11 levels. Zone 0 is pure black with no detail, Zone 1 is the first perceptible value lighter than black, Zone 5 is medium gray, and so on up to Zone 10, which is pure white.

[Figure 6.20]
An exposure meter tells photographers how to expose an area to produce a medium gray tone, or Zone 5, but adjusting the exposure to achieve other values is up to the creative control of the photographer.

Photographers use a light meter, as shown in Figure 6.20, to check the brightness of a particular area, such as a patch of snow. The meter displays a recommended exposure that brings the snow to Zone 5. If the photographer wanted the snow to be printed in Zone 8, she could open the aperture by three stops compared to what her meter suggests.

To a practicing photographer, there's a lot more to the Zone System than this. Photographers use special filters that darken the sky by a certain number of stops, develop and print the film in different ways to achieve different levels of contrast, and, as a last resort, adjust the brightness of different areas of the shot while printing in a darkroom. Throughout this process, every possible step is taken to adapt and control whatever light is available into the tones that the photographer wants to achieve in the final print.

How do we translate this into 3D graphics? How can we focus on controlling which tones appear in our images as carefully as a professional photographer? A good place to start is to look at a histogram.

Using Histograms

A *histogram* is a chart showing how frequently each possible tone appears in an image. Most paint and compositing software has a histogram function.

Figure 6.21 shows a typical histogram. For each of the 256 possible levels of brightness in the image, a vertical column is plotted. The height of each column is determined by the number of pixels in the image that use the tone. The columns on the left show the number of pixels using black and dark values, and the height of the columns on the right shows how many pixels use brighter tones, up to pure white on the extreme right.

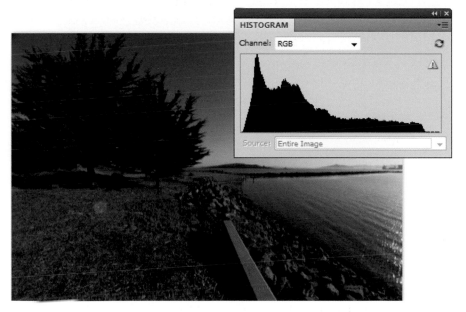

[Figure 6.21]
A histogram shows how you are using the tones in your rendered image.

You can view a histogram of one of your renderings, a live-action frame, a texture map, or a photograph. A histogram is useful for spotting some common problems in renderings or photography. For example, Figure 6.22 shows the histogram of an underexposed scene. All of the taller columns are on the left side of the image, showing that all of the dominant tones in the image are very dark. Most of the available tones that could be used to separate the sky from the ground, or give shape and definition to the trees, aren't being used. As a result, most of the image looks uniformly dull and dark.

[Figure 6.22]
Underexposure appears as a concentration on the left side of the histogram.

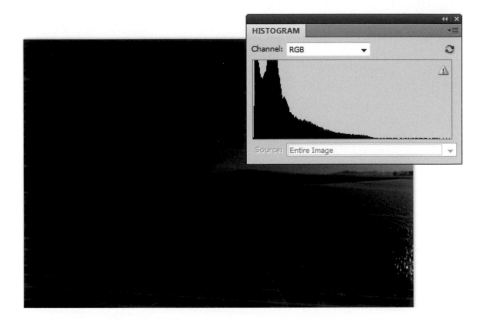

Photoshop's Levels tool includes a histogram as a part of a powerful tool for changing the brightness and contrast of an image. As shown in Figure 6.23, immediately beneath the histogram are three triangles you can slide into new positions along the histogram. The black triangle represents the level that will become black in the output image, and the white triangle represents the level that will become pure white. Between them, the gray triangle represents what will become medium gray. This triangle automatically stays at a midpoint between the black and white triangles as you drag them around; if you drag the gray triangle, then you will also be changing the gamma of your image.

[Figure 6.23]
You can adjust Photoshop's Levels tool to isolate one zone of brightness found in a 3D scene.

The cool thing about the Levels tool is that you can use it interactively to explore the different zones of your image. For example, Figure 6.23 shows the triangles framing the brightest tones in a scene. This causes every tone that is darker than where the black triangle points to disappear from your image, which lets you see only where the brightest tones are used. You can also frame just the darkest part of the image by moving the white triangle to the left. If you are planning to composite 3D elements into a live-action plate, it is especially important to check that the black levels and white levels match the background plate.

In general, try to take advantage of the full range of tones available to you so that a histogram from most of your renders shows columns in each zone. Students learning to light scenes often produce underexposed images in an effort to hide flaws in their scenes and make the lighting look more "subtle." Even if you are trying to depict a night scene or a dark closet, be selective with your lighting. To convey darkness, use high contrast and dark shadows rather than simply underexposing the whole scene.

Exposure Value

The *Exposure Value (EV)* calculates the overall brightness of your exposure. The EV is not a separate factor in the exposure, but a result of all three factors (f-stop, shutter speed, ISO) put together.

If you are in fully manual exposure mode using a real camera, you choose the f-stop, shutter speed, and ISO for yourself. A display on the camera indicates the EV that results from your decisions. You cannot adjust the EV directly when you are in a fully manual exposure mode; the EV is just a display that shows you how the bright the shot will appear, compared to the camera's own metering.

If you are in an automatic exposure mode where the camera is automatically setting at least one of the three factors for you, then the EV becomes an adjustable preference you can set. In this case, when you set the EV to a neutral value of 0, the camera tries to adjust the f-stop, shutter speed, or ISO to make the image as close as possible to a middle-gray value according to its exposure meter. If you set an EV of 2, you are saying that you prefer the image to be exposed two stops brighter when the camera makes its automatic adjustments.

When you adjust the EV to be one stop brighter on a camera in a fully automatic mode, you may not know whether the camera will open up the aperture by one stop, use a shutter speed one stop slower, or use an ISO that is one stop brighter. The camera could make any of these adjustments for you to achieve your preference of getting an image that is one stop brighter.

The EV is displayed on most cameras as a relative (not absolute) scale. An EV of 0 means a neutral value—that is, the image is as close as possible to medium tones—according to the light meter. Higher numbers indicate overexposure and lower numbers indicate underexposure, according to the light meter.

The term EV has another meaning: an absolute exposure value, which specifies combinations of shutter speed and f-stop. On this scale, 0 EV refers to a 1-second exposure taken at f/1 or any equivalent combination of shutter speed and f-stop (such as a 30-second exposure at f/5.6). The absolute EV scale does not specify the ISO film speed and does not take into account scene brightness. The absolute scale of EV values was written back in the days of film photography, and you are much less likely to see it implemented than the relative scale that's common in most digital cameras.

Bracketing

Bracketing is the process of photographing a set of multiple exposures at different exposure values. Many cameras have an automatic bracketing function so that at the push of the shutter release, a number of exposures (often three or five) will be taken, each offset by a given number of EV. For example, the camera could take one shot at –2 EV, one at 0 EV, and one at +2 EV. This would give you a choice of exposures when you went to select and process your shots.

Going beyond basic automatic bracketing, 3D artists often shoot sets of images taken over a much wider range of exposure values in order to assemble High Dynamic Range Images (HDRI). HDRI will be discussed more in Chapter 8, but to capture all of the colors and tones of light in a scene, from the darkest to the lightest, you need to employ manual bracketing and take advantage of some of what you've learned in this chapter about camera exposure.

To manually bracket shots for HDRI, put the camera on a tripod and set it to full manual mode with a low ISO such as 100. Focus the camera and set it to manual focus to leave it at your desired focal distance. Set your white balance to a fixed setting, such as daylight if you are outdoors.

Set the aperture to a medium f-number such as f/5.6 and leave it there. As you know, changing the f-stop also changes the DOF and puts different things into focus, creating images that can't be aligned perfectly.

Bracket your shots by changing the shutter speed. Start with a slow enough shutter speed so that almost the whole scene looks overexposed to make sure you are capturing all possible detail, even in the darkest shadow areas. Then move in increments of about 2 stops, changing to faster and faster shutter speeds for each shot in the sequence. For example, you might move from an 8-second exposure to a 2-second exposure and then to a ½-second exposure. Keep shooting darker and darker versions of your shot until you can see the full color in even the brightest light sources, as shown in Figure 6.24.

[Figure 6.24]
Bracketing the shutter speed (not the aperture) when you shoot a set of shots that can be assembled into an HDRI. Note that in the top image, you can see the color in even the brightest tones of the image, and nothing is overexposed.

If the sun is visible in the scene, you may run into a situation in which even the quickest shutter speed your camera offers is not brief enough and the sun is still overexposed. In this case, a set of ND (neutral density) filters comes in handy. An ND filter is like putting sunglasses on your camera; it darkens everything by a specified number of stops. Stack on the ND filters as needed until even the sun shows a deep orange color and nothing is so overexposed that it looks desaturated.

Matching Lens Imperfections

In real life, lenses aren't perfect. Even the best lens can't reproduce the world around it as clearly as the virtual camera that renders our 3D scenes. Here's a look as some of the flaws of real lenses and how to match or simulate them in 3D.

Lens Distortion

In most 3D rendered images, every line that is modeled as a straight line appears perfectly straight in the final rendering. This is not true in photography. In a real photograph, lens distortion often causes straight lines to appear bent.

The amount of curvature you get depends on what kind of lens you use. On many zoom lenses (lenses that have an adjustable field of view), zooming out to a wider angle causes moderate *barrel distortion,* in which the center of the image is bowed outward and the edges and corners are compressed. More extreme curvature is seen in shots taken with a *fisheye lens,* which covers a very wide field of view but often greatly curves and distorts the image, as shown in Figure 6.25.

On many zoom lenses, barrel distortion appears when the lens is zoomed out, but the opposite problem, *pincushion distortion,* appears when the lens is zoomed in. Pincushion distortion warps an image inward, making the center smaller, and is usually a result of an attempt to correct for barrel distortion in zoom lenses.

[Figure 6.25]
A fisheye lens causes curvature in an image, as seen where the vertical tower appears bent.

In visual effects, if you want to combine 3D renderings with a live-action plate, matching the lens distortion of the original shot becomes a pressing issue. Motion tracking software that matches real camera moves often includes image-processing functions to correct for lens distortion. The workflow is to undistort the background plate after it is digitized, composite in your 3D elements, then redistort the image if you need to.

Even for entirely 3D content, by adding some barrel or fisheye distortion to shots that use a very wide field of view you can make the shots more believable. Figure 6.26 shows the difference that a little distortion can make.

[Figure 6.26]
A 3D scene rendered with a wide field of view (left) can sometimes be made more natural by simulating barrel distortion (right).

Although 3D software can simulate real camera lenses and lens distortion, you can also render without distortion and then warp the rendered frames in a composition program. Most compositing software includes warping functions that can simulate barrel distortion.

Adding barrel distortion has an added benefit in some shots: When the camera pans or tilts, the distortion almost resembles a perspective shift. If you are trying to sell a 2D matte painting as if it is a more fully modeled 3D environment, then you don't want a pan or tilt to simply appear as if the background is scrolling by. By adding a pan or tilt along with some barrel distortion, you can create a much more natural integration of 2D backdrops, and help them look like larger spaces filmed with a wide-angle lens.

Chromatic Aberration

A lens artifact closely related to barrel distortion is called *chromatic aberration (CA)*. CA appears in an image as colored fringes around bright lines or high-contrast edges, as shown in Figure 6.27.

CA occurs as light is focused through a lens, because different wavelengths of light are refracted at different angles. For example, red light refracts through the lens at a different angle than blue light, focusing at a different point on the film or sensor. This is the same principle that allows people to split light into a rainbow using a prism. However, in a camera, having different colors of light fall out of alignment on the film or sensor creates colored fringes of CA. Because CA is more prevalent in cheaper lenses, you might simulate it if you're processing your renderings to resemble camcorder footage. You're not likely to see as much CA in background plates shot for feature films.

[Figure 6.27]
Chromatic aberration appears as colored fringes around high-contrast edges in a photograph.

You can simulate CA using the same kind of outward warping as you use to simulate barrel distortion, but you need to do it one color channel at a time, with slightly more distortion on the red channel and slightly less distortion on the blue channel.

In addition to CA applied to the image itself, you can also see CA on bokeh and blooms. If you are using a custom bokeh map, offset a warmer colored copy of the image to one side and a cooler colored copy of the image to the other side of the map to create the impression of CA in your bokeh effects.

Vignetting

Vignetting is another flaw that is common in many lenses, and most visible and pronounced in cheaper zoom lenses. Vignetting simply makes the edges and corners of the frame darker than the center of the image.

Some directors intentionally produce this effect for creative reasons, such as when they are showing the point of view of a killer who is following someone, or in a flashback to make a memory appear more faded. Sometimes directors actually smear Vaseline around the edges of a filter in front of the camera, which causes the edges of the frame to become both dark and blurry.

Most compositing programs can correct minor vignetting in a background plate or match it by darkening the edges of 3D elements. Vignetting is also offered as an option in some 3D camera models.

In some shots, you can also achieve a sort of natural vignetting through how you light or compose your image. If you light a shot so that the main subject toward the center of the frame is brighter, and the edges and corners fall off into darkness, then the audience's attention is focused toward the center of frame. Sometimes shots can be framed with a dark wall or corner in the foreground, creating a naturally dark frame for the subject. In these kinds of cases, you can have the compositional benefits of vignetting without introducing anything that looks like a bad lens artifact.

Lens Flares and Halation

For years, *lens flares* have been considered an overused cliché in computer graphics. Use lens flares only where they are very clearly motivated, such as when the sun or another very bright light is directly visible in the scene, or in scenes where characters being out in the bright sun is a story point. Figure 6.28 shows a photograph in which the sun's reflection on a building caused a lens flare.

If you use a lens flare, render it as a separate pass. To do this, simply hide everything else in the scene except the light that is making the lens flare, and render it as a separate file sequence. This way, you can add or screen it over your rendering in a compositing program, and you won't risk rerendering a full scene just to adjust a lens flare.

In many cases, you can avoid lens flares and instead simulate *halation* (also known as *specular bloom*), which is the glow and occasional streaks of light visible around bright light sources. Halation is caused by light reflecting off the back of the film plane of the camera or scattering through the film itself. As with lens flares, it is a good idea to render light glows separately and add them in the composite.

In widescreen movies that are filmed in an anamorphic film format (where a special lens squashes the image horizontally so that it fits on the film), the halation scatters light on the film while the image is squashed. When projected, the halation is stretched out horizontally, so that glows around lights appear to be elongated bars or streaks instead of circular glows.

[Figure 6.28]
Even though most 3D artists consider lens flares tacky and overused, they can be used sparingly in places where they are motivated by a bright enough light.

Use special effects described in this section only in situations where you really need them. If you find yourself tempted to run your footage through lots of filters to change the look, most likely it is because you aren't happy with the original lighting and shading, and you should go back and fix those problems instead of trying to hide them behind lots of filters. Before you fixate on imitating every possible flaw that could exist in a photograph, try to learn from the best that photography has to offer, and craft well-exposed images where every tone counts.

Exercises

To grow as a 3D artist, take every chance you get to study more about photography and cinematography.

1. The EXIF data embedded in many digital photographs is a terrific learning resource. Whether you are looking at digital pictures you took yourself or at JPEG files that were shared over the Web, this embedded information lets you see what exposure settings were used, as well as what camera was used, the focal length of the lens, and a great deal more about how, when, and where the picture was taken. On Windows, right-click an image, choose Properties, and look under the Details tab. You can see the f-stop, shutter speed (exposure time), ISO, and more data, and you can even edit the data if you need to correct any of it. On a Mac, right-click an image and choose Get Info to see basic EXIF data, but you can see more embedded information using File Viewer from the Mac App Store. On portable devices, numerous apps are now available that let you view embedded EXIF data.

    By reading the EXIF data, you can learn from your own mistakes and from others by reviewing the EXIF data from pictures you like, as well as from pictures that didn't come out very well. If a picture looks too noisy, check what ISO setting was used and see if it could have been shot with a slower shutter speed or a wider aperture instead. If a picture has a lot of visible motion blur or camera shake, check to see what shutter speed (exposure time) was used. If you like a soft-focused background, check what f-stop was used that caused the results you like.

2. Spend some time with a camera that has full manual controls. Try taking some shots indoors and outdoors using full manual mode just to practice adjusting each parameter for yourself. Professional photographers use all different exposure modes, and shooting in manual mode is not necessarily the best choice for every shooting situation, but it is great for practice and as a learning experience. Also try aperture priority and taking a picture of someone or something with the widest f-stop, a middle value, and the narrowest f-stop; see for yourself how it changes the DOF and clarity of the image. In shutter priority mode, try shooting a moving subject such as a fountain with very fast and very

slow shutter speeds, and look at the differences. Set yourself up with a tripod and try shooting a full set of images to create an HDRI.

3. Watch a movie using a computer or media player software that has a frame grabbing function. Many 3D artists build up a collection of reference images from their favorite movies. Stop and examine a scene filmed at night. Where are the brightest and darkest tones? How deep is the DOF? When the background falls out of focus, can you see any bokeh effects? Bring some images into a program with a histogram function. Did the movie use all of the tones that were available? What would the scene look like if you adjusted the levels to change the exposure?

CHAPTER SEVEN

Composition
and Staging

Some of the most important decisions the director and cinematographer make in filming a scene concern composition and staging. *Composition* refers to the layout of the entire shot; *staging* is the arrangement of objects and characters within the frame. Good composition and staging are kcy ingredients in any compelling professional image. In effect, they act as subtle cues from the director, helping guide a viewer's eye. Composition and staging are governed by a set of artistic rules and cinematic conventions that you can apply in 3D graphics when adjusting your camera, lights, layout, and animation.

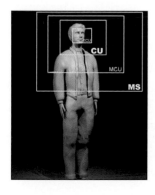   

Types of Shot

Your first decision in planning a shot is what will be shown in the frame. If two characters are interacting, will you show both of them in the frame or just a close-up on one of them? How much of the environment around them will be visible? Do you want to draw the audience's attention to any particular area? You can plan your digital productions using the vocabulary that filmmakers use to describe each shot.

Shot Sizes

One of the major distinctions between types of shots is the *shot size*, which identifies how large an area is visible within the frame. From the smallest area to the largest, here are the five most common shot sizes:

- An *extreme close-up (ECU)* makes a very small detail—such as only part of a character's face—fill the screen.

- A *close-up (CU)* is a shot framed tightly on a specific area, like a character's face.

- A *medium close-up (MCU)* widens the scope further. A character's head and shoulders constitute a medium close-up.

- A *medium shot (MS)* shows a broader area than a close-up. Often a medium shot shows a character's upper body, arms, and head.

- A *wide shot (WS or WIDE)* shows a broad view of an entire location, subject, or action. Often a wide shot shows an entire character from head to toe, or a whole group of characters.

The yellow boxes in Figure 7.1 show the areas of a character typically covered by these shot sizes. These are only general guidelines—actual shot sizes are relative to the size of the subject or environment you are portraying. For example, in an animation of a football game, a wide shot might show the whole stadium, but in a film starring animated insects, a wide shot might cover only a few inches of space.

Wider shots can show whole environments, capture broader actions, or show the positions of multiple characters at once. Medium shots and close-ups help draw the audience into the scene and reveal details or facial expressions.

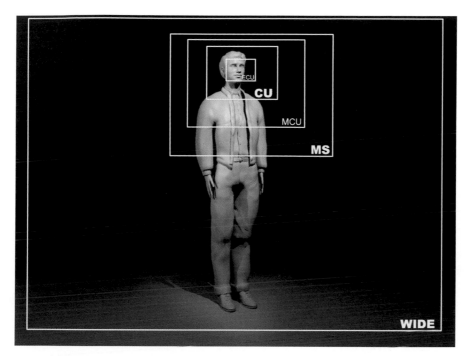

[Figure 7.1]
An ECU (extreme close-up), CU (close-up), MCU (medium close-up), MS (medium shot), and WS or WIDE (wide shot) are common shot sizes used for rendering characters.

You can give your audience an idea of the overall scene with an *establishing shot*, which is usually a wide shot that sets up the scene and shows surroundings that might not be appear in each close-up. For example, an establishing shot might show the exterior of a building, providing context for the interior scene that follows.

A *reaction shot* shows a character's response as she watches or reacts to some other event. Usually a close-up of the character is used to show her reaction. Reaction shots in action sequences keep the audience engaged in the human side of a story. Even if you are animating an enormous scope of events, the audience will care more about what is happening if you show the reaction of individual characters being affected by the action.

Z-Axis Blocking

A shot can function as both a close-up and a wide shot at the same time by using a technique called *z-axis blocking*: populating a scene with subjects at varying distances from the camera. Figure 7.2 shows an example of z-axis blocking, with one character in close-up, walking toward the camera, while other characters remain in the background. Z-axis blocking may sound like a computer graphics term, but in reality cinematographers were using the phrase long before the advent of 3D rendering.

POV Shots

A *point-of-view (POV)* shot creates the illusion of viewing the scene from a character's perspective.

POV shots are easy to set up in 3D: You just position the camera right between a character's eyes. If a character is moving, group or constrain the camera to follow any character motion, such as by parenting the camera to the head bone, or animate the camera to simulate the character's gaze. Often you will want to hide the character whose POV is being shown; you usually don't need to show body parts, such as arms and hands moving as the character walks, in a POV shot.

Here are some ideas for how you can use POV shots in your animations:

- Seeing a scene from a character's point of view can help an audience better identify with the character or sympathize with his position in a scene. For example, if something is going to jump out and surprise a character, it might be animated to appear suddenly and leap toward the camera (in other words, from the character's POV), surprising the audience.

- A POV shot can capture an action or event dramatically. For example, if a character is falling down a hole, you can animate the camera so it moves through space just where her head would be.

- You can use a POV shot for comic effect in some animations by animating the camera with an attribute of a character. For example, an animated camera might imitate the motion of a staggering drunk or a bounding dog.

- A POV shot can show a character's view when he looks through a gun sight, telescope, or keyhole. Often POV shots such as these are processed after you render to imitate the shape of the telescope or keyhole, or to simulate the distortion or focus of a viewing device.

- A POV shot can be a convenient shortcut also, because while the audience is watching the view through the character's eyes, they don't see the character himself, so you don't have to animate or render him in that shot.

- It's a standard horror- and suspense-film convention to show the POV of a killer or monster as it stalks its next victim. The use of the POV shot prevents the audience from seeing the actual killer; they see only the killer's-eye-view of the unwitting victim.

Have fun using POV shots, but remember that they can be very noticeable, and sometimes even distracting, if overused.

Two-Shots

Specific types of shot can be put together to help you stage a conversation, interview, or other scenes in which two characters are facing each other.

A two-shot is simply a shot with two characters, as shown on the left side of Figure 7.3. Although this is a convenient, straightforward way to show both characters, it can look flat and uninteresting. To make a scene more visually diverse, use a two-shot as an establishing shot, and then cut in to close-ups and *over-the-shoulder* shots.

Over-the-Shoulder Shots

An *over-the-shoulder (OSS)* shot is a close-up or medium shot on one of the characters, which also shows just enough of the other character—a portion of his back and shoulder, generally—to indicate his position. The center and right images in Figure 7.3 illustrate this. Even though you can't see the face of the character whose back appears in the foreground, his presence serves to frame the shot and establish the spatial relationship between characters.

[Figure 7.3]
The shot/countershot structure can start with a two-shot (left) and then alternate between OSS coverage (center, right) of the characters.

A series of shots that alternate between an OSS of each character, sometimes also including tighter close-ups of the characters, is called shot/countershot coverage. This is a common and effective way to capture almost any kind of interaction between two characters, whether they're exchanging words, bullets, kisses, or punches. Once you start looking for it, you will see shot/countershot coverage used over and over in movies and television programs.

Rendering OSS shots of each character and adopting *shot/countershot* instead of a fixed two-shot for the full scene can create a more engaging, cinematic look for your animation. For a dialogue scene, this approach has an added bonus: You may be able to skip some of the facial animation on one of the characters during a shot by framing it so the audience is watching the other character react to what the first says.

Camera Angles

Where you place the camera can change the appearance and function of your shot. Your *camera angles* come from the positions you choose for the camera and which way you aim it.

The Line of Action

If you are rendering a scene from several different camera angles and plan to edit the different shots together into a seamless sequence, then it is vital that you make all of your camera angles come from camera positions on the same side of a *line of action*. A line of action is the path along which your subjects are looking or traveling, or an imaginary line between two characters who are interacting. For example, in Figure 7.4, the line of action is shown by the yellow line between the two characters.

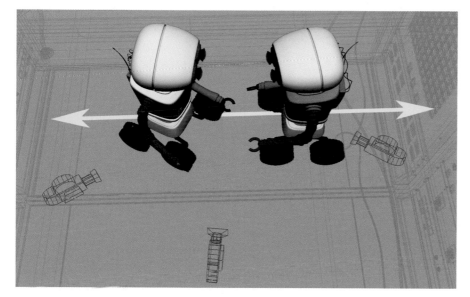

[Figure 7.4]
To maintain screen direction, all camera shots are taken from the same side of an invisible line of action.

Do not cut to any angle on the characters filmed from the other side, because that reverses the direction that the characters appear to be facing and can confuse the audience. This rule is also called the *180-degree rule*, and cutting between shots from opposite sides of the line of action is also called *breaking the 180*. For example, if a character is facing toward the right side of the screen, in the next shot do not choose a camera angle that suddenly makes her appear to face to the left, because if you do she will appear to have turned around.

Imagine a character who is traveling or in a chase. If he is running toward the right side of the screen in one shot, then he should continue to run toward the right side in every shot. Do not cut to any camera angles that reverse his screen direction, because that could create the misimpression that he has turned around. If you really need to get the camera to the other side of the line of action, use a camera move and have the camera travel across the line during a shot. Football fans are familiar with this concept from the way football games are televised: All of the cameras are normally put on the same side of the stadium. On occasion, a camera is used on the opposite side to capture action that is not visible otherwise. To avoid confusion, whenever they cut to a camera on the opposite side of the line of action, the words "Reverse Angle" are superimposed on the screen.

Perspective

Perspective is the point of view or position you choose for your camera. Whenever the camera is in a different position, it shows the scene from a different perspective.

Figure 7.5 shows three different perspectives of a person standing in front of a bridge. To maintain close-ups of a similar size in each perspective, different lenses were used when the camera was at different distances from the subject: A telephoto lens was used when the camera was farther away (left), a normal 60mm lens was used at 3 meters from the subject (middle), and a wide-angle lens was used when the camera was close to the subject (right). Although you will notice barrel distortion in the shot taken with the wide-angle lens, remember that the lenses themselves do not change the perspective—lenses only magnify part of the scene as seen from the perspective of the current camera position.

Notice how the bridge appears to loom right behind the woman in the left image, but on the right, from a closer perspective, the bridge seems much farther away and we see more of it. Figure 7.6 shows a similar comparison in 3D. The left image was rendered with the camera positioned close to the chess pieces, but with a wide angle of view. On the right, the camera has been positioned much farther away from the chess pieces but has been given a narrower angle of view.

[Figure 7.5]
A shot from a distant perspective (left) compresses space; a shot from 4 meters away appears more normal (center); and a shot from a close-up perspective tends to expand space and distort features (right).

[Figure 7.6]
Spaces seem expanded, as if there is a great deal of space between each pawn, from a close-up perspective (left), whereas space looks compressed from a distant perspective (right), as if the pawns were stacked close together.

Moving the camera far away from the subject seems to compress or flatten space. This effect is useful if you want to make a character appear lost in a crowd, to make a space seem cramped, or to make objects appear closely stacked together. If you zoom in on a subject from a distant perspective, you see a much smaller slice of the background behind the subject, which can be useful if you want to accentuate something in the background.

Moving the camera close to the subject distorts distance. It can even make a character's facial features appear to stick out farther; for instance, it can exaggerate the size of a person's nose. Most photographers back off by about

3 or 4 meters when they are trying to take a flattering portrait, instead of sticking the camera right in the subject's face. However, you don't want to back off too far, because even though you can compensate for extreme distance with a telephoto lens, doing so tends to flatten a person's face so that horizontal features such as ears appear to stick out.

When you position the camera close to your characters and zoom out to cover the action from the close perspective, you get a broader view of the background behind the characters. You might want to see more of the environment around a character, but sometimes if you do so, you will need to build a more complete set or add more trees to your scene to fill up the visible area.

When you render with the camera near a character, you can also make action appear to move more quickly or cover a greater distance. This is especially true for motion directed toward or away from the camera. Getting the camera right into the middle of the action makes animation appear more dynamic and puts the audience closer to the perspective of the characters.

If you animate a camera's position and field of view at the same time, in opposite directions, you can produce a disturbing effect. For example, if the shots shown in Figure 7.6 were frames in an animation and you simultaneously moved the camera toward the subject and zoomed out to compensate, the perspective would shift oddly during the shot. This effect has been used in horror movies to make a hallway appear to grow longer in front of a character as he struggles to run down it.

If you want to choose a natural-looking perspective, think about where a person might be standing within the 3D space to watch your scene, and position the camera at the same distance. For example, if a scene takes place indoors, do not position the camera much farther back than the size of an actual room naturally allows. In filming live-action movies, walls are often removed from sets in order to film scenes from a more distant perspective than would be possible otherwise. Even when this is done, however, the camera itself is usually only a few feet beyond the missing wall.

It is important to note that your perspective on a scene changes only when the camera moves to a new position. Perspective does not change as the result of the camera's zoom or field of view. When the camera is left in the same position, the perspective is the same, no matter how telephoto or wide-angle your lens is. Choosing a longer focal length for your camera in 3D graphics gives you the same perspective as you get if you had rendered with a short focal length and then cropped the image down to the close-up you wanted.

High-Angle and Low-Angle Shots

The most normal-looking shots are the ones you take with the camera at eye level. When you move the camera to different heights, you can create other camera angles that are sometimes more interesting or dramatically useful.

A *low-angle shot*, one where the camera is positioned below your character and is looking up at her, can make a character look bigger, stronger, nobler, or more honest. Low-angle shots can also exaggerate the size of environments and architectural spaces.

A *high-angle shot*, one where the camera is aimed downward from a position above the character, can make a character look sly, small, young, weak, confused, cute, or childlike. Figure 7.7 shows how a character looks from a high angle (left) and a low angle (right).

[Figure 7.7]
A character is perceived differently from a high angle (left) than a low angle (right). Images by Andrew Hickinbottom, www.andrewhickinbottom.co.uk.

Creating Camera Moves

If you want to animate more realistic and natural camera moves, study the most popular types of moves used with a real camera:

Pan: The camera rotates from side to side so that it aims more to the left or right. The camera does not change location in a pan; it only faces a different direction. Panning is one of the most common and subtle of all camera moves.

Tilt: The camera rotates to aim upward or downward without changing the position where it is mounted. Both a tilt and a pan can be executed while the camera is mounted on a tripod.

Zoom: The camera's lens is adjusted to increase or decrease the camera's field of view so a portion of the scene can be magnified without moving the camera. A *zoom in* narrows the field of view to create more of a close-up, while a *zoom out* widens the field of view.

Dolly: The camera's actual position changes; for instance, it moves alongside a subject or travels closer to a character during a scene. A *dolly in* moves the camera physically closer to the subject to create more of a close-up. A *dolly out* backs the camera away from the subject. Dollying is considered more dramatic but also more noticeable than zooming, because a dolly actually changes the camera's perspective.

Rack focus: A camera's focal distance changes during a shot so that subjects at a different distance from the camera come into or fall out of focus, as shown in Figure 7.8. This is also called a *focus pull*.

[Figure 7.8]
A rack focus directs the audience's attention by changing the focus during the shot.

Many of these common types of camera move do not involve actually changing the camera's basic position. When the camera pans, tilts, zooms, or rack focuses, it can remain mounted in the same place, on a tripod—you only aim the camera in a different direction or adjust the lens.

Even when it is on a stationary tripod, however, when a real camera is tilted or panned, the center of rotation is usually not exactly at the optical center of the camera's lens. Instead, the pivoting head of a tripod rotates below where the camera is attached; the camera is on top of this center of rotation, and the lens is toward the front. This offset creates a small perspective shift when the camera is panned or tilted.

Even if your default 3D camera uses the same terminology for camera moves as a traditional camera on a tripod, your moves might not be completely identical to the real thing. The default way a camera is created in 3D graphics makes the camera rotate around the exact center of the lens when you pan or tilt. If you group your camera to a parent node positioned underneath the camera and a bit to the back, and then you rotate that node for panning and tilting, you'll see a slight perspective shift while the camera pans or tilts, instead of a flat "scrolling" effect.

Motivations for Camera Moves

Constant camera motion can be distracting. Only use a camera move when it is motivated by an action or event in the story. Here are some times when a camera move might be motivated:

- When a character or vehicle is moving, you can pan or dolly the camera to follow the character's motion.

- You need a moving camera for POV shots from moving characters and vehicles.

- Use a moving camera to dolly into an environment as a way to explore the space, especially when you are trying to acquire sweeping establishing shots with a new environment.

- For dramatic effect, sometimes you might want a camera to move slowly toward a character to emphasize certain actions or dialogue. When the camera dollies in from a medium shot to a close-up, the audience's attention is focused on the subject being approached.

You don't need to animate the position of the camera if alternatives, such as panning to follow your animation or simply cutting to a new shot, will do just as well. An unmotivated camera move can distract the audience instead of helping you tell the story.

Natural-Looking Camera Moves

An old attitude toward animating the camera in 3D was that you needed to carefully imitate the types of real dollies and cranes on which a movie camera was traditionally moved. 3D artists used to be afraid that if they used any physically impossible camera moves, their animation would seem unrealistic. However, in recent years, filmmakers have begun to use 3D graphics, motion-control camera rigs, digital compositing, and other technologies to create seemingly impossible camera moves in live-action films.

In modern productions, live-action footage is stabilized both with physical devices, such as a Steadicam stabilizing mount, and also digitally to remove any unwanted frame-to-frame vibrations from the footage after it is shot. If the director wants a smooth camera move, then the camera move can look smooth and seamless, even in live-action footage shot in real locations.

The widespread use of 3D graphics to previsualize motion pictures has further encouraged live-action directors to plan their movies using all kinds of camera motion that would have been seen only in 3D animation or video games in the past. Audiences are growing accustomed to seeing the camera fly through scenes in ways that would have seemed remarkable in previous decades.

Of course, you still need to make sure that any camera motion helps tell your story instead of distracting from it. Learn to imitate and use old, conventional camera moves when they meet your needs. But if it fits your story for the camera to fly through a keyhole or follow action out the window of a moving car, go ahead and animate the camera whichever way best fits your scene.

In editing, cutting between two moving camera shots can sometimes be distracting. Even if the camera motion within each of the shots looks natural, editing between a camera moving in one direction and a camera moving in a different direction can be jarring in the cut. When animating a camera move, begin with a well-composed static shot before you ease into the move. When the move is complete, make sure the camera comes to rest at another well-composed static shot. One exception to this rule is if you have an entire sequence of shots set in and around a moving car, and the camera is following along with the car's motion in each shot. In this case, it might appear perfectly natural to cut between different shots that all travel along with the car.

For natural-looking camera moves, think of yourself in the role of a camera operator watching a scene. Often, something needs to begin to happen, such as an actor starting to move, before the camera operator can react to it and move the camera to follow the action. Camera motion looks most natural if it begins just after the motion it is intended to follow, as if the operator needed a fraction of a second to react to the motion. Also, when a camera pan comes to an end, it can slightly overshoot its mark and then slightly correct backward a fraction of a second later, as a human operator sometimes does when aiming a handheld camera.

Improving Your Composition

After you have decided on the size and angle of your shot, some principles can help you balance and improve your composition. Where you place key elements within the frame can make the difference between an average or even boring rendering and a rendering with a composition that makes your work look more professional. When you carefully compose a shot, you also serve the art of storytelling by helping direct the viewer's eye to different parts of the image.

The Rule of Thirds

Placing a subject dead-center in a frame does not look very natural or interesting and generally produces a bad composition. Your rendering looks better composed if you place your subject off-center.

A useful guideline when composing a shot is to picture the frame divided into thirds, both horizontally and vertically, as shown in Figure 7.9. This is known as the *rule of thirds*. Your shot is better composed if you position the subject along one of the lines (shown in black) or position a subject that you want noticed exactly at a point where two lines intersect (shown in red).

[Figure 7.9]
To follow the rule of thirds, align subjects to break the composition into thirds instead of halves, and put centers of interest at the points marked in red.

If you have a horizon line in the scene, put the horizon one-third or two-thirds of the way up the frame; this looks much better than if you place the horizon in the center, which can appear to split the rendering in half.

Using Positive and Negative Space

Most images can be said to consist of both positive space and negative space. *Positive space* is the part of the frame that shows the main subject or foreground objects. *Negative space* is the background or the area around the subject. Composition is a balance between the positive and negative space. The left side of Figure 7.10 shows the negative space in black and the positive space in white.

Examining your image for positive and negative space can often help you improve your composition. For example, if all of your positive space is clustered in one area or aligned in a single row, or if large areas of your frame are empty, you might consider reframing the shot. Doing so will allow you to achieve more balance between positive and negative space.

[Figure 7.10]
The negative space (shown in black) and the positive space (white) are equally important shapes in your composition.

Sometimes you need negative space in a shot to create a greater sense of balance or closure. For example, in a close-up or medium shot, if you have a character's face or eyes looking to one side, this creates a powerful vector that directs the audience's attention to that side of the frame. To balance your composition, you usually want to leave negative space in front of your character, in the direction that she is looking. Camera operators sometimes call this extra space *look space* or *nose room*. The top image in Figure 7.11 is a balanced, complete rendering with negative space, which gives the audience room to follow the direction of the character's gaze.

Without look space, or with the negative spaces distributed elsewhere, viewers cannot follow the direction a character is looking, and the composition seems cropped, unbalanced, or incomplete. In fact, a viewer can even interpret the character's pose differently based on where the negative space is. In the unbalanced lower image in Figure 7.11, the woman appears to be deliberately turning away, isolating herself from her surroundings. With no change to her pose, the shift in composition gives the character a more sullen, introspective appearance in the lower frame.

[Figure 7.11]
A balanced composition (top) leaves "look space" for a character (shown in yellow). An unbalanced composition (bottom) can trap your eye in the side of the frame.

Graphic Weight

Everything that appears in your rendering has a *graphic weight*. The graphic weight of an area or object is the amount, relative to other objects in the frame, that it attracts attention or dominates the composition. Bold or bright items that contrast against the surrounding scene have the greatest graphic weight. Sharp edges and shadows have more graphic weight than soft, gradual transitions. People naturally look at other people, so a person in the shot or parts of the person, such as the eyes, are natural centers of interest, which take on greater graphic weight. Larger items have more graphic weight than smaller details. Areas near the edge of the frame also can have greater graphic weight.

To judge which objects in your scene have the most graphic weight, just glance at the whole rendering and notice where you find yourself focusing. Arrange objects with a high graphic weight carefully in your frame to achieve a balanced composition.

As with positive and negative space, analyze your composition to determine which parts of it have the most graphic weight. Which parts of the image first catch your eye? How well distributed are they within the frame? If a viewer is "reading" the image from left to right, is there anything interesting on the left side to draw his eye back, or does it come to rest on the right side of the frame? Scan your image from left to right, noticing what catches your eye; this thought process can lead you to find better ways of laying out your scene.

Your lighting can increase or decrease the graphic weight of parts of your scene. Areas of your rendering that are dimly lit, washed out, or lack contrast have less graphic weight, whereas areas with more shading, contrast, or color stand out. If part of your scene needs more graphic weight, add colored light or extra highlights and contrast.

In a film or television production, motion catches the eye and lends greater graphic weight. Even more important than motion itself is where the audience's eyes had been focused in the previous shot. When there is a cut from one shot to another, people's eyes are still looking at the area that grabbed their attention in the last shot. Especially in rapidly edited sequences, it is a good idea to pick up each new shot with the subject of interest positioned close to where the viewer is already looking. In everyday life, people tend to focus most of their attention on a small area in the center of their visual field, keeping only a vague impression of what is outside that area in their peripheral vision. When you allow viewers of a movie the same comfort and keep their attention focused through multiple shots, you enable them to remain immersed in your film instead of being jolted by each shot as if they were being presented with a completely different scene.

Lines

Another way to examine and improve your composition is to picture the dominant lines within the shot. Look at any line, whether it is the horizon, a fence, or the edge of a shadow, and think about where it leads. People's eyes naturally follow lines within the image, so by placing an interesting subject along a line, or by having lines within your composition point to a subject that you want a viewer to notice, you help direct people where you want them to look.

Diagonal lines are dynamic. They add excitement and interest to a composition. Lines that are just horizontal and vertical look boring in comparison. Figure 7.12 shows how much more dramatic a scene looks when it is tilted at an angle, in comparison to a standard two-shot.

[Figure 7.12]
Changing the dominant lines in your image to diagonal (instead of just horizontal and vertical) makes for a more dynamic composition.

Curved lines are soothing. An S curve can even be graceful and elegant. Employ curves when you want to make a scene look organic and natural, and save the straight edges for designs that need to look high-tech or as if they are obviously created with computer graphics.

Jagged lines and sharp corners look threatening. They can add excitement to an image, but they also can make a place or a character look less hospitable. Don't create any angles so sharp that they look as if they could cut you—unless, of course, you are trying to make a threatening image.

Tangencies

A *tangency* is a place where two lines meet within your composition, such as where an edge of one object aligns with an edge of another object, or where a shadow falls along an edge in a surface. In 3D graphics, objects often come into perfect alignment by accident, and this can reduce the impact of your composition.

When two lines become tangent, they essentially become the same line in your composition; this can cause your scene to lose definition. The left side of Figure 7.13 is plagued with undesirable tangencies. The top of the cube lines up with the horizon behind it, and the cube's shadow lines up with a square on the chessboard. Even the upper-left edge of the cube is aligned with a line on the chessboard. On the right, both the camera and light are adjusted to fix these problems. Notice how the cube appears to pop out from the picture and looks more 3D in the right image.

[Figure 7.13]
On the left, tangencies hurt the composition. On the right, changing the camera and light angles fixes the tangencies and makes the cube look more three dimensional.

Framing for Film and Video

As you work in different media, you need to frame your work for different film and television formats.

Formats and Aspect Ratios

The actual frames in which you arrange your scene can have different proportions, depending on the format of film or television for which you are rendering your graphics. The proportion of the width to the height of an image is called its *aspect ratio*. For example, if the width of an image is exactly twice its height, it has an aspect ratio of 2:1. Aspect ratios are sometimes written as a single number, the result of dividing the width by the height. For example, 4:3 can be expressed as a 1.33 aspect ratio.

Here are the most popular aspect ratios used in film and television production, in order from the narrowest aspect to the widest:

1.33: Old standard definition television sets have a 1.33 (spoken out loud as "one three three") aspect ratio. This was also an aspect ratio for older motion pictures, including many silent films.

1.66: This aspect ratio ("one six six") is less popular in the United States but still is used for movies in some parts of the world.

1.78: HDTV and earlier widescreen television systems have a 1.78 aspect ratio, but they are commonly referred to as 16:9 ("sixteen by nine"). This allows viewers at home to see an aspect ratio closer to some of the most popular widescreen presentations in movie theaters.

1.85: The most popular aspect ratio for motion pictures is 1.85 ("one eight five").

2.35: The second most popular aspect ratio for feature films is 2.35 ("two three five"). This aspect ratio is sometimes called *Cinemascope* or *Panavision*, which are trademarks for specific formats that use a 2.35 aspect ratio.

When you know the aspect ratio and the horizontal resolution of a shot, you can determine the vertical resolution by division. For example, if you are rendering a film frame that is 2,048 pixels across and the aspect ratio is 1.85, the height in pixels would be 2,048/1.85, or 1,107.

Film Formats

Photographic film is becoming obsolete. Every year, it is replaced to a greater extent by digital photography and digital cinema. However, this has already been a slow, gradual transition, and some artists continue to shoot film as a matter of personal preference. Movies are still distributed on film as well as in digital formats, because movie theaters haven't all invested in digital projectors yet. Many effects studios offer filmmakers a *digital intermediate process*, in which filmed images are digitized, manipulated, and then recorded onto film again for distribution. As a result, productions that are shot and distributed on film can benefit from the full range of digital color correction, effects, and compositing. Visual effects professionals are likely to deal with some footage shot on film, as well as footage shot digitally, for years to come.

Thirty-five millimeter motion picture film used to be standardized at the 1.33 aspect ratio, and television sets were initially designed with a 1.33 aspect ratio for the sake of compatibility with film. However, in the 1950s, Hollywood studios felt threatened by the growing popularity of television and devised widescreen movie formats as a gimmick to differentiate their films from smaller television screens. Different studios, which owned the theater chains as well, developed different methods for fitting a wider image onto regular 35mm film.

Common 2.35 film is shot and projected with an *anamorphic lens*, which is designed to squeeze the image horizontally so it fits onto the 35mm film, as shown in Figure 7.14. This format is popular for films shot outdoors with sweeping panoramas, and is often used in bigger-budget films. When anamorphic film is projected, the projector is fitted with an anamorphic lens that widens the image into its full 2.35 aspect ratio.

[Figure 7.14]
An anamorphic widescreen image is scaled down horizontally by a special camera lens to fit on regular 35mm film and requires an anamorphic projector lens to expand it to its original width in the theater.

Although 2.35 has its advantages, modern movie theaters are commonly being divided into many smaller screens to show different films at once. A movie screen cannot be made any wider than the size of the theater, so when showing widescreen movies, the width of the screen remains the same as for other aspect ratios, but the image is less tall. A similar thing happens when 2.35 films are adapted for HDTV; either the sides of the image are cropped off beyond the 1.78 frame or the top and bottom of the screen are left black.

When films are shot with a 1.85 aspect ratio, they usually are not shot anamorphically. Instead, the widescreen image is fit into the center of the film frame, as shown on the left side of Figure 7.15. In the theater, only the center part of the film is projected onto the screen. This means that a lot of the film stock is wasted. The center of the film frame—including grain and dirt—is enlarged to fill the screen.

[Figure 7.15]
A 1.85 widescreen format uses only the center part of the film frame, and sometimes the top and bottom are cropped off (left). When 1.85-format footage is shot full gate (right), it captures extra image areas at the top and bottom that are not projected in theaters.

Films that will be projected in a 1.85 aspect ratio are often exposed *full gate*, as shown on the right side of Figure 7.15. When film is shot full gate, this means that extra image area is recorded above and below what will be seen in theaters, filling the full negative with an image, even though only the center part will be projected in theaters.

When visual effects need to be added, the entire film frame is often digitized full gate. This gives visual effects artists extra image area to work with. Instead of always using the center of the digitized background plate in your final composite, with a full gate image you can shift the entire shot to reframe higher or lower. You can even animate the position of the background image to simulate camera shake or small camera moves, which is all very handy for making it appear as if the camera has reacted to a visual effects element or a CG creature that you are adding to the shot.

Shooting full gate also provides extra image area that can be revealed when a widescreen film gets adapted for television.

In footage that is shot digitally, one advantage to shooting at 4K (capturing frames with a resolution of about 4,000 pixels horizontally) is that the extra image resolution allows you to crop the image slightly. You can reframe shots, create simulated camera shakes, and otherwise enjoy the flexibility that you would have had with footage that was shot on film and digitized full gate.

Adapting to Non-Widescreen Video

When films or other widescreen programming was adapted for standard television or home video, the 1.66, 1.85, or 2.35 aspect ratios needed to be converted for display on 1.33 screens. This process is becoming less common, because most new home video releases are widescreen (16:9) format instead of 1.33.

The technique of *letterboxing* is one approach to adapting widescreen images to standard 1.33 video. A letterboxed image consists of the original widescreen composition, shown in its entirety, with a black area above and below the image that fills the rest of the taller-screen format. The left side of Figure 7.16 shows a full 1.85 image as it would appear when letterboxed in a 1.33 television frame. Letterboxing is a faithful way to preserve the composition of a widescreen film, but many home viewers don't like to lose inches off their television picture.

[Figure 7.16]
A 1.85 frame can be converted to 1.33 by letterboxing (left) or pan and scan (right).

Another technique, called *pan and scan*, was commonly used and is still used occasionally to adapt widescreen footage for television. This process involves going through a movie and selectively cropping off portions of the left and right of each shot. Usually only the center of the image appears on television. If something significant is happening on the left or right side of the frame, then instead of showing the center, the image can pan sideways to show what had been the left or right side of the widescreen frame. Either way, the picture that fills the TV screen is really just a portion of the full scene that was shown in theaters. The right side of Figure 7.16 shows the cropped 1.33 composition that would result. This practice is seen by some as an unnecessary modification of a filmmaker's original work, especially when it is done to classic films whose directors cannot be a part of the film-to-video conversion.

The pan and scan process also can involve animating the area that gets cropped from each frame. For example, a shot on video might virtually pan across the original film frame, starting with the left side of what was filmed and ending with the right side of what was filmed. This is supposed to appear similar to the results of the original film camera having panned, but it appears more as if you are scrolling across the image. When watching movies on video (which are not letterboxed), sometimes you notice small horizontal pans that were added in the process of converting widescreen films to video.

If a film was shot full gate, then you can crop the taller 1.33 aspect image from an area that goes beyond the widescreen image. In this case, the television viewer is simply seeing more of what was above or below the main action than was shown in theaters.

Cropping and Overscan

You can't expect every pixel of your image to make it onto the screen. When digital images are sent to a film recorder, between 15 and 30 rows of pixels can be cropped from each edge of the image in the film recording process. Also, when movies are projected, the theater adjusts the projector so that the image more than completely fills the screen, cropping off even more from the edges of the frame.

In television, a similar cropping problem occurs when a process called *overscanning* crops a portion of a video signal off of the screen. A television picture tube overscans an image by projecting a slightly larger picture than the size of the actual screen. Overscanning was designed into early televisions to hide fluctuations of picture size that could result from variations in the electrical current powering the television receiver. The amount of overscan and the centering of the image vary greatly between televisions.

Even though most new HDTVs are capable of showing a full widescreen image without overscan, most sets have a button that cycles through multiple modes for enlarging and cropping into the scene. You have no guarantee that someone viewing your work won't see a version that's scaled or cropped in some way to fill the frame with no letterboxing visible.

Make sure you keep important actions in the center 90% of the screen, because some viewers might miss them if they happen too near the edge. Be even more careful if you are putting text or titles on video, because viewers would certainly notice any letters or lines of text that were cut off and not completely visible on the screen. As a rule of thumb, text should be kept in the center 80% of the image to keep it safe from overscan. Most 3D software has optional guides to safe-image areas that can be displayed in your viewport to help avoid cropping important elements.

Exercises

You can frame and reframe your shots in an infinite number of ways. Study the composition and framing in your favorite movies, and see if you can explore or rethink the composition in your own work.

1. The power of using different lenses, from wide-angle to telephoto, is one that's often overlooked by 3D artists. Instead of always using the same field of view and just moving the camera, try to take advantage of wide-angle lenses, with the camera placed very close to the action, to accentual motion toward and away from the camera. Also try using telephoto lenses, with the camera far away from your subject, to compress space from a distant perspective.

2. The scene with the robots used in some figures in this chapter is a Lighting Challenge scene, modeled by Juan Carlos Silva, that is available for you to download from www.3dRender.com. Feel free to use this scene when creating your own personal work.

3. As recommended in other chapters, it's a great idea to build up your own library of still images captured from your favorite movies. Take a look at some of your favorite stills with an eye for composition and staging. Where is the camera positioned? What is the center of interest with the greatest graphic weight? What kinds of line are used in the composition, and how do they affect the image?

CHAPTER EIGHT

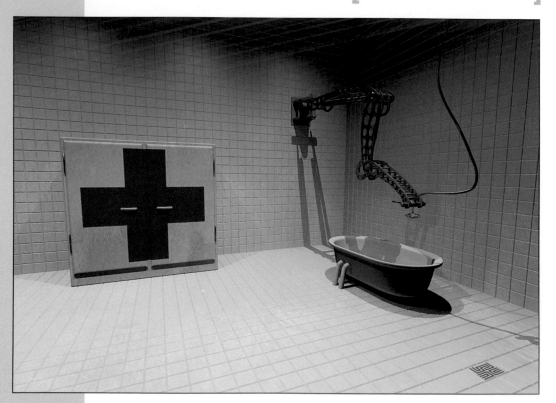

The Art and Science of Color

When you want to play with your audience's emotions, few tools are more powerful than an intelligent use of color. This chapter will explore the visual power of color in your 3D art. The right color scheme can create or enhance a mood, or even change the meaning of an image. But the use of color also has a technical side; this chapter will delve into digital color reproduction and ways to choose realistic colors for different types of light source. We will start with one of the most important lessons a 3D artist needs to master in order to light, render, and composite images convincingly: You need to understand and correctly use a *linear workflow*. This lesson necessitates a technical beginning for a chapter that will combine both art and science. You need to get started with a linear workflow before addressing other issues, such as designing color schemes, because adopting a linear workflow can change how you pick and assign colors.

Working in a Linear Workflow

A *linear workflow* is an approach to the entire process of preparing texture maps, choosing surface colors, lighting, rendering, and compositing that allows all software calculations to maintain a direct, uniform relationship between digital color values and actual light intensities.

If you don't fully understand that definition yet, don't worry. In order to understand what a linear workflow is, we have to start with what it is not. You need to understand what factors cause other workflows to break down and become less believable and consistent. Especially in the 1990s and 2000s, a lot of people were working without a linear workflow; they got into bad habits while they attempted to compensate for the lack of a linear workflow in how they lit and composited scenes. After we talk about what went wrong, we'll talk about how to do it right, and how modern graphics software allows you to take advantage of a linear workflow. You'll then be able to enjoy all of its benefits, without needing any of the old-school work-arounds in your lighting and compositing.

Understanding Gamma

Where do all of the problems come from that cause people to create graphics without a linear workflow? It starts with your eyes. The human eye does not detect brightness uniformly. In a dimly lit room, even the smallest amount of light, such as the flicker of a candle, is noticeable. In a bright outdoor environment, it takes far more light being added to the scene for you to notice a change in the illumination. Televisions and computer monitors are accordingly designed to deliver a nonlinear response to their input signals. Figure 8.1 shows a graph of the relationship between an input voltage and the amount of light displayed on a monitor. The red line is the actual relationship, called a power log function. The straight black line in the center shows what a linear response to the input signal looks like.

[Figure 8.1]
Graphing output brightness (vertical axis) compared to input intensity or voltage (horizontal axis), the red line represents the response of most monitors, the black line represents a linear response, and the dashed blue line represents a gamma of 2.2 as used in the sRGB standard.

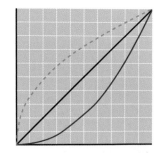

The image displayed by the monitor is black when the input voltage is 0, and it's white when the input voltage is 100%. However, in between black and white, it does not proceed linearly. At a 50% input value, instead of showing a 50% brightness, the monitor displays a brightness of less than 25%. This kind of relationship between input signals and output brightness is still used in modern flat-panel monitors with digital inputs. Even though the standards are similar to what was used in early televisions and cathode-ray tube (CRT) monitors, they are actually an efficient use of the digital signal, not just a relic of ancient standards.

The images displayed on televisions and monitors look correct because they are *gamma corrected* before they are sent to the display. For example, when you capture a JPEG image with a digital camera, the camera performs the necessary gamma correction for you, storing an image that has the gamma already baked into the data. When the JPEG image is displayed on a monitor, it comes out looking correct. The correction is a standard gamma of 2.2, which compensates for the power log relationship applied by the monitor. The gamma relationship is shown in Figure 8.1 as a dashed blue line, and as you can see, it mirrors the response curve of the monitor itself.

The makers of different computers, monitors, computer software, and cameras have agreed upon an industry standard called sRGB so that images can be captured, shared, and displayed correctly if they have the gamma correction of 2.2 built in to them.

So far, no problem, right? Images are created by cameras, stored, and displayed, so they appear correctly.

The Problem with Incorrect Gammas

A problem arises because 3D rendering software and 2D paint and compositing programs work internally as if they are dealing with linear data. But in reality, the images that you give the programs as input (such as texture maps and background images) are not linear; they have built-in gamma correction. Rendering and compositing programs work with this data as if it is linear, however, and then they produce output that is not gamma corrected. Your output is not gamma corrected overall, but it is displayed on your monitor at a gamma of 2.2, as if it was. Adding to the confusion, although your lighting is displayed at the wrong gamma, the texture maps within the scene may be displayed at the correct gamma. This can fool you into thinking that the only problem is that your lights aren't bright enough and cause you to readjust your lights to compensate for the incorrect output.

You can see the problem in how light falls off. A quadratic decay (also called inverse square) is the most physically correct setting for a light, but if you view the rendering at the wrong gamma, it won't look correct. Figure 8.2 shows a situation that should be simple: A single fluorescent ceiling panel is lighting part of an office. An area light coming from the ceiling panel ought to light the scene well. When an area light with quadratic decay is placed right below the panel, it produces enough light so that a part of the upper wall is overexposed already. We don't want to turn up the light any brighter if parts of the scene are already overexposed, and yet the light clearly isn't illuminating the full area that a big panel of light such as this should cover.

As shown in Figure 8.3, turning on global illumination helps, but not as much as it should. Even with global illumination, the area right under the light still looks unrealistically dark.

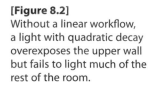

[Figure 8.2]
Without a linear workflow, a light with quadratic decay overexposes the upper wall but fails to light much of the rest of the room.

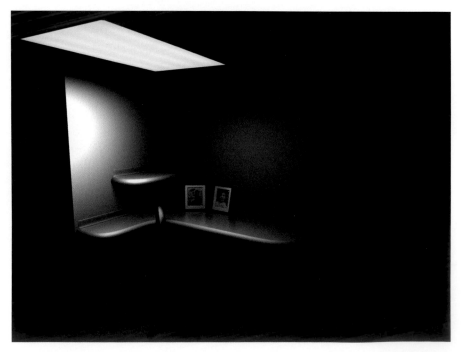

[Figure 8.3]
Without a linear workflow, global illumination fails to spread the light as far as it should.

Global illumination uses a physically correct inverse square distribution of light, so just like the area light with quadratic decay, global illumination is another thing that can fail to work correctly without a linear workflow.

Working without a linear workflow, some people learn to live with this kind of initial output and work though the situation with a series of cheats. For example, they add other fill lights to the scene from other angles, use a less realistic decay setting or no decay at all on the ceiling light, or adjust the global illumination to appear brighter. Certainly they can brighten the scene, but when they do, it no longer looks as if it is lit entirely by the ceiling panel.

Another time when your output can look wrong without a linear workflow is when you add two lights together to illuminate the same area. A surface lit by both lights can sometimes look more than twice as bright as the surfaces lit by just one of them. Also, if you have two lights emitting beams of fog and the beams cross, then the area where the two beams overlap can look more than twice as bright as the beams look individually.

The real problem in all of these cases is that the renderer is internally computing linear color values, but the output is being displayed as if it is an sRGB image that already has gamma correction applied. Applying a gamma correction of 2.2 to the image may actually help brighten it so it looks more like a realistic decay of light. Unfortunately, the texture maps, such as the framed pictures and the floor tile pattern, already look correct without any more gamma correction because they are created with the gamma of 2.2 built in. So, gamma correcting the whole scene after it is rendered can make the textures look pale and desaturated because the texture maps are essentially gamma corrected twice.

Fixing the Linear Workflow in Three Steps

Luckily you can fix all the problems just described by using a linear workflow. The *linear workflow* is not just a correction you apply to the image at one point in the creative process, but instead is an entire approach of how to deal with images. Here are three key steps that I'll cover in the following sections:

1. Convert source images such as texture maps that have built-in gamma correction and the colors assigned to materials and shaders into linear values.

2. Your software already renders the scene using entirely linear values; you just need it to produce files that remain linear and are not gamma corrected upon output.

3. Make sure that any compositing you do to the layers and passes you render are done in linear space. Finally, at the end of the compositing process, adapt the result to suit your output device, which usually means you need to convert it to gamma 2.2 to fit your monitor.

Throughout this process, you need to be able to work on your monitor. You need to see the colors that you are selecting in your 3D software and see accurate test renders of your scene. This means you need windows in your 3D program that are able to read linear data but show it to you on your monitor as sRGB.

The good news about the linear workflow is that many artists and software companies have been taking it seriously in recent years. Some 3D programs, such as Cinema 4D, now work in a linear workflow by default for new scenes. Other programs, such as Maya, support a linear workflow after you adjust a few settings that are documented in the manual. Search the Web for the name of almost any graphics program followed by the words "linear workflow," and you'll find 3D artists talking about what settings to use and how to take advantage of this process.

What happens when the sample scene we were discussing earlier with the fluorescent panel is rendered with a linear workflow? Figure 8.4 shows the results. Just one light, with quadratic decay, and with global illumination turned on to bounce the light back up to the ceiling, lights the office nicely, just as you'd expect.

[Figure 8.4]
With the linear workflow, a single light with quadratic decay and global illumination works to convincingly light an office.

Now let's focus on the three steps of the linear workflow and how to make sure they work correctly.

Starting with Linear Textures and Colors

The first step in a linear workflow is to make sure that the texture maps and other sources of color that are provided to your renderer are all converted into linear color values.

When you activate a linear workflow in a 3D program, this usually includes the option or default behavior of setting the input gamma for your texture maps. When a texture map has a standard sRGB gamma of 2.2 (which makes it look correct on a regular computer monitor without any extra color correction applied), just set the input option to sRGB, and the software will remove the gamma correction for you when the texture map in imported. Figure 8.5 shows this setting in Cinema 4D's Project Settings window.

Be cautious when you are importing textures that are designed to be used as bump maps, displacement maps, normal maps, or are otherwise not a natural color image. These should generally be linear data already, so you do not need to convert them from sRGB. Your software may be smart about this, but make sure you do not see any shift in your bump maps when you adjust the input color profile. If maps change that you don't want to change, then you may need to set those textures to be considered linear instead of sRGB so that they don't receive unnecessary gamma correction.

[Figure 8.5]
Activating a linear workflow lets you specify the input color profile of your texture maps.

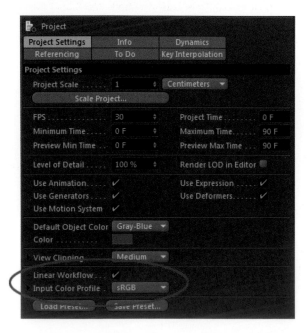

You also want to make sure your input colors are adjusted for a linear work-flow when you are choosing and mixing surface colors. Some programs, such as 3ds Max, have an option you can choose that has gamma correction affect color selectors; this way you can pick a color that looks correct on your monitor, without having the monitor gamma built in to the values sent to the renderer. If your software doesn't have an option to do color correction on your color picker, then another solution to this problem is to pick colors in sRGB that look good on your monitor, then apply a gamma correction to the colors before they are used in the shader, as shown in Figure 8.6.

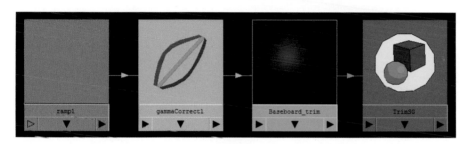

[Figure 8.6]
A gamma correct node with a value of 0.4545 can adjust surface colors from the sRGB color space into a linear value.

The gamma correction to turn an sRGB (gamma 2.2) color into linear is 1/2.2 or 0.4545. You should choose to add a gamma correction node after a color choice or an input texture map only if you don't have any other way to ask your software to remove gamma correction from the texture or color. If in future versions of your software other options are added and you are able to use another approach, then the extra gamma correction nodes in your old scenes would only be a source of confusion.

Rendering Linear

Internally, your renderer is already computing linear data. To continue with a linear workflow, you need to make sure that your output files preserve all of this information without gamma correction, and that what you see in your Render View or Render Window gives you an accurate preview, corrected for accurate display on your monitor.

Strictly speaking, if you know that you won't do any compositing after you render, you can set your 3D software to output gamma-corrected sRGB images and still have a linear workflow that ends in your 3D program.

However, if you plan to do any compositing or post-processing of your images, it's best to keep your data linear all the way through the compositing process, and set your 3D software to output linear data without gamma correction, as shown in Figure 8.7.

[Figure 8.7]
Shown in Maya's settings for a linear workflow, your output files should be linear, so no gamma correction is applied.

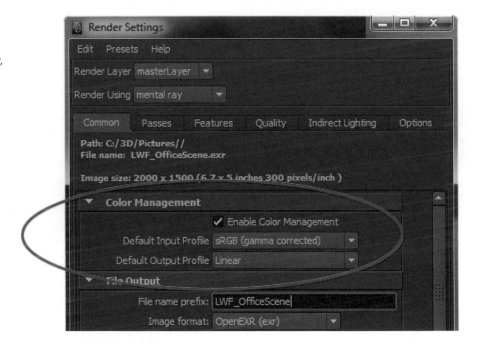

Don't worry that some versions of Maya label the output profile as "Linear sRGB" (instead of just "Linear"). It is still linear and not gamma corrected.

Apart from your render settings, you need to make sure that no other gamma corrections are applied, such as through a Mental Ray lens shader. The mia_exposure_simple lens shader is created automatically when a Mental Ray Physical Sun and Sky environment is created, and it sets an output gamma of 2.2. Delete this lens shader if you want to maintain a linear workflow into compositing.

Later in this chapter we'll focus on types of digital color representation, such as 8-bit, 16-bit, and 32-bit data. For now, choose the .exr file format with 32-bit floating point or 16-bit half-float as an ideal way to output your rendered elements. You can use these in almost all leading compositing programs.

Even after you are rendering linear data, you still need to make sure that your Render View shows you images with the correct gamma for your monitor. Figure 8.8 shows the Render View Color Management options in Maya to display images on standard sRGB monitors, while linear images are being rendered.

If you can set your Render View to display full 32-bit floating point data, this will also help you adjust the exposure of the image after it is rendered and preview what the lighting would look like with an increased or decreased exposure value.

[Figure 8.8]
Set your Render View or Render Window to correct from linear renderings to an sRGB display that looks correct on your monitor.

Compositing in a Linear Workflow

Chapter 11 talks more about compositing. However, to state the situation briefly, you will also be happy to work in a linear workflow while you are compositing.

Compositing without a linear workflow tends to create output that looks much too bright whenever you add two images together. Some people working without a linear workflow even avoid using a natural "Add" operation when they put together layers; instead they use a "Screen" operation to attempt to fix the problem. This means that different lights rendered as separate passes do not add together in the same way that they would have if they had been rendered together in a single pass.

When you are working with a linear workflow, not only can you use "Add" operations convincingly, but blooms and glows you add around light sources will look softer and more natural.

Because you are working with images that don't have the gamma of 2.2 built in to the data, you need to have your viewer window adjust to display images with gamma correction.

The final step of your compositing process is gamma correcting your image for your final output device, which usually means assigning a gamma of 2.2 for standard sRGB monitors. By saving this step for the end of your process, you have maintained a linear workflow from the start to the finish of your production.

Color Mixing

Colors in 3D graphics software are generally stored as RGB (red, green, blue) values, three numbers representing the levels of red, green, and blue that combine to make up the color. In this book, RGB values are shown on a scale of 0 to 1 unless otherwise noted. For example, {0,0,0} represents pure black and {1,1,1} represents pure white.

Additive Color: RGB

Red, green, and blue are called the *additive primary colors* because any color of light can be represented by combining red, green, and blue light in varying proportions. When red, green, and blue light are added together in equal proportions in a rendering, they form white light, as seen in Figure 8.9.

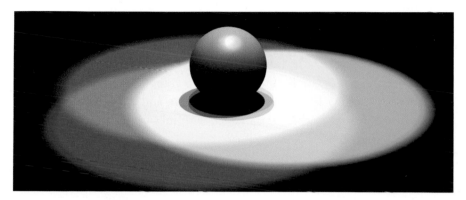

[Figure 8.9]
The additive primaries combine to form white illumination.

Between the additive primary colors are the *additive secondary colors*, created when any two of the additive primaries are both present in equal amounts. As shown in Figure 8.10, the additive secondary colors are yellow {1,1,0}, cyan {0,1,1}, and magenta {1,0,1}.

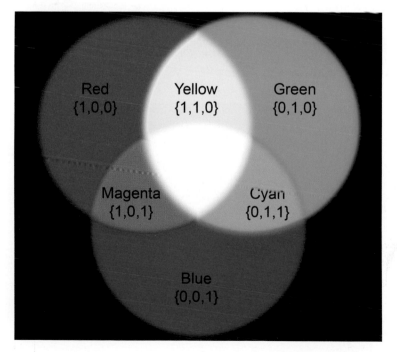

[Figure 8.10]
The additive secondary colors—yellow, magenta, and cyan—exist where any two additive primaries overlap.

The additive secondary colors can also be called the *complements* of the additive primaries. *Complementary colors* are pairs of colors that are opposite from each other on a color wheel. Cyan is the complement of red, magenta is the complement of green, and yellow is the complement of blue.

Subtractive Color: CMYK

Printed output creates colors differently than a computer monitor does. A monitor starts out black and then adds red, green, and blue light. A printer starts with white paper, which is darkened with inks in the *subtractive primary colors:* cyan, magenta, and yellow.

The three subtractive primary ink colors can produce any hue, but when combined, they produce brown, not black. To compensate for this, most full-color printing uses four ink colors: cyan, magenta, yellow, and black, abbreviated CMYK (yes, the K stands for blacK). The black ink can produce crisp text and also reinforces the shading of the color image. Take a look at Figure 8.11, where you can see a conventional four-color printed image up close; this image was created by adding cyan, magenta, yellow, and black dots to the paper.

Adjusting Hue, Saturation, and Value

Most graphics programs let you select colors by HSV (hue, saturation, value) instead of by directly setting RGB values. However, HSV color selection is

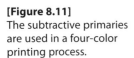
[Figure 8.11]
The subtractive primaries are used in a four-color printing process.

entirely an interface feature in most programs; the values that are actually stored and used for internal calculations are in RGB.

The advantage of HSV is that it provides a way to select colors that is more intuitive for most artists. When we think about colors, we tend to group and describe them based on their hue (is it more red or more orange?), their saturation (is it a pale pink, almost gray, or a bold, saturated red?), and their value (is it dark or bright?). Using hue, saturation, and value as the three ways to organize and describe colors makes sense to us visually. Figure 8.12 shows how colors appear when they are organized by HSV as opposed to RGB.

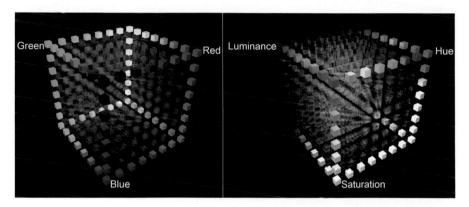

[Figure 8.12]
RGB color (left) mixes red, green, and blue, while HSV (right) varies the hue, luminance, and saturation.

Your 3D graphics software performs internal calculations in RGB. It is much quicker to simulate colored lights illuminating colored surfaces using only three possible wavelengths of light (red, green, and blue) instead of a continuous spectrum of many possible wavelengths.

When Light Color Meets Surface Color

Colors are mixed during a rendering in two very different ways. As shown at the beginning of this chapter, when different lights overlap, their colors are *added* together. When colored light illuminates a colored surface, however, the light color is *multiplied* with the surface color. For example, if you make a surface orange {1,.28,.08}, it reflects 100% of the red light that illuminates it, 28% of the green light, and 8% of the blue light. You can think of a surface color as a filter that controls how much red, green, and blue light an object reflects.

Note that when light colors are multiplied by surface colors, this usually makes them less bright. This is because colors are being multiplied by a fractional value less than one. Some software optionally expresses RGB values on a scale of 0 to 255 instead of 0 to 1, but the renderer's internal color multiplication is still always performed with color values expressed on a scale of 0 to 1. This standard of using a 0 to 255 scale is based on a limitation that no longer exists in most modern rendering software—there used to be only 256 possible shades of each color. Expressing RGB values in fractions with more digits of accuracy is more precise than the 0 to 255 scale, but many programs give you a choice. Whether you choose an interface where 255 represents a full brightness or 1 represents a full brightness is up to you and won't affect your rendering.

If you set any of the color values for a surface to 0, then the surface reflects 0% of the light of that color. Figure 8.13 shows some of the problems that this can cause. On the left, a white light illuminates spheres of many colors, and all the colors are visible. On the right, the light is pure green {0,1,0}, and where it illuminates a sphere with a pure red {1,0,0} color, the result is black. The result is predictable because the purely red surface reflects 0% of the green light, and the light does not emit any red. However, in real life, colors are rarely this pure, and you'd expect a bright enough light to illuminate surfaces of any color.

[Figure 8.13]
A white light uniformly illuminates six Lambert-shaded spheres (left), but some spheres appear black in the render when a green light illuminates them (right).

When you sample colors from an evenly lit photograph, you tend to find that objects usually reflect some amount of red, green, and blue. When you look at something painted bright red, you might not notice any of the green there, but as shown in Figure 8.14, there is a green component of the color.

Picking colors from a photograph can be a great starting point from which to root your color scheme in realistic colors. Most graphics programs include an eyedropper or sampler tool. Sampling material colors works best with images that are evenly lit with white light. A color you sample from a picture will not exactly match the original surface color, because what you sample is influenced by the lighting in the photograph (as well as by the white balance of the camera—something we discuss later in this chapter). Reflections also can tint the colors you sample.

Often a surface that you call "black" still reflects at least 15% or 20% of the light that hits it, so realistic RGB values for a piece of black rubber might be {0.17,0.16,0.19} instead of {0,0,0}. Likewise, a "white" piece of paper doesn't really reflect 100% of the light that hits it, so a color of {0.82,0.76,0.79} may be more realistic than {1,1,1}.

[Figure 8.14]
Colors sampled from a photograph show that even what looks like a pure red can actually have green and blue in it.

Beginners in 3D graphics often err on the side of choosing surface colors that are too saturated or too close to pure black or pure white, and thereby they create surfaces that don't respond realistically and consistently to light. Keep most of the red, green, and blue values on surfaces roughly between 0.2 and 0.8; then you leave room to use your lighting to determine most of the brightness values in the scene, instead of having some surfaces that always appear much bolder or respond to light differently from others. This is a very generalized rule of thumb; on some projects you might want to use more muted pastel colors, and in other projects bolder colors might be a creative necessity.

Even when you don't use extremely pure RGB colors, if your light color is a complement of your surface color, it makes your surface appear darker. Figure 8.15 shows roses lit by a red light (left) and a green light (right). In the red light, the petals look bright, but the stems and leaves appear dark. In green light, the stems and leaves appear brighter, but the petals appear dark.

Complementary color lights can also appear to desaturate a surface color. If you use blue light to illuminate a character with pink skin, the skin looks grayer and less saturated than it does in a white or pink light.

With all of the ways that colored lights and differently illuminated surfaces can add complexity to your scene, it's easy to have 3D scenes that are a mishmash of many different tints. As an artist, sometimes you need to control what colors appear in your scene and focus on using colors that come from a clearly defined color scheme.

[Figure 8.15]
Lit by red light (left) the petals look brighter, while in green light (right) the leaves look brighter.

Developing Color Schemes

The most striking images you can create have a clearly defined *color scheme* instead of colors from all over the palette. The color scheme—the total set of colors that appear in an image as a whole—creates a first impression and helps set the mood for the scene. When a new scene begins in a movie, the audience may perceive the color scheme first, before they even interpret all of the shapes and subjects depicted in the image.

You can develop a strong color scheme by choosing a small, consistent set of colors, and coloring every element in the scene with one of these specific colors. Often, you'll give different kinds of objects in your scene the same colors to maintain your color scheme. For example, in Figure 8.16, the entire composition consists of a few shades of blue and a few shades of yellow.

By reusing the same set of colors, you "tie together" the image. In this figure, the yellow of the moon is picked up and reused for the stars, and similarly colored dots appear on the building. Because the artist adhered to a limited color scheme, every part of this image is unmistakably unified.

When you add a new color to an object or a light, you are not just setting one color, you are also adding to the color scheme of your image. For example, in Figure 8.16, the entire scene would have looked different if any object were bright green or red. People interpret each color in relation to

[Figure 8.16]
The color scheme helps unify the composition. Scene by Jorge R. Gutierrez, www.super-macho.com.

the rest of the color scheme, so you need forethought to design the most effective color scheme for your rendering.

Color Contrast

A color scheme can use *color contrast* to make some colors seem to "pop" from a scene and grab the viewer's attention. Figure 8.17 is a good example of color contrast: It's hard to look at the image without your eye being drawn immediately to the orange ball. The contrast between the orange and the rest of the color scheme, not just the color's own hue or saturation, makes it pop.

Exclusivity

Concentrating a color in only one area increases color contrast. If orange had been squandered elsewhere in Figure 8.17, then the orange ball would not carry the same graphic weight or attract the viewer's eye as readily.

[Figure 8.17]
The exclusive use of orange in one part of the image immediately catches your eye.

Complementary Colors

Color contrast is most visible when colors are surrounded by their complements. As noted earlier, complementary colors are pairs of colors that are opposite each other on a color wheel, as shown on the left side of Figure 8.18. This provides a maximum amount of contrast and makes the purple color appear to be even stronger and more noticeable.

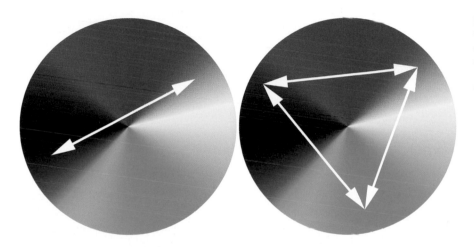

[Figure 8.18]
Complementary colors (left) are pairs from opposite sides of the color wheel, but some artists like to pick color schemes from three points around the wheel (right).

The reason complementary colors are called "complementary" instead of just "opposite" is that they work so well together. If you design two characters who will spend a lot of screen time together, or should look as if they belong together, consider giving them complementary colors.

Instead of just a pair of two colors, sometimes you can find three or more colors for your color scheme by picking colors evenly spaced around the color wheel, as shown on the right side of Figure 8.18.

Contrast over Time

In animation, if you plan for how colors are seen over time, it can give them greater impact. For example, a bright, fiery explosion of red and yellow looks even more intense if the environment is dark blue just before the explosion. The blue soothes the audience, their eyes adjust to the dimly lit scene, and then: Wham! When the explosion hits them, it looks twice as bright and colorful as it would have without the contrast.

Cutting between scenes presents another chance to take advantage of color contrast. Especially if you have several things going on at once, if you give each location a different color scheme, it helps orient the audience after a cut. For example, if some action takes place in a police headquarters under greenish light, while other action is happening in the criminal's base, if you add an orange tint to all the scenes in the criminal base, it makes it easy for the audience to recognize each location instantly.

Meanings of Colors

Why is the logo of a bank, insurance company, or hospital likely to be blue, while the logo of a fast-food restaurant is likely to be yellow or orange? The colors you choose in your color schemes can convey subtle impressions and trigger different associations in your audience.

Warm and Hot Colors

People generally describe red, orange, and yellow as *warm* colors, as opposed to blue and green, which are *cool* colors. The boldest, most saturated reds and oranges are considered *hot* colors.

Red may trigger alarm because it is the color of blood and fire. People hesitate to go through a red door or push a red button. Signs with strong warnings or prohibitions often use red, as do fire exits. Figure 8.19 shows the different feeling you get from hot colors compared to cool colors.

[Figure 8.19]
Hot colors cause excitement (left), while cooler colors suit soothing scenes (right).

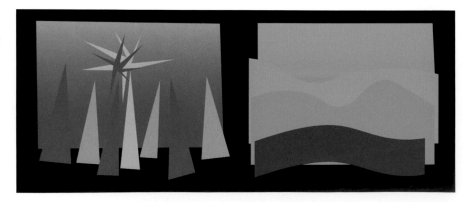

Hot colors are generally thought to be spicy, exciting, zippy, and attention-grabbing. A sports car looks faster if it's red. A fast-food restaurant might use orange or yellow in its logo and décor to capture this spirit, or to make customers feel like hurrying up and leaving their tables more quickly.

Yellow, the color of the sun, is often considered a bright, cheerful color as well. If you cut to a scene that is dominated by bright yellow, the audience expects a happy point to be reached in the story.

Although some associations are universally recognized, such as yellow being the color of sunshine, others are very culturally specific. In the United States, the color red is associated with communism so strongly that campaigns on the political left avoid using predominantly red color schemes in their commercials, posters, or bumper stickers. When they use red at all, it is usually balanced with plenty of blue and white, so they are using all three colors from the American flag. In Canada, however, red and white are the national flag colors, so political ads and banners widely feature red-based color schemes and are seen as nothing but patriotic.

Any experience that people have in common can lead to common color associations. The expansion of global media exposes much of the world to a common body of images and color choices through film, television, art, fashion, and advertising. Red is globally recognized not just as the color of natural constants like blood and fire, but of brand names like Coca-Cola.

Cool Colors

Blue and green are considered soothing and relaxing. In many environments, the water, sky, grass, and trees are composed of blues and greens, and they function as a sort of neutral background.

Deeper, bolder blues can look solid and majestic. This may be one reason why many banks and insurance companies use blue logos. While a color scheme dominated by red can say "fear me," a deep ocean blue seems to say "trust me."

A scene bathed in blue light can take on a sad feeling. Even very subtle tints in a scene's lighting can help create impressions about a scene. A blue-tinted light can create the impression of winter or night air, and make a location or a person look colder.

Green is a fascinating color in that it can look very natural or very unnatural. Green is the color of much of our natural environment, a symbol of nature itself. However, if a person turned green he would look very sick, a light green is often used in the walls of hospitals, and green-tinted illumination from fluorescent tubes is disturbing. Figure 8.20 takes advantage of a green cast to create an image that suggests sickness. Of course, without color contrast, the green wouldn't be as noticeable, so at least a little bit of red is used to help accentuate the green. It uses only two small areas of red—first on the cabinet, then on one tile in the lower-right corner—to help balance the composition so that your eye isn't stuck at the cabinet.

Contextual Associations

Within a narrative film, you can redefine the meanings of specific colors, like any other symbol. In a larger animation, characters or groups of characters can have their own color schemes, and you might use it in their home environment, costumes, props, or even skin colors. Once an audience is subconsciously accustomed to certain colors appearing with your villains, any new element you introduce into the film appears sinister if it uses the

[Figure 8.20]
Vaclav Cizkovsky's rendering sets a mood with a green light.

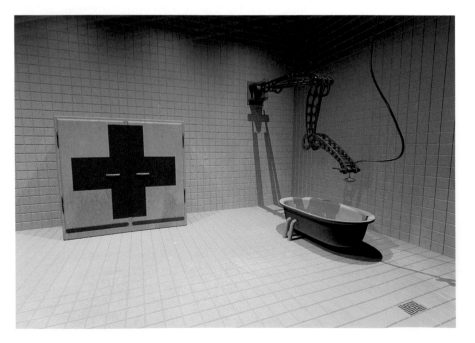

villains' colors. Like musical motifs, color schemes can follow not just characters, but themes, emotions, or any other recurring aspects of a film.

In storytelling, it helps to occasionally move away from the most obvious color meanings. For example, if you want to make a robot look evil or threatening, the most obvious cliché is to make its eyes glow red. Chances are, however, that your audience has already seen that done before, so you might try something fresher and have your robot do something evil without flashing a red light.

Color and Depth

Often people perceive cool colors as being farther away and hot colors as being nearby. For example, even with no other depth cues, most people find it easier to see the left side of Figure 8.21 as a frame with a hole in the middle, and they see the right side as being a small box in front of a larger square.

There are different theories about why this happens. One reason may be that, in natural environments, many subjects are seen against blue sky or green foliage backgrounds, so people naturally consider blue- and green-colored areas to be background. People might also focus more attention in nature on things with warmer tones, such as a red piece of fruit, a wound, or the flesh tones of a person or animal, rather than on colors of foliage or sky.

[Figure 8.21]
All other factors being equal, red tends to appear closer to us than blue.

Another reason that blue may appear to be farther away is due to chromatic aberration in people's eyes. When light is refracted through the lens of a human eye, different wavelengths are refracted at different angles. To correct for the difference, human eyes must focus to a slightly closer distance to see a red subject than they do to see a blue subject in the same position.

In a rendering, you can effectively increase the sense of depth in a scene by washing your background with a blue light and lighting the foreground with red. Naturally, this is not something that is appropriate or plausible in every scene. Take a look at Figure 8.22. When I lit a section of subway tunnel, I could have used almost any color of signal lights to illuminate the scene, but I chose a red foreground and a blue background because it adds punch to the scene.

[Figure 8.22]
Red light in the foreground enhances the sense of depth in a rendering.

Tinted Black-and-White Images

Even some black-and-white images can benefit from the use of color. You can produce a tinted black-and-white image in almost any paint or compositing program by first removing any color or saturation, and then assigning a hue and saturation to the entire image.

Even before color film was invented, filmmakers recognized the emotional impact of color. Some early black-and-white movies have scenes tinted with colored dyes. For example, footage of a building on fire was tinted with a dip in red dye and then spliced back into the film. Black-and-white photographs are also sometimes tinted with colored oils.

Even without intentional colorization, very old photographs turn yellow with age, and people associate a yellow or sepia tone with an older image. I tinted Figure 8.23 with a sepia tone to make it appear more nostalgic, like an old photograph.

[Figure 8.23]
Tinting a black-and-white image can make it look older or more nostalgic.

Using Color Balance

If you want to accurately simulate the way a light source would appear if it were really photographed, then you need to start by understanding the idea of *color balance*.

Colors of light do not directly translate into the tints that are reproduced in a photograph. Instead, the colors that appear in a photograph are relative to the color balance of the film being used.

The color balance of the film determines what color of light appears to be white light. *Indoor film*, which is film color balanced for use with regular lightbulbs, makes light from a regular lightbulb look white but what you see outdoors appear blue, as shown in Figure 8.24.

On the other hand, *outdoor film* makes daylight and the outdoors look normal, but indoor lightbulbs appear yellow or red in color, as shown in Figure 8.25.

Color balancing is not unique to film. You can accomplish a similar adjustment, called *white balance*, electronically on video cameras and digital cameras.

Even your own vision automatically adjusts to compensate for different colors of light. For example, imagine that you are wearing a white shirt at night in front of a campfire, where everything is lit by red firelight. Once you grow accustomed to the light, you perceive the shirt as being white, even though you see red when you look at the shirt in the red light of a fire. In much the same way that the automatic white balance of a digital camera adjusts the signal to respond to colored light, your brain compensates for different colors of light and manages to perceive a white shirt where it sees red.

Most 3D rendering programs do not have controls to simulate different color balance. Instead, you need to mentally take color balance into account when you adjust the color of your lights. This means that you must know two things before you can pick a realistic light color: the characteristic color of the type of light source you want to represent, and the color balance you want to simulate in your rendering.

[Figure 8.24]
An indoor (3,200°K) color balance makes what you see through the door appear blue.

[Figure 8.25]
An outdoor (5,500°K) color balance makes daylight appear normal, but light from indoor bulbs appears red or orange.

The color of a light and the color balance of photographic film are both described by a *color temperature*, which is measured in degrees Kelvin. This is the standard system filmmakers and photographers use to discuss colors of light. It is worth taking a few minutes to understand color temperatures and photographic color balancing, so you can pick more realistic colors for the lights in your 3D scenes.

Understanding Color Temperatures

Working in the late 1800s, the British physicist William Kelvin found that as he heated a block of carbon, it glowed in the heat, producing a range of different colors at different temperatures. The black cube first produced a dim red light, changed to a brighter yellow as the temperature increased, and eventually produced a bright blue-white glow at the highest temperatures.

Today, color temperatures are measured in degrees Kelvin, which are a variation on Centigrade degrees. Instead of starting at the temperature water freezes, the Kelvin scale starts at *absolute zero*, which is –273 Centigrade. Subtract 273 from a Kelvin temperature and you get the equivalent in Centigrade.

Color temperatures attributed to different types of lights are not the actual temperature of the light source. They are just a description of the light's color, which is made by comparing it with the color that you would see if you heated a block of carbon to that temperature.

Table 8.1 shows the color temperatures correlated with a variety of types of light source that you might encounter in the real world. The low color-temperature values (starting with the match and candle flames) tend to appear more reddish, and the higher numbers tend to appear more blue.

So how do you convert these color temperatures into RGB colors for your lights? The answer depends on the color balance of film that you are trying to simulate. If your light source has exactly the same color temperature as the color balance you choose for the scene, then your light color can be white or gray. But this isn't usually what happens—in most scenes, you will need a range of different color lights.

SOURCE	DEGREES KELVIN (°K)
Match flame	1,700–1,800
Candle flame	1,850–1,930
Sun, at sunrise or sunset	2,000–3,000
Household tungsten bulbs	2,500–2,900
Tungsten lamp 500W–1,000W	3,000
Quartz lights	3,200–3,500
Fluorescent lights	3,200–7,500
Tungsten lamp 2,000W	3,275
Tungsten lamp 5,000W, 10,000W	3,380
Sun, direct at noon	5,000–5,400
Daylight (sun and sky)	5,500–6,500
Sun, through clouds/haze	5,500–6,500
Sky, overcast	6,000–7,500
RGB monitor (white point)	6,500
Outdoor shade areas	7,000–8,000
Sky, partly cloudy	8,000–10,000

[Table 8.1] Color Temperatures of Different Light Sources

Simulating Different Color Balances

Despite the names "indoor" and "outdoor," it is the dominant light source, not the location, that determines your color balance. If you are indoors but the scene is lit mainly by daylight entering through a window or door, then you may want to use a 5,500°K color balance despite being indoors. Conversely, if you are outdoors but a scene is lit mainly by artificial lights (especially at night), then you may want to use a 3,200°K color balance.

Table 8.2 shows sample RGB values to use for different kinds of lights as they appear with an outdoor (5500°K) color balance. RGB values are available shown in both the 0 to 255 scale and in 0 to 1 scale.

Table 8.3 shows sample RGB values you can use to simulate indoor (3,200°K) film. Typically you choose from this list if you want to use regular household bulbs to light a scene and you want the bulbs to seem like normal white light.

[Table 8.2] RGB Values for Light Sources at 5500°K Color Balance

SOURCE	RGB (0–255)	RGB (0–1)
Match flame	177,94,88	.69,.37,.35
Candle flame	180,107,88	.71,.42,.35
Sun, at sunrise or sunset	182,126,91	.71,.49,.36
Household tungsten bulbs	184,144,93	.72,.56,.36
Tungsten lamp 500W–1,000W	186,160,99	.73,.63,.39
Quartz lights	189,171,105	.74,.67,.41
Fluorescent lights	191,189,119	.75,.74,.47
Tungsten lamp 2,000W	192,186,138	.75,.73,.54
Tungsten lamp 5,000W, 10,000W	192,189,158	.75,.74,.62
Sun, direct at noon	192,191,173	.75,.75,.68
Daylight (sun and sky)	190,190,190	.75,.75,.75
Sun, through clouds/haze	189,190,192	.74,.75,.75
Sky, overcast	183,188,192	.72,.74,.75
RGB monitor (white point)	174,183,190	.68,.72,.75
Outdoor shade areas	165,178,187	.65,.70,.73
Sky, partly cloudy	155,171,184	.61,.67,.72

[Table 8.3] RGB Values for Light Sources at 3200°K Color Balance

SOURCE	RGB (0–255)	RGB (0–1)
Match flame	188,174,109	.74,.68,.43
Candle flame	191,181,120	.75,.71,.47
Sun, at sunrise or sunset	192,186,138	.75,.73,.54
Household tungsten bulbs	192,189,154	.75,.74,.60
Tungsten lamp 500W–1,000W	191,190,169	.75,.75,.66
Quartz lights	191,191,183	.75,.75,.72
Fluorescent lights	191,197,189	.75,.77,.74
Tungsten lamp 2,000W	186,190,191	.73,.75,.75
Tungsten lamp 5,000W, 10,000W	182,187,191	.71,.73,.75
Sun, direct at noon	174,183,190	.68,.72,.75
Daylight (sun and sky)	166,179,188	.65,.70,.74
Sun, through clouds/haze	159,173,184	.62,.68,.72
Sky, overcast	254,254,255	1.0,1.0,1.0
RGB monitor (white point)	143,159,185	.56,.62,.73
Outdoor shade areas	134,147,189	.53,.58,.74
Sky, partly cloudy	124,134,193	.49,.53,.76

If you don't want to type in RGB values, you can download a version of these tables with columns of RGB colors instead of numbers and pick colors directly from the appropriate column (go to www.3dRender.com/light).

Color Temperature Caveats

Even in realistic, "accurate" photographs, the hue (and saturation and brightness) of a light can be portrayed in many different ways. Different kinds of film, different brands of digital cameras, and digital cameras that are adjusted with different settings all record colors differently.

The direction that color temperatures run seems counterintuitive to many people. As discussed earlier, in our common life experience we think of blue as a cooler color than red. Because of this, the idea that the lowest color temperatures represent red colors and highest temperatures represent blue colors is the opposite of what most people would guess. This difference is just because most people's everyday life experiences don't include super-heating a block of carbon above 5,000°K until it glows blue.

Color temperatures indicate the shift from red to blue only; they don't tell you about the amount of green in a light. In many cases, a fluorescent light tends to appear greenish when compared to other lights. Tables 8.1 to 8.3 include the greenish tint in the RGB values listed for fluorescent lights. However, many manufacturers tint their fluorescent tubes to filter out the green to make them more pleasant looking, so different brands of fluorescent tubes have different hues.

Even with stable, consistent types of light, such as tungsten spotlights, cinematographers can *gel* the lights, which means they place transparent, colored plastic sheets in front of the light, as you can see in Figure 8.26. Cinematographers also place gels outside of windows when they shoot indoors, and photographers often use colored filters on cameras. Even after scenes are shot, directors exert additional creative control through a *digital intermediate process*, a stage in the film creation process in which all of the images are processed as digital files. In short, the light colors you see in a movie or on TV will not be the same as they are in these tables if the cinematographer doesn't want them to be.

Perhaps the only constant rule that you can determine from studying color temperatures is that a source listed with a lower color temperature should always appear redder than a source that has a higher color temperature. For example, in Figure 8.27, the light coming in from the window appears to be bluer in color than the light from the lamp. In a real photograph, how much more red lamp light appears than daylight varies according to the settings on the camera, the type of bulb in the lamp, and other factors, but the fact that an interior bulb appears redder than daylight is a constant factor.

[Figure 8.26]
Colored gels mounted in front of lights can adjust a light's color temperature.

[Figure 8.27]
In a mixed lighting situation, daylight naturally appears to be bluer than interior lamps.

Some 3D graphics programs include menus of color temperature settings for lights but not for the color balance of the camera. They may have chosen to always simulate 5,500°K outdoor film or some other color balance, but be cautious when using these presets, as they may not be based on the color balance most appropriate for your scene. You may get a more appropriate color for your lights if you use a color from one of the earlier tables, or pick a color from your background plate.

Picking Colors from Pictures

Color temperatures may be your only resource if you start from scratch when you light an all-CG scene. However, if you have an image available to you as a starting point, take advantage of it.

In some studios, the art department initially works out colors, and produces a colored storyboard or some other color illustration of each main scene in your production. You can pick colors directly from that image and apply them to lights. Of course, if you do this, you need to test-render and make sure that final colors, including the colors from the shaders, come together to form colors that match the illustration.

When you work in visual effects, you often integrate a rendered element into a live-action background plate. Picking colors directly from the plate should be your first choice in how to set colors for your lights. For instance, you can give fill or rim light from the sky a color you sample from the sky in the background plate, and you can assign bounce lights a color you sampled from the ground in the background plate. If some elements such as the sun are not visible in the plate, you may need to make a warmer color for your sunlight based on the color temperature tables you saw earlier.

Working with Digital Color

When rendering final images, professionals render animation as a series of uncompressed images, creating a numbered image file for each frame of an animated sequence. Many high-end productions are rendered in Open EXR (.exr) file format, but older standards such as TIFF (.tif) and TGA are still used in some places as well. Rendered images generally have at least three channels (red, green, and blue) and usually have a fourth channel when an alpha channel is rendered. Alpha channels store transparency information; Chapter 11 describes how useful alpha channels are in compositing.

The amount of accuracy and memory used per channel varies between the common standard of 8 bits per channel, up to the most versatile alternative of 32-bit-per-channel High Dynamic Range Images (HDRIs).

8-Bit Color

With 8-bit color, your red, green, and blue channels (and an alpha channel if you have one) can each have a range of 256 possible levels, sometimes expressed as a value from 0 to 255 for each channel. In total, 256 values for each of your red, green, and blue channels gives you over 16 million possible colors.

Don't confuse the number of bits per channel with total bits per pixel. When each pixel has a red, green, blue, and alpha channel, there are four times as many bits per pixel as bits in each individual channel. Graphics cards, which use standard 8-bit color (8 bits per channel), are usually advertised as supporting 24-bit color or 32-bit color, which simply means 24 or 32 total bits per pixel, when you add together all the 8-bit channels.

Earlier in this chapter we discussed why a standard gamma of 2.2 is used on many digital images, including most files that use 8 bits per channel of color, such as JPEG files. We mentioned compatibility with televisions and monitors as one reason, but in reality, modern displays can be programmed with different gamma curves if need be. Having a gamma of 2.2 built in to the RGB values also helps them efficiently use the limited 256 levels of brightness available. If they used the 256 levels linearly, then they would waste too many of the levels on highlight tones that are difficult to tell apart, whereas dark tones could move through larger, more visible steps between each brightness level.

16-Bit Color

16-bit color uses twice as much disk space as 8-bit color, but it allows for thousands of possible values for each channel, instead of just 256.

When you render at 16 bits per channel, you allow yourself a greater range of adjustment to the colors and tones in an image during the compositing stage of a project. For example, if 3D elements have been rendered to match night-time background plates, but a change in the script requires that you brighten and color-correct them to match a daytime scene, you can handle this kind of extreme color boost better if you rendered the elements at 16 bits per channel rather than the standard 8.

A problem called *banding* sometimes appears if you brighten a dark image too much in a paint or compositing program. Figure 8.28 shows an example of this: You can see the stripes or steps in brightness created instead of con-tinuous tones in the image, and you can see gaps in the histogram, which indicate the lack of intermediate tones between the different brightness levels.

Banding is a problem that is 256 times more likely to be visible with 8-bit color than with 16-bit color. With 16-bit color you have many more inter-mediate tones stored with your image, so even if you adjust the brightness of an image during compositing, you are not likely to see banding.

HDRI

High Dynamic Range Images (HDRIs) commonly use 32 bits (4 bytes) per channel to store a full floating-point value to represent the red, green, and blue components of an image.

Rendering in HDRI takes four times as much disk space as rendering in 8-bit color, but it doesn't add much to your rendering time, and it allows you the most creative control over your elements during compositing.

Switching from 8-bit to 16-bit increases only the *precision* of the data stored, which gives you more gradations between 0 (black) and 1 (white). Switch-ing to HDRI gives you more than precision—it increases *dynamic range*, the difference between the brightest and darkest tones that can exist in an image. HDR images store values that can go above 1 (brighter than pure white) or below 0 (darker than pure black).

What good is HDRI? If a value is brighter than the brightest tone a monitor can display, why store it?

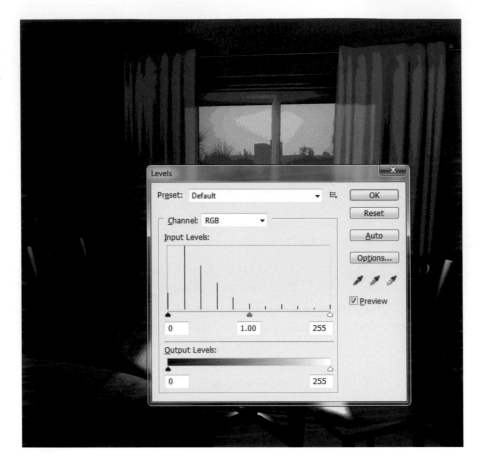

[Figure 8.28]
Banding is visible, especially in the sky outside the window, when an underexposed 8-bit image is brightened after it is rendered. Gaps in the histogram are a sign of banding.

When you render in 8-bit or 16-bit color, overexposed areas in your scene become *clipped*, or rounded down to a value of 1, because they cannot go beyond the highest value those file formats can store. A clipped area has no detail, because all of the pixel values are 1, without any variation. Figure 8.29 shows how you can spot a clipped image by its histogram. The "cliff" on the right side of the histogram shows that tones have built up to a maximum value. If you reduce the brightness of the image after it is rendered, the clipped area becomes a flat, untextured area, as you can see on the right side of the figure.

[**Figure 8.29**]
An 8-bit image is clipped in the overexposed area (left) and the clipped areas lack detail when darkened in a paint or compositing program (right). A sharp cliff on one side of the histogram is a warning sign of clipping.

On the other hand, if you render in HDRI, detail and texture are stored in every part of the image, including the overexposed areas, such as the tabletop in Figure 8.30, where values above 1 are stored at each pixel. In compositing, you can reduce the brightness of overexposed areas, and when you do, all of the original texture and detail is revealed, as shown on the right side of Figure 8.30. This side has the same brightness reduction applied as the right side of Figure 8.29 had, but the adjustment looks much better here because the original file was rendered as an HDR image.

[**Figure 8.30**]
When images are rendered in HDRI (left), even an overexposed image can be darkened convincingly to reveal additional detail and texture (right).

Half Floats

Full 32-bit floating point files are an ideal way to render your images, because they allow you to adjust and post-process the most with little risk of clipping or banding. However, this does create large files (four times as large as when you use 8-bit color) that take up more disk space and require time to load during compositing operations.

A great compromise, called *half floats,* is supported in the Open EXR (.exr) file format. A half float (or half-precision floating point) value still stores high dynamic range data, just like a 32-bit floating point value does, only it stores it with less precision and uses only half as many bits per channel.

Even though a half float uses 16 bits per channel, it is not the same as 16-bit color. Regular 16-bit color does not store out-of-range values above pure white, so it can create clipping. Half floats store any floating point number, including values above pure white, so you are only sacrificing some precision (in terms of not having as many decimal places of accuracy in each value), not dynamic range.

Half floats have far more intermediate steps than 8-bit color, and in practice, even when you process and manipulate half float images in compositing, you are unlikely to see any banding or problems because you used half floats instead of full 32-bit floating point.

Because half floats are supported as a part of Open EXR, the most popular standard file format for high-end 3D rendering, rendering frames as half floats is an ideal sweet-spot for many productions. It achieves a balance between the greatest possible flexibility during compositing and files that are not any bigger than they need to be.

Compact Data Formats

Sometimes you want to convert your images into more compact data formats after rendering, using file formats such as .jpg, .gif, and .png. Although .png files use standard 8-bit color as described earlier, you may also deal with indexed color in .gif files, or lossy image compression in .jpg files.

Indexed Color

The least memory-intensive type of digital color is *indexed color,* which means that you use a limited number of colors in your image, and that all the colors you use are included in a color look-up table (CLUT). During the 1980s, indexed color was the only color mode that most personal computers supported, so even 3D graphics had to be rendered into indexed color. Most paint programs allow you to convert graphics into indexed color so you can create .gif files for websites.

The number of bits used per pixel determines the colors in the CLUT. Table 8.4 shows the number of colors available for each number of bits per pixel.

BITS PER PIXEL	NUMBER OF COLORS
1	2
2	4
3	8
4	16
5	32
6	64
7	128
8	256

[Table 8.4] Number of Colors Supported by Bits per Pixel

Generally you don't use the CLUT approach above 8 bits per pixel. You can re-create the table above by computing 2 raised to the number of bits to derive the number of colors from the number of bits per pixel (for example, two to the eighth power, or 2^8, is 256). Figure 8.31 shows a CLUT for an image reduced to 8 bits per pixel, or 256 colors.

You will find using indexed color .gif files on websites useful for icons or diagrams where you want a small file, but you don't want to use any compression that could blur the image.

[Figure 8.31]
A color look-up table (CLUT)
shows the colors that can
appear in an indexed color
image.

Compressed Images

After you render your frames, often you need to compress them in order to display them on the Web or for other purposes. JPEG (.jpg) is by far the most common compressed image format for Internet display. When you save your file as a JPEG, you get to choose between higher quality images that are stored as larger files, and lower quality images that are very compact but can be blurred or have compression artifacts.

JPEG uses *lossy compression,* meaning that the image itself degrades when it is compressed. Often a small amount of compression isn't noticeable but it does change the image, and greater amounts of lossy compression soften the image and can add blocky artifacts to it. Many other file formats use *lossless compression,* meaning the images are stored in a more compact and efficient way, but every pixel remains the same color as the original when the file is opened. Lossless compression can be especially efficient on images that have large blank areas in them. However, lossless compression doesn't make files as small and quick to download as JPEGs can be.

Even if a compressed image is your final product, you should also archive your original uncompressed image in case you want to edit or print a full-quality copy in the future.

Exercises

Color is fun to explore—seize every opportunity to play with it and learn more about its impact on your work.

1. For each program you use (not just your 3D software, but also 2D compositing programs), check the documentation or web resources to see how to best adjust it to work in a linear workflow. If you've been using a file format that only supports 8 bits per channel, such as TGA, then it's a good idea to upgrade to Open EXR (.exr).

2. Try lighting a scene with light from two or more different sources. A set with a window that allows natural light to enter can be ideal, because then natural light comes through the window and blends with the lamps indoors. When a viewer cannot see the light sources in the shot, can you make the type of light clear from the colors you use?

3. Usually, your goal in created 3D renderings is to try to get the colors right when you first render an image, but it's also possible to color-correct images during compositing. In fact, during the digital intermediate process, feature films are routinely processed and digitally color-corrected. For example, sometimes entire scenes are tinted blue-green and only the character's skin, fire, and explosions are kept as a warm orange. This reduces some action scenes into a color scheme of just two colors, no matter how the footage looked when it was first shot. This really isn't the way color is assigned in most 3D scenes, but just as an exercise to explore color, try running some previously created 3D scenes through a paint and compositing program and changing the colors in a way that reduces the color scene to just two or three colors. Make several variations so that you have some choices beyond the clichéd example of everything being reduced to teal and orange.

CHAPTER NINE

Shaders and Rendering Algorithms

This chapter gives you a look under the hood of your rendering software. You'll see what your software is doing through the main stages of rendering your scene and learn how to achieve the best image quality and rendering speed. The rendering process starts with *shading,* setting up how your surfaces respond to light, and we will explore various kinds of shaders and shader adjustments. We will also look inside *anti-aliasing* functions, which determine how your scene is sampled and filtered to produce smooth, high-quality renderings. This chapter also explores different *rendering algorithms,* the basic approaches that software uses to produce images, such as raytracing, Reyes algorithms, and different types of global illumination (GI).

Shading Surfaces

Shaders are definitions of how 3D objects respond to light that describe their surface appearance or how they will be rendered. *Shading* is the process of designing, assigning, and adjusting shaders to develop unique looks for the objects in a 3D scene. Figure 9.1 shows some of the variety that you can achieve by assigning different shaders to an object.

[Figure 9.1]
Four spheres with different shaders respond differently to light. These examples show some of the things that you can do by adjusting attributes discussed in this chapter.

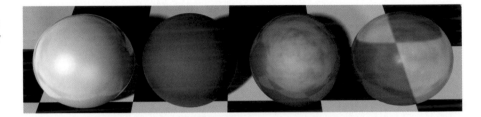

Some 3D programs use the word *material* in reference to their built-in selection of shaders and use the word *shader* only in reference to the optional plug-ins available for a renderer. Although materials and shaders may be listed separately in your software's interface, all definitions of surface appearances provided to the renderer are really shaders.

Diffuse, Glossy, and Specular Reflection

The three most common ways that light reflects off a surface are shown in Figure 9.2. *Diffuse reflection* (left) is when light scatters uniformly in all directions. *Glossy reflection* (center) preserves the directionality of light rays but still causes some scattering or softening. *Specular reflection* (right) perfectly preserves the sharpness of the light and reflects all rays without scattering.

[Figure 9.2]
Light reflects in a diffuse, glossy, or specular manner.

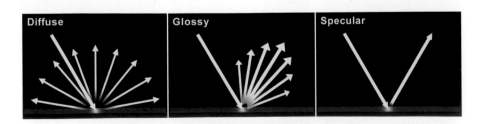

Figure 9.3 shows how diffuse, glossy, and specular reflection appears on surfaces. Diffuse reflection (left) gives materials a matte appearance so that they don't show any reflections or highlights. Glossy reflections (center) are soft, and diverging rays naturally make reflections appear softer with distance, as you can see in the mug's reflection on the ground. Specular reflections (right) are crisp and mirror-like.

[Figure 9.3]
A scene rendered with entirely diffuse (left), glossy (middle), and specular (right) reflections.

Most surfaces show some combination of diffuse, glossy, and specular light transmission. Real surfaces do not reflect light in a perfectly specular way. Even a mirror shows some glossy or diffuse light reflection. Likewise, materials in real life are not completely diffuse.

If you look at a real material and you can't spot any reflections or highlights on it, move your head back and forth. As your point of view shifts sideways, you see highlights and reflections change and travel over the surface, visually separating them from the diffusely reflected light. Moving your head from side to side readily shows you how glossy the pages of this book are (if you're reading this as an e-book, make sure you turn on some lights that can reflect off the screen; you'll see how glossy the screen is when you move your head). Sometimes you will find a material such as a brown paper bag, and think that it is mainly diffuse, but when you look at it in a well-lit room and shift your head from side to side, you will see that it actually has broad highlights.

Diffuse, Glossy, and Specular Reflection in Shaders

Many common shader parameters fall into a category of simulating diffuse, glossy, or specular reflection.

Your main surface color controls diffuse shading. When we ask "what color is that?" we mean the color of the diffuse reflection, not the highlights, reflections, or other components of the shading.

Many shaders also have a parameter called *diffuse,* which is simply a multiplier for the surface color. In this case, cutting in half the value of the diffuse setting reduces your diffuse brightness just the same as cutting in half the brightness of the surface color.

Specular highlights are intended to look like a specular reflection of a light source. Outside of computer graphics, however, there isn't really any difference between reflections and specular highlights. Highlights are just a part of what reflects off a surface, such as the reflection of a light source or other bright area. In computer graphics, starting in the early days of 3D rendering, specular highlights simulating the reflections of lights have been added as a standard part of many surface shaders, and they are rendered through a different algorithm from the optional raytraced reflections that you might also use. As a result of this, shaders offer separate controls for the appearance of raytraced reflections compared to the appearance of specular highlights, but be aware that these are supposed to look like the same thing. Whatever influences the appearance of specular highlights on a real surface also influences the reflections you see of other objects. To render a surface with bright specular highlights but without any raytraced reflections is actually a cheat, because this is something that you will not find in real life.

It also may surprise you to hear that most specular highlights are actually a glossy reflection, not a specular one. If a light is a point source that comes from an infinitely small point in space, then a perfectly specular reflection of it would be an infinitely small dot, probably much smaller than a pixel. To correct for this, most shaders allow you to adjust the highlight size. Although a highlight size can be considered a realistic simulation of the roughness of a surface, most often it is used as a cheat to hide the fact that your light sources are infinitely small. Once you add a highlight size, the specular highlight actually spreads out to become a glossy reflection of the light source.

Standard raytraced reflections are perfectly specular, which means that they are perfectly focused. *Glossiness,* also called *reflection blur* or *soft reflections,* enables you to make raytraced reflections that blur with distance. See the

"Raytracing" section, later in this chapter, for more on rendering glossy reflections.

Most GI techniques can be considered diffuse-to-diffuse light transfer, meaning that the light diffusely reflecting off of one object adds to the diffuse illumination of another. Caustics are an exception—they can be described as specular-to-diffuse light transfer. When light reflects off a surface in a specular or glossy way, caustics carry that illumination into the diffuse shading of other objects.

The Microfacet Model

You use a *microfacet model* to understand what makes real materials diffuse, glossy, or specular. A microfacet model simulates the roughness or jaggedness of surfaces on a microscopic level. The tiny details or facets on a rough surface are what scatter the light in different directions to produce a glossy or diffuse light transmission. Several popular shaders, including *Cook-Torrance,* are programmed based on a microfacet model of surfaces.

Figure 9.4 shows the difference that microscopic roughness can make. On a rough surface (left), parallel rays of light enter and are each reflected to different angles, producing diffuse reflection. On a smoother surface (middle), the rays are scattered less and retain some of their directionality, producing a glossy reflection. A perfectly smooth surface (right) allows all of the rays to reflect in parallel, producing a perfectly specular reflection.

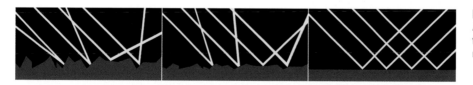

[Figure 9.4]
A microfacet model of diffuse, glossy, and specular reflection.

The property of a surface that causes a specular highlight to spread out is called *roughness*. Roughness does not always appear as big, visible bumps. Microscopic roughness in a surface's structure can make a surface appear smooth, while still diffusing reflected light. For example, the surface of a rubber pencil eraser diffuses light due to a microscopic roughness to its structure, even though it looks and feels smooth. In this sense, any surface with a matte finish instead of a glossy finish can be said to be rough.

Specular Highlights

A common misconception is that specular highlights are centered in the brightest point of the diffuse shading. In reality, the positioning of the specular highlights is derived separately from the diffuse shading. Diffuse shading is based on the position of a surface and its angle relative to the light. Specular shading, on the other hand, is calculated only from a specific camera angle. It is based on the angle between the light, the surface, and the camera. Because of this, specular highlights are an example of *view-dependent shading*.

View-dependent shading is any effect that varies depending on the camera angle from which it was rendered. Specularity, reflections, and refraction are all examples of *view-dependent shading*; they seem to shift across a surface when you view it from different angles. Contrast this with *non-view-dependent shading,* such as diffuse shading and cast shadows, which can be computed without regard for the camera angle.

Realistic Specularity

Big, bright, airbrushed-looking specular highlights are one of the most conspicuous clichés of 3D graphics. Specular highlights appear fake in many renderings because they are often misused or poorly adjusted. However, almost all surfaces in the real world exhibit some degree of specularity, and using it appropriately can add realism to your renderings.

You can improve the quality of your shading if you give your specular highlights an appropriate size, color, shape, and position. When adjusting your specular highlights, your best bet is to find a real-world example of the material you are trying to simulate, and study how it responds to light. By studying reference images or a sample of a real material, you can adjust your specular highlights based on real-world observations instead of preconceived notions or software presets.

Highlight Size

In real life, the size of a highlight depends on two things: the light source and the surface. A bigger light source, or a light source positioned closer to the surface being lit, produces a bigger highlight. The type of surface also influences the size of a highlight. Materials with very smooth, hard surfaces, such as metals and glass, have smaller, tighter highlights. Rougher surfaces, such as paper and wood, have broader (although less intense) highlights.

Try to make each highlight look like a reflection of the light source that motivates it. If the light source is small or far away, then the highlight should be small, as shown on the top of Figure 9.5. If you are simulating a large light source and it is close to the object, then you need to increase the highlight size on the shader until you have a very large specular highlight, as shown on the bottom of Figure 9.5.

Unmotivated specular highlights can be very noticeable and distracting. If there is no light below an object, you don't expect to see a highlight on its underside. Specular highlights that aren't motivated can still be eye-catching and will distract viewers and detract from the realism of your scene. If you need to add an extra fill or bounce light from an angle where highlights wouldn't be motivated, set those lights not to emit specular illumination.

Specular Color

In most cases, you should leave your shader's specular color as a shade of gray. A white or gray specular color means that the color added by specular shading will be based on the color of the light source, which is usually the most natural source of color for a specular highlight.

Colored specularity is necessary only for metallic surfaces. In this case, give the specular color a tint similar to the color of the metal itself. Figure 9.6 is a photograph of a brass fixture. Notice how the highlights and the reflections are all tinted to the brass color. Often metals have a very dark diffuse color so that they can receive most of their color and shading from the colored specularity.

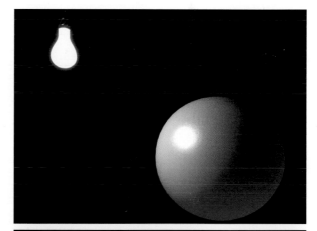

[Figure 9.5] Adjust the size of a highlight until it visually matches the size and distance of the light source.

[Figure 9.6]
Only a metallic reflection
uses colored specularity
and tint reflections.

The Fresnel Effect

The French physicist Augustin-Jean Fresnel (1788–1827) advanced the wave theory of light through a study that showed how light was transmitted and propagated by different objects. One of his observations is now known in computer graphics as the *Fresnel effect*—the observation that the amount of light you see reflected from a surface depends on the viewing angle.

For example, in Figure 9.7, note how the side window is full of reflections, such that you can't see through it. The windshield, on the other hand, does not appear reflective and is more transparent. Of course, both pieces of glass are equally reflective materials. It is the angle from which you view the glass that changes how much reflection you see.

[Figure 9.7]
The Fresnel effect makes the side window look more reflective than the front in this photograph.

Figure 9.8 shows another common occurrence of the Fresnel effect. If you look straight down at a pool of water, you don't see very much reflected light on the surface of the pool. From such a high angle, without seeing reflections, you can see down through the surface to the bottom of the pool. At a glancing angle (for instance, when you look at the pool with your eye closer to water level, from the edge of the water surface), however, you see much more specularity and reflections on the water surface and might not be able to see what's under the water at all.

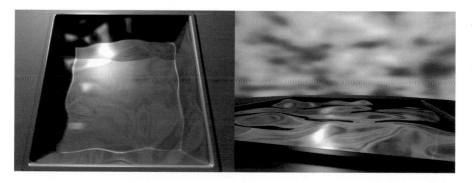

[Figure 9.8]
The Fresnel effect increases reflection and specularity on surfaces viewed at a glancing angle (right).

You don't see your reflection in a painted wall if you look at it straight on. However, at a glancing angle, as shown in Figure 9.9, you can clearly see reflections of the window and light bulb at the end of the hallway. Many, if not most, surfaces become somewhat reflective when viewed from the correct angle. Even pavement on a street can appear reflective if you are viewing it from a low enough angle.

[Figure 9.9]
Even surfaces that don't look reflective when viewed head-on show reflections at a glancing angle.

A shader that allows you to vary the specularity and other parameters according to the viewing angle of the surface is often called a *Fresnel shader*. A Fresnel shader lets you specify a specular color you want to appear on parts of a surface that directly face the camera, and another specular color to appear on parts of a surface that are perpendicular to the camera. Besides specular color increasing at the edge of an object, the specular highlight size and reflectivity also increase.

Another way you can create the Fresnel effect is by linking the surface angle (or *facing ratio*) of an object to the shader attribute that needs to change, such as the specular brightness, as shown in Figure 9.10.

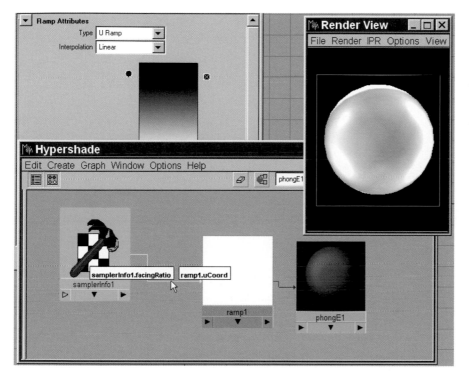

[Figure 9.10]
In Maya's Hypershade window, the Facing Ratio attribute of a surface is linked through a ramp into the surface's specularity. The intermediate ramp allows the center-to-edge specularity to be edited as a gradient.

Something else common in film production is also named after Augustin-Jean Fresnel. He invented the Fresnel lens, designed to project beams of light from lighthouses. Still popular today, Fresnel lenses are built into the front of film and television lighting equipment; filmmakers call this type of focusable lighting instrument a *Fresnel*.

Anisotropic Highlights

The microscopic roughness responsible for diffusing light is not always randomly distributed and doesn't always scatter all light randomly in all directions. Some surfaces have a structure of small grooves or scratches running in a particular direction, instead of random bumpiness. Brushed steel, human hair, phonograph records, DVDs, compact discs, and some wooden objects are examples of surfaces with grooves that affect their shading. Reflections and highlights are stretched out in a direction perpendicular to the grooves in the surface, for a result called *anisotropic shading.* Surfaces that spread reflected light evenly in all directions are called *isotropic*—Figure 9.11 shows isotropic surfaces on the left and anisotropic surfaces on the right.

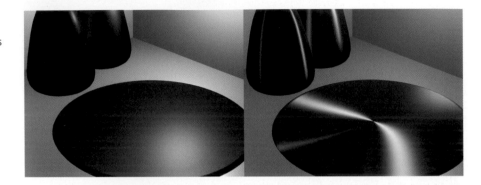

[Figure 9.11]
Isotropic shading (left) spreads specular highlights uniformly in all directions, whereas anisotropic shading (right) causes specular highlights to elongate.

On a microfacet level, you can picture rays that run across the grooves getting scattered widely, similar to what is shown running across Figure 9.12. However, rays that run along the grooves (vertical in Figure 9.12) are reflected in parallel without scattering. This broadens the highlights running *across* the grooves, while it leaves highlights smaller and more focused where they run *along* the grooves. The way the highlights would be stretched out running across the grooves, while they could remain focused running along the grooves, causes the anisotropic appearance of the surface.

[Figure 9.12]
The microfacet structure on an anisotropic surface shows rays scattering only when they run across the grain of the surface.

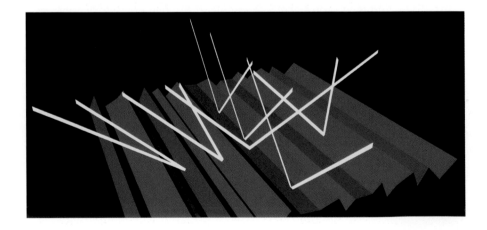

Physically Based Shaders

Physically based shaders are accurate models of how light is transmitted by surfaces. They are written so that materials respond realistically to a wide variety of different lighting situations, without your needing to tweak them much to achieve a realistic look.

With basic shaders such as Phong and Blinn, you can achieve realistic-looking results after you tweak both your shaders and your lights a great deal. However, this doesn't guarantee that the shaders will look good when you move them into a different lighting setup, such as lighting a car by day in one scene and by night in another. A physically based shader is designed to respond realistically to light so that you can adjust the lighting mainly through the lights, which hopefully will mean that you spend less time adjusting shader parameters to achieve believable results.

Energy Conservation

One key aspect of physically based shaders is that they support *energy conservation*. This means that the amount of light that reflects off the surface is consistent, no matter how diffuse, specular, or glossy the material becomes. For example, as the shader is adjusted to simulate a shinier surface, the highlights and reflections become brighter, but there is also less diffuse reflectance.

Energy conservation in the shader is a different approach compared to what you may be accustomed to in non–physically based shaders, which tend to let you adjust diffuse and specular light and reflectivity separately, as if they were independent variables.

Some physically based shaders do allow a user the option of cheating by making adjustments that do not respect energy conservation. However, if you chose to do this, you are breaking the physically correct nature of the shader.

BRDF and BSSRDF

A real surface's *bidirectional reflectance distribution function (BRDF)* describes how it reflects or absorbs light from different angles. Most common shaders, such as Lambert, Phong, and Blinn, provide a simple, generalized BRDF.

Some renderers also come with a shader called BRDF, which is designed to mimic real responses to light based on data collected from real-world measurements.

In real life, every material has a unique BRDF that represents how it reflects or absorbs light when illuminated or viewed from different angles. A BRDF can be measured from specific, real-world materials. Researchers have constructed special rigs that can photograph a material sample, or a person's face, from a variety of camera angles, with light hitting the material from different angles. From this, they can digitize a *light reflectance field*, which a BRDF shader can use to match how a real material responds to light from all directions and viewing angles.

BRDF is based on the assumption that light reflects off a surface at the same point where it hits. As discussed in Chapter 5, translucent materials rendered with subsurface scattering are brightened by light transmitted through objects. Light can hit one point on an object and travel through it to come out on the other side. When you add scattering to a BRDF, you get a *bidirectional surface scattering reflectance distribution function (BSSRDF)*. This is quite a mouthful, but all it means is a shader that can be based on measured data about realistic light transmission, and that also includes support for realistic translucency.

Figure 9.13 shows the difference between BRDF and BSSRDF. On the right, you can see how BSSRDF allows light to be scattered within a surface before it is transmitted out at a different point from where it entered.

[Figure 9.13]
BRDF (left) reflects light off a surface, whereas BSSRDF (right) includes scattering within the surface.

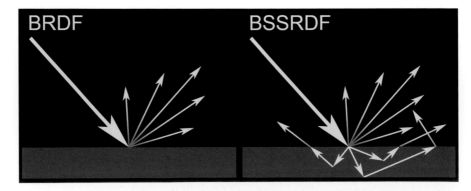

Creative Control vs. Unnecessary Tweaking

In the entertainment industry, the use of physically based shaders is a relatively recent trend on many productions. Traditionally, a production's top priority would be to use shaders that allowed complete creative control. To allow this, each aspect of the shader, such as its specular highlight size, color, and brightness, had to be a separate set of variables, so that you could tweak and adjust each separately. The downside of this is that you needed to perform an enormous amount of tweaking to create realistic results.

As software gets better and computers get faster, the approach of lighting scenes more the way a live-action cinematographer would light scenes is becoming popular with more productions: use GI, use soft raytraced shadows and real area lights positioned where you need them, and use shaders that respond to light realistically so that you can achieve realistic results much more quickly and easily. This approach often requires more computing power to complete an image, but at the same time it uses less human labor and fewer versions between the one where you plan your lighting design until you receive final approval from your client or director.

You still need the ability to tweak and cheat parts of the process, even when you are working with GI and physically based shaders. But the important part is that you are starting out with realism based on the physics of real light transmission, and from there you only tweak things as needed to meet the creative needs of your production.

Anti-Aliasing

Anti-aliasing is a critical component of high-quality rendering. You need to adjust anti-aliasing at least twice during each project. The first time is when you start doing quick test-renders, when you choose low-quality settings just to get images to render quickly. Later, you have to adjust it again to achieve the quality output you need for final renderings. Any time you are doing test-renders to see whether a shadow or reflection is too noisy, use full-quality anti-aliasing to inspect the image quality.

Without anti-aliasing, jaggy or stair-stepped artifacts appear along diagonal edges, and textures can appear to crawl or jitter during animation.

Anti-aliasing makes rendered images look smooth, natural, and more similar to a photograph.

The two main components of anti-aliasing are over-sampling and filtering.

Over-Sampling

Over-sampling means collecting more data than you need. When a renderer over-samples a scene, it computes more points or rays than the number of pixels in the final image.

Figure 9.14 shows an area of 8 pixels by 8 pixels in which a polygon needs to be displayed. To render the image without over-sampling, the renderer takes only one sample (shown as a yellow dot in the left side of the figure) per pixel. If the sample hits the polygon, the corresponding pixel takes on the sampled color from the polygon. If the sample hits the background, then the pixel gets the background color. The right side of the figure shows the results. Without over-sampling, the polygon is represented in a blocky, stair-stepped manner.

Figure 9.15 shows a small amount of over-sampling, what happens when you use four samples per pixel. Where the edge of the polygon passes through a pixel, some of the samples hit it and others miss. The results are averaged together for each pixel, which produces intermediate shades of gray. On the right side of Figure 9.15, you can see the output shaded with an average of four samples per pixel.

[Figure 9.14]
A single sample per pixel (left) produces stair-stepped output (right).

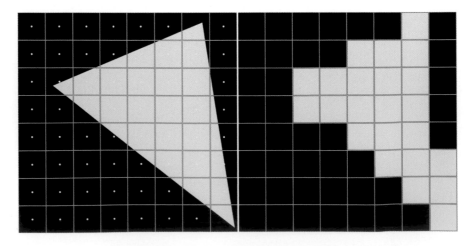

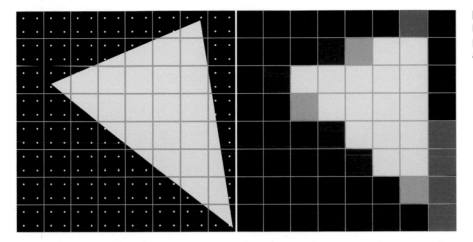

[Figure 9.15]
Four samples per pixel (left) produce more accurate anti-aliased output (right).

Anti-aliasing through over-sampling does not blur your image. It actually uses shading to represent a subpixel level of detail, thus adding detail to your image. Using more over-sampling never makes your image softer—it only makes it more accurate. The only downside to over-sampling is that more samples take longer to compute and slow down your rendering.

Adaptive Over-Sampling

Adaptive over-sampling varies the number of samples taken in different parts of the image. The renderer takes more samples where a significant number of edges need anti-aliasing, and fewer samples in smooth areas where over-sampling is unlikely to make much of a difference. With adaptive anti-aliasing, instead of setting one number for a consistent amount of over-sampling, you choose both a minimum and a maximum level.

The renderer begins by taking the minimum number of samples, shown as large red dots in Figure 9.16. The renderer then needs to determine where additional samples are needed. A common way to do this is by measuring contrast between the samples. The renderer compares the colors of each sample with its neighbors to see how different their color values are. Where neighboring samples differ in color by more than a *contrast threshold* that you set, more samples must be taken. The yellow dots show the additional samples that are taken in high-contrast areas. The process continues until the level of contrast between new samples is less than the contrast threshold or the maximum amount of over-sampling has been achieved.

[Figure 9.16]
Adaptive over-sampling
uses extra samples only
where they are needed.

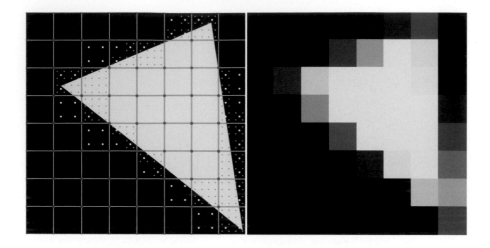

[Figure 9.16]
Adaptive over-sampling uses extra samples only where they are needed.

Notice that only the minimum samples (red) are placed uniformly over the image. The next level of samples (yellow) appears only where there was contrast between the initial samples. The samples taken at the maximum level (green) appear only where contrast existed between previous samples. All of these samples are averaged together to compute a color for each pixel. As a result, the edge of the polygon has been thoroughly sampled, but extra time hasn't been wasted taking too many samples of empty space.

Adjusting the Contrast Threshold

When you lower your contrast threshold, you tend to get more anti-aliasing. As you raise the contrast threshold, more subtle color changes are less likely to trigger additional over-sampling, so you tend to get less anti-aliasing.

Most renderers let you set the contrast threshold as a set of red, green, and blue values. For maximum efficiency, you have to remember that red, green, and blue are not equally important. In an RGB image, the brightness is not derived equally from the three color channels. Instead, green is the most important component to the brightness of your image, red is less important, and blue is the least significant. A small change in your green channel is much more noticeable than a numerically equivalent change in your blue channel. To take this into account, instead of setting the red, green, and blue of the contrast threshold to the same number, choose values that take the importance of the different color channels into account, such as a contrast threshold of 0.2 red, 0.15 green, and 0.3 blue.

If you are able to set a contrast threshold for differences in the alpha channel as well, this should be the lowest number, such as half the green value.

Under-Sampling

Under-sampling means sampling fewer points or rays than the number of pixels being rendered. This can cause blurry images or lower image quality. However, under-sampling is often used in conjunction with adaptive over-sampling. For example, in Mental Ray, where negative numbers refer to under-sampling, the minimum number of samples is often set to –2, with the maximum at 0 or 1, in order to render quick tests or previews. This way the renderer begins sampling the image with an initial under-sampling pass, but then in areas of high contrast it takes more samples, heading into an area of over-sampling where needed.

There is a danger that the initial under-sampling could entirely miss thin lines, causing gaps within the animation. Even when used as an adaptive minimum, under-sampling is safe only for tests, not final production work.

Filtering

Filtering is the process of constructing the final image out of your subpixel samples. Most programs offer a choice of different filtering types, which are ways to reconstruct your image, most of them weighted to rely most on samples within the pixel, but also factoring in local samples from adjacent pixels.

Using filtering takes relatively little extra rendering time, compared to over-sampling. Filtering lets you get the smoothest possible image from a limited number of samples.

When used in small amounts, a little filtering can smooth out jagged edges and help create a more natural image. However, on a subpixel level, filtering is very similar to blurring an image with a Photoshop filter. As a result, too much filtering can make your image blurry. Any time you activate or increase the level of filtering, test-render at least a small portion of your image to make sure you haven't turned it up too high and softened the image too much.

Rendering at Higher Resolutions

An alternative way to achieve good anti-aliasing is to render at a higher resolution than you will need for your final product. For example, if your final image is going to be 720 pixels wide, render at 1,440 pixels. When you are finished rendering and compositing your shot, the last step in your composite is to scale down the image to your final size. You can regain some of that render speed that you lose in rendering at higher resolutions by using lower quality anti-aliasing.

Rendering at a higher resolution and then scaling down is a manual way to make your own over-sampling. Of course, if you render the entire image at four times the resolution, the over-sampling you create is not adaptive, but the quality is just as high. If you also want to create some filtering, blur the high-resolution image a bit before scaling down.

If you work this way, your image files end up much bigger and use up more network bandwidth, I/O time, and storage space. However, this allows you to work at a higher resolution during compositing and retouching, and then scale down only after image processing is completed. This provides you with potentially higher quality in the compositing process, because you can perform operations such as rotations or matte extraction at high resolution before you scale down the image.

If you create media at any lower resolution for display within an app on a phone or on the Internet, bear in mind that different versions of the app or website might be created in the future that could require graphics at a different resolution. Mastering all of your work at a higher resolution gives you the flexibility to output your work again at a different resolution by just changing the scaling parameters at the end of your composite so that all of your rendering, compositing, and retouching can be reused in the next version.

Raytracing

Raytracing is an optional part of the rendering process that simulates the natural reflection, refraction, and shadowing of light by 3D surfaces.

The process of raytracing is backward in comparison to real life. In real life, light originates at a light source, bounces around the scene, and eventually reaches the camera. In raytracing, rays begin at the camera and are fired from the camera out into the scene.

To begin a raytracing process, the renderer divides the camera's field of view into an array of pixels, based on the resolution of the image being rendered. For each pixel, a ray is projected from the camera, sampling one point from any objects that it hits, as shown in Figure 9.17. With anti-aliasing, more than one point may be sampled per pixel, further multiplying the amount of work your raytracer needs to do.

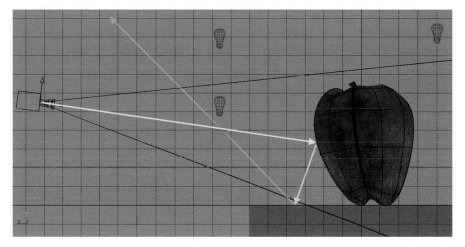

[Figure 9.17]
In raytracing, a ray (shown in yellow) starts at the camera, then bounces off visible objects.

When the ray hits an object, the raytracer checks the object to see if it is reflective or refractive, or whether it is receiving shadows, which the raytracer would need to compute by sampling other rays. If the object is reflective, for example, then after computing the diffuse and specular shading of the point on the surface, the raytracer would send an additional ray shooting off the object into 3D space; it would check along this ray whether any other object would appear reflected at the point being rendered.

If it encountered another reflective object, then it would cast another ray from that object, further extending the amount of rendering work it was doing for that pixel.

Raytracing Acceleration Structures

Raytracing software spends a great deal of time searching through space to

- Find out whether a ray will hit any model between a light and a point on a surface that might receive a raytraced shadow

- Find out which object will appear in a particular pixel of a reflection

- Find out what objects a ray will hit after refracting through glass

All of this searching must be done for each bounce of each ray, for every pixel in your scene.

To quickly determine which objects are present in a particular area of 3D space, a raytracer needs to sort all of the geometry in the scene into lists of polygons or other basic components based on their location. These lists are called *raytracing acceleration structures*. They take time to compute and use up a lot of your computer's memory, but without them, raytracing would take much longer than it already does.

A renderer begins creating raytracing acceleration structures by tessellating all of the surfaces in the scene into polygons. Any NURBS or subdivision surfaces are divided into polygons, and any displacement mapping is divided into more polygons. All of these polygons are then sorted into lists, which are sorted into smaller lists by subdividing the space they occupy. The process continues until all of the lists are reasonably short, or until a limit to the depth of sorting is reached.

Adjusting your raytracing *recursion depth* or *oct tree depth* is a trade-off between memory use and rendering speed. If you have enough free RAM during your rendering process, and you want to potentially speed up the raytracing a little, you can increase this setting. If your raytracing is using up all of your computer's memory so that it is crashing or swapping data out from the hard disk, then turning down this setting can help save some memory and avoid swapping. However, turning down the recursion depth too low if you aren't out of memory can lead to slower render times.

Raytraced Reflections

Raytraced reflections serve a very similar role to specular shading. Raytraced reflections provide reflections of other objects in the scene, while specular shading simulates a reflection of a light source. Both of these things should look as if they are reflecting the same world, in the same way.

Often a raytraced reflection of something bright makes a more realistic highlight than a specular highlight from a light, because you can better control the shape of a raytraced reflection. Figure 9.18 compares an apple with only a specular highlight and an apple with a raytraced reflection of a window. To add a reflection, just build a simple model in the shape you want and position it near a light source. The model you build to appear in the reflection can be just one polygon, and you can give it any texture map. As long as it is bright enough and the rendered surface is reflective, your custom shape will show up in your rendering.

[Figure 9.18]
An object can show reflected light with a specular highlight (left), a raytraced reflection (middle), or both (right).

Integrating Reflections and Specular Highlights

Often you'll want both specular highlights and raytraced reflections on a surface. The key is to make sure that reflections and highlights work together so that they look like part of the same reflection.

If you use colored reflectivity to simulate a metallic surface, usually the color of the reflection should be the same as the specular color.

If you look at the scene reflected in a surface, you should see a complete scene in the reflection; make sure the highlights that are visible are only in the places where you expect a light source within the reflected scene.

The Surrounding Environment

If a reflective object is surrounded by empty black space, no reflection should appear, no matter how reflective you made it. When you use raytraced reflections, you must give reflective objects something to reflect.

A common beginner's mistake with raytraced reflections is failing to build a complete scene that goes all the way around your model. Some 3D artists are in the habit of building rooms with only three walls, leaving the fourth side open so that the camera can look through the opening. A reflective object in such a three-walled room would have a black square missing from its reflection. If the camera needs to look through the fourth wall, you can set that wall to be invisible to *primary rays* or *primary visibility*, but leave it visible in reflections.

Glossy Reflections

Standard raytraced reflections produce perfectly specular reflections of other objects. Often the reflections can appear unrealistically crisp.

Glossiness, also called *reflection blur* or *reflection softness*, is an option in most raytracers that scatters or randomizes reflected rays to produce a naturally blurred reflection. When glossiness is applied, raytracers randomize and shoot rays over a range of different directions when rendering a reflection.

Glossy reflections can initially appear with some dithering or noise from all of the randomly scattered reflection rays. To correct this, raise the number of samples or rays that are cast in the reflection. Calculating more rays can greatly increase rendering time, but it produces a smoother, more realistic reflection.

Reflection Limits

In a scene where there any many reflective or refractive surfaces, there is a risk that a raytracer could get caught in an infinite loop, forever tracing a ray from one surface to another. Figure 9.19 shows a situation where mirrors on each wall of a room reflect one another. In order to render the mirror on the right, the raytracer must include the reflection of the left mirror, which in turn requires a calculation of the left mirror's reflection of the right mirror, which again reflects the left mirror, and so on. As the rays of light seem to bounce infinitely between mirrors, the scene could take an infinite amount of time to raytrace.

[Figure 9.19]
Mirrors facing each other can create an infinite loop in raytracing.

To prevent the renderer from looping endlessly, the number of raytracing steps needs to be strictly limited. Because raytracing can have such a huge impact on your rendering time, many programs limit the number of reflections twice. First, they are limited globally in your rendering settings, where you set a maximum number of reflections and total raytracing steps. Second, raytracing is also limited per shader; a reflective shader will have a *reflection limit* (also called a *recursion depth* or *trace depth*) set as a raytracing option.

If you need to see light inter-reflect several times between surfaces, use a higher number on both the shaders and your global settings. Raising these numbers can make raytracing slower, but using too low a value can hurt the realism of your scene by causing missing reflections within reflections. You don't want the audience to notice a missing reflection if they spy a reflective object while looking in a mirror, but you also don't want to slow down your rendering by tracing unnecessary steps that don't add appreciably to the image.

A sensible approach to adjusting your reflection limits is to test-render your scene, starting with high enough values on your shaders and your render settings so that you are sure you are seeing all visible reflections. You might start at 8, then raise them by 1, and see if there's any noticeable difference between the two values. If you are still noticing a difference that you care about, use an even higher value. If you can't see a difference you care about, try lowering the numbers and see if lower values such as 3 or 4 look good to you. You may notice the difference in rendering speed as you make these adjustments, but make sure your values are high enough that you aren't omitting anything the audience will miss.

Shadows

Chapter 3 described how raytraced shadows differ from *shadow-mapped* (also called *depth-mapped*) shadows. Here is a summary of the main differences:

- Shadow-mapped shadows generally render more quickly and use less memory than raytraced shadows.

- Raytraced shadows can remain crisp and accurate at any resolution rendering, whereas shadow maps have a limited resolution.

- Transparent and transparency-mapped objects can cast transparent shadows with raytracing. Most implementations of shadow maps ignore the level of transparency in an object.

- When raytraced shadows are made soft, they become diffused with distance in a very realistic way—but at a substantial cost in rendering time. Soft shadow maps are filtered uniformly and appear less realistic.

Flip back to Chapter 3 if you want to read more about shadows.

Depth Mapped Shadows and Raytracing

Depth mapped shadows are completely compatible with raytracing. You can continue to use depth mapped shadows when you switch over to using raytracing; you can see them in raytraced reflections and through refractive surfaces, without making any special adjustments.

If a scene is already using raytracing for other effects such as reflections or refraction, then the extra memory it takes up has already been used, and therefore, using raytraced shadows can be just as efficient a solution as depth maps. However, if your scene includes elements such as hair, fur, or dense foliage, you may want to exclude those from any raytracing and use depth mapped shadows for the shadows of those elements.

Trace Depth and Number of Shadows

Raytraced shadows do not necessarily appear in reflections or through refractive surfaces unless the light's *ray depth limit* (also called *trace depth* or *number of shadows*) is high enough. A level of 1 makes the shadow appear when it is seen directly, but not in reflections. A level of 2 makes the shadow also appear indirectly in reflections or refractions. Setting the light's ray depth limit higher makes the shadow visible even through multiple layers of refractive glass or in a reflection of a reflection, as long as you add a level for each layer of glass, which can be necessary in scenes with lots of glassware or environments full of metal, chrome, or mirrors. As with the reflection limits for your reflectivity itself, it's worth test-rendering your scene to see how high a value you need to make sure there aren't any noticeable missing shadows in your reflections.

Transparency and Refraction

When making an object transparent, you have the same concern as you do with raytraced reflections: The object's surroundings affect the shading. A transparent surface left in limbo in an all-black environment appears darker as it becomes more transparent. Make sure that you will be able to see another object or background behind the object once it becomes transparent.

Refraction is a raytracing effect that adds a lens-like distortion to the image seen through a transparent surface. Just like an optical lens, when using refraction, your 3D models focus rays differently depending on their shape and proportions. The models in Figure 9.20 focus rays differently due to their different shapes. How concave or convex a model is, and whether you look through a single surface or both a front and back surface, will produce completely different refractions.

Index of Refraction

Besides the shape of the model, the other factor governing refraction is a number called the *index of refraction*. Figure 9.21 shows an object rendered with several different index of refraction values. A value of 1 gives you no refraction, allowing rays to pass straight through the object. As you set values further above or below 1, the amount of refraction increases. For a convex surface, such as a sphere, values above 1 make it enlarge the refracted image, like a magnifying glass, while values below 1 make the refracted image shrink.

[Figure 9.20]
All using an IOR of 1.44, differently shaped models produce different refraction effects.

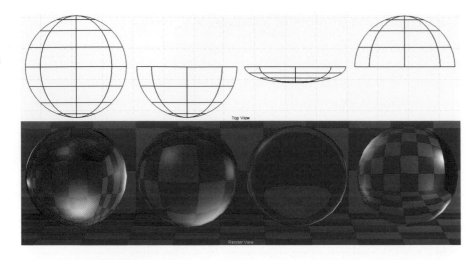

[Figure 9.21]
From left to right, vases are rendered with an index of refraction of 1 (no refraction), 1.04, 1.15, and 1.44 (glass). There is no difference in the transparency of the vases—the black edges appearing on the right are purely a function of refraction from the environment.

Table 9.1 lists some common materials and their indices of refraction (IORs). Refraction happens when light leaves one kind of material and enters another, such as leaving air and entering glass, or leaving water and entering air. Because of this, IOR values are all relative to two materials and describe light bending as it travels out of one material and into another. The values in Table 9.1 are based on the listed material surrounded by air, with one exception: The listing of "Air (from under water)" might be used at a water surface when looking up at air, or on bubbles of air seen underwater.

MATERIAL	INDEX OF REFRACTION (IOR)
Air (from under water)	0.75
Air/Neutral	1.00
Smoke	1.02
Ice	1.30
Water	1.33
Glass	1.44
Quartz	1.55
Ruby	1.77
Crystal	2.00
Diamond	2.42
Daylight (sun and sky)	5,500–6,500
Sun, through clouds/haze	5,500–6,500
Sky, overcast	6,000–7,500
RGB monitor (white point)	6,500
Outdoor shade areas	7,000–8,000
Sky, partly cloudy	8,000–10,000

[Table 9.1] Useful Index of Refraction (IOR) Settings for Materials

The numbers in Table 9.1 are useful starting points, but you will probably make most adjustments based on sight. You need to see the refraction on your own model before you can be sure that the index of refraction gives you the look you want.

Colored Refraction

In real life, different frequencies of light refract at different angles. You'll recall from Chapter 6 that this difference is what's responsible for chromatic aberration in lenses. Blue light tends to refract as if a material had a slightly higher index of refraction, and red light tends to refract as if the material had a slightly lower index of refraction. The rainbows of colors that you see through a prism or in a diamond come from this effect in refraction.

Some shaders contain an option called *dispersion* or *chromatic aberration* that adds multicolored refraction. Figure 9.22 shows the difference that colored refraction makes.

[Figure 9.22]
Without optical dispersion
(left) refraction works in
black and white, whereas
with optical dispersion
(right) you see different
wavelengths of light
refracted differently.

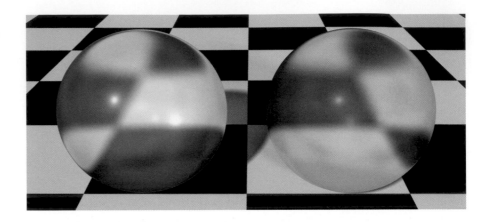

Refraction Limits

As with reflections and raytraced shadows, you must also limit refraction.
However, at times you need to set refraction limits quite high so the audience can see through all of the refractive surfaces in a scene. Figure 9.23
shows a scene where a refraction limit of 2 (left) is not enough to see
through a rack of glass plates. Upping the limit to 8 (right) allows us to
look through all of the plates.

[Figure 9.23]
Too low a trace depth (left)
makes some objects seem
less transparent, whereas a
higher trace depth (right)
lets you see through all the
refractive objects.

Count how many surfaces you need to see through that are refractive, and
set the refraction limits on the shader. Set global limits on the number of
refraction steps to be high enough for the audience to see through all of
the layers in your scene. As with all trace depth issues, you need to do test-
renders to see how many steps you really need.

Reyes Algorithms

A *Reyes algorithm* is the heart of Pixar's RenderMan, which for years has been considered a leading renderer for high-end feature film work. Other renderers have also adopted Reyes and Reyes-type algorithms.

The core elements of a Reyes renderer were originally developed in the 1980s by by Lucasfilm's Computer Graphics Research Group, the initial group of people who later became Pixar Animation Studios.

Reyes stands for *Renders Everything You Ever Saw.* That acronym was conceived by a researcher while swimming in the waters of Point Reyes, an area near Lucasfilm in Marin County, California. The algorithm was designed to make possible a high level of detail, smooth curved surfaces, displacement mapping with pixel-level detail, motion blur, and depth of field—all key aspects of producing realistic graphics for film—within the speed and memory limitations of that era's computers.

Reyes renders curved surfaces, such as those represented by NURBS or subdivision surfaces, by dividing them into *micropolygons*, small quadrilaterals each about one pixel in size or smaller. Each curved surface is divided into exactly enough micropolygons to appear completely smooth at the rendered resolution. If a shader is applying displacement mapping, the displacement will also be broken down into micropolygons.

Next, the software evaluates the shader and assigns a color and opacity to each micropolygon. It applies all of your lighting, shadows, and texture mapping at this stage. For example, a specular highlight might cause a white micropolygon. If a part of a texture map contains a green pixel, it can contribute to a green micropolygon.

The renderer samples shaded micropolygons in screen space to produce the rendered image. Sampling the micropolygons after they have been shaded does not take very long. It is important to contrast this with popular raytracers such as Mental Ray, which need to shoot twice as many rays into the scene, which requires twice the render time, so they can double the amount of over-sampling. As a result, you can achieve fine-quality anti-aliasing easily with a Reyes algorithm without causing as big a slowdown as you could experience in Mental Ray. You can also achieve effects such as motion blur and depth of field, which typically require a large number of samples to render smoothly, without adding inordinately to the rendering time. This makes rendering with both motion blur and depth of field a practical solution in a Reyes renderer like RenderMan, whereas users of other software often try to render without effects like these and then simulate them during compositing.

A Reyes algorithm typically divides an image into *buckets,* or groups of about 16 pixels by 16 pixels. Division into micropolygons, shading, and rendering are done one bucket at a time. As a result, entire objects or scenes of micropolygons do not need to be stored in memory at once; instead you can create them as needed for each bucket and then clear them from memory after the bucket is rendered.

The RenderMan Interface Standard

When Pixar created RenderMan, they didn't just create a piece of rendering software. They also created the *RenderMan Interface standard.* In much the same way that HTML is a language to describe websites or PostScript describes printed pages, the RenderMan Interface standard was created as a way to describe a 3D scene to be rendered.

Key components of the RenderMan Interface standard are

- .rib (RenderMan Interface Bytestream) files, which contain scene descriptions

- A shading language to describe RenderMan shaders in .sl files

Companies other than Pixar also make their own *RenderMan-compliant renderers,* which follow the RenderMan Interface standard and can produce renderings from the same files as Pixar's RenderMan. These other RenderMan-compliant renderers include RenderDotC, 3Delight, and Aqsis (which is free). Most major animation and modeling packages can output files to be rendered in a RenderMan-compliant renderer, either natively or through a plug-in.

Reyes and Raytracing

Historically, most Reyes rendering has been done without raytracing. In many feature films that you have seen rendered with Reyes algorithms, all of the shadows have been depth mapped shadows and all reflections have been reflection maps. A main idea behind Reyes algorithms—rendering one bucket at a time without needing to hold polygons in memory for the whole scene—works well if rays are not bouncing around the scene requiring random access to other objects in a reflection, refraction, or shadow.

In more recent years, raytracing is common in feature film production. Full support for raytracing and GI has been added to Pixar's RenderMan and other RenderMan-compliant renderers so that today raytracing often coexists with the Reyes algorithm. However, some studios still employ raytracing only when it is needed and combine it with non-raytraced elements when some parts of a production don't need raytracing and can be rendered faster without it.

Global Illumination

Global illumination (GI) is any rendering algorithm that simulates the inter-reflection of light between surfaces. When rendering with GI, you don't need to add bounce lights to simulate indirect light, because the software calculates indirect light for you based on the direct illumination hitting surfaces in your scene.

Contrast the term global illumination with *local illumination*. Most rendering software uses local illumination as the default, unless you activate a GI function. In local illumination, your rendering software considers only the surface currently being rendered and the lights directly illuminating it without taking into account any other surfaces.

Using local illumination, if you add a single light to a scene, pointing down at the floor, then all of the light in the scene will be down where the light is aimed. This is illustrated on the left side of Figure 9.24.

Simply using raytracing, such as for raytraced shadows and reflections, is generally not considered GI. Even though a raytraced reflection can fit with the broad definition of having indirect light contribute to the rendering of a surface, only techniques in which indirect light can add to the diffuse illumination of objects are generally referred to as global illumination.

[Figure 9.24]
With local illumination (left), only the light coming from the light source itself illuminates the scene. Adding global illumination (right) allows indirect light from other surfaces to contribute to the illumination.

On the right side of Figure 9.24, you can see that light is bouncing off the walls and other colored objects, adding indirect illumination to the scene. I did not need to add bounce lights manually; the software performed the entire simulation of indirect light.

A phenomenon called *color bleeding* is visible in many renderings with GI. In real life, color bleeding is always happening around us as light reflects off of differently colored surfaces. However, color bleeding is a subtle effect that is often unnoticeable. The situation in which you can most readily see color bleeding is when a brightly colored surface is much more brightly lit than a nearby white or gray surface. Figure 9.25 is a photograph in which natural color bleeding is visible. In the photograph, a sunbeam illuminates a red carpet brightly enough to cause red light to bounce up onto the white sofa.

Sometimes GI renderings contain an unrealistic amount of color bleeding. For example, in Figure 9.26, the green cube almost appears to glow and illuminate the rest of the scene. The culprit is usually too much saturation in the shader, too bright a color for your GI scale, or too high a photon intensity coming from your lights.

The basic workflow for lighting with GI starts out the same as for lighting without it. Start by using a linear workflow, as described in Chapter 8. Add direct lights, such as practical lights that represent ceiling lights in your set, light from the sun, and light from the sky. Then, instead of adding bounce lights, turn on and adjust your software's GI; it essentially adds all of the bounce lighting for you. Figure 9.27 shows an example of this process. In this example, only one light is used: a single area light positioned just below the ceiling panel. After that, GI is responsible for all of the indirect light.

[Figure 9.25] A bit of color bleeding is visible when a sunbeam brightens a red carpet right below a white sofa in an otherwise dim room.

[Figure 9.26] Too much color bleeding, making an environment look as if it had been painted with a glossy paint, can be a problem in badly adjusted GI.

[Figure 9.27] Only one light is used in this scene, so areas such as the ceiling appear dark when rendered with local illumination only. Turning on GI illuminates the rest of the scene with indirect light.

The difference between a test-render with only local illumination and your final render with GI can be dramatic. If you plan to use GI, your own light sources can leave much of the scene in shadow. Your initial test can look contrasty and bleak, with large black areas where the lights aren't aimed directly. The GI fills in the black areas, making the whole scene brighter and softening the illumination so that it wraps around more of the geometry in the scene.

There are a number of different types of GI, including *radiosity, photon mapping, final gathering,* and *caustics.*

Conventional Radiosity

Radiosity was one of the first types of global illumination to be implemented in commercially available rendering software. Although it is not the best or the most popular technique in modern software, the word *radiosity* became very famous. Some people have even incorrectly referred to all GI solutions as radiosity, just because they heard of radiosity first. As an example of this, the lighting style that simulates GI by adding bounce lights became known as *simulated radiosity* because of radiosity's early popularity.

Radiosity is calculated progressively so that light can bounce as many times as you need to create a refined, accurate simulation of real lighting. The number of bounces in a progressive radiosity solution is limited only by the amount of time available to compute the radiosity solution; it keeps running and calculating more light bounces forever, or at least until you interrupt it.

Radiosity is usually calculated by storing shading information for each vertex of the polygonal objects in a scene. Figure 9.28 shows how a scene is subdivided during the radiosity calculation. More vertices are added where additional detail is needed in the shading, such as at the edges of shadows or highlight areas.

A disadvantage of this approach is that the resolution of your geometry is linked with the resolution of your GI solution. It is difficult to compute a quick approximation of the lighting for a scene with a high polygon count. The radiosity solution and subdivision of the geometry are also very difficult to recompute at each frame for an animated sequence if major objects in a scene are moving.

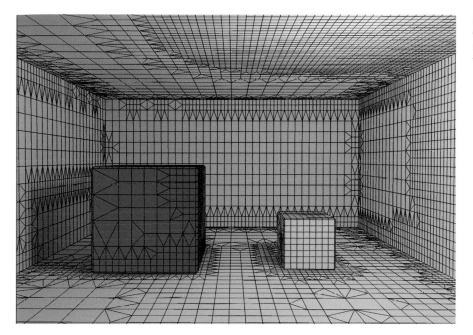

[Figure 9.28]
Conventional radiosity stores irradiance information in polygon vertices.

Radiosity never became a very popular GI solution in the entertainment industry, but it did become popular with architects. Architects often need to render *fly-throughs*, animations in which nothing moves except for the camera, and for that they can compute radiosity only once and use the solution in every frame of the animation. In the film industry, animation usually involves moving geometry, so other GI solutions, such as photon mapping, have become more popular.

Photon Mapping

You can render the same kind of results that conventional radiosity calculates via *photon mapping*. With this approach to GI, the renderer creates a separate data type—the *photon map* to store the GI solution. The resolution of a photon-mapped solution is independent from the resolution of the geometry.

The speed and accuracy of photon-mapped GI depends on the number of photons you use. Extra photons take longer to compute, so for quick test-renders while you are setting up GI, start with a lower number of photons. When you render with fewer photons, the results look blotchy, as shown on the left side of Figure 9.29; the individual photons seem like paintballs splattered onto every surface in the scene. As you turn up the number of photons, the results become smoother, more realistic, and less blotchy, as shown on the right side of the figure—however, keep in mind that rendering with a higher photon counts takes longer.

[Figure 9.29]
Photon mapping with a low photon count (left) is very blotchy but gets smoother with a high photon count (right).

You can think of photons in a photon map as very small particles of light. Photons can bounce around a scene in a GI solution and are stored in a photon map where they bounce off of each surface. Photons don't necessarily duplicate all of the rules of real physics. For example, photons in CG can vary in size from pixel-sized dots up to the size of golf balls or sometimes basketballs. You can use a small number of photons set to a larger size for quick tests, and then use more photons for a more accurate final rendering. Most software has an adjustable photon size or radius, and also can choose a size automatically if the radius is left at 0. In this case, the size varies depending on the number of photons and the size of the surface to be covered.

You can set as many lights as you want to emit photons. Ideally, all of the lights that are responsible for direct illumination in your scene should emit photons. It does not take any longer to render with two lights each emitting 50,000 photons than to render with one light emitting 100,000 photons, so don't worry about distributing your photon emission among the relevant lights. Your brightest lights should generally emit the most photons, while you may need fewer photons for dimmer fill lights.

By itself, photon mapping can produce good results if you use enough photons. However, smooth renders sometimes require a huge number of photons, which makes them very slow to render. To solve this problem, use photon mapping in conjunction with final gathering.

Final Gathering

Final gathering is a rendering option you can use in conjunction with photon-mapped GI to smooth out your results, producing continuous illumination instead of the blotchy output you get when you use photon mapping alone. The left side of Figure 9.30 shows a scene with photon-mapped GI; on the right, you can see the smoother results of turning on final gathering.

[Figure 9.30]
Final gathering smoothes out photon-mapped GI.

Final gathering does two basic things:

- If you're using photon-mapped GI, it filters and smoothes out the result to prevent blotchiness.

- It functions as a GI solution unto itself, adding an extra bounce of indirect light.

Final gathering performs both of these tasks by starting at each point on a surface being rendered, and looking in all directions to see what is visible from that point. You adjust how many rays or samples are taken by final gathering to determine how many different directions it looks in the scene. When final gathering is sampling rays in different directions, it looks at the color and illumination on nearby surfaces to add to the GI, and it also looks at nearby photons in a photon map so that it can filter and smooth out photon-mapped GI.

To use final gathering in conjunction with photon mapping, usually it's best to save the final gathering step for last. Adjust your photon-mapped GI until the photon intensity (brightness) looks good to you and you have a number of photons that accurately capture all of the indirect light bounces that you need in the scene. If the GI still looks a little blotchy, then, as a finishing touch, turn on final gathering to smooth out the results.

You can also use final gathering by itself, without any photon-mapped GI. This is an approach that keeps getting more and more viable. In the Mental Ray renderer, final gathering was used mainly to smooth out photon-mapped GI, but with each newer version of the software, the final gathering function became more powerful and capable. It now lets you adjust the number of bounces that final gathering calculates so that indirect light can bounce from one surface to another a number of times, not just for a single bounce. This can greatly simplify the process of setting up GI, because you don't need to set each light to emit photons or worry about the number of photons emitted into your scene. An increasingly popular approach to rendering GI is just to turn on final gathering by itself and adjust it in the render settings until the quality is high enough that it doesn't look blotchy.

Unbiased Renderers

Modern renderers employ different caching schemes to store information about indirect illumination. Photon mapping was the first popular example, but different software also offer irradiance maps, light caches, baked spherical harmonics, and other approaches. New software is always being written with different acceleration techniques, but the main idea behind all of them is to allow GI rendering to be completed more quickly. Such techniques provide a quick way to sample the amount and color of the indirect illumination around any point being rendered, without requiring the software to recompute shading on all the nearby objects just to evaluate their contribution to the indirect light. These solutions can work well, but they also can introduce artifacts into renderings and create a level of indirectness in how the GI is calculated that might make the solution differ from the most realistic possible output.

An *unbiased renderer* is a renderer that does not use any of these caching approaches. Instead, it works more straightforwardly with a technique such as *path tracing,* which starts at the camera, shoots a number of rays per pixel, and then, through randomized sampling, computes the indirect and direct light contribution to each pixel. When you use such a renderer with physically based shaders and position lights where real lights would exist in the scene, the result can look just like a photograph. The only artifact you should see is noise, resembling a grainy photograph, when too few paths are traced; but employing more samples fixes this. Once you use enough samples, the renderer is not biased with any other artifacts that can cause blurring or blotches due to caching techniques or incomplete sampling of the indirect light.

Variations on unbiased rendering include *bidirectional path tracing,* which computes rays of light starting at the light sources as well as starting at the camera. Both kinds of path tracing can converge on the correct result when enough rays are sampled. Computing rays in both directions might sound less efficient, but it actually can show gains in overall efficiency.

Software algorithms can be optimized in many ways to maximize quality, so the lack of caching mechanisms does not mean that all unbiased renderers are equal in speed or performance. Sometimes rendering without a caching or acceleration structure has been dismissed as "brute force" rendering, as if it were too slow to use in a real production. The popularity of Solid Angle's Arnold software in a growing number of feature film productions shows that unbiased renderers are now mainstream tools in film production. As path tracing becomes possible even in real-time for some scenes, hardware and software advances are rapidly putting to rest the need to compromise our output in pursuit of faster rendering times.

A great increase in productivity and efficiency is possible when lighting artists can think more like live-action cinematographers who are focusing on positioning and adjusting lights, rather than spending much of their time performing technical adjustments and cheats designed to speed-up rendering, trying to reduce artifacts, or trying to simulate more convincing bounce lighting. Although newer rendering techniques can demand more computation per frame than rendering techniques used in previous years, they also allow lighting artists to produce more believable output with less human labor.

Caustics

Caustics are a visibly different type of indirect light compared to other kinds of GI. They are a type of indirect light that remains focused, instead of being diffusely scattered in all directions. Caustics are distinctive in that they have a shape or pattern, instead of being scattered into soft, diffuse illumination.

Whereas the previous sections have described approaches to simulating diffuse-to-diffuse light transfer, caustics simulate specular-to-diffuse light transfer. By diffuse-to-diffuse light transfer, I mean the situations in which light diffusely reflects off of one surface, and that contributes to the diffuse illumination of another surface. Specular-to-diffuse light transfer is when light is bounced off of a mirror or other shiny surface and casts a pattern that contributes to the diffuse illumination of another surface.

In addition to indirectly reflected light, caustic patterns can also be created by refraction. When light refracts through glass, water, or other transparent media, the pattern it forms is a caustic pattern.

When you start looking for them, you will see that caustics are all around you in the real world:

- Light that refracts through a lens, magnifying glass, or prism is a caustic effect. You often see refracted caustics on top of a table next to glasses and bottles.

- Beams of light reflecting off a mirror are caustics, as are all the little glints of light reflected off a disco ball.

- Any shiny or highly specular surface creates caustic effects when hit by a bright light. On a sunny day, a car's chrome bumper or a building's window will create caustic patterns on the ground.

- The throw pattern of lights with built-in reflectors, including flash-lights and car headlights, are broken up with caustic patterns from the reflected light. (This kind of effect is commonly simulated by mapping a cookie onto the light, but in real life, these are caustic patterns.)

- Caustic patterns are perhaps best known for being the patterns reflected onto walls near water surfaces (as shown in Figure 9.31) or refracted into shimmering patterns on the bottom of swimming pools.

[Figure 9.31]
Caustics are best known
for shimmering water
reflections.

Figure 9.32 shows two photographs of real-life caustics. On the left is an
example of refracted caustics, caused by light traveling through a transparent bottle. On the right is an example of reflected caustics, caused by light
bouncing off windows and metal panels on a building. You can see the most
caustic patterns during hours when the sun is low in the sky, creating a lot
of contrast between surfaces that receive sunlight and areas in shadow where
caustics show up.

One way that some renderers compute caustics is through photon mapping.
If your renderer uses photon mapping to render caustics, then you will find
that issues discussed earlier for photon-mapped GI apply to caustics. Turning
up the number of photons emitted from a light makes more accurate, less
blotchy caustic patterns. Rendering caustic photons along with final gathering provides smoother, more accurate results than photon-mapped caustics
by themselves.

Figure 9.33 shows what a difference caustics can make in rendering a scene that features a transparent product.

Back in Chapter 3, I mentioned that an advantage of raytraced shadows was that they pass through transparent surfaces so that the shadow is lighter, and the shadow can even pick up a color when the light shines through colored transparency. If you are going to use caustics, however, the caustics themselves offer a more complete simulation of light refracting through the transparent object. The raytraced shadow can become fully black, even though the object is transparent, and the caustics you add fill in the shadow area with the light that has refracted through the object. Figure 9.34 shows the key light illumination (including a black shadow) and the caustics pass that were used in Figure 9.33. Luckily, the feature of having transparency included in raytraced shadows (called "direct illumination shadow effects" in Mental Ray) is turned off by default when you activate caustics, so the refracted caustics are all the light that crosses through into your shadow areas.

[Figure 9.33]
Without caustics (left), the bottle looks dry and opaque. Adding caustics (right) conveys the impression that light has refracted through the liquid. This scene is Lighting Challenge #11, modeled by Anthony Thomas.

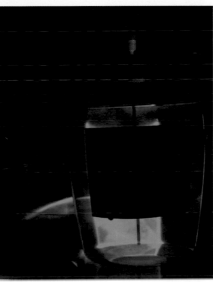

[Figure 9.34]
The key light (left) has a completely black shadow, with no shadow transparency effect. The caustics (right) add a simulation of light refracting through liquid.

You can use caustics in conjunction with full GI to add convincing glints of indirect specular light to the bounced diffuse added by other GI techniques. Caustics are relatively quick and simple to add and tend to render faster than full GI. Also, they are often the brightest, most noticeable part of the indirect lighting in a scene. Because of this, even if you have a scene in which you are not using GI, it still makes sense to include caustics if you might have glints of light created by reflective, shiny, or transparent surfaces.

Figure 9.35 shows the fill light pass and occlusion pass that I used to simulate indirect lighting. I created an occlusion sandwich with this fill light and occlusion, with the key light pass from Figure 9.34 added on top. Adding the caustics completed the impression of light refracting through a green liquid.

[Figure 9.35]
A fill layer (left) and occlusion pass (right) are the other necessary ingredients for an occlusion sandwich.

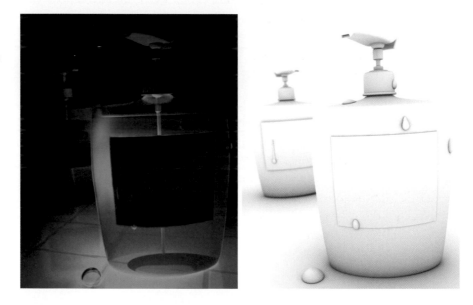

Exercises

If you want to become truly obsessive about realistic rendering, try to think throughout the day of how you would render everything that you see around you.

1. The caustics example used in the last three figures of this chapter uses a Lighting Challenge scene that you can download from www.3dRender.com/challenges and try lighting yourself. Once you start thinking about caustics, you see them all around you, especially when you are around water or in cities during times when the sun is low in the sky. If you haven't been using them in your renderings, this is a good time to start.

2. Look at the surfaces in the room around you. If you were re-creating them in 3D, how many of them would need to be reflective? Of those, how many would use a glossy reflection? For the surfaces that you didn't see as reflective, do any of them become more reflective when viewed at a glancing angle?

3. People often guess what material something is supposed to be made out of based on the context. They guess that a shader assigned to a car is supposed to be painted metal and that the shader on the tires is supposed to be rubber, even if both shaders look a bit more like plastic. If you want an honest opinion about your shaders, assign some of them to a ball (or other primitive shape), so that when you show them to people, they do not get any hints from context; then ask other people what material they think each ball is made of.

CHAPTER TEN

Designing and Assigning Textures

Texture mapping is the art of adding variation and detail to 3D surfaces that goes beyond the level of detail modeled into the geometry. This chapter will discuss the types of textures you can create, how to align textures with your models, and different ways to create textures.

As noted in the Introduction of this book, you can download this chapter from the Registered Products tab on your Account page at www.peachpit.com. Refer to the book's Introduction for further details.

CHAPTER ELEVEN

Rendering in Layers and Passes for Compositing

Professional productions created with 3D graphics are usually not rendered all as a single image. Instead, it's more common to split a scene into separate elements called layers or passes, which you can combine together into a completed final shot using compositing. If you are working on visual effects for movies or television, then you need to composite the 3D elements that you light and render into live-action scenes to seamlessly integrate your creations into real environments. Compositing isn't just for visual effects production, though. Companies making productions that are entirely animated also split their 3D scenes into multiple layers or passes, which are rendered separately, and then assemble them into complete shots through compositing.

  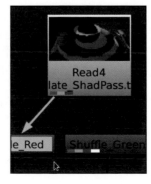 

You can split up a scene in different ways: You can split your scene into different render layers that each contain different objects, such as foreground and background layers; you can split your scene into different render passes that each contain an aspect of the scene such as reflections, occlusion, or global illumination; or you could render lighting passes so that the illumination from each light source was rendered into its own pass. All of these approaches are discussed in this chapter, along with the creative options that each approach opens up to give you greater creative control over your final product.

In order to apply the techniques discussed in this chapter, you need some compositing software. A dedicated node-based compositor such as Nuke would be ideal for all of your 3D compositing, but there are many other choices. Some 3D programs, including Softimage, Houdini, and Blender, include built-in node-based compositing, so you can render elements and composite them all within the same program. Maya comes bundled with Maya Composite (formerly called Toxik), which is a node-based compositing package suitable for putting together your render layers and passes. After Effects is immensely popular for motion graphics, but you can also use it for compositing and visual effects work. For the purpose of learning how to composite together what you render, you can even use Adobe Photoshop. Photoshop is designed to work primarily with still images, not animated sequences; however, you can perform all of the necessary operations with it to assemble multiple layers and passes. I've included notes in this chapter about how to use Photoshop to practice compositing.

Rendering in Layers

Rendering in layers just means you organize the objects in your scene so that they render into different image files, instead of rendering one image that includes the full scene. Here are some common examples of how you can split a scene into layers:

- Render animated characters in one layer, and render the set or environment around them into another layer.

- Sort objects into render layers based on distance from the camera to render foreground, midground, and background layers.

- Split very bright objects, such as the sky, neon tubes, or other light sources, into separate render layers from other objects so that you can later apply blooms or glows around them in compositing.

As a simple example of rendering in layers, Figure 11.1 shows how you could render the robot. The robot appears over a black background (left) and is rendered with an alpha channel (right). The *alpha channel* is the channel of the image file that stores transparency information that you can use in compositing.

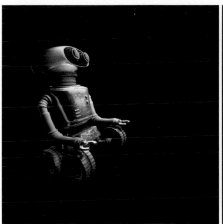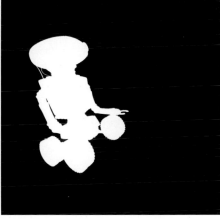

[Figure 11.1]
A foreground layer (left) is rendered along with an alpha channel (right).

The other layer is just the background image, showing everything in the scene that appears behind the robot, as shown in Figure 11.2. The foreground and background layers are both part of the same 3D scene, are staged and animated together, and are rendered using the same camera. During rendering, however, you can render the layers one at a time.

When compositing, you layer the foreground image from Figure 11.1 over the background image from Figure 11.2. The parts of the robot image marked by white pixels in the alpha channel will be opaque, and the parts of the image that have black pixels in the alpha channel will be transparent. The composited result is shown in Figure 11.3.

[Figure 11.2] The background layer includes everything but the character.

[Figure 11.3] Compositing the foreground layer over the background forms a complete scene.

Why Bother with Layers?

Rendering in layers clearly involves more setup work than rendering all the objects in a scene at once. You might wonder why most professional productions are rendered in multiple layers. Couldn't busy professionals skip the process of rendering in layers and save more time by not needing to composite? Actually, there are several advantages to rendering in layers:

- Rendering in layers makes large, complex scenes possible. Your computer's memory can be overloaded if all objects have to be rendered at once. Without layers, huge projects could either slow down the computer as it swaps data from its hard drive or crash it completely.

- Using held layers (discussed later in this section) saves rendering time compared to rerendering static objects for each frame of your animation.

- For high-quality character animation, most of your rerenders are likely to apply to the character, not the background. In this case, you can quickly rerender the character as a foreground layer without rerendering the full scene.

- For a soft-focused background, you can sometimes get away with blurring the background layer in your compositing program instead of rendering with a slow depth of field (DOF) effect in 3D.

- For maximum rendering efficiency, you can render different layers using different software settings. For example, you might use motion blur and raytracing on layers where you need them. You may render more distant objects, or objects that you plan to blur during compositing, in a manner more optimized for speed.

- You can perform last-minute fixes, such as adjusting the color or brightness of a part of your scene, more easily by adjusting individual layers in your composite, rather than rerendering your whole scene.

- To work around bugs, limitations, or incompatibilities in your software, split different effects into different render layers. For example, if you use an effect that does not render through a transparent surface, you can render the effect as a separate layer and then composite the transparent foreground layer over it.

Although including layer rendering and compositing in your pipeline takes effort to set up, it can save time and money once it becomes a regular part of your workflow.

Using Layer Overrides

In many cases, you need some shader or setting in your scene to change when a particular render layer renders. Many programs support overrides, either as a built-in feature of their render layer management, or as an available plug-in that manages render layers. If you don't have software support for overrides that accompany render layers, you can still make the same changes to scene settings or shader assignments, but you need to make them manually before you render each layer.

One common type of override is to change the visibility of an object or group in a particular render layer. Notice that in Figure 11.3 the robot casts a shadow and a reflection onto the ground. If you want a character to cast shadows and reflections into a render layer, then the character needs to be present in that render layer. A layer override lets you set a character so it is not directly visible, even though it is present to cast shadows and appear in raytracing in that layer. Figure 11.4 shows the render layer overrides I added to the robot as it appeared in the background layer. In Maya, overrides are indicated by using orange text in the parameter names. I only needed to override the setting to make it not directly visible, and I left all the other settings at their defaults.

[Figure 11.4]
Layer overrides let you tweak visibility or other settings for objects in specific render layers.

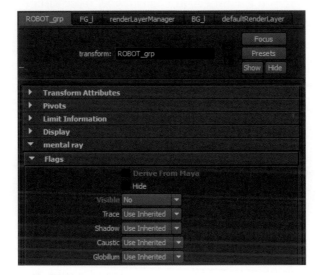

Holding Layers

If the camera is static and you are rendering a layer in which nothing moves during the shot, then you can *hold* the layer. Holding the layer means rendering the layer only at one frame (usually the first frame of the shot), and then compositing that still image together with the fully animated layers. Because the held layer needs to be rendered only once, instead of being rendered again at all the other frames of the shot, this saves a lot of rendering time.

If you have groups of objects in your shot that don't move or change at all, then you can put those in a separate render layer and hold that layer. However, this is something that you'll find possible in some scenes, but not in others. If the environment around the robot appeared in an animated feature, it's likely that the director would ask you to make some of the lights on the walls flicker or blink, or to animate the giant fan on the ceiling so that there was motion in the set. In high-quality productions, it is only possible to hold layers in a small minority of shots, because so many of the environments are likely to be animated in some way.

Matte Objects

The easiest way to break down your scene into layers is to start with the farthest objects back and work your way toward the front of the scene. However, sometimes objects don't fit neatly into a back-to-front ordering. For example, imagine you are splitting the grass into a different layer from the egg in Figure 11.5; the grass is both in front of and behind the egg.

When one layer surrounds another in space and it isn't clear what is in front of or behind the surrounded layer, you may need to render some of the objects as *matte objects*. A matte object is an object that renders pure black and also appears pure black in the alpha channel. Many shaders have an *alpha* or *matte opacity* setting that you can turn down to pure black for a black alpha.

[Figure 11.5]
The grass layer extends into both the foreground and the background around the egg.

Figure 11.6 shows the grass rendered with the egg as a matte object. In this case, the grass layer is composited over the egg layer to produce the result in Figure 11.5. Even though the grass layer is composited over the egg, the hole in the grass layer cut by the matte object ensures that the egg appears to be in front of some of the grass.

[Figure 11.6]
Rendering the egg as a matte object; it appears as a black hole in the grass layer (left) and its alpha channel (right).

You can achieve similar results if you render the egg with the grass as a matte object, so that the egg had the grass cut out of it. In this case, you composite the egg layer over the grass layer, instead of the other way around. Using the ground and ground coverings as matte objects is common in rendering animated characters so that when their feet are composited over the ground, the bottoms of their feet can be occluded by appropriate parts of the terrain.

An alternative approach to rendering with matte objects is to include all of the objects in all the layers, and in each layer, make all of the objects be matte objects except for the main subject of the layer. Figure 11.7 shows an example of this approach. The set is rendered with the robot as a matte object (left), then the robot is rendered with the set as a matte object (center). You can create a complete composite (right) by simply adding together the two layers in a compositing program. If you take this approach, then you don't even need to use any alpha channels to combine the layers; simply add the layers together to get a perfect composite no matter which objects are in front of or behind other objects.

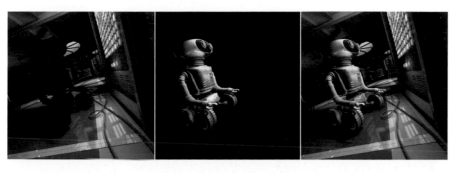

[Figure 11.7]
An alternative way to render layers uses the character as a matte object in the background layer (left) and the environment as a matte object in the character layer (center), so both can be added together with no alpha channel needed (right).

Adding Glows

A *glow* (also called a *bloom*) is a softly brightened area that surrounds bright spots in your image. Although most 3D software offers the option of adding glows around objects or lights in your rendering, it's best to add glows during compositing instead. Adding glows during compositing gives you a quick, efficient, and highly controllable way to adjust the size, brightness, and saturation of each glow as you add it to the completed scene.

If you plan to add glows during compositing, it's useful to render the brightest light sources in your scene as a separate layer. Figure 11.8 shows the ceiling lights and lit-up control panels rendered as a separate layer. Just blur this image and add it to your composite, and you'll get nice glows around each bright light source, as shown in Figure 11.9.

If you're using Photoshop to add glows, then the blending mode is called Linear Dodge instead of just Add. Photoshop's Field Blur filter gives you nice control over bokeh-like effects that let you create little beads of light around light sources; you may like this kind of glow better than what you get from an ordinary Gaussian blur. You may also wish to boost the saturation of your blurred light sources to bring out the color of colored lights.

[Figure 11.8] Light sources that need glows around them are rendered as a separate layer.

[Figure 11.9]
Glows are added around
all the light sources in
the scene.

If you have rendered a character as a separate layer, then you can choose
to add glows to the background before you composite the character over it,
so that the glows don't cover the character himself. If a glow exists entirely
in the background, then it can resemble what you see if a light illuminates
a foggy area of the atmosphere. When you add glows in the foreground so
they can extend in front of your characters, they look more like the halation
that occurs when some lenses and filters spread out the illumination from a
bright light source.

When you render light sources as a separate layer, include other parts of
the scene as matte objects so that the lights are hidden in any place where
something comes in front of them. Figure 11.10 shows candle flames that

I've rendered in different ways. On the left, I rendered the flame as a separate layer. The foreground candle is present as a matte object. You can see that its wick cuts out a hole from the bottom of the flame in the foreground, and its stick blocks parts of the out-of-focus flames in the background. I've formed a complete scene by adding the flames layer to the image of the candles without flames (center). Even with bokeh effects in the render, the flame still lacks the natural softness that a glow can add. When I blur a copy of the flames layer, boost its saturation to bring out the warmth of the candle light, and add it on top of the composite, I get a more natural-looking candle-lit environment (right).

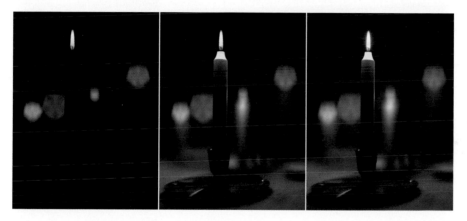

[Figure 11.10]
A candle flame layer is rendered with the candle as a matte object (left) and added into a scene (center). Adding a blurred copy of the flames layer creates a nice glow around the flames (right).

If the sky is visible in a scene, usually you should split it into a separate layer. One reason for splitting scenes into layers is that it gives you more creative control over adjusting colors and tones within your compositing program. Usually the sky has very different tones than any of the layers in the foreground, so having the sky as a separate layer lets you experiment easily with changes; you can brighten the sky, adjust its hue or saturation, or adjust tones on the foreground layers without affecting the sky.

Once you have the sky as a separate layer, it also helps to add a glow around the sky that wraps around the edges of other layers in front of it. After blurring the sky layer, sometimes you may want to mask out the sky itself so that the sky glow only covers the objects near the sky and doesn't brighten the sky itself. Figure 11.11 shows a sky layer that has been multiplied by the alpha channel of the foreground layer so that only the parts of the sky glow that extend over the foreground are visible (left). Compare the scene without any sky glow (center) to the result with the sky glow added (right); you'll see the subtle increase in realism that's gained by integrating the architecture with the sky in this way. The difference is most visible in the upper-right area of the images.

[Figure 11.11]
A sky glow bleeding over the edges of the foreground (left) can enhance a back-lit scene. Compare the scene before the sky glow is added (center) to after (right).

Alpha Channel Issues

Before you rely on an alpha channel for a composite, always inspect the alpha channel itself. If you're running After Effects, just press Alt+4 to view the alpha channel of any element. If you're running Nuke, just press the A key while your mouse pointer is over a viewer.

If you're using Photoshop, be careful: In many file formats, when you open a file, alpha channels are deleted and replaced with a layer transparency effect. This makes it difficult to view and edit the alpha channel, and it also makes it impossible to see the pixels of your RGB image that exist where the image gets marked as transparent. Luckily, in recent versions you are given a choice when opening an OpenEXR file: You can keep alpha channel "As Alpha Channel" or "As Transparency." As long as you make sure that the files you render are in OpenEXR format and you choose "As Alpha Channel" when opening them, you will be able to view and inspect your alpha channels in Photoshop.

Figure 11.12 shows one of the kinds of problem you might encounter in an alpha channel: The robot's eyes appear gray instead of pure white. When you composite the robot over a background, the pure black in the alpha channel marks areas where you will only see the background. Pure white marks areas where you will only see the robot. But shades of gray in the alpha channel represent partial transparency. They would allow some of the background layer to show through the robot. If the robot's head was pure glass all the way through, you'd expect some transparency in the alpha channel, but in this case, where the robot has a solid metal head with glass lenses for eyes, this is clearly a mistake. In this case, I just increased the shader's matte opacity to fix the problem.

You'll come across four common situations in which you expect to see gray tones in an alpha channel:

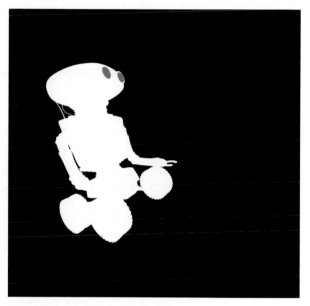

- Partially transparent objects, such as a windshield of a car, are represented with gray tones in the alpha.

- The edges where objects are anti-aliased against a background are represented as gray shaded pixels. Hair, fur, and fine vegetation create some of the most complex edges for objects and create larger areas with intermediate shades in the alpha when they are anti-aliased against the background.

- Moving objects rendered with motion blur get their blurs depicted as shades of gray in the alpha.

[Figure 11.12] Transparent holes in the alpha channel located at the robot's eyes are an example of the kind of mistake you need to look for when checking your alpha channels.

- The edges of objects that are out of focus when rendered with DOF are represented as soft gray gradients.

If you are rendering with a *premultiplied alpha channel*, then these effects are visible in both the RGB and the alpha channels. Along an anti-aliased edge, the edges of the object are blended with the background color (usually black) so that you can see the anti-aliasing applied in the color image, as well as in the alpha channel.

Rendering over a black background with a premultiplied (or *premult*) alpha channel is the default behavior of most 3D graphics software and is the most common way that layers and passes are rendered in professional production work.

When an image has a premultiplied alpha channel, it means that the alpha channel exactly fits together with the red, green, and blue channels of the image. In images with a *non-premultiplied alpha channel* (or *straight alpha channel*), the alpha channel is completely independent from the color channels, and can be any matte or mask.

In many renderers, you can turn off the premultiply option if you do not want a premultiplied image. Figure 11.13 shows a glass bowl of ice cream and a moving spoon. The transparent glass bowl, the anti-aliased edges of the objects, and the motion blur on the spoon all add complexity to the alpha channel (left). The RGB image is shown rendered premultiplied (center) and not premultiplied (right). You can see that the premultiplied image looks smoother and more realistic because the RGB colors have been combined with the black background color in all of the places that there was gray in the alpha.

[Figure 11.13]
Motion blur and anti-aliasing blend smoothly with the background in a premultiplied image (left) but do not blend with the background color in a non-premultiplied image (center). The alpha channel (right) does not change.

The alpha channel shown on the left side of the figure does not change between premultiplied and straight renderings. In the premultiplied color image, objects appear anti-aliased against the black background, and motion blur blends the spoon with the background color. Without premultiplication, the coverage and transparency is stored exclusively in the alpha channel, and the colored pixels in the image are never blended with the background. You can see this difference in the transparent bowl, the moving spoon, and all of the anti-aliased edges.

Compositing with Straight Alpha Channels

Non-premultiplied alpha channels come from a tradition of matting or masking in live-action compositing. When images are filmed or photographed, they don't include an alpha channel. In the compositing process, mattes that are rotoscoped or keyed off a green screen can be stored in an alpha channel, but this does not change the color channels in the original image. As a result, compositing processes designed for dealing with filmed elements tend to expect an alpha channel to be a separate, arbitrary mask, with no direct connection to the color channels in the image.

Different programs have different ways of dealing with straight alpha channels. Photoshop is built around the assumption that all alpha channels and layer masks are straight. When you import an element into After Effects, it lets you specify whether the element has a straight or premultiplied alpha channel. In node-based compositing programs such as Nuke, you can use a straight alpha channel as the mask input to a keymix node, using the alpha channel just as if it were the output of a keying operation.

Rendering with straight alpha channels limits your compositing in several ways. Here are some of the drawbacks to working with straight alphas:

- Images do not appear anti-aliased until they are multiplied with the alpha channel.

- A pair of layers, each matting the objects shown by the other layer, does not add together correctly if they aren't rendered premult (shorthand for premultiplied), because the color channels are not anti-aliased against the matte objects.

- If you blur your images during the composite—to simulate DOF or motion blur, for example—the color can fall out of alignment with the alpha, causing colored fringes around your images.

However, there can be advantages as well:

- Some editing and simpler compositing programs handle straight alphas more easily than premultiplied.

- You can apply some color-correction operations more accurately to color channels that are not premultiplied. For example, if you gamma-correct a straight image, edge pixels that are 50% transparent in the alpha still receive the appropriate color correction. In a premultiplied image, the transparent edge pixels would be multiplied with the black background color, so the gamma correction would treat them as if they represented darker tones, and would not adjust the edge pixels the same way as the pixels that were not transparent.

- Images that you multiply with the background during compositing generally don't need to be premultiplied in rendering. You should render elements such as occlusion passes (discussed later on) without premultiplication.

Compositing with Premultiplied Alpha Channels

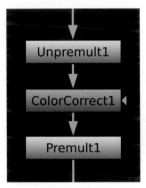

[Figure 11.14]
When needed, you can un-premultiply an image prior to color correction and premultiply it again afterward.

It is generally faster and simpler to composite with premultiplied alpha channels than it is to work with images that have not been premultiplied. In Nuke, a Merge (Over) node works perfectly for putting a foreground layer over a background, guided by the foreground layer's premultiplied alpha channel. Photoshop doesn't expect alpha channels to be premultiplied, but if you use a premultiplied alpha channel to delete the background from a layer, the function Matting > Remove Black Matte will perfect the key according to the premultiplied alpha channel.

If you render premultiplied layers, you can always switch them to un-premultiplied and back in a compositing program. Figure 11.14 shows the Unprmult (as in "un-premultiply") and Premult nodes in Nuke. You don't need to use these often. They are useful, however, if you encounter a color-correction operation that doesn't look consistent in half-transparent edge pixels around a layer. If some combination of extensive color-correction operations leave you with visible fringes around the edges of a premultiplied layer, you can fix this problem by un-premultiplying before the color correction and premultiplying again after it, as shown in Figure 11.14.

If you are rendering 3D graphics and passing off layers to someone else for compositing, you may encounter a compositor who is more used to working with straight alphas than premult. Take it as a warning that your compositor is unfamiliar with premultiplied graphics if you hear him say, "Your mattes were a little off, but I fixed them" (this means they may have pushed the edges in by a pixel or two, which does not really fix a problem and can badly degrade motion blurred frames) or "Could you possibly render this over a different color than black?" (which means they're having problems separating the image from the background because of being unaccustomed to premultiplied alpha channels).

A good test to make sure that your alpha channel compositing is working flawlessly is to render a scene of a white object in a white environment, as shown in Figure 11.15. If you render the foreground object against a black background as one layer and render the environment as another layer, you should be able to composite the two together seamlessly, without any darkness creeping into the edge pixels around the foreground object.

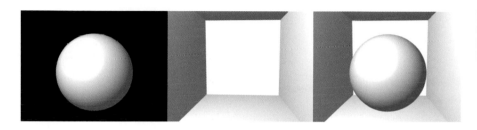

[Figure 11.15]
Check to avoid black matte lines in a composite, even between two white objects.

If you aren't sure how to get a particular compositing program to work with premultiplied alpha channels, a fallback solution will work in any application. Instead of using the alpha channel to layer your foreground over the background, use the alpha channel to cut a black hole in the background, as shown in Figure 11.16.

With the black hole cut in the background, you can then add your foreground as the layer on top. Figure 11.17 shows how a simple Add operation (or Linear Dodge in Photoshop), without using any matte or mask, puts your foreground over the background without any dark fringes or matting errors.

[Figure 11.16]
Using an alpha to cut a hole in the background prepares it for the addition of another layer.

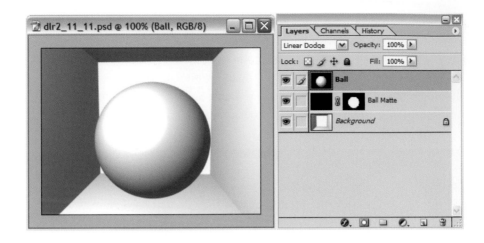

[Figure 11.17]
You can add a layer on top of a composite, without needing any masks, if you have already used its alpha to black out the background.

Rendering in Passes

Rendering in passes is the process of rendering different attributes of your scene separately. Passes are often named after the attribute of the scene that they isolate, such as a shadow pass, which shows just the shadows in the scene. Whereas rendering in layers just means rendering different objects separately, rendering in passes isolates aspects of the scene such as parts of your lighting, shadows, or depth information. Ten common types of passes that you can render are

- Diffuse

- Specular

- Reflection

- Shadow

- Ambient

- Occlusion

- Beauty

- Global Illumination

- Mask

- Depth

Rendering in passes is not exclusive of rendering in layers—you can do both at the same time, such as rendering a specular pass for your foreground character layer. In some programs, the system for managing render layers can also used to set up your passes.

Rendering Diffuse Passes

A *diffuse pass* is the full-color rendering of your subject, including diffuse illumination, color, and texture, but *not* including reflections or highlights, which will be rendered as separate passes. Because a diffuse pass includes the diffuse illumination from lights, surfaces are shaded brighter where they face a light source and darker where they face away from a light source. Figure 11.18 is the diffuse pass for the spaceship; it includes the basic texture and shading, but lacks highlights and reflections.

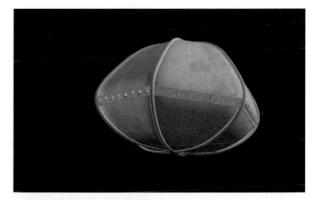

Many programs include a preset to render a diffuse pass as a single function. If you need to set up diffuse pass rendering without a preset, you can do it by modifying the shaders so they are not reflective and don't have specular highlights. Another approach to setting up a diffuse pass is to modify the lights so they do not emit specularity and globally turn off raytraced reflections.

[Figure 11.18] The diffuse pass of the spaceship.

Rendering Specular Passes

Specular passes (or *highlight passes*) isolate the specular highlights from your objects. You can render specular passes by turning off any ambient light and making the object's diffuse shading and color mapping pure black. The result, as shown in Figure 11.19, is a rendering of all the specular highlights in the scene, without any other types of shading.

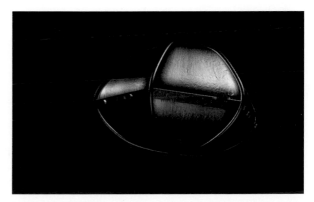

Rendering a separate specular pass allows you more creative control over how the highlights are rendered. For example, in Figure 11.19 I added

[Figure 11.19] The specular pass of the spaceship.

a bump map to vary and soften the highlights. I did not keep the bump map there when I rendered the diffuse pass; I applied it only for the highlights. You may also move your lights to different positions if it makes better highlights. Naturally the lights should come from the same general angle as the lighting that you used in the diffuse pass, but there's nothing wrong with cheating a little bit to make a better-looking rendering.

During your composite, having specular highlights as a separate pass allows you to have control over their color and brightness so that you can adjust the highlights to match the rest of your composited scene. Don't clip large areas of your highlights into pure white. Your specular pass works best if highlights run through different shades of gray, which allows it to look realistic when it is added together with other passes.

You can also use separately rendered highlights to control visual effects, such as glows added in compositing. Adding a blurred copy of your specular pass creates glows around your highlights, as shown in Figure 11.20. This way, glows do not take any test-renders to adjust, and they can be adjusted in context with the final composite.

[Figure 11.20]
A specular pass (left) can be blurred (middle) to add a glow to the composite (right).

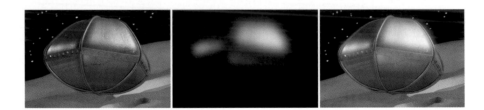

Rendering Reflection Passes

A *reflection pass* can include self-reflections, reflections of other objects, or reflections of the surrounding environment. Often you need to render several reflection passes, especially if you want to isolate raytraced reflections on different objects.

To set up a reflection pass showing the reflections of the environment onto the spaceship, I gave the spaceship a shader that does not show diffuse illumination or specular highlights (I gave it a black color and a highlight size of 0) but is reflective. I made the objects that it needs to reflect invisible to primary visibility but left them visible in reflections. The result shows only the reflections on the spaceship, without any diffuse or specular illumination. The reflection pass for the spaceship is separate from any other reflection passes, such as reflections of the ship on a reflective ground surface.

Compositing Reflections

You can composite reflection passes, diffuse passes, and specular passes together with an Add operation (or Linear Dodge in Photoshop), as shown in Figure 11.21. This way, lighter areas of your reflection and specular passes brighten your diffuse pass, and black areas have no effect.

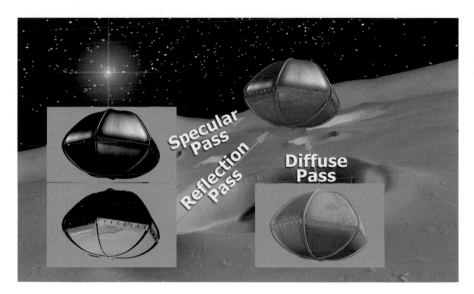

[Figure 11.21]
Diffuse, specular, and reflection passes are added together in the final composite.

Some people use Screen instead of Add as the compositing mode when combining these passes. Instead of adding the values as $a+b$, a Screen operation calculates $1-(1-a)*(1-b)$. Add is more realistic and accurately re-creates the results of rendering diffuse, specular, and reflections all at once in a 3D program. However, especially for people who are compositing without using a linear workflow, Screen is a popular choice because it is less likely to reach pure white too soon and suffer from clipping problems in bright areas. When you add two medium gray values together, the result is pure white. This is what you would expect, and it looks perfectly normal when you are using a linear workflow. If you are compositing without a linear workflow, however, colors in gamma-corrected images with a brightness on the screen of about 25% can have a numeric value of 50%. As a result, when you add two tones together that both look like darker gray, the result moves up to white. The best solution to this problem is to adopt a linear workflow, as described in Chapter 8, but people compositing without a linear workflow often choose to use Screen instead of Add as a workaround.

Adding Reflections to Real Objects

Sometimes your 3D object casts a reflection onto a real-world surface, such as a shiny floor, a countertop, or a water surface. In this case, render the cast reflection as a separate reflection pass received by a 3D model of the real surface, such as the grid in Figure 11.22.

For the effect of rippling water, you might add a bump map to a reflective water surface object, which distorts a reflection as shown in Figure 11.23.

[Figure 11.22]
A plane is positioned to receive a reflection pass.

[Figure 11.23]
Bump mapping distorts the reflection to make it more watery (right).

When keying the reflection over a surface, adjust it in your compositing program to match the tones of existing reflections on the surface, as in Figure 11.24. Reflections that have too much color and contrast can look unrealistic, so color correction is usually necessary to match any real background sequence.

[Figure 11.24]
The reflection is graded to match the water's colors.

Rendering Shadow Passes

A *shadow pass* is a rendering that shows the locations of shadows in a scene, without including all of the illumination from the lights that cast these shadows.

Unlike the other kinds of passes discussed in this chapter, it is not safe to assume that you'll be able to re-create your full scene in compositing if you split your shadows into a separate pass. If you start with passes that contain lights that don't cast shadows and then use shadow passes to darken them, it may not be possible to composite together a version of the scene that looks as natural as the output you can achieve if you don't try to split out your shadows at all.

There may be times when you need to render shadow passes. In visual effects, when a 3D model casts shadows onto a ground surface that's part of a live-action plate, then you need to render a shadow pass, and the compositor will use that pass to darken parts of the filmed image of the real ground. In very specialized cases within 3D animation, you may have a situation where the ground is moving past the camera very quickly with motion blur, but the camera is travelling along with the character, so you want the character's shadow on the ground not to be blurred. One approach to this kind of tricky situation might be to render separate shadow passes. But, other than cases where rendering a shadow pass is really the only solution you can think of to a problem, your best bet is to avoid using them.

Advice on rendering shadow passes in this section should help you get the best results possible, but you are likely to get even better results if you render your lights and shadows together whenever possible. Especially when modern rendering techniques rely on shadows appearing in reflections and contributing to global illumination, rendering all of your lights with shadows turned on is usually better than relying on separate shadow passes to darken parts of the scene during compositing.

In scenes with multiple lights casting shadows, it is important to keep the different shadows separated when rendering shadow passes so that you can control their appearance, color, and softness separately during the composite.

The scene on the left side of Figure 11.25 is lit by multiple light sources. A shadow pass that lumps them all together (right) does not allow you to isolate them and manipulate them separately in the composite. This kind of shadow pass is a quick preset in some programs, but it puts all of your shadows together into the alpha channel of the shadow pass image. Since the lights casting these shadows may have different colors and intensities, a single alpha channel full of overlapping shadows is not going to be enough to let you add convincing shadows to a composite.

Another way to render a shadow pass is to set up render layers with up to three lights per layer, and make each light render a shadow using a unique false color. Using layer overrides, set the light's color to black, but give each light a shadow color such as red, green, or blue. This means that the only things that render are shadows colored red, green, or blue, as shown in Figure 11.26.

[Figure 11.25]
A scene with several overlapping lights (left) could produce an unmanageable number of overlaps in a shadow pass (right).

[Figure 11.26]
Shadows split into red, green, and blue pack three shadow passes into one.

The trick of using a black light color and a red, green, or blue shadow color doesn't work in every program. You may need a workaround, such as giving the light a negative intensity and a negative shadow color.

Regardless of how you set it up, packing three shadows into each shadow pass is more efficient than rendering shadow passes with only one shadow each, and it is more versatile than a shadow pass in which multiple shadows cannot be separated. During the composite, you can separate the red, green, and blue color channels into separate elements and use them like three separate shadow passes. Figure 11.27 shows how to do this in Nuke using three Shuffle nodes. Each node is set to isolate one color channel. In the node isolating the red, for example, the red channel is shuffled into the red, green, and blue output.

[Figure 11.27]
You can split the three color channels into three gray-scale images and use them like separate passes.

Rendering Ambient Passes

An *ambient pass* (also known as a *color pass*) shows the color and texture maps on your surfaces but does not include any diffuse shading, specular highlights, or reflections. An ambient pass shows every object as if it is uniformly lit by ambient light, so objects appear in a consistently flat, uniform tone, as shown in Figure 11.28. The colors in rendered pixels in an ambient pass are the colors from the corresponding pixel of a texture map, or the exact surface color of untextured objects, without any influence from light colors.

[Figure 11.28]
A completely uniform ambient pass shows the surface colors of each object.

In Maya, you can use an ambient light with its Ambient Shade parameter set to 0 to light an ambient pass uniformly. Other than this, you generally do not need any light sources present in an ambient pass. To create an ambient pass in 3ds Max, turn off all other lights and add a light set to ambient only. You can also create an ambient pass by rendering a diffuse pass with Diffuse Texture Element Lighting unselected.

Your ambient pass can look very uniform by itself. Usually, when you light an image, you want to see more shaping of the round forms and more definition in your lighting than an ambient pass provides. However, remember, this is just one pass that you can use within your composite. When you multiply it with an occlusion pass, that adds soft shading between the objects. You can add other passes, such as diffuse passes, specular passes, or other lighting passes, on top of this to add directionality and variety. You can even render a mask pass that lets you isolate particular objects in your scene, and only make your ambient pass contribute to some objects and not others. With all of the flexibility that you (or the compositor you're working with) can find in the compositing process, sometimes a simple, completely uniform ambient pass can be useful, even if it doesn't look like beautiful lighting all by itself.

There's more than one way to render an ambient pass. For Figure 11.29 I used light linking to link the ambient light to some of the models but not others. In this figure I also turned up the Ambient Shade parameter of the ambient light to 0.5; this makes objects a little brighter on the side facing the ambient light, instead of giving them completely uniform lighting. This kind of ambient pass lets you add a little extra light to certain objects, such as to simulate translucency or subsurface scattering in objects that need it.

[Figure 11.29]
A selectively lit ambient pass brightens some objects in the scene.

To add more variety to the scene, you can also render an ambient pass with a variety of colors and shades in the ambient lighting. Figure 11.30 shows an example of this. For this pass I used multiple lights, each with a different color and brightness, to add illumination. The volume lights are set to emit ambient light and are not set to emit diffuse or specular light, but they provide a base of illumination that can help add colored fill and bounce illumination to selected areas of the scene without brightening areas that you might want to remain dark.

[Figure 11.30]
An ambient pass lit with multiple colored lights gives a selective boost to certain areas of the scene.

Rendering Occlusion Passes

We discussed *occlusion passes* in Chapters 3 and 4, along with the suggested compositing approach I call an occlusion sandwich. Figure 11.31 shows an occlusion pass of this book's cover scene.

[Figure 11.31]
An occlusion pass for the full scene. Note that the reflective mirror shader and refractive glass vase keep their reflective and refractive appearance so that occlusion can appear within reflections and through refraction.

[Figure 11.32]
When occlusion passes are rendered for layers, they should be rendered over a white background and should not be premultiplied.

Because occlusion passes are designed to be multiplied with other passes, they should be rendered without premultiplication. This won't be a visible difference for passes that fill the frame, but when you render an occlusion pass for an individual foreground layer, make sure you render without premultiplication, as shown in Figure 11.32.

If you render a foreground occlusion pass premultiplied over black, then the anti-aliased edges of the character get blended with the black background color; if the character moves with motion blur or falls out of focus with DOF, the blurred edges create a thicker area that becomes extra dark. When you composite your occlusion pass into your scene by multiplying it, the dark areas of the occlusion darken the lighting from the layers underneath. This creates dark edges around your character in the composite. By rendering occlusion passes over a white background without premultiplication, you make sure this won't happen. Like multiplying any value by the number 1, multiplying an image with pure white has no effect on your composite. White edges in your occlusion pass do not cause unwanted edge darkening.

Rendering Beauty Passes

A *beauty pass* is really just a name for a complete rendering of your scene, including all of the attributes, such as reflections, highlights, and shadows. Whether you knew it or not, when you were rendering your scene before you broke it down into passes, you were rendering a beauty pass. Figure 11.33 shows a beauty pass of the cover scene, complete with caustics and final gathering.

[Figure 11.33]
A beauty pass is just a full rendering of the scene, including all attributes such as shadows, reflections, and caustics.

A beauty pass can be made redundant if you render other passes that can be composited together to re-create it. For example, if you render multiple lighting passes separately, then you can add them together to re-create the beauty pass, and you won't need to render the beauty pass itself.

However, a beauty pass can also serve as the starting point for your composite. For example, if you have a beauty pass you may also render a lighting pass that will guide areas where you want to add glows to the beauty pass, a depth pass that will guide where you'd add some fog or haze, or a mask pass that will let you isolate and brighten or darken particular objects in the beauty pass. In some projects, rendering the beauty pass plus a few other passes may still allow you to put finishing touches on your scene during compositing.

Rendering Lighting Passes

A *lighting pass* is an optional part of multipass rendering that adds a great deal of flexibility and control to the compositing process. An individual lighting pass shows the influence of one light (or one group of lights) on a layer. You can create it by rendering your scene with just one light (or one group of lights) visible and all the other lights hidden. Figure 11.34 shows four lighting passes rendered for the cover image of this book.

[Figure 11.34]
Clockwise from the upper left, four lighting passes show the key and spill, a light on the door in the reflection, the shadow of a man in the reflection, and a bounce light.

Add together the lighting passes in your compositing program and you can re-create the beauty pass. However, compared to rendering the beauty pass all at once, the approach of rendering different lighting passes separately gives you more creative control over how you render the passes and how you composite them together. You can render the different lighting passes using different render settings. For example, you might not turn on global illumination or final gathering for some of the passes if you don't want some of the lights to contribute to the indirect illumination in the scene. You also can adjust these passes differently in the composite, such as the way I darkened the layer with the reflection of the door to make the back of the room appear very dark.

You probably won't have time to render separate lighting passes from each light on each layer in every scene. Here are some of the situations where it is worthwhile to render separate lighting passes:

- Your key lights are often worth isolating. This way, you can multiply your other lights with an occlusion pass but add the key light on top of your occlusion sandwich so it doesn't get darkened by the occlusion.

- Always separate lights that you plan to process in any way during the composite, such as a specular light that will trigger a glow effect around bright highlights.

- Isolate lights that you plan to animate during the composite. For example, you can render a flash of light from an explosion as a separate lighting pass. You can animate the brightness and color of the lighting layer in your compositing program, instead of animating the brightness and color of the light itself in your 3D software. It's much faster to change an animated variable in your composite and recomposite your scene than it is to rerender your scene for each change you'll need in animated lighting.

- Any light that you're worried about should be rendered in a separate pass. If you are worried the light may appear too bright or need to be faded off in one part of a shot, then you'll be able to do to this to the lighting pass during the composite. If you are worried that the light has a light leak and may appear in a place where it shouldn't, then it's easier to fix this kind of problem while compositing if the light is in a separate pass. (In an ideal world, problems like this would be solved in 3D before your final rendering. But when you're short on time, rendering in passes and compositing allows you to make quick fixes at the last minute.)

Be careful if you have any materials or shaders in your scene that use ambience or incandescence. Those objects can appear bright even if you have no lights illuminating them. This creates a problem if they appear in more than one lighting pass because they will be bright in each pass, and once you add all of your lighting passes together, the shaders that have their own ambience or incandescence will become much too bright in the composite. The safest approach is to set the ambience or incandescence of this kind of shader to zero, and then render the ambience or incandescence from them in just one layer with a layer override to turn their ambience or incandescence back up to the level you want in that layer. This ensures that these self-illuminating shaders don't add extra illumination to any of your other layers or passes.

Rendering Global Illumination Passes

A *global illumination pass* isolates the indirect light added to your scene by global illumination. You can render any kind of global illumination, including final gathering and caustics, as a separate pass, as shown in Figure 11.35.

[Figure 11.35]
A global illumination pass (left) shows only indirect light added through final gathering. A caustics pass (right) shows the light that has refracted through the vase.

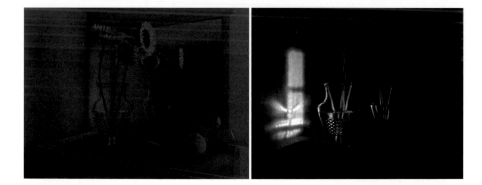

You can add global illumination passes on top of others that do not include global illumination. Adjusting the balance between direct and indirect light in your scene can be a very slow process if you have to rerender your scene with global illumination for every change and adjust the intensity of the global illumination or photons each time. It is easier to get your scene looking the way you want it if you render your global illumination separately, so you can brighten, darken, or tint it interactively in the composite.

Caustics cast from moving objects are especially likely to change brightness from frame to frame, so having them on a separate layer lets you adjust their brightness in context after they are rendered.

If your renderer doesn't make it easy to split out the global illumination into a separate pass, there's an alternative approach to isolating it. Render your beauty pass twice, once with global illumination turned on and once with it turned off. In your compositing program, isolate the global illumination as the difference between these images using a subtract operation (subtraction is also called difference in Photoshop and After Effects, or a minus operator in a Nuke merge node). Once you have isolated your global illumination, you are free to adjust its brightness, color, or saturation before you add it back into the scene. You can also use this approach to isolate caustics by rendering a beauty pass once with caustics and once without, and then using the difference between these images as a caustics pass.

Rendering Mask Passes

A *mask pass* (sometimes called a *matte pass* or *alpha pass*) provides you with masks that show the location of different objects in your scene.

You already get an alpha channel with each layer you render, which you can use as a mask for any kind of effect in your compositing program. If you want to render more masks at once, you can use more of the channels of your image. By giving one object a solid red color, another a solid blue color, and another a solid green color, you get three extra channels of masking information, in addition to your alpha, in a single pass. Figure 11.36 shows a mask pass that uses all three color channels to mask out areas of the scene that might need color correction.

In a compositing program, you can split the red, green, blue, and alpha channels into separate masks to control color correction, or any other effects or adjustments that you want to confine to specific objects in your scene. Depending on how many objects or types of object require separate masks, you may need to render several mask passes for a scene.

It's OK to reuse a color; for instance, you can use red for two different objects in a pass. As long as the objects don't touch or overlap during the shot, you can draw a simple roto mask or selection around one of them to isolate it if you ever need to.

[Figure 11.36]
A matte pass may look
like modern art, but it's
actually useful in letting
you color-correct individual parts of your scene.

[Figure 11.36]
A matte pass may look like modern art, but it's actually useful in letting you color-correct individual parts of your scene.

Rendering Depth Passes

A *depth pass* (also called *Z-depth* or a *depth map*) stores depth information at each point in your scene. A depth pass is an array of values measuring the distance from the camera to the closest subject rendered at each pixel. These are three main uses for depth passes:

- You can use a depth pass to simulate fog, haze, or atmosphere in the composite.

- You can use a depth pass to guide a distance-blurring effect to fake DOF or bokeh in the composite.

- You can render your scene in multiple layers, with a depth pass for each layer, and use the depth information to guide a depth-based composite, putting objects from different layers into the correct space in the scene.

A depth pass of the space scene is shown in Figure 11.37. Brighter shades of gray represent parts of the scene that are closer to the camera.

[Figure 11.37]
A depth pass rendering of
the spaceship scene.

Depth maps are worth rendering for any environment that needs atmospheric or DOF effects to be simulated during compositing. Even for scenes where there is not much visible fog or dust, having a depth map lets you tint your scene to cooler or less saturated colors with distance, adding an impression of *atmospheric perspective*—the color shift that you are used to seeing in natural environments.

Types of Depth Passes

Most renderers have an option to render a Z *depth buffer*, also called a *depth channel*, along with any render layer. This extra information is rendered simultaneously along with the color image and the alpha channel, giving you an extra pass of information that doesn't add much to your total rendering time.

The Z depth itself is not an image; it doesn't store a color or shade for each point, but instead stores a floating point number representing the camera-to-subject distance. It can be converted to an image, but the resulting image only represents a part of the data using 256 levels of gray.

A traditional Z depth buffer is limited because it stores only one distance measurement for each pixel of your rendering. Anti-aliased edges are not represented correctly, and neither are other cases where more than one object contributes to the value of a pixel, such as transparent objects or the soft edges of motion-blurred objects. Using traditional Z depth information often causes jagged edges in your composite.

As a workaround to avoid traditional Z depth buffers, some artists make a rendering that is sometimes called a *simulated depth pass*. Simulated depth passes are really the output of a regular rendering. They do not involve floating-point distance measurements. To set up a simulated depth pass rendering, you need to give all of the objects in your scene a flat, constant white color, with no shading. Then you must activate a *depth-fading* or *fog effect* to fade your scene toward black at greater distances from the camera. This kind of image does not have enough accuracy to perform *depth-based compositing,* putting together objects from different render layers according to their depth in the scene, but it is adequate for adding some fog or haze based on distance, and it can be anti-aliased like any regular image.

A newer and more sophisticated alternative to traditional Z depth buffers is called *deep compositing.* This approach renders deep images that store multiple samples at each pixel, oversampling the distance as well as color and opacity. This means that you have greater accuracy than a traditional Z depth buffer and will not get jaggy edges to depth-based compositing. Having reliable depth-based compositing available means that you can organize your scene into layers however you want, and all of the objects will be integrated at the correct depth within the scene when they are composited together. The deep image files that are rendered take up a great deal more disk space than regular images, although compression is a part of the deep file format that tries to reduce file sizes. Deep image rendering is currently supported by software including RenderMan and Houdini, and deep compositing is supported in Nuke and plug-ins such as Bokeh from Peregrine Labs.

Pass Management Features

An old way to set up passes is to modify your whole scene for each pass you want to render. For example, making a specular pass you would change all the shaders in the scene to black out the diffuse illumination and show only specular highlights. This works in any program and enables you to set up any pass you need, but it is not very efficient. You may end up saving several versions of your scene, one modified to render each pass that you need. If the modeling or animation changes, you then need to modify each of these scene versions before rerendering your passes. While 3D artists have set up multipass rendering manually like this in the past and it does work, most modern 3D software has added pass management features that make dealing with passes much easier and more efficient.

Most high-end 3D programs include pass management functions that can speed and simplify rendering in layers and passes. The advantage of having pass management built into the software is that you can configure and maintain many pass descriptions at once in a 3D scene. Different passes and layers may include different shaders, lights, and objects, or can include overrides to change render settings, shader values, or attributes of specific objects. As a result, you can have one scene but flip through different layers and passes, each of which is ready to render as soon as a version of your animation is complete.

Rendering Many Passes at Once

Most 3D software can render at least a color image, an alpha channel, and a depth pass at the same time. To render more passes than that, sometimes passes must be rendered in serial, one after another. However, some renderers can be programmed to output many passes at the same time, instead of each pass as a separate rendering task. Mental Ray's support for Frame Buffers and RenderMan's support for Arbitrary Output Variables are examples of this. While rendering one main image (the beauty pass), these features also let you simultaneously write out many other image files, containing specularity, reflections, shadows, global illumination, multiple masks, or even different lights in isolation. A limitation of these approaches is that they only work with certain shaders that can write data to multiple outputs. However, if rendering many passes in parallel is an option for you, it can save a huge amount of time.

Matching Live-Action Background Plates

A *background plate* is usually a sequence of frames digitized from live-action film or video into which you will add your computer graphics elements.

Many 3D programs have an option to view background plates within an animation window (an *image plane* or *rotoscope background*), showing how your subject will be aligned with the background. Once your 3D scene is aligned with the camera angles from the real-world shot, you face the challenge of matching the lighting from the real-world environment. Matching the direction, color, and tone of the light sources in the real scene is essential to integrating your 3D rendered passes with the photographed background plate.

Reference Balls and Light Probes

A set of reflective and matte balls can be ideal reference objects to help measure the position and color of lights on a location. Mirrored balls are sold as lawn ornaments, ball bearings, and housings for ceiling-mounted security cameras. For a ball with a matte finish, plaster is ideal, but a Styrofoam ball from a craft store can be more portable and affordable. You may need to paint the ball gray and attach a piece of wire to hold it in place.

Using Matte Balls

A photograph that shows the matte ball in a lighting environment can be great for picking the color of light that reaches your subject from each direction, as shown in Figure 11.38. Ideally, this image should be shot with the same camera as your final background plate and digitized at the same time with the same settings.

[Figure 11.38]
A matte-finished gray ball is positioned between a fire and window to probe different colors in the scene.

For the most accurate color matches, pick specific RGB color values from the image of the ball, as shown in Figure 11.39. You can then assign these RGB colors directly as colors for your lights from corresponding directions.

[Figure 11.39]
RGB colors picked off the reference ball give an accurate color match to 3D lights.

When developing the scene's lighting, import the ball image as a background in your 3D program and create a 3D sphere in front of it. Using your 3D sphere as a reference, adjust lights from each direction to make the shading of the 3D sphere match the shading of the ball in the background plate.

Studying the colors reaching a point in a real-world environment is a great exercise for anyone working in 3D lighting. Even if you don't need to match the lighting of a background plate right now, this process is worth trying a few times, just so you get a better feel for the colors of real-world lights.

Using Mirror Balls

A picture of a reflective ball in an environment, like the one shown in Figure 11.40, helps you more precisely determine the angle and relative brightness of each light, and guides you in creating highlights and reflections for your object. It is best if you shoot the reflective ball from the same camera position as your final background plate.

[Figure 11.40]
A mirror ball captures a reflected image of the surrounding environment for reference or for use as a reflection map.

As with the matte ball image, you can bring the reflective ball image into your 3D program. If you make a shiny 3D sphere, you should be able to see highlights from your brighter lights and match these to the highlights in the reflective ball.

An added bonus to having a picture of a reflective sphere in your environment is that you can use it to develop a reflection map for your object, as shown in Figure 11.41. In many programs, the best way to project your acquired image is as a planar projection onto the side of a large sphere surrounding your 3D scene; make the sphere render reflections only.

Light Probe Images

A traditional approach to matching natural light from a real environment is to use an array of directional lights. Once you have properly adjusted each light to match the color and brightness from each direction, this approach can produce realistic renderings and seamless lighting matches.

Another approach to re-creating a real-world lighting environment is to use a *light probe image* recorded on the same location as your background plate. Unlike ordinary photographs of a reflective ball, light probe images are *High Dynamic Range Images (HDRI)*, meaning that they can capture an exposure latitude greatly exceeding the range of one visible image, and are ideal for image-based lighting. To photograph light probe images, cameras are programmed to shoot a series of images at different exposure settings, exposing for the brightest light sources all the way down to the darkest, as shown in Figure 11.42. Unless you use HDR images, all of the brighter lights in your scene may appear clipped as pure white highlights, with no record of their

[Figure 11.42]
An HDRI indicates accurate colors at multiple levels of exposure.

relative brightness or color. Using HDRI, a light probe image can accurately record the color and relative brightness of every light source.

Other Approaches to Matching Lighting

You can't always use probes and reflective balls on the set, nor can you expect every production to stop and wait for you to set up special reference shots. Sometimes you won't even be able to visit the location where background plates were filmed.

Even if you do get to measure the lighting with different kinds of balls, the lighting in the scene may change without you getting a chance to remeasure it. Also, balls in one location in a scene may fail to give you the information you need about lighting in another point—you'd need an infinite number of probes to fully measure the light at every point in space.

If you can go to the set or shooting location, you can use other techniques to assist in matching the lighting:

Take a camera to the set. Take reference pictures of the set and the lighting around it; flat-on pictures of walls or floors for possible use in texture mapping; and wide-angle or panoramic pictures to create reflection maps.

Take a measuring tape to the set. Ask early in the production if you can have blueprints for the set, but don't trust the original plans to be accurate. Take a measuring tape and record enough information so that you can build an accurate 3D model of the set if necessary.

Watch for changes during the course of the production. In a studio, lights are adjusted, and even the walls and set pieces are moved between shots. Outside, the weather and time of day create more changes.

If you cannot go to the shooting location, or your background plate comes from stock footage or other sources, you still can match the lighting using other techniques:

Study shadows in the background plate. When you match their length and direction in 3D, your lights are in the right places.

Use an object in the background plate to find light colors. Try to find a white or gray object in the background plate from which you can pick RGB values.

Try to find reference objects in the background plate that can be made into a matching 3D model. By aligning the 3D model with the real object, you can compare how illumination and highlights hit your 3D model until it receives the same illumination as the background plate.

Every production creates different challenges, but with this basic set of tricks, you should be able to match the lights from any background plate.

Managing Colors in Your Composite

We discussed the linear workflow in Chapter 8. Your compositing software is a part of your linear workflow just as much as your 3D software is.

Color management in programs such as After Effects and Nuke allows you to read in images that you rendered in linear space without gamma correction but see the images gamma-corrected on your monitor while you work with them. Enable color management in your viewer window and you'll get a choice of monitor profiles or LUTs (look-up tables) for your display. Here you can choose sRGB or a gamma of 2.2 to match a standard monitor.

If you rendered without gamma correction and stored them as 16 bits per channel (half float) or 32 bits per channel (floating point) High Dynamic Range (HDR) files, then there are many benefits to keeping all your data in this color space while you work on your composite.

If you reduce the brightness of a layer or pass during compositing, values that had been brighter than pure white (color values above 1.0) in your file can be darkened into the visible range of tones, revealing detail in your highlights that would have been hidden without HDR data.

Blurs, blooms, and glows appear much more realistic and photographic as they respond to the HDR data.

When you add together two lighting passes, the additive compositing function matches the results you would have gotten by rendering the lights together in your 3D software. (If you try compositing without a linear workflow, the results of an add function often become too bright, with harsh transitions into white areas.)

When you color-correct an element or increase its brightness or exposure, the extra precision makes banding artifacts less likely, and it lets you reveal parts of the image that might have been too dark to notice in your original passes.

These advantages make working with floating point, linear data the norm in high-end work on feature films. Despite these advantages, there are reasons that not everyone works this way.

Using more bits per channel requires more memory and more time as your compositing software reads, writes, and processes data. You need a fast computer or a lot of patience to work with the larger files.

Compositing programs differ widely in terms of how many of the functions are written to support HDR data or how well they support it. Although some programs like Nuke were written originally to support HDR, high-bit-depth data, many other programs operate without a full set of image-processing operations or filters available when you are compositing with HDR data.

Some people try to render HDR linear data into OpenEXR files, but they find that it hampers their workflow on their specific software or hardware too much; as a result, they go back to rendering 8-bits-per-channel, gamma-corrected PNG files or QuickTime movies. Doing this is fine for some projects, and it still allows you to maintain a linear workflow while in your 3D software. But if you are learning about what's possible in compositing, make sure you at least give a full linear approach a try.

The process of converting an HDR image into a standard image is called *tone mapping*. Tone mapping doesn't need to be an elaborate process. You can set your compositing project's output settings to render out files that are 8 bits per channel and gamma-corrected for your final output (often using an sRGB gamma of 2.2), and the viewable portion of your data is written out so that it looks like what you saw in your viewer window.

If you're running Photoshop, when you convert a file from 32 bits per channel to 8 bits per channel, you see an HDR Toning dialog box with multiple tone-mapping approaches available. The Exposure and Gamma method is the most straightforward; it allows you to set your output gamma and do a last-minute exposure adjustment if necessary, before the data is clipped down to 8 bits per channel.

Other tone-mapping algorithms actually multiply different parts of your images by different brightness levels, trying to make both the brightest highlights and the darker shadow tones visible at once. This kind of effect is popular with some photography hobbyists who like the "high dynamic range" look in their photographs, but it sometimes causes artifacts such as dark outlines surrounding a bright sky. In most productions, a more straightforward conversion is better than the fancier, adaptive approaches to tone mapping.

Choosing Your Approach

Every production is different.

For some kinds of production, you may get away with little or no compositing. You could render your shots entirely in one layer whenever possible. Even if you try to minimize the amount of compositing you do, you may still use a compositing program for a few steps after you render:

- Use a noise reduction filter in some parts of the scene if a soft shadow, soft reflection, or DOF effect is a bit noisy when rendered.

- Perform color correction or adjustments to tones and contrast if they help improve the look or the continuity of your production.

- Add optical effects, such as blooms around bright light sources, which tend to be quick and easy to add during compositing.

- Perform any last-minute fixes you have to do before a deadline.

Another minimal approach some people take is to render a beauty pass, so they have a complete image rendered of each frame, but also render masks of different objects and passes such as reflections, specularity, and diffuse illumination. Renderer features such as Mental Ray's Framebuffers or RenderMan's AOVs (Arbitrary Output Variables) make it efficient to output some of these extra passes along with your main beauty pass, so you have them as extra elements if you need them. This way, you don't necessarily need to do anything to a shot during compositing—but if you do want to adjust anything, you have the extra passes available that let you adjust colors and tones on individual models separately, or add or adjust reflections, specularity, or other aspects of the scene.

Instead of trying to reduce or avoid compositing, however, some artists relish the opportunity to split scenes into multiple layers and passes, because reassembling their scenes from a versatile set of elements is a part of their creative process. For them, how they adjust the color and tone of each pass is an important part of their looks-development process. Some people even render in more layers and passes when they are initially developing the look of their production, and then, after they have adjusted things in their compositing program and gotten the look approved, they go back into their 3D software and adjust shaders and lights to match the changes they had previewed through compositing adjustments.

As a lighting artist, you may not choose to use all of the types of passes or layering approaches available to you, but you should certainly understand what kinds of things are possible through compositing. Practice splitting out lights into separate layers and adjusting their colors and brightness as you add them together in your compositing program. Learn to take advantage of separate occlusion passes and put lights into the most appropriate layer of an occlusion sandwich.

This chapter has covered many types of layers and passes. Don't think of these as obligatory steps you have to follow. Instead, you should view the wealth of choices available to you as an invitation to experiment, explore, and see how you can improve your own productions using layers, passes, and compositing.

Exercises

1. You can find jobs doing 3D lighting and rendering at a variety of companies. Some companies create content that consists entirely of computer graphics, such as animated feature films or cut scenes for video games. Other companies create content that combines computer graphics with live-action background plates, such as to create visual effects for movies or television, or to create architectural visualizations putting 3D buildings into real environments. You'll be able to find work at more companies if you have both kinds of work in your portfolio. If you've been focusing on all 3D content so far, then a great project to branch out into is to integrate a 3D rendered vehicle into a real environment. You can grab a vehicle model from Lighting Challenge #9 at www.3dRender.com/challenges and work on putting it onto a real highway. Vehicles are great subjects because they are reflective, so they show the reflection environment as well as the lighting environment that you put around them.

2. Come back to one of the 3D scenes you were rendering for the exercises in a previous chapter —it doesn't matter much which one—and try to split it into more passes than you used originally. Experiment with splitting more of the lights into separate lighting passes and adding them together in the composite. When you're putting them back together, experiment with fading each layer in and out from the composite, or brightening some layers to a brighter level than you have used originally. In many cases, the process of interacting with your scene in this way leads to a version you like better than the original beauty pass.

CHAPTER TWELVE

Production Pipelines and Professional Practices

Launching a career in 3D lighting and rendering involves a lot of decisions. What skills can you contribute to a production pipeline? Will you specialize in just lighting or also try to master other crafts? Which other skills best complement lighting? How different is it working in a large studio compared to a smaller company? This chapter presents some of the issues and challenges you will encounter in the working world, including collaborating with other lighters to designing lighting on large teams, and integrating yourself into the sometimes complex production pipelines of film studios.

Production Pipelines

To create feature films, effects and animation studios must organize hundreds of employees to complete large amounts of animation and effects on ambitious schedules. At this scale, a *production pipeline*—the system whereby artists across departments contribute to a computer graphics production—is necessary.

This section outlines the positions and departments typically found in either visual effects studios (that combine computer graphics with live-action) or computer animation studios (that create scenes entirely out of computer graphics), and how these departments work together as part of a production pipeline.

Planning an Animated Feature

In an animation studio, the story department works with the director and editor to plan out how the story will develop, how it will be told, and how it will be broken down into individual shots and sequences. The layout department then sets up all of the shots in the movie with their composition, camera angles, and camera moves.

Story

Story is one of the most important of all departments. If a story is not engaging, it won't matter to the audience how great the modeling or animation or lighting is; high production values cannot save a weak story.

Screenwriters write a screenplay or script for the movie. Often they write many drafts of the script during story development. However, the drafts do not predict every gag or action sequence, nor how all of the events unfold in an animated film. These things are worked out visually by story artists.

Story artists work primarily on paper. They come up with ideas for how a sequence or portion of the story can be presented and draw *storyboards*, small sketches of each shot in a sequence, as shown in Figure 12.1.

When a story artist has drawn a set of storyboards for a scene in the movie, he presents his ideas in what's called a *pitch* to the director. The director may approve the scene or ask for other ideas or changes. Even an approved sequence is likely to have more changes made over time.

A storyboard panel is drawn for each shot in a movie. For some shots, more than one storyboard panel is drawn—for instance, when a camera moves or when different subjects enter or leave the frame during a shot. An animated feature film might have 1,800 shots in it, but story artists may draw thousands of storyboard panels while a film is being developed as they design different versions of scenes and ideas for gags, and plan for scenes that don't make it into the final cut of the movie. Individual storyboard panels, as shown in Figure 12.2, don't necessarily look exactly like the completed shot. Story artists draw these panels before set designs, character designs, or other aspects of the film have been finalized, so they only provide a rough preview of what will eventually appear on the screen.

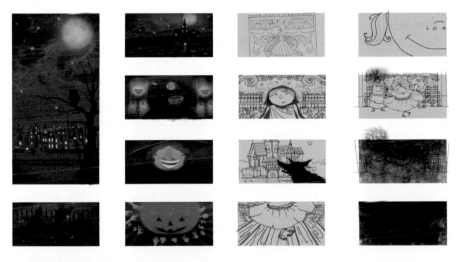

[Figure 12.1]
Miguel Ortega and Tran Ma drew storyboard images for each shot in their film, *The Green Ruby Pumpkin.*

[Figure 12.2]
One panel from the storyboard shows an early conception of the shot with Dorothy and two other characters arriving on the porch.

The *story reel* (also called an *animatic*) is a preview of the entire movie that the story department creates before the film is animated. Working with the film's editor, the story department creates the story reel by editing together the storyboard panels that represent each shot in the movie. If a camera motion is not well represented by still images, the story department may create multiple drawings for a shot, or sometimes they create moving graphics using compositing programs to pan or tilt through a large storyboard panel. The story and editorial departments also create a temporary soundtrack for the story reel. Because the actors who will voice each character may not have been cast yet, the director, animators, or other available crew may volunteer to record temporary dialogue for the story reel.

The director usually watches many versions of the story reel, trying to make sure a well-paced telling of the film's story is developed before animation begins. Watching a 90-minute story reel gives you a much better impression of how a movie will actually appear in theaters than simply reading a 90-page script does. Often, in the story reel phase, sequences are shortened, consolidated, or eliminated to help move the story forward or shorten the film. On large productions, it can save many millions of dollars to make these decisions while sequences exist only as little digitized pencil drawings instead of after they are fully animated and rendered. When movies are released on Blu-ray or DVD, as an extra feature on some discs, you can watch deleted scenes from the movie. This is your chance to see what scenes look like when they are still in the form of a story reel.

The film's editor keeps working throughout the production of the movie. When shots are animated, the editor replaces the still pictures digitized from the storyboards with moving animation tests and sometimes makes small adjustments to the timing. As the reel becomes a more and more complete preview of the film, the producer may screen it for a test audience to get feedback, and more changes are sometimes made based on test screenings. Eventually, fully lit and rendered footage replaces the animation tests, professional actors record final dialogue, and the story reel evolves into the final cut of the film.

Layout

After the story department completes storyboards and adds them to the reel, *layout artists* are responsible for positioning or animating the 3D camera to compose shots. Layout artists are the first in the pipeline to actually create a 3D scene for each shot in the movie. Using storyboards or story reels as a guide, they work in close consultation with the director to frame each shot. Sometimes a layout artist makes several different versions of a camera move to show the director so that he can pick the best way to cover a scene. After the modeling department has built sets and character models, layout artists also load the necessary models into the shot and put them into position.

Sometimes a layout artist roughly animates a character, at least translating the character from one place to another if that motion is an important part of the shot. Even though the temporary motion they add will be replaced with full character animation by an animator, the composition and animated camera moves made by a layout artist will be a part of the final film.

Preparing for Visual Effects Shots

Visual effects studios start their productions differently than feature animation studios. Instead of creating sequences from scratch like an animation studio, effects studios intgrate computer graphics with live-action film.

Previsualization

Previsualization, or *previs* (pronounced *"pree-viz"*), is a way of previewing live-action or visual effects shots with simplified 3D graphics to plan sequences and camera moves before they are filmed. Some companies offer previsualization services to directors to help plan complex sequences prior to filming. Some directors even previsualize an entire feature film before shooting it. Using previs, directors can work out camera angles, figure out exactly how action scenes or stunts should be staged, and generally make live-action film production faster and more efficient.

The best previsualization is done before any footage is shot, but visual effects studios also do previs of visual effects sequences for shots where background plates have already been filmed. Previs helps determine where 3D elements and effects will appear, which models or miniatures need to be built, and how *practical effects* (effects elements filmed in real life such as smoke or explosions) should be filmed.

Previsualization artists must be able to work quickly and responsively, and frequently they need to work alongside the director, moving the camera and changing elements of the scene at the director's request.

Match Move and Virtual Sets

The *match move* department does the work of aligning the 3D camera with the real camera used to film live-action footage. For any shot where a real actor is going to be composited into a 3D rendered environment, or where a computer-generated creature will be composited into a live-action shot, you need to make sure that the camera within your 3D software matches the position, camera angle, and lens of the real camera.

Figure 12.3 shows a completed shot containing a real actress, who was filmed in front of a green screen, composited in front of two digital characters, in a computer-generated environment. The actress is filmed from a high angle, as if the scene were filmed from the point of view of the taller woman who has answered the door. For this shot to work, you need to render the 3D elements from a matching camera angle, as shown in Figure 12.4.

If the cinematographer shooting the live-action footage moves the camera during the shot, then match move artists will create a 3D scene with an animated camera that duplicates the real camera's motion, frame by frame. This task is called *3D camera tracking* and can be done with commercially available software such as 3D-Equalizer (www.3dequalizer.com), built-in features of some compositing programs or 3D animation packages, or proprietary software at some studios.

[Figure 12.3]
This frame from *The Green Ruby Pumpkin* shows an actress composited in front of a computer-generated background scene.

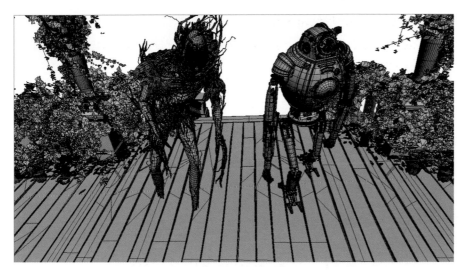

[Figure 12.4]
The Scarecrow, the Tin Man, and the porch are viewed from a camera angle that matches the live-action plate. You can view this short online at monster-sculptor.com along with information about how Miguel Ortega and Tran Ma created the film.

Besides matching the camera itself, match move artists also create *virtual set models* (sometimes also called *match move geometry*), which are carefully measured models of the sets that are used in filming a live-action scene. For example, if a scene shows 3D creatures chasing real actors through a real house, then match move artists create an accurately built reproduction of the floor, walls, and other main surfaces that are visible in the live-action footage. Match move artists then superimpose their virtual set models over the filmed footage, as in Figure 12.5. If the wireframe models remain aligned with the filmed set throughout the shot, then this verifies that the 3D camera is accurately matched with the real camera.

Even though the virtual set models are not visible in the final product, other departments use them to maintain integration with the live-action footage. For example, character animators stage action and position characters relative to the virtual set. Effects artists may use virtual set models as a part of the dynamic simulation of smoke, fire, water, or other effects that are limited by walls and furniture. Lighting artists use the virtual set to align light positions with windows and lamps in the real set. They also render shadow and reflection passes using the virtual set geometry so composited shadows and reflections follow the shape of walls, doors, or terrain visible in the shot.

Being a match move artist is often considered an entry-level position. After someone starts in match move, he can gain experience working in the pipeline and working with the company's software, and later, he may move into other departments such as modeling, animation, or lighting.

The head of the match move department is usually one of the few visual effects studio employees who travels to different shooting locations with the crew. On location, she can take detailed measurements of the real set and camera location, measure distances, or survey the location terrain. For some shots, the department head may place tracking markers in the scene that appear in the footage to facilitate 3D camera tracking. These markers are later retouched out of the shot by the rotoscoping department.

Rotoscoping

In shots that combine 3D animation with live-action footage, sometimes the 3D creature or character needs to appear in the background, behind actors or objects that were filmed in the real world. To accomplish this, an artist needs to create a *matte* at each frame of the shot, indicating the exact shape and location of the real-world people or objects that appear in the foreground. Drawing these animated mattes is called *rotoscoping* (or *roto*).

Once a *rotoscoper* (or *roto artist*) creates animated mattes for actors in the foreground, compositors have an easier time inserting 3D elements behind the actors. Roto elements are also used for other effects, such as casting the shadow of a 3D character onto a human actor or blurring, sharpening, or color-correcting different parts of a scene.

It would be very difficult to preview the interaction of a 3D character and a human actor if you couldn't see them composited together, so animators need roto elements as early in production as possible, even for test-renders of their animation. Lighters also need a preview of the final shot, including being able to see 3D elements behind rotoscoped live-action elements. Often rotoscopers develop a very rough, quick version of the roto first; they distribute this to lighters and animators to help preview the appearance of the shot as it is developed. Eventually, a more final, accurate roto needs to be developed before the compositor begins to combine the final elements.

Rotoscoping can be very labor intensive, because it involves tracing the outlines of moving people on a frame-by-frame basis, trying to match every aspect of the movement and the motion blur. Being a roto artist is often an entry-level position at a studio, and after starting in roto, employees are often promoted to texture painting, compositing, or other positions. Besides rotoscoping animated mattes, roto artists also do routine retouching such as removing dust and scratches from digitized film frames, or removing tracking points from the shot.

Core Departments

Thus far we have focused on the differences between animated feature production and visual effects production. These two different kinds of projects began in different ways. However, once you get beyond their starting points, many of the same core departments are involved in any computer graphics pipeline for common tasks such as designing and building models, animating characters and effects, and determining the look of the rendered images.

Art Department

The art department is responsible for developing concepts and designs for all the scenes, creatures, characters, and effects produced at the studio.

Work produced by artists in the art department can include concept sketches that show what a scene or character might look like; small sculptures called *maquettes*, which convey the final designs for characters; and color storyboards (sometimes called *color scripts*), which define the color schemes to be used throughout the production.

Traditional artists do most of the work in the art department. Many work without computers, drawing on paper or sculpting models out of clay. Others use digital tools such as 2D paint programs to illustrate their designs. However, almost all of the work ends up in digital form: Either flat artwork is scanned into digital images, or 3D scanners are used to digitize hand-sculpted maquettes into 3D models. In some cases, the artists are credited as *concept artists* (who develop designs for imaginary environments, creatures, or vehicles) or *character designers*. All of the work that the art department produces is ultimately subject to approval by the director of the film, who can make suggestions, request changes, or ask for new versions.

Working with pencil, paper, and only simple art supplies, concept artists can sketch out many ideas for what characters can look like, as shown in

Figure 12.6. The art director and director review concept art; they give feedback, ask for changes, and approve the appearance of different characters.

Designing on paper saves time compared to designing everything in 3D. For example, if a script calls for a dog character, a concept artist can draw several pictures of what the dog may look like and show them to the director. If the director wants some changes, the artist can produce new drawings quickly; sometimes they make new sketches or modify existing drawings as they talk. If people jump straight into 3D without an approved character design on paper, the process of modeling the dog in 3D, texturing it, rigging it, and adding fur can take weeks of work. All of this work is wasted if the director wants a redesign.

Concept artists often design a full packet of images showing the appearance of a creature, character, or set. The packet may include drawings from multiple angles, or separate drawings of different close-up details or facial expressions. Other common items artists include in packets are reference photographs that show what materials, textures, or details of a model may

[Figure 12.6]
Concept art shows the appearance of characters that could appear along with Dorothy in *The Green Ruby Pumpkin*.

look like; look along the bottom of Figure 12.7 for an example. Once the director has approved reference photographs, they are shared with the artists in other departments who actually model, shade, and texture the design.

3D sculpting tools such as Autodesk Mudbox and Pixologic ZBrush have slightly blurred the line between design and modeling. Instead of fine artists and sculptors designing characters, then passing off those designs to the modeling department to build 3D models, sculptors in some art departments have started digitally sculpting creatures and characters themselves. Figure 12.8 shows a troll character being sculpted in Mudbox; this kind of work can be done either by a modeler in the modeling department or by a sculptor in the art department.

A key position on any film is the *art director*, who is not just the head of the art department but also helps the director create the look and feel of the overall film. In live-action film, an art director is involved in all aspects of costume and set design, set decoration, matte paintings, makeup, and all other creative aspects of the film. In a computer-animated film, the art director is involved in all of these issues and, in addition, she approves the modeling, shading, textures, and lighting.

[Figure 12.7]
Miguel Ortega and Tran Ma sketched ideas for the Tin Man character, along with reference photos of classic cameras that inspired the appearance of his head.

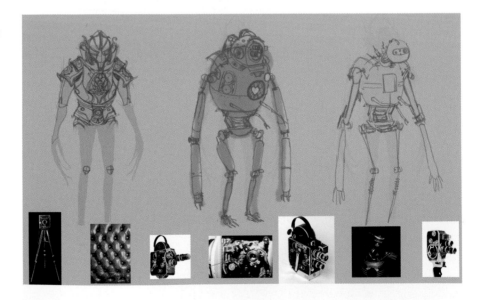

[Figure 12.8]
The troll character was sculpted in Mudbox by Miguel Ortega and Tran Ma.

Even after the colors and appearance of each sequence are initially planned in the color script or concept art from the art department, scenes still evolve substantially as they are actually shaded and lit. The art director stays involved and gives feedback in reviews of lighting and shading, but ultimately, it is the director who guides the development of the final shot.

Modeling

The modeling department can begin building digital versions of creatures, characters, and environments as soon as the director approves the art department's designs.

Modelers work with a variety of starting points. In some cases, they are given detailed designs for their models from the art department; in other cases, they are asked to find reference images and build things according to those images. Sometimes modelers also begin with digitized data made by putting an actor, a maquette, or other objects into a 3D scanner. After digitizing a model, the modeler then needs to clean up the data, fill in any areas that were not digitized correctly (for example, a whole-body 3D scanner can not capture an actor's hair very well), and make sure that the topology and level of detail meet the production's needs. In any situation, modelers need good judgment and a fair dose of creativity. Modelers often need to produce models that have more detail than any drawings or reference photograph they are given. Figure 12.9 shows the model of the Tin Man that Miguel Ortega and Tran Ma built; it was based on much simpler concept art.

[Figure 12.9]
The Tin Man character was
modeled in Maya by Miguel
Ortega and Tran Ma.

[Figure 12.9]
The Tin Man character was modeled in Maya by Miguel Ortega and Tran Ma.

Modelers usually need to shepherd a model through several different revisions before everyone is happy, have each version reviewed, and then respond to different notes and feedback from the director and art director.

Because modeling happens early in the production, it is a good complementary skill to have in addition to lighting and rendering. At many companies, people who work as modelers or set decorators early in a production switch to another task such as lighting later on.

Set Decorating

In an animated feature or for many visual effects sequences, a complex 3D world needs to be arranged and populated with many 3D models. After modelers build models of household items, trees, plants, and other objects that will appear in a movie, it is the job of a *set decorator* to place many copies of these models throughout the scene. Some studios have a *digital backlot* (an archive of old 3D models), which they can reuse on different shows; as a result some sets are decorated with a mix of recycled and new models that have been built just for the current show.

Set decorators rely on sketches and feedback from the art department, as well as their own aesthetic judgment, to go from a small library of plant species models to a full jungle, or from a directory of household props into a cluttered room that looks as if it belongs in the story.

Set decorators are very aware of where the camera is positioned and how it moves throughout a sequence. They try to dress detail into the specific areas that will be visible in the shot, filling in background areas with larger objects only where necessary. If a location is going to be visible only in a single shot, then a set decorator may follow the cone of the camera and dress props or foliage only in the area that will be visible, as shown in Figure 12.10. Even for a single shot, however, it's a good idea to have vegetation slightly beyond the camera's view because it can still cast shadows that are visible in the shot; also, any shot may need to survive small changes to the framing that may be made later in the production.

[Figure 12.10]
Set decorators fill a 3D scene with models where the camera is aimed (camera is shown in green), sometimes leaving other areas blank.

Character Rigging

Character rigging is the process of turning a 3D model into a character that is ready to be animated. In the character rigging department, a *character technical director (TD)* assigns an internal skeleton to a character, setting up the relationship between each bone and joint in the poseable skeleton and corresponding parts of the character model. At different companies, character TDs may be known as physiquers, riggers, or puppeteers.

The character TD also adds the controls and sliders that the animator adjusts in order to pose the character. She may create sliders for dozens of factors, such as how wide a creature's left upper eyelid is opened, or how much extra bulge a muscle gets. Figure 12.11 shows the Tin Man rigged with controls that an animator can grab and drag to pose the character.

[Figure 12.11]
The Tin Man is shown here with rigging, including handles that can be manipulated by animators to pose the character.

To be a character TD, you must be familiar with human and animal anatomy, and even more familiar with the company's animation package. Switching between brands of animation software might take only a few weeks of training for an animator, but a character TD needs to master far more of the minutia of the package.

Character Animation

Character animation has been practiced since the early days of motion pictures, using hand-drawn animation (also called 2D) and stop-motion animation (posing models, dolls, or clay figures at different frames). In modern production companies, the practice of meticulously planning a character's performance frame by frame is applied in 3D graphics using the same basic principles and aesthetic judgments that were first developed in 2D and stop-motion animation. If motion capture is used at the studio to digitize the motion of real actors, then a great deal of an animator's time is also spent cleaning up the motion-captured performance and completing the portions of the motion that may not have been digitized, such as the eyes and hands.

Unlike many other parts of the pipeline, character animation is a position that it's best to focus on full-time. You don't often see people moving in and out of character animation to do other jobs around the studio. Instead, most animators focus on character animation in their education, and then they get a job doing just character animation for all their studio years.

Effects

It is the job of an *effects TD* (sometimes called an effects animator or effects artist) to produce elements such as flowing or splashing water, dust, avalanches, hurricanes, smoke, flames, and sometimes hair and fabric motion. Effects animation often relies on dynamic simulations, procedures used to calculate motion based on the physical parameters of the effect being simulated. Effects TDs may use a commercial package such as Maya or Houdini to set up a simulation, or they may use proprietary software developed at their company.

Effects need tight integration with character animation, and generally an artist who is working on effects for a shot doesn't start until the character animation is completed. For example, if an animated whale is going to spray water off its tail, the effects TD producing the water spray needs to start with the character animation as the basis of her dynamic simulation. If the character animation changes, she will probably need to redo the effect. With every effect, from hair and clothing motion to volcanic explosions, the exact timing must look right relative to the other action in the scene.

Shading

As described in Chapter 9, *shading* is the process of developing shaders or surface descriptions that determine how each model responds to light. As soon as the modeling department completes a model and it is approved, the shading department goes to work creating shaders for the surfaces. Figure 12.12 shows the Tin Man with shaders assigned that make parts look like metal, glass, and other materials.

Assigning shaders to surfaces is generally the work of a shading TD.

Some shading TDs are programmers with advanced computer skills, whereas others are basically artists who can get their work done entirely by linking together and adjusting existing shading nodes. For many objects, shading TDs assign pre-existing shaders and adjust them to represent common surfaces, especially if they are just props or set pieces.

[Figure 12.12]
Shading by Miguel Ortega and Tran Ma makes the Tin Man character look as if he's made of real materials.

In many cases, shading TDs also assign texture maps to surfaces. In some companies, the same group of artists do both texture mapping and shading. At large studios, texture painters may paint original texture maps, but a shading TD may do basic texturing, such as creating a tiling metal texture to help a surface look like metal.

Texture Paint

As soon as shaders are created on a surface, *texture painters* go to work creating maps for it.

Texture painters develop texture maps using a variety of tools and sources:

- Painting maps from scratch in a 2D or 3D paint program.

- Basing all or part of a map on a scan or photo of a real-world surface.

- Starting the map with a photo of a painted maquette from the art department.

- Projecting images from the live-action portion of a film onto 3D models and modifying as needed.

- Mixing procedural patterns and noises.

Texture painters can use these techniques in various combinations depending on the type of maps they need to create. Even when digitized or procedural sources are used, texture painters almost always need to paint into and manipulate an image to produce their final set of texture maps.

After she assigns maps to the model, the texture painter creates a turntable test to show the mapping from all sides. She can use a frame from a live-action scene as the background image in the test to show how well the model integrates with the real environment.

In some companies, texture painting (unlike shading) is done within the art department. No matter how departments are organized, texture paint is a stage at which the art director is involved in reviewing the appearance of models.

Lighting

A *lighting artist* (also called a lighter, a lighting TD, or a lighting animator) working within a production pipeline has to think first and foremost about lighting, but also about bringing together all of the elements of a shot that other departments created. In most companies, lighting TDs assemble the latest version of the animation, the effects, the camera moves, the shaders, and the textures into scenes that they render every day.

Many lighting TDs show their work each morning in screenings called *dailies,* where they receive feedback on the lighting of their shots. By the end of the day, a lighting TD strives to create a new version of the lighting that addresses each of the concerns mentioned in dailies. They then leave shots to render overnight so they can be ready to screen the next day in dailies. This cycle repeats until the shot is approved.

Because lighting is a later part of the production pipeline, a lighting TD inherits changes from many different people. At times it seems that the farther down the production pipeline you are, the more people can potentially make a mistake that causes problems with your shot. However, most studios have developed systems for managing different versions of their assets (an *asset* is anything someone has created, such as a model, an animation, a shader) so that a TD has the ability to select an earlier version of an asset if a new version causes problems. An asset management system should also help prevent changes that are made while a shot is rendering from appearing in some frames but not others. Very often, though, a lighting TD is the first one to see a problem, and he will need to ask someone in another department to fix whatever element isn't holding up in his renderings.

The creative head of the lighting department is the director of photography (DP) on the film. It is her job to give lighting artists notes on their work on a daily basis, and she reviews sequences with the director of the film. Although the director needs to approve each sequence and shot, the DP spends more time than the director does reviewing each iteration of the lighting work while it is in progress. The DP also guides lighting artists in getting their work ready for the director's approval.

At some studios, lighting TDs are involved in rendering scenes for stereoscopic viewing, so they need to render two versions of each frame—one for the left eye and one for the right eye—for when the movie is shown in stereoscopic 3D. Lighting TDs may be expected to do their own fixes to minor problems in animation and simulation, such as places where a button accidentally cuts through the fabric of shirt.

At some companies, lighting TDs also do their own compositing, although for feature films visual effects, compositing is generally a separate department from lighting. In animation studios, compositing can be a simpler process than it usually is in visual effects. At times, all that a compositor needs to do is layer together a background and perhaps midground and foreground layers, and then maybe add glows around some of the light sources. In many animation studios, lighting TDs do their own compositing, and there is no compositing department.

Compositing

Compositors take rendered images from lighting TDs, live-action filmed plates, and rotoscoped masks, and composite them all together to form completed images that will appear in the film. Even in studios where compositing is a separate department from lighting, lighting TDs need to create at least an initial composite of their render layers. This is needed so they have a version to show in dailies and so the compositor has something to use as a rough starting point.

Compositors perform image processing on 3D elements such as slightly blurring the edges of the 3D model where it needs to blend with the filmed imagery, color-correcting any of the passes, and adding film grain to match live-action footage. In visual effects studios, compositors also need to manipulate live-action footage. They take multiple actors who are filmed in front of a green screen, as shown in Figure 12.13, and composite them into a 3D environment like the one in Figure 12.14. They also composite 3D characters into live-action plates, composite shadows from the characters into the live-action plate, and composite in dust kicks where the characters' feet hit the ground. Compositors also remove elements from the shot that do not belong, such as telephone lines in the background of a historical drama, or markers that were added to the set for 3D camera tracking.

Some visual effects studios provide a *digital intermediate process* to filmmakers, which means that they digitize filmed footage for general retouching, color correction, timing adjustments, and other 2D manipulation, and then they output the adjusted footage to film again. These services give directors who shoot film access to most of the creative possibilities of working with digital images. A digital intermediate process does not involve all of the 3D-graphics-related departments, so the compositors work with footage that has not gone through the rest of the pipeline.

[Figure 12.14]
This still from *The Green Ruby Pumpkin* shows the actors composited into the scene.

Grading and Final Output

To make the film as seamless as possible, the director and DP can improve the continuity by making adjustments during the process of *color grading*.

Color grading software, such as Autodesk Lustre or DaVinci Resolve, gives them a chance to review sequences of the film in context and adjust whatever colors or regions of the shots are needed in order to fine-tune the colors and tones in every shot. The person who operates this software, adjusting footage as requested by the director and DP, is sometimes called a *colorist*. The colorist can use the software to track any objects, or select any regions of the frame, in order to adjust their brightness or color.

Color grading allows tones in a movie to be optimized for several different formats. For example, the stereoscopic release may need a boost to the brightness of the midtones so that the movie doesn't look too dark and muddy in 3D projection.

Photographic film is an obsolete technology and has been replaced in most situations by digital cameras and digital projection. However, the film industry's switch to digital has not been a quick or complete transition. Instead, the industry is slowly evolving toward less film and more digital. Even though less footage is shot and projected on film every year, both technologies are likely to coexist for many years to come. Some studios have their own film scanners (for digitizing footage off film) and film recorders (for recording digital images onto film), and the department that does the input and the final output in multiple formats may still be named the "film I/O department," even if the same department also masters files in digital formats for digital distribution.

Even animation studios, which don't need equipment to digitize film frames, still have a department that focuses on outputting final images onto film, digital cinema, and different video formats, while trying to maintain the highest possible quality and a consistent look on each format. This department also deals with the challenging issue of keeping color displays accurately calibrated throughout the studio so that everyone can see images that are as close as possible to the final output.

Visualizing Production Pipelines

Using the departments described in this chapter, you can imagine the production pipeline of a visual effects studio, as shown in Figure 12.15.

At an animation studio, on the other hand, the pipeline is not centered around live-action film; instead it revolves around developing original art and stories, and putting together computer-generated shots. A generalized pipeline for an animation studio is shown in Figure 12.16.

Although you see similar jobs at many places, no two studios have identical pipelines. Some studios have unique departments to fill specific needs, such as a creature department that builds physical models to use on film sets. Other companies provide film and television editing services to clients as well as effects. Studios can change their pipelines and add new departments at any time. For example, a particular film may need a department dedicated to clothing and hair simulation, or another film may need a department focused on rerendering shots as stereo pairs for a release in a stereoscopic 3D film format. Also, many small studios—and some large ones—try to consolidate several jobs into one wherever they think it might improve efficiency.

[Figure 12.15]
A visual effects pipeline is focused on integrating computer graphics with live-action film.

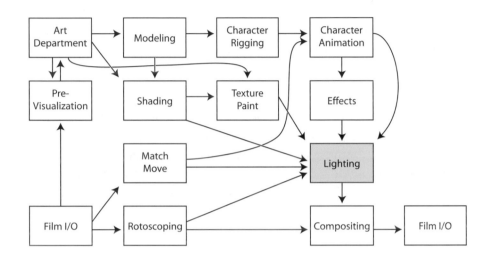

[Figure 12.16]
An animated feature pipeline is focused on creating an original story and art.

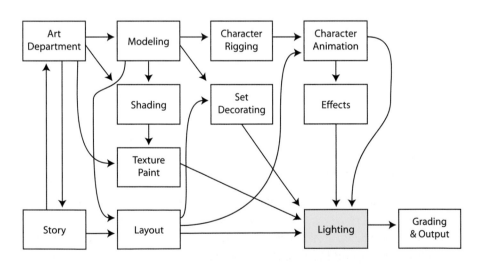

Lighting on Larger Productions

In an animated feature, you need to work as a part of a team of lighting artists, and in total your department needs to light about 1,800 shots for the film. You need to maintain continuity between these shots so that they all fit together into a continuous experience for the audience. And you need to find an efficient way to light many shots without wasting too much time on any individual shot in the movie. There are several strategies you can use to divide up and share work efficiently in a longer production.

Defining Key Shots

A very popular and effective strategy for lighting a sequence is to pick out a small number of *key shots* that you will light first. Suppose a sequence in a movie contains 35 shots featuring two characters interacting in one location. In this scenario, you could select two or three shots from the sequence to use as key shots. When you look through the sequence, you can select key shots based on a number of criteria:

- You almost always need to pick a wide shot that shows the broadest view that is used of the set.

- If the camera aims in different directions on different shots, such as for shot/counter-shot coverage of two characters, then choose at least one key shot with the camera aimed in each direction.

- If a character moves from one location to another during the sequence, then include at least one key shot with the character in his initial position, and another that shows the character in his final position.

- If any event during the sequence changes the lighting, such as a door opening or a car turning on its headlights, make sure you have key shots before and after the change.

Having to work on wide shots sometimes seems unfortunate. Often a wide establishing shot only appears for a few seconds at the beginning of a scene and then never again, yet lighting this shot can take up a significant portion of the time you spend lighting the sequence. Luckily, once the lighting of the widest shot is completed and approved by the director, the basic lighting on the full set is established. You can use this basic lighting as a good start-ing point for lighting many other shots in the sequence.

Lighting key shots is a process that you should start as early as possible, usually as soon as you have characters in the set with shaders and textures installed. Often, when you start key lighting early, you find problems that other departments need to fix. For instance, you may need to ask for some shaders to be adjusted, or you may find that some parts of a set are not look-ing right when you render them with lighting. As you work on your key lighting, the sets, characters, and animation in your shots keep changing from day to day.

As the sequence becomes more complete in "upstream" departments (the departments you depend on to provide animation, sets, shading, and what-ever else goes into the scenes you are lighting), you can seek final approval of the key shots from the director. This way, you may get more notes on how the director wants the shots to look; these notes are valuable to receive early while you still have time to address them.

Once these key shots are approved, you duplicate the lights from the key shots into all of the other shots in the sequence and render them with the lighting they inherited from approved key shots. With so much preliminary work completed, you should be able to proceed quickly and efficiently, only making changes you need to make to get those shots approved.

Sharing Light Rigs

As discussed in Chapter 5, a *light rig* is simply a group of lights that may be saved together into the same file and that serve a similar purpose. For exam-ple, if a car in the film sometimes has its headlights and taillights turned on, then you can create a light rig for all of the car's lights. You can constrain the lights to different points on the car model and test-render to see how they look on the car itself, what pattern of light the headlights throw onto the road, and how they illuminate other parts of the environment around the car. Once you have all of these lights looking good, you can save and share this entire group of lights as a light rig for the car's practical lights.

You can also create light rigs for sets. Many sets contain lamps or light fixtures, so a light rig could include practical lights constrained to each of these. Make sure you also include lights for the sun and sky when you are making light rigs for any windows or outdoor locations. Include bounce lights in any set rigs you make, unless a production is using global illumination (GI) to create bounce light in that set.

Make sure to include all the standard lights that might illuminate the character in a character light rig. Because you can always hide or delete lights if you don't need them, it's best to make a rig complete with rim lights from the left and the right; kicks from the left and right; a key, fill, and bounce light; and any special lights that contribute to the character's look, such as a specular lights for the character's eyes or fur.

Once you have shared light rigs for each set and each character, you've completed much of the work in lighting most shots. When it comes time to light an individual shot, you can render it lit by the set rig lights, then make some of the character rig lights visible as necessary. If you've already test-rendered and fine-tuned rig lights, then they can make your lighting work go much faster. Small details, such as using light linking to make sure rim lights won't illuminate parts of a character's mouth, or having a light constrained to a character's eyes that makes an appealing eye highlight, can save a lot of time compared to adjusting each light from scratch while you're lighting each shot.

Using Referencing

Referencing is a function of many 3D programs that allows you to assemble assets such as lights, characters, sets, and effects into a 3D scene, even though these assets are each stored in separate files. If you have a 3D scene file for each shot in the movie, referencing allows that file to remain reasonably small, because instead of holding all of the assets that will appear in the shot, it just contains references that instruct your 3D program to load assets from other files. Referencing is essential when you're working on larger projects, because different artists may be working on editing different assets at the same time. For example, while you are designing the lighting that is referenced into some shots, an animator may also animate characters that appear in those shots.

The best way to use referencing for lighting is to start by lighting a full sequence at a time. For the purpose of lighting, the *sequence* is all of the shots that take place at a certain location at a certain time and have similar lighting. Create a reference in all of the shots in the sequence so that all the shots will load in lights from your sequence lighting file.

While you are lighting a sequence, all of the shots in the sequence inherit the same version of your lighting, and you shouldn't stop to make any local changes that apply to individual shots. Develop lighting that works for the overall set or environment first, and then add lights as you need to for the characters in the sequence.

There may be small details that you can't get exactly right while setting up lights for the whole sequence. For example, a character might turn too far away from his key light in some shots so he isn't lit well, or rim lights might not be adjusted perfectly for each of the camera angles. When lighting a whole sequence at a time, don't worry about small issues that will be easier to adjust one shot at a time, just try to establish the overall lighting, colors, and tones for the sequence.

During sequence lighting, you'll often need to produce a *contact sheet,* an image you assemble that shows thumbnail-sized images from every shot in a sequence. Many studios have scripts that assemble contact sheets automatically, based on a list of all the shots in a sequence. For longer sequences, sometimes only one frame is shown from each shot; however, showing two frames per shot (usually first and last) can better represent your sequence, especially for shots with camera moves.

When you show sequence lighting to the DP and the director for their initial comments, sometimes you may only show a contact sheet, perhaps accompanied by a few full-resolution still images, without showing any shots in motion. This way, their comments will only apply to the overall lighting and colors in the sequence; they won't focus on issues that may need to be addressed in individual shots.

After the director approves your sequence lighting, break up the sequence into packets. A *packet* of shots is a subset of the shots in the sequence that have a great deal in common. For example, you can put all the close-ups of a particular character into a packet, or all of the shots in which the camera is facing a particular direction can become a packet. Give each shot in a packet a reference to a packet lighting file. Your packet lighting file will contain new lights that only shots in that packet need, and it will also contain adjustments and modifications to the sequence lighting.

When you light a packet of shots, you work on the packet lighting file in much the same way you did on the sequence lighting. If your packet consists of characters facing a certain direction, seen from a certain angle, you may need to swing the angle of the key light around a bit, cheating the key light so that it makes the characters look as good as possible. Rim lights and specular lights are very angle-dependent, and often you need to adjust them at the packet level.

Each shot receives lights from the original sequence lighting, as well as from packet-level lighting. For many shots, the lighting will be almost completed by the lights it inherits. However, you still need to perform the final stage of lighting individual shots. To light individual shots, render the shot with the lights it has inherited, and then add or adjust lights as needed to make that particular shot look its best.

In shot lighting, pay attention to how the lighting influences the composition of the shot. In many shots, you see a close-up of a character, with a small portion of the set visible in the background behind her. To make the character read well on screen, sometimes you may need to brighten or darken the background in places to increase contrast between her and the set. You may want to reduce highlights where they appear near the edge of frame, to avoid distracting the audience from the center of attention in the shot. Sometimes having some darkness near the frame edges creates a natural sense of vignetting and draws people into the middle of the shot.

Even if two shots have the same camera angle, each shot still has unique animation. Test-render the animation in each shot, and make sure that highlights fall in a natural location in the character's eyes and that interior surfaces of the mouth are visible without becoming unnaturally bright. You often need to fine-tune rim lighting for each shot to make sure the rim is positioned in exactly the right place to outline the character without over-lighting any more than a thin rim.

Every shot in the movie eventually needs to be approved by the DP and the director. Present a lit shot to them in context whenever possible, playing the shot along with the shots that preceded it or follow it in the film, as well as any shots that are similar to it and are already approved. Make sure that the contact sheet for the sequence is updated with latest lighting and also show the contact sheet. Before you show a shot to the director, first show the shot's location on the contact sheet, before you play it along with the surrounding shots; this way everyone is clear about exactly where the shot fits into the overall sequence.

Using referencing to sequence and packet lighting files helps you maintain continuity between shots and work efficiently without spending too much time on each individual shot. However, not every shot in a movie benefits from this approach. Some shots are so unique that you have to treat them as "one offs" and light them from scratch, all with one level of lighting.

Mixing Approaches

The three approaches described here (lighting key shots, creating light rigs, and referenced lighting) are not mutually exclusive. Instead, most productions mix and match some of each technique, in whatever ways make the most sense for their project.

Even if the primary approach to lighting a movie is based on light rigs, some shots inevitably end up getting lit earlier than others. Often these are shots that will appear in an early trailer for the movie or are used as test shots in developing certain effects. Once a few shots like this are lit early, they are used like key shots, with lighting rolled back into sequence-level lighting files or exported as light rigs to be used in other shots.

Almost every production ends up using light rigs to share working light setups between shots and sequences. At any level of lighting, including lighting sequences, packets, or key shots, a lighting artist takes advantage of available rig lights if they exist already, or exports lights into light rigs if the artist thinks they may be useful to another artist on the production.

Advancing in Your Career

Working in computer graphics puts every artist in the "Alice in Wonderland" situation of having to run very fast just to stay in the same place. Keeping up with today's technology requires that you rethink and revise even your most tried-and-true techniques, and that you invest the time in testing new ones. To move your career forward, you should always be learning and growing. Even after you land your dream job at a famous studio, you need to think about how to improve your skills and explore ways to make yourself more valuable in the future.

Even after a project is delivered, before you put away your files, load up the scenes (no matter how sick you are of them) and experiment with a few more renderings. You may want to render a high-resolution print of the scene for your own portfolio, or experiment with other ways the scene could look, without needing to match your client's expectations. If you don't have any scenes available from productions you just finished working on, the Lighting Challenge scenes from www.3dRender.com/challenges are always ready for you to practice shading, texturing, lighting, and rendering.

If possible, work on personal projects, no matter how brief or simple, to stretch what you can achieve. You may have some downtime in between major projects to do your own work. Perhaps you are fortunate enough to be reading this book while you are still a student so that you can experiment with each of the techniques and concepts covered here. Your semesters as a student are special times when you are free to design and develop whatever projects you can dream up. You may never again be in this position during your professional career. Seize these opportunities to express your personal vision and establish yourself as a computer graphic artist.

I hope the information and techniques covered in this book stay with you and help you improve your work. You know the motivation and visual function of each light in your scenes, and you name them accordingly so other artists can understand your light rigs. You can tell good lighting from bad by how well it shapes and defines forms, draws the viewer's eye to the desired center of interest in each shot, and avoids distracting artifacts that could detract from the scene. You use and understand a linear workflow. You can optimize your lights, shadows, and scene settings to render as quickly as possible while still looking good. You study any light you see in real life and can imagine how to match its qualities in 3D. You know a spill light from a kick, how to aim a rim light, and what to look for in lighting a character's eyes. You know what GI can do for you and how to do without it when necessary. You know how to take advantage of compositing, whether you use it as an integral part of your looks development process, or just as a tool for perfecting your images and adding a few finishing touches.

All of this information is only useful if you put it into action and practice each technique until you are proud of your results. Creating a great showreel isn't quick or easy, and it shouldn't be. The compelling images on your showreel don't just demonstrate your talent, they also prove that you have practiced and perfected your craft. This field never stops changing, and you should never stop exploring the evolving tools. Whether it's for pay or for pleasure, never stop creating new images and trying new techniques.

Read More Online

As an appendix to this book, an additional section "Getting a Job in 3D Graphics" is available for download on the publisher's website. To download it, visit the Peachpit website (peachpit.com), sign in, and register this book. Once you are registered, go to Account, select the Registered Products tab, and click the "Access Bonus Content" link.

Index

Note that Chapter 10 is included in the files you downloaded with this book (see the Introduction for details). In this index, the page numbers for Chapter 10 begin with "10:" and pages are numbered sequentially for that chapter.

Numbers

1.33 aspect ratio, 259–260, 262–263
1.66 aspect ratio, 259, 262
1.78 aspect ratio, 259, 261
1.85 aspect ratio (widescreen), 259, 261–262
2D
　casting into 3D space. see Projections
　paint program for creating texture maps, 10:25–10:26
　procedural textures, 10:51
2.35 aspect ratio, 259–262
3:2 pulldown, 222
3D
　building 3D models, 422
　casting 2D into 3D space. see Projections
　cheating in, 5–9
　paint program for creating texture maps, 10:25
　pass management software, 399
　procedural textures (solid textures), 10:51
　reference spheres, 401–402
　sculpting tools, 422
　surfaces. see Texture maps
　texture map resolution and, 10:49–10:50
3ds Max, shadows-only light, 69
8-bit color, 302
16-bit color, 302–303
32-bit color. see HDRIs (High Dynamic Range Images)
35 millimeter film, 260
180-degree rule, for camera angle, 245

A

Acceleration structures, retracing, 332
Adaptive oversampling, 327–328
Additive color, 278–280. see also RGB (red, green, blue)
Adobe After Effects. see After Effects
Adobe Photoshop. see Photoshop
After Effects
　color management, 405
　compositing with straight alpha channels, 375
　noise reduction filters, 214
　rendering with, 362
　viewing alpha channels, 372

Algorithms
　for calculating shadows, 73
　for rendering. see Rendering software and algorithms
Alpha channels
　adjusting contrast thresholds, 328–329
　compositing with premultiplied alpha channels, 376–378
　compositing with straight alpha channels, 374–376
　layering and, 10:39
　matte objects and, 367
　rendering issues, 372–374
　working with digital color, 302
Alpha mapping, 10:10–10:11
Alpha passes. see Mask passes, in rendering
Ambience mapping, 10:7–10:9
Ambient (color) rendering passes, 386–389
Ambient light, 38–39
Ambient occlusion, 91–92
Ambient shade option, from Maya, 39
American Standards Association (ASA), 222
Anamorphic lens, for 2.35 aspect ratio, 260
Angles
　camera angles. see Camera angles
　controlling spotlights, 26–27
　increasing dramatic impact, 188
　of light, 4
　occlusion and spread or sampling angle, 94
　shadows revealing alternate, 57–58
　for soft raytraced shadows, 88
Animated feature
　layout of, 414–415
　planning, 412
　storyboard for, 412–414
　visualizing production pipeline for, 434
Animation
　character animation, 427
　illuminating characters. see Character illumination
　procedural textures and, 10:51
　setting keyframes for focal distance, 206
　when to applying lighting to project, 21
Anisotropic highlights, 321–322
Anisotropic shading, 321–322

Anti-aliasing
　filtering, 329
　oversampling, 326–329
　overview of, 325–326
　rendering at higher resolution to achieve good, 330
　undersampling, 326–329
Aperture of lens, 202. see also F-stops
Aperture priority, 223
Aperture ring, on cameras, 203
Area lights
　indirect light without global illumination, 135
　lighting large areas, 141
　in simulation of sky illumination, 125–127
　for soft raytraced shadows, 87
　types of lights, 32–34
Art department, 420–423
Art directors, 422
Art work, basing scene lighting on, 20
Artifacts, depth map bias and, 77–78
ASA (American Standards Association), 222
Aspect ratios, 259
Atmosphere (participating media)
　creating with lighting, 148–151
　underwater effect, 151–154
Attenuation. see Decay

B

Background, rendering in layers and, 363–364
Background plates
　light probe images, 403–404
　matching live action to, 399–400
　matte balls as reference object, 400–401
　mirror balls as reference object, 402–403
　other approaches to matching lighting, 404–405
　reference objects in, 400
　starting creative process and, 20
Baking
　procedural textures into maps, 10:53–54
　shadows and occlusion, 104–106
Banding problem, 8-bit and 16-bit color and, 302
Barn doors, spotlight options, 28–29
Barrel distortion, in camera lens, 230, 232

Beauty rendering passes, 391–392
Bidirectional path tracing, 351
Bidirectional reflectance distribution function (BRDF), 323–324
Bidirectional surface scattering reflectance distribution function (BSSRDF), 324
Black and white images, tinting, 293
Blooms (glows), rendering in layers, 369–372
Blue. *see* RGB (red, green, blue)
Blur. *see* Motion blur
Bokeh effects
    camera lens and, 209–212
    computational expense of, 213–214
    with Photoshop, 369
Bounce lights. *see also* Indirect lighting
    following character movement, 185–186
    functions of, 173–175
Bracketing approach, to exposure, 229–230
BRDF (bidirectional reflectance distribution function), 323–324
Breaking the 180, camera angles and, 245
Brightness
    of area lights, 32
    EV (Exposure Value) in calculating, 228
    key-to-fill ratio and, 166
    physically based lights and, 35–36
    qualities of light, 4
BSSRDF (bidirectional surface scattering reflectance distribution function), 324
Buckets, of pixels, 342
Bump first strategy, for painting texture maps, 10:42
Bump mapping, 10:13–10:15

C

Camera angles
    high-angle and low-angle shots, 249
    line of action, 245–246
    motivation for camera moves, 251–252
    natural camera moves, 252–253
    overview of, 244
    perspective and, 246–249
    shutter angle, 215–216
    types of camera moves, 250–251
Camera moves
    motivation for, 251–252
    naturalness of, 252–253
    types of, 250–251
Camera projections, 10:23–10:24
Cameras
    3:2 pulldown, 222
    blurring rapidly rotating objects, 218–219
    bokeh effects, 209–212

bracketing approach to exposure, 229–230
chromatic aberration of lens, 233
comet tail myth, 217–218
computational expense, 213–214
depth of field and hidden image areas, 212–213
determining area in focus, 208
EV (Exposure Value), 228–229
exercises, 236–237
film speed and grain, 222–223
first frame problems, 217
focus pull, 205–206
focusing, 204–205
f-stops and depth of field, 202–204
histograms in setting exposure, 225–227
hyperfocal distance, 209
interlaced and progressive scans, 219–220
lens breathing, 207–208
lens distortion, 230–232
lens flares and halation, 234–235
lighting matching and, 404
match focal length of real lenses, 206–207
overview of, 201–202
reciprocity in exposure settings, 223–224
rendering motion in separate video fields, 221
shutter speed and shutter angle, 214–216
vignetting flaw in lens, 233–234
Zone System of exposure, 224–225
Career as graphic artist, 441–442
Cathode-ray tube (CRT) monitors, 269
Caustics, indirect light and, 352–356
Character animation department, 427
Character designers, 420
Character illumination
    creating light rigs for, 183
    letting performance guide the lighting, 187–189
    lighting cornea of eye, 197–198
    lighting eyes, 193
    lighting hair, 192–193
    lighting iris of eye, 195–196
    lighting pupil of eye, 196–197
    lighting sclera of eye, 193–194
    making lights move with character, 185–186
    for multiple characters simultaneously, 186–187
    overview of, 182
    splitting out lights, 184–185
    subsurface scattering, 189–192
    testing frames, 189
    using set of lights, 183–184
Character rigging department, 425–427

Character technical directors (TD), 425–427
Characters, adding definition to, 161–163
Cheating
    in 3D, 5–9
    defined, 5
    light linking and, 49–50
    in live actions, 9
Chromatic aberration (CA)
    color refraction and, 339
    of lens, 233
Clipping, HDRIs and, 304–305
CLUT (color look-up table), 307–308
CMYK (cyan, magenta, yellow, and black), 280
Color
    balance. *see* Color balance
    color scripts created by art department, 420
    correcting color shifts in tiling maps, 10:34–10:36
    depth, 291–292
    digital. *see* Digital color
    dramatic impact of, 188–189
    exercises, 275–277
    managing in composition, 405–407
    mixing. *see* Color mixing
    overview of, 267
    picking from pictures, 301
    refraction, 339–340
    rendering linear data, 275–277
    schemes. *see* Color schemes
    specular color, 317–318
    starting linear workflow, 274–275
    of sunlight, 113
    temperature. *see* Color temperature
    understanding gamma, 268–269
Color (ambient) rendering passes, 386–389
Color, of shadows
    as diagnostic tool, 67–68
    natural color, 64–66
    shadow color parameter, 66–67
Color balance
    adjusting, 118
    caveats regarding color temperature, 299–301
    color temperature and, 296–297
    overview of, 294–296
    picking colors from pictures, 301
    simulating indoor/outdoor color balances, 297–299
Color bleeding, 132, 344–345
Color contrast
    complementary colors and, 287
    exclusivity and, 286
    over time, 287–288
    overview of, 286–288
Color first strategy, in painting texture maps, 10:41–10:42

Color grading production department, 432–433
Color look-up table (CLUT), 307–308
Color mapping
  color first strategy, 10:41–10:42
  overview of, 10:4–10:6
Color mixing
  additive color (RGB), 278–280
  HSV (hue, saturation, and value), 280–281
  light color and surface color, 281–284
  overview of, 278
  subtractive color (CMYK), 280
Color schemes
  color and depth and, 291–292
  color contrast and, 286–288
  contextual associations and, 290–291
  cool colors, 289–290
  overview of, 285–286
  tinted black and white images, 293
  warm and hot colors, 288–289
Color temperature
  adjusting color balance, 118
  caveats regarding, 299–301
  color schemes and, 288–289
  dividing space into different lighting treatments, 147
  physically based lights and, 35
  qualities of light, 3
  simulating indoor/outdoor color balances, 297–299
  understanding, 296–297
Colorists, 432–433
Comet tail myth, 217–218
Compact data formats, 306
Complementary colors, 280, 284, 287
Composite, from Maya, 362
Composition. see also Rendering
  adapting widescreen to standard video, 262–263
  camera angles and, 244
  color management, 405–407
  core production departments, 431–432
  cropping and overscan, 263–264
  examining dominant lines, 257–258
  exercises, 264–265
  formats and aspect ratios and, 259–262
  graphic weight and, 256–257
  high-angle and low-angle shots, 249
  line of action, 245–246
  in linear workflow, 278
  motivation for camera moves, 251–252
  natural camera moves, 252–253
  OSS (over-the-shoulder) shots, 244
  overview of, 239

perspective, 246–249
POV (point-of-view) shots, 242–243
with premultiplied alpha channels, 376–378
rule of thirds, 253–254
shadows enhancing, 58–59
shot sizes, 240–241
with straight alpha channels, 374–376
tangency of lines, 258
two-shots, 243
types of camera moves, 250–251
use of positive and negative space, 254–255
z-axis blocking, 241–242
Compositors, 431–432
Compression, image compression, 308
Computational expense, of DOF and bokeh effects, 213–214
Concept artists, 420–421
Cone angle, controlling spotlights, 26–27
Constant mapping, 10:7–10:9
Contextual associations, color schemes and, 290–291
Continuity, maintaining on long projects, 12
Contrast
  adaptive oversampling and, 327
  adjusting contrast threshold, 328–329
  letting performance guide the lighting, 188
  shadows adding, 59
Control, creative. see Creative control
Cookies
  creating light effects with, 50–51
  creating throw pattern of light with, 142
  faking shadows, 107–108
Cook-Torrance shader, 315
Cool colors, 289–290
Coordinates. see UV coordinates
Creative control
  in computer graphics, 16–17
  vs. unnecessary tweaking, 325
Creative process, starting, 20
Crop regions, saving rendering time, 22
Cropping, overscan and, 263–264
CRT (cathode ray tube) monitors, 269
CU (close-up)
  combining close-ups and wide shots using z-axis blocking, 241–242
  shot sizes, 240–241
Cubic projections, 10:24
Cucoloris. see Cookies
Custom (deformable) projections, 10:24
Custom shaders, 10:53
Cyan, magenta, yellow, and black (CMYK), 280
Cylindrical projections, 10:22–10:23

D

Daylight
  adding indirect light, 119–121
  adding skylight, 116–118
  adding sunlight, 112–113
  overview of, 112
  representing spill from sun, 115–116
  simulating skylight using IBL, 123–124
  simulating skylight without using dome lights, 121–122
  using depth map shadows, 114–115
  using raytraced shadows, 114
  using sun and sky shaders, 122–123
Decals
  adding realistic dirt to model, 10:40–10:41
  creating for texture maps, 10:38–10:39
Decay
  inverse square (quadratic) decay, 41–44, 139
  options, 44–46
  overview of, 41–42
  softness of light and, 4
  sunlight and, 113
  types of, 42
  when to use no decay, 44–45
Deep focus, DOF (depth of field) and, 203
Deep shadow maps, in RenderMan, 80, 115
Depth
  color and, 291–292
  defining with lighting, 146–148
Depth map bias
  artifacts and, 77–78
  light leak issues, 78–79
Depth map shadows
  advantages of raytraced shadows, 82–83
  creating daylight, 114–115
  raytraced shadows compared with, 336
  raytraced shadows compatibility with, 336–337
Depth maps
  depth map bias, 77–79
  framing, 75–77
  light leak issues, 78–80
  overview of, 73–74
  resolution and memory use, 74–75
  soft shadows using, 80–82
  transparency support and, 80
Depth of field. see DOF (depth of field)
Depth passes
  atmospheric perspective from, 149
  overview of, 396–397
  types of, 397–398

Design
    challenges in lighting, 13–14
    cheating in 3D, 5–9
    cheating in live action, 9
    creative control and, 16–17
    direct and indirect light, 5
    directing the viewer's eye, 12
    emotional impact of, 13
    enhancing shaders and effects, 11
    maintaining continuity, 12
    making things believable, 10–11
    making things read, 10
    motivation and, 2
    qualities of light, 3–5
    visual goals, 9
    workspace setup, 15–16
Detail shadow maps, from Mental Ray, 115
Diffuse mapping. *see* Color mapping
Diffuse passes, rendering in, 379
Diffuse reflection
    controlling, 46–48
    microfacet model of reflection shaders, 315
    overview of, 312–313
    shaders and, 313–315
Digital backlot, 424–425
Digital color
    8-bit and 16-bit, 302–303
    compact data formats, 306
    compressed images, 308
    half floats, 306
    HDRIs (High Dynamic Range Images) and, 303–305
    indexed color, 307–308
    overview of, 301–302
Digital intermediate process
    compositing and, 431
    in film creation, 299
Direct lighting, 5
Directional lights
    adding spill light, 128–129
    augmenting skylight, 117
    matching natural light, 403
    simulating skylight without using dome lights, 121–122
    simulating sunlight, 127–128
    for soft raytraced shadows, 88
    types of lights, 29–30
    when to use no decay, 44
Directionality, modeling with light, 158–161
Dispersion. *see* Chromatic aberration (CA)
Displacement first (bump first) strategy, for painting texture maps, 10:42
Displacement mapping
    overview of, 10:11–10:12
    special cases in occlusion passes, 95–96

Displays. *see* Monitors
Distance, using lighting to show, 144
Distance falloff. *see* Decay
Distant lights. *see* Directional lights
Dmap filters, softening depth map shadows, 80–82
Dmaps. *see* Depth maps
DOF (depth of field)
    atmospheric perspective from DOF effect, 151, 154
    computational expense of, 213–214
    f-stops and, 202–204
    hidden image areas and, 212–213
    overview of, 202
    reciprocity between exposure controls, 223–224
Dolly, types of camera moves, 250–251
Dome lights
    simulating skylight, 116–117
    simulating skylight without using, 121–122
Drop off. *see* Decay

E

ECU (extreme close-up) shots, 240–241
Effects
    core production departments, 427–428
    enhancing, 11
Effects TD (technical director), 427–428
Emotional impact, lighting design and, 13
Environment sphere light source, 31
Environmental lighting
    adding global illumination, 128–134
    adding illumination to point light source, 138–139
    adding indirect light, 119–121, 128
    adding skylight, 116–118, 124–125
    adding spill light, 128–129
    adding sunlight, 112–113, 127–128
    avoiding spills, 140
    creating atmosphere, 148–151
    creating distance effect, 144
    defining depth, 146–148
    dividing space into different lighting treatments, 145–146
    excluding elements of window geometry, 127
    IBL (image-based lighting) approach, 123–124
    for large areas, 141
    night scenes, 143–144
    practical lights, 138
    representing spill from sun, 115–116
    set lighting, 139–140
    simulating skylight using area lights, 125–127
    simulating skylight without using dome lights, 121–122

throw pattern of, 142
underwater effect, 151–154
using depth map shadows, 114–115
using raytraced shadows, 114
using sun and sky shaders, 122–123
working without global illumination, 134–138
Establishing shots, 241
EV (Exposure Value), 228–230
Exposure
    bracketing approach, 229–230
    EV (Exposure Value), 228–230
    film speed. *see* Film speed
    f-stops in. *see* F-stops
    histograms in setting, 225–227
    reciprocity between exposure controls, 223–224
    shutter speed in. *see* Shutter speed
    three main aspects of, 202
    Zone System, 224–225
Exposure Value (EV), 228–230
EXR file format
    Open EXR, 306, 406
    working with digital color, 301
Extreme close-up (ECU) shots, 240–241
Eyes
    in character illumination, 193
    lighting cornea of, 197–198
    lighting iris of, 195–196
    lighting pupil of, 196–197
    lighting sclera of, 193–194

F

Faking
    shadows, 102
    subsurface scattering, 192
Falloff angle, controlling spotlights, 26, 28
Feedback loop, in scene refinement, 21–23
Fill lights
    functions of, 171–173
    indirect light and, 135
    key-to-fill ratio, 166
    lighting multiple characters simultaneously, 186–187
    making lights move with character, 185–186
    occlusion sandwich technique and, 97–99
    sky domes for, 31
    in three-point lighting, 164–167
Film formats, 260–262
Film speed
    defined, 202
    EV (Exposure Value) and, 228
    grain and, 222–223
    reciprocity between exposure controls, 223–224

Filters
anti-aliasing and, 329
exposure settings and, 224
noise reduction filters, 214
softening depth map shadows, 80–82
Final gathering, 349–350
First frame problems, 217
Flatbed scanners, 10:30–31
Floating point values, depth map shadows and, 74
Focal length
DOF (depth of field) and, 203
lens breathing and, 207
match focal length of real lenses, 206–207
setting the focus, 204
Focus pull, 205–206, 250–251
Focusing cameras. see F-stops
Follow focus, 205
Foreground, rendering in layers, 363–364
Formats
adapting widescreen to standard video, 262–263
aspect ratios and, 259
compact data formats, 306, 406
digital color and, 301
film formats, 260–262
Frame rates, 214
Frames, testing, 189
Fresnel effect, 318–321
Fresnel shaders, 320
Front projections, 10:23–10:24
F-stops
bokeh effects, 209–212
computational expense and, 213–214
defined, 202
depth of field and hidden image areas, 212–213
determining area in focus, 208
EV (Exposure Value) and, 228
focus pull, 205–206
hyperfocal distance, 209
lens breathing, 207–208
matching focal length of real lenses, 206–207
overview of, 202–204
reciprocity between exposure controls, 223–224
setting the focus, 204–205

G

Gamma
correction, 275
problems with incorrect gammas, 269–272
understanding, 268–269
Gels, color temperature and, 299–300

GI (global illumination)
adding indirect light, 119–121
ambient light compared with, 38–39
caustics, 352–356
creating indoor natural light, 128–134
creating indoor natural light without using, 134–138
final gathering and, 349–350
inverse square (quadratic) decay and, 42
models as light source and, 37
overview of, 343–346
photon mapping approach to, 347–349
problems with incorrect gammas, 270–271
radiosity and, 346–347
right use of, 183
unbiased renderers, 350–351
GIF files, 306
Global illumination passes, 394–395
Glossy reflection
glossiness and, 314
microfacet model of reflection shaders, 315
overview of, 312–313
raytraced reflections and, 334
shaders and, 313–315
Glows (blooms), rendering in layers, 369–372
Gobo. see Cookies
Grain, of film, 222–223
Graphic weight, of objects, 256–257
Green. see RGB (red, green, blue)
Groups, organizing lights into, 23

H

Hair, character illumination and, 192–193
Halation (specular bloom), 234–235
Half floats, color formats and, 306
Hard shadows
compared with soft, 69–71
when to use, 71–72
HDR (High Dynamic Range), 405–406
HDRIs (High Dynamic Range Images)
bracketing approach to exposure and, 229
creating, 201
digital color and, 303–305
IBL (image-based lighting) and, 124
illuminating scene with, 121
light probe images, 403
working with digital color, 302
HDTV
interlaced and progressive scans, 219–220
resolution of texture maps and, 10:48

Hemispheric sampling, ambient occlusion and, 91–92
High Dynamic Range (HDR), 405–406
High Dynamic Range Images. see HDRIs (High Dynamic Range Images)
High-angle shots, in composition, 249
Highlight passes, in rendering, 379–380
Highlights. see also Specular highlights
light linking for, 48
specular lights and, 181–182
Highpass filters, correcting luminance and color shifts, 10:34–10:36
Histograms, adjusting exposure, 225–227
Holding layers, 366–367
Horizontal tiling, 10:38
Hot colors, 288–289
HSV (hue, saturation, and value), 280–281
Hue, saturation, and value (HSV), 280–281
Hyperfocal distance, 209

I

IBL (image-based lighting)
simulating skylight, 123–124
sky domes and, 31
Icons
for directional lights, 29
for point lights, 25
IES (Illuminating Engineering Society), 35–37
Illustrations, basing scene lighting on, 20
Image compression, 308
Image planes, in 3D software, 399
Image-based lighting (IBL)
simulating skylight, 123–124
sky domes and, 31
Incandescence mapping, 10:7–10:9
Index of refraction (IOR), 337–339
Indexed color, 307–308
Indirect lighting
adding global illumination, 128–134
caustics and, 352–356
creating daylight, 119–121
creating indoor natural light, 128
overview of, 5
without global illumination, 134–138
Indoor film, color balance and, 294–295
Indoor lighting
adding global illumination, 128–134
adding indirect light, 128
adding skylight, 124–125
adding spill light, 128–129
adding sunlight, 127–128
area lights in simulation of sky illumination, 125–127
dividing space into different lighting treatments, 145–146

Indoor lighting *(continued)*
excluding elements of window
geometry, 127
working without global
illumination, 134–138
Infinite lights, 128–129
Interlaced scan, 219–220
International Organization for
Standardization (ISO), 222
Inverse square decay
adding illumination to light source,
139
overview of, 41–44
problems with incorrect gammas, 270
IOR (Index of refraction), 337–339
ISO (International Organization for
Standardization), 222
Isotropic reflection, 322

J

Jitter frames, caused by 3:2 pulldown, 222
JPEG files
8-bit color, 302
compact data formats, 306
lossy compression, 308
understanding gamma, 269

K

Kelvin, color temperature measured in,
296
Key lights
creating daylight effect, 112
functions of, 168–171
key-to-fill ratio, 166
lighting multiple characters
simultaneously, 186–187
occlusion sandwich technique and,
99–101
testing, 171
in three-point lighting, 164–167
Key shots, defining for large production,
435–436
Keyframes, setting for focal distance, 206
Kick lights
functions of, 180–181
lighting multiple characters
simultaneously, 186–187

L

Label maps. *see* Decals
Layer overrides, rendering in layers,
365–366
Layered textures. *see* Decals
Layout
of animated feature, 414–415
when to applying lighting to, 21

Lens breathing, 207–208
Lens distortion, 230–232
Lens flares, 234–235
Lenses, camera
bokeh effects, 209–212
chromatic aberration, 233
distortion, 230–232
flares and halation, 234–235
match focal length of real lenses,
206–207
vignetting flaws, 233–234
Letterboxing, 262
Levels tool, Photoshop, 226–227
Light angle, for soft raytraced shadows, 88
Light color, vs. surface color, 281–284
Light functions
bounce lights, 173–175
fill lights, 171–173
key lights, 168–171
kick lights, 180–181
overview of, 167–168
rim lights, 176–180
specular lights, 181–182
spill lights, 175–176
Light leaks, fixing, 78–80
Light linking, 48–50
Light Material, from VRay, 38
Light meters, for setting exposure, 224
Light probe images, 403–404
Light radius, for soft raytraced shadows,
87–88
Light rigs
creating, 183
sharing for large production,
436–437
Lighting, on large productions
defining key shots, 435–436
mixed approach to, 440
overview of, 435
referencing and, 437–440
sharing light rigs, 436–437
Lighting artist, 430–431
Lighting basics
ambient light, 38–39
area lights, 32–34
cookies, 50–51
decay, 41–46
diffuse and specular light reflection,
46–48
direct and indirect light, 5
directional lights, 29–30
exercises, 51–53
feedback loop in scene refinement,
21–23
light linking, 48–50
models as light source, 37–38
naming lights, 23
overview of, 19
physically based lights, 35–37
point (omnidirectional) lights, 24–26

qualities of light, 3–5
sky dome light source, 31
soloing and testing lights, 40–41
spotlights, 26–29
starting creative process, 20
types of lights, 24
version management, 24
when to applying lighting to
project, 21
Lighting department, 430–431
Lighting passes, 392–394
Line of action, camera angles and,
245–246
Linear workflow
compositing and, 278
inverse square decay and, 44
overview of, 268
problems with incorrect gammas,
269–272
rendering linear data, 275–277
starting with textures and colors,
274–275
steps in problem correction,
272–273
understanding gamma, 268–269
Lines
examining dominant lines in
graphic images, 257–258
tangency of, 258
Live action
cheating in live action
cinematography, 9
matching to background plates,
399–400
starting creative process for live-
action footage, 20
studying real life in process of
creating believable lighting,
10–11
Local illumination, contrasted with global,
343, 345–346
Look-up tables (LUTs)
color look-up table (CLUT),
307–308
displays and, 405
Lossless compression, 308
Lossy compression, 308
Low-angle shots, in composition, 249
Lumens
area light intensity in, 35–36
brightness settings of physically
based lights, 35–36
Luminance, correcting in tiling maps,
10:34–10:36
Luminosity mapping, 10:7–10:9
LUTs (look-up tables)
color look-up table (CLUT),
307–308
displays and, 405

M

Macro lens, 207
Mapping surface attributes. *see* Texture maps
Maquettes, concept work by art department, 420
Mask passes, in rendering, 395–396
Match move department, in production pipeline, 415–419
Materials, 36, 312. *see also* Shaders
Matte balls, as reference object, 400–401
Matte passes. *see* Mask passes, in rendering
Mattes
    drawing animated (rotoscoping), 419–420
    rendering in layers and, 367–369
Maximum distance, occlusion and, 93–94
Maya
    ambient shade option, 39, 387
    Composite, 362
    Hypershade window, 321
    Ray Depth Limit parameter, 86
    shadows-only light, 68–69
    support for linear workflow, 273
MCU (medium close-up) shots, 240–241
Medium close-up (MCU) shots, 240–241
Medium shot (MS), 240–241
Mental Ray
    detail shadow maps, 115
    Framebuffers, 408
    ray tracing, 341
    undersampling, 329
Microfacet model
    of anisotropic surface, 322
    of reflection shaders, 315
Micropolygons, in Reyes rendering, 341
Mirror balls, as reference object, 402–403
Mirrors, occlusion passes and, 96
Modelers, 423–424
Modeling department, in production pipeline, 423–424
Modeling with light
    adding definition to character, 161–163
    directionality of light, 150–161
    making things read, 10
    overview of, 158
Models
    aligning maps with, 10:17
    as light source, 37–38
Monitors
    calibrating, 15–16
    CRT (cathode-ray tube), 269
    LUTs (look-up tables), 405
Motion blur
    blurring rapidly rotating objects, 218–219
    comet tail myth, 217–218

first frame problems, 217
    shadows and, 89–90
    shutter angle and, 216
    shutter speed and, 214
Motivation
    for camera moves, 251–252
    cheating as departure from, 5
    direct and indirect light, 5
    lighting design and, 2
    off-screen space impacting lighting, 2–3
    qualities of light, 3–5
MS (medium shot) shots, 240–241

N

Naming lights, 23
Negative lights, faking shadows and occlusion, 102–104
Negative space, in composition, 254–255
Night scenes, creating, 143–144
Noise reduction filters, 214
Normal mapping, 10:15–10:16
Nuke
    color management, 405
    compositing with premultiplied alpha channels, 376
    compositing with straight alpha channels, 375
    inspecting alpha channels, 372
    as node-based compositor, 362
    noise reduction filters, 214
    occlusion sandwich technique and, 97
NURBS surfaces
    implicit UV coordinates, 10:19–10:20
    poles and, 10:43–10:45
    Reyes rendering curved surfaces and, 341
    subdivision surfaces, 10:12, 332

O

Occlusion. *see also* Shadows
    ambient occlusion, 91–92
    baking, 104–106
    distance settings, 93–94
    faking, 102
    negative lights in faking, 102–104
    occlusion sandwich technique, 97–102, 136–138
    overview of, 91
    rendering in separate pass, 92
    sampling and, 95
    special cases, 95–97
    spread (sampling angle) setting, 94

Occlusion passes, 92, 389–390
Off-screen space
    lighting shaped by, 2–3
    shadows indicating, 59–60
Offset filters
    correcting luminance and color shifts, 10:34–10:36
    creating tiling maps and, 10:33
Omnidirectional lights. *see* Point lights
Opacity settings, shaders and, 367
OpenEXR, 306, 406
OSS (over-the-shoulder) shots, 244
Outdoor film, color balance and, 294–295
Overrides, using layer overrides, 365–366
Oversampling
    adaptive, 327–328
    adjusting contrast threshold, 328–329
    overview of, 326–327
Overscan, cropping and, 263–264
Over-the-shoulder (OSS) shots, 244

P

Packets, breaking shots into, 438–440
Painting texture maps
    color first strategy, 10:41–10:42
    displacement first strategy, 10:42
    in layers, 10:42–10:43
    Paint programs, 10:25–10:26
    stylized textures, 10:45–10:48
Pan, types of camera moves, 250–251
Pan and scan technique, in adapting widescreen to standard video, 263
Path tracing, 351
Penumbra angle, controlling spotlights, 26, 28
Penumbra of light, softness and, 4
Per-face texturing (Ptex), 10:20–10:21
Performance, guiding lighting, 187–189
Perspective
    positioning camera and, 246–249
    POV (point-of-view) shots, 242–243
    of shadows, 63
Perspective projections, 10:23–10:24
Photographic textures
    capturing, 10:27
    flatbed scanners for capturing, 10:30–31
    shooting tips, 10:28–10:30
Photometric lights, 35–37
Photon mapping
    approach to GI, 347–349
    final gathering used in conjunction with, 349–350
Photorealism, 10–11

Photoshop
    adding glows, 369
    alpha channel issues, 372
    compositing in, 362
    compositing reflections, 381
    compositing with premultiplied
        alpha channels, 377
    compositing with straight alpha
        channels, 375
    creating texture maps, 10:25–10:26
    Levels tool, 226–227
    occlusion sandwich technique and,
        97
    Polar Coordinates, 10:43–10:45
    rendering with, 362
    tone mapping and, 406–407
Physically based lights, 35–37
Physically based shaders
    BRDF/BSSRDF, 323–324
    creative control vs. unnecessary
        tweaking, 325
    energy conservation and, 323
Pincushion distortion, 230
Pixar RenderMan. see RenderMan
Pixels
    dividing images into buckets or
        groups of, 342
    oversampling, 326–327
    undersampling, 329
Planar projections, 10:21–10:22
PNG files
    color management, 406
    compact data formats, 306
Point lights
    adding illumination to light source,
        138–139
    area lights contrasted with, 32
    types of lights, 24–26
Point-of-view (POV) shots, 242–243
Poles, in texture maps, 10:43–10:45
Polynomial texture mapping (PTM),
    10:16–10:17
Portal lights, 33
Positive space, in composition,
    254–255
POV (point-of-view) shots, 242–243
Practical lights
    adding illumination to light source,
        138–139
    avoiding spills, 140
    defined, 124
    for large areas, 141
    overview of, 138
    set lighting, 139–140
    splitting out lights, 184–185
    throw pattern of, 142
Premultiplied alpha channels, 373–374
Previsualization, preparing for visual
    effects shots, 415
Primary colors, additive, 278

Procedural textures
    3D textures, 10:51
    animation of, 10:51
    appearance of, 10:52–10:53
    baking into maps, 10:53–54
    overview of, 10:50
    resolution independence,
        10:50–10:51
Production pipelines
    art department, 420–423
    character animation, 427
    character rigging, 425–427
    compositing, 431–432
    effects, 427–428
    grading and final output, 432–433
    layout, 414–415
    lighting, 430–431
    match move and virtual sets,
        415–419
    modeling, 423–424
    overview of, 412
    planning animated feature, 412
    previsualization, 415
    rotoscoping, 419–420
    set decorating, 424–425
    shading, 428–429
    storyboard, 412–414
    texture painting, 429
    visualizing, 433–434
Progressive scans, shutter speed and,
    219–220
Projections
    camera, 10:23–10:24
    other types, 10:24
    overview of, 10:21
    planar, 10:21–10:22
    spherical and cylindrical,
        10:22–10:23
Ptex (per-face texturing), 10:20–10:21
PTM (polynomial texture mapping),
    10:16–10:17

Q

Quadratic decay. see Inverse square decay
Qualities of light, 3–5

R

Raccoon eyes, issues in character
    illumination, 170
Rack focus, 205, 250–251
Radiosity, approach to GI, 346–347
Ray depth limit, 337
Ray Depth Limit parameter, Maya, 86
Raytraced reflections
    glossiness and, 334
    integrating with specular highlights,
        333

overview of, 332–333
    perfectly specular nature of, 314
    reflection limits, 334–336
    surrounding environment and, 334
Raytraced shadows
    area lights and, 87
    compatibility of depth map shadows
        with, 336–337
    creating daylight, 114
    depth map shadows compared with,
        336
    how they work, 84–85
    light angle and, 88
    light radius and, 87–88
    overview of, 73, 82–83
    sampling and, 88–89
    soft raytraced shadows, 86–87
    trace depth and, 85–86
Raytracing
    acceleration structures, 332
    overview of, 330–331
    reflections. see Raytraced reflections
    refraction and, 337
    Reyes algorithm and, 342–343
    shadows. see Raytraced shadows
    transparency and refraction,
        337–340
Reaction shots, 241
Realism
    area lights and, 33
    inverse square decay and, 42
    photorealism, 10–11
    physically based lights and, 36
    of specular highlights, 316
Rect lights. see Area lights
Recursion depth, raytraced reflections and,
    335–336
Red. see RGB (red, green, blue)
Reference images (or objects)
    in background plates, 400
    light probe images, 403–404
    making things believable, 10
    matte balls as, 400–401
    mirror balls as, 402–403
Referenced lighting, approach to large
    production, 437–440
Reflection blur. see Glossy reflection
Reflection limits, raytraced reflections,
    335–336
Reflection of light
    adding to real objects, 382–383
    anisotropic highlights, 321–322
    BRDF/BSSRDF, 323–324
    diffuse and specular, 46–48,
        312–315
    Fresnel effect, 318–321
    global illumination. see GI (global
        illumination)
    glossy, 312–315
    isotropic reflection, 322

raytraced reflections, 332–336
reflectors for, 133–134
Reflection passes, in rendering, 380–383
Reflection softness. *see* Glossy reflection
Reflective objects
    creating night scenes, 144
    in occlusion passes, 96
Refraction
    color refraction, 339–340
    index of, 337–339
    limits, 340
    overview of, 337
Refractive objects, in occlusion passes, 96
Renderers, 37
Rendering. *see also* Composition
    choosing approach to, 407–408
    exercises, 409
    layered approach. *see* Rendering in
        layers
    linear data, 275–277
    motion in separate video fields, 221
    pass approach. *see* Rendering in
        passes
    saving rendering time, 22–23
    software and algorithms for.
        see Rendering software and
        algorithms
Rendering in layers
    adding glows (blooms), 369–372
    advantages of, 364–365
    alpha channel issues, 372–374
    compositing with premultiplied
        alpha channels, 376–378
    compositing with straight alpha
        channels, 374–376
    holding layers, 366–367
    matte objects and, 367–369
    overview of, 362–363
    using layer overrides, 365–366
Rendering in passes
    ambient passes, 386–389
    beauty passes, 391–392
    depth passes, 396–398
    diffuse passes, 379
    global illumination passes, 394–395
    lighting passes, 392–394
    management features, 398–399
    mask (matte) passes, 395–396
    multiple passes simultaneously, 399
    occlusion passes, 92, 389–390
    overview of, 378–379
    reflection passes, 380–383
    shadow passes, 384–386
    specular passes, 379–380
Rendering software and algorithms
    anisotropic highlights, 321–322
    anti-aliasing, 325–326
    caustics, 352–356
    diffuse, glossy, and specular
        reflection, 312–315

exercises, 356–357
filtering, 329
final gathering, 349–350
Fresnel effect, 318–321
global illumination, 343–346
microfacet model of reflection
    shaders, 315
oversampling, 326–329
overview of, 311
photon mapping approach to GI,
    347–349
physically based shaders, 323–325
radiosity and GI, 346–347
raytraced reflections, 332–336
raytracing, 330–331
raytracing acceleration structures,
    332
rendering at higher resolution to
    achieve good anti-aliasing, 330
Reyes algorithm, 341–343
shaders, 312
shadows, 336–337
specular color, 317–318
specular highlights, 316–317
transparency and refraction,
    337–340
unbiased renderers, 350–351
undersampling, 326–329
RenderMan
    AOVs (Arbitrary Output
        Variables), 408
    deep shadow maps, 80, 115
    interface standard, 342
    Reyes algorithm and, 341–342
    tessellation and, 10:12
Resolution
    depth map shadows and, 74–75
    interlaced and progressive scans
        and, 219–220
    rendering at higher resolution to
        achieve good anti-aliasing, 330
    resolution independence with
        procedural textures, 10:50–10:51
    saving rendering time, 22
    of texture maps, 10:48–10:50
Resolution independence, 10:50–10:51
Revisions, feedback loop in scene
    refinement, 21–23
Reyes algorithm
    overview of, 341–342
    raytracing and, 342–343
    RenderMan Interface standard, 342
    tessellation and, 10:12
RGB (red, green, blue)
    additive color, 278–280
    adjusting contrast threshold,
        328–329
    color matching from reference
        balls, 401
    HSV compared with, 280–281

light color and surface color and,
    282–284
models as light source and, 37
premultiplied alpha channels and,
    374
scale for, 282
simulating indoor/outdoor color
    balances, 297–299
Rim lights
    character definition and, 163
    functions of, 176–180
    lighting multiple characters
        simultaneously, 186–187
    making lights move with character,
        186
    in three-point lighting, 164–167
Rotoscope background, in 3D software,
    399
Rotoscoping, drawing animated mattes,
    419–420
Roughness property, specular highlights
    and, 315
Rule of thirds, in composition, 253–254

S

Sampling
    occlusion and, 95
    raytraced shadows and, 88–89
Saturation, in HSV, 280–281
Scaling up area lights, 32
Scanners, 10:30–31
Secondary colors, additive, 279
Selective lighting, 48–50
Set decoration department, 424–425
Set decorators, 424–425
Set lighting, practical lights, 139–140
Set of lights, in character illumination,
    183–184
Shaders
    alpha or opacity settings, 367
    anisotropic highlights, 321–322
    controlling diffuse and specular
        reflection, 46–47
    custom, 10:53
    diffuse, glossy, and specular
        reflection, 312–315
    enhancing, 11
    Fresnel effect, 318–321
    microfacet model of reflection
        shaders, 315
    overview of, 312
    physically based lights and, 36
    physically based shaders, 323–325
    specular color, 317–318
    specular highlights, 316–317
    sun and sky shaders, 122–123
    transparency support and, 189–191
    volumetric fog shader, 150, 152
    VRay's Light Material, 38

Shading
core production departments, 428–429
overview of, 311–312
Shading TD (technical director), 428–429
Shadow color parameter, 114
Shadow maps. *see* Depth maps
Shadow objects, 106–107
Shadow passes, in rendering, 384–386
Shadow softness filters, 80–82
Shadows
adding contrast, 59
adding drama with, 188
algorithms for calculating, 73
appearance of, 62
area lights and, 32–33
in background plate, 404
baking, 104–106
cookies in faking, 107–108
defining spatial relationships, 56–57
depth map. *see* Depth map shadows
directional lights and, 30
disclosing new angles, 57–58
enhancing composition, 58–59
exercises, 108–109
faking, 102
hard and soft, 69–72
indicating off-screen objects, 59–60
integration function of, 60–61
motion blur and, 89–90
natural color, 64–66
negative lights in faking, 102–104
point lights and, 25
raytraced. *see* Raytraced shadows
shadow color parameter, 66–67
shadow objects, 106–107
size and perspective of, 63
sky domes and, 31
soft shadows, 4
spotlights and, 26
using shadow color as diagnostic tool, 67–68
using shadows-only light, 68–69
walls creating, 61–62
Shadows-only light, 68–69
Shots
defining key shots for large production, 435–436
OSS (over-the-shoulder) shots, 244
packets of, 438–440
POV (point-of-view) shots, 242–243
preparing for visual effects shots, 415
shot sizes, 240–241
two-shots, 243
z-axis blocking, 241–242
Shutter angle, 215–216

Shutter priority, 223
Shutter speed
3:2 pulldown, 222
blurring rapidly rotating objects, 218–219
comet tail myth, 217–218
defined, 202
EV (Exposure Value) and, 228
first frame problems, 217
interlaced and progressive scans, 219–220
overview of, 214–216
reciprocity between exposure controls, 223–224
rendering motion in separate video fields, 221
Sky dome light source, 31
Skylight
adding to daylight effect, 116–118
adding to indoor natural light, 124–125
area lights in simulation of, 125–127
IBL simulation of, 123–124
night scenes, 143–144
simulating without using dome lights, 121–122
Soft reflections, 314
Soft shadows
compared with hard, 69–71
depth maps and, 80–82
raytraced shadows, 86–87
softness of light and, 4
when to use, 72
Softness
area lights and, 32–33
controlling spotlights, 28
qualities of light, 4
sky domes and, 31
Soloing lights
making adjustments and, 40–41
saving rendering time, 22
Spatial relationships, shadows defining, 56–57
Specular (spec) lights, 181–182
Specular bloom (halation), 234–235
Specular color, 317–318
Specular highlights
anisotropic highlights, 321–322
Fresnel effect, 318–321
integrating retraced reflections with, 333
overview of, 314, 316–317
realism of, 316
roughness property and, 315
size of highlights, 316–317
specular color and, 317–318
specular mapping and, 10:6–10:7
Specular mapping, 10:6–10:7
Specular passes, in rendering, 379–380

Specular reflection
controlling, 46–48
microfacet model of reflection shaders, 315
overview of, 312–313
shaders and, 313–315
Spherical projections
overview of, 10:22–10:23
poles and, 10:43–10:45
Spill lights
adding spill from sun, 115–116
avoiding spills, 140
creating indoor natural light, 128–129
functions of, 175–176
Splitting out lights
character illumination, 184–185
separating diffuse and specular reflection, 47–48
Spotlights
depth map shadows and, 75–76
types of lights, 26–29
using cookie to tint edges of, 142
Spread angle
controlling spotlights, 26, 28
occlusion and, 94
SRGB standard, 269, 272
Staging, 239. *see also* Composition
Stencils. *see* Decals
Storyboard, for animated feature, 412–414
Subsurface scattering
faking, 192
mapping variation, 191–192
overview of, 189–191
Subtractive color (CMYK), 280
Sunlight
adding spill light, 128–129
creating daylight effect, 112–113
creating indoor natural light, 127–128
directional light simulating, 29
when to use no decay, 44
Surface color, vs. light color, 281–284
Surface normal, bump mapping and, 10:13

T

Tangency, of lines in graphics, 258
Telephoto lens, 206
Terminator
as edge of visible illumination, 160
subsurface scattering, 190
Tessellation, 10:12, 332
Testing frames, 189
Testing lights, 40–41
Texture maps
aligning with models, 10:17
assigning UV coordinates, 10:17–10:19
baking shadow into, 104–105

bump mapping, 10:13–10:15
capturing photographic textures, 10:27–10:31
color first strategy, 10:41–10:42
color mapping (diffuse mapping), 10:4–10:6
converting into linear color values, 274–275
correcting luminance and color shifts in tiling maps, 10:34–10:36
creating with paint programs, 10:25–10:26
decals and, 10:38–10:41
displacement first strategy, 10:42
displacement mapping, 10:11–10:12
exercises, 10:55
extending tiling maps, 10:36–10:38
horizontal and vertical tiling, 10:38
incandescence mapping (luminosity, ambience, or constant mapping), 10:7–10:9
making maps for multiple attributes, 10:41
normal mapping, 10:15–10:16
overview of, 10:3–10:4, 359
painting in layers, 10:42–10:43
painting stylized textures, 10:45–10:48
poles and, 10:43–10:45
polynomial texture mapping, 10:16–10:17
procedural textures, 10:50–10:54
projections, 10:21–24
Ptex (per-face texturing), 10:20–10:21
resolution of, 10:48–10:50
specular mapping, 10:6–10:7
tiling maps, 10:31–10:33
transparency mapping, 10:9–10:11
using implicit UV coordinates, 10:19–10:20
Texture paint department, 429
Textures, in linear workflow, 274–275
TGA file format, 301
Three-point lighting
avoiding formulaic approach, 167
overview of, 164–165
tweaks and modifications, 166

Throw pattern
of practical lights, 142
shape of light, 4
TIFF file format, 301
Tiling maps
correcting luminance and color shifts, 10:34–10:36
extending tiling, 10:36–10:38
horizontal and vertical tiling, 10:38
overview of, 10:31–10:33
Tilt, types of camera moves, 250–251
Tinted black and white images, 293
Tone mapping, HDR (High Dynamic Range), 406–407
Trace depth
overview of, 337
raytraced reflections and, 335–336
raytraced shadows and, 85–86
Transparency
refraction and, 337–340
shaders and, 189
shadows and, 80
special cases in occlusion passes, 96
Transparency mapping, 10:9–10:11
Turntable tests, 10:7
Two-shots, 243

U

Unbiased renderers, 350–351
Undersampling, 329
Underwater effect, creating, 151–154
Upstage key, 166
UV coordinates
aligning texture maps with models, 10:17–10:19
Ptex (per-face texturing) and, 10:20–10:21
using implicit, 10:19–10:20

V

Value, in HSV, 280–281
Version management, 24
Vertical tiling, 10:38

Video
3:2 pulldown, 222
adapting widescreen to standard video, 262–263
frame rates, 214
interlaced and progressive scans, 219–220
rendering motion in separate video fields, 221
View-dependent shading, specular highlights and, 316
Viewer, directing eye of, 12
Vignetting, lens flaws, 233–234
Virtual radius, for soft raytraced shadows, 87–88
Virtual set models, in production pipeline, 417
Visual effects, visualizing production pipeline for, 434
Volumetric fog shader, 150, 152
VRay's Light Material, 38

W

Wagon wheel effect, 219
Walls, shadows created by, 61–62
Warm colors, 288–289
Watts, vs. lumens in measuring brightness, 36
White balance, 294
WIDE shot. see WS (wide shot)
Wide-angle lens, 206
Widescreen, adapting to standard video, 262–263
Wild walls, 9
Workspace, checking lighting and setup of, 15–16
WS (wide shot)
combining close-ups and wide shots using z-axis blocking, 241–242
shot sizes, 240–241

Z

Z-axis blocking, 241–242
Z-depth. see Depth passes
Zone System, of exposure, 224–225
Zoom, types of camera moves, 250–251